James Halliday's

AUSTRALIAN WINE GUIDE

James Halliday's

AUSTRALIAN WINE GUIDE

1986
EDITION

ANGUS & ROBERTSON PUBLISHERS

*Unit 4, Eden Park, 31 Waterloo Road,
North Ryde, NSW, Australia 2113, and
16 Golden Square, London W1R 4BN,
United Kingdom*

*First published in Australia
by Angus & Robertson Publishers in 1986
First published in the United Kingdom
by Angus & Robertson (UK) Ltd in 1986*

ISSN 0817-0215

*Cover illustration by Barbara Rodanski
Cover photograph by Per Ericson*

*Typeset in 9/10 and 11/12 Garamond
by ProComp Productions Pty Ltd, South Australia*

*Printed in Australia
by The Dominion Press – Hedges & Bell*

Contents

How to Use This Guide

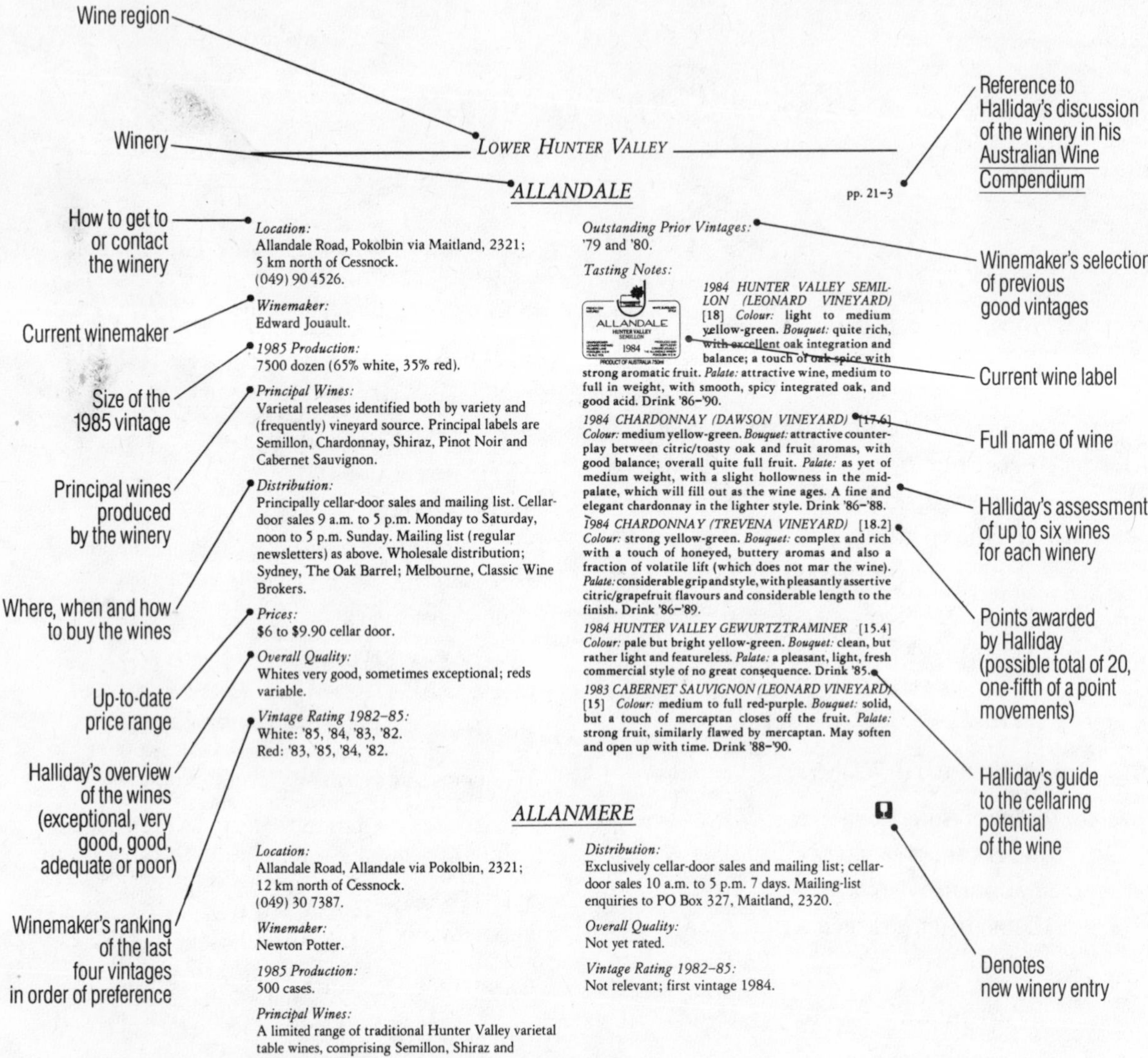

LOWER HUNTER VALLEY

ALLANDALE

pp. 21–3

Location:
Allandale Road, Pokolbin via Maitland, 2321;
5 km north of Cessnock.
(049) 90 4526.

Winemaker:
Edward Jouault.

1985 Production:
7500 dozen (65% white, 35% red).

Principal Wines:
Varietal releases identified both by variety and (frequently) vineyard source. Principal labels are Semillon, Chardonnay, Shiraz, Pinot Noir and Cabernet Sauvignon.

Distribution:
Principally cellar-door sales and mailing list. Cellar-door sales 9 a.m. to 5 p.m. Monday to Saturday, noon to 5 p.m. Sunday. Mailing list (regular newsletters) as above. Wholesale distribution; Sydney, The Oak Barrel; Melbourne, Classic Wine Brokers.

Prices:
$6 to $9.90 cellar door.

Overall Quality:
Whites very good, sometimes exceptional; reds variable.

Vintage Rating 1982–85:
White: '85, '84, '83, '82.
Red: '83, '85, '84, '82.

Outstanding Prior Vintages:
'79 and '80.

Tasting Notes:

1984 HUNTER VALLEY SEMILLON (LEONARD VINEYARD) [18] *Colour:* light to medium yellow-green. *Bouquet:* quite rich, with excellent oak integration and balance; a touch of oak spice with strong aromatic fruit. *Palate:* attractive wine, medium to full in weight, with smooth, spicy integrated oak, and good acid. Drink '86–'90.

1984 CHARDONNAY (DAWSON VINEYARD) [17.6] *Colour:* medium yellow-green. *Bouquet:* attractive counter-play between citric/toasty oak and fruit aromas, with good balance; overall quite full fruit. *Palate:* as yet of medium weight, with a slight hollowness in the mid-palate, which will fill out as the wine ages. A fine and elegant chardonnay in the lighter style. Drink '86–'88.

1984 CHARDONNAY (TREVENA VINEYARD) [18.2] *Colour:* strong yellow-green. *Bouquet:* complex and rich with a touch of honeyed, buttery aromas and also a fraction of volatile lift (which does not mar the wine). *Palate:* considerable grip and style, with pleasantly assertive citric/grapefruit flavours and considerable length to the finish. Drink '86–'89.

1984 HUNTER VALLEY GEWURTZTRAMINER [15.4] *Colour:* pale but bright yellow-green. *Bouquet:* clean, but rather light and featureless. *Palate:* a pleasant, light, fresh commercial style of no great consequence. Drink '85.

1983 CABERNET SAUVIGNON (LEONARD VINEYARD) [15] *Colour:* medium to full red-purple. *Bouquet:* solid, but a touch of mercaptan closes off the fruit. *Palate:* strong fruit, similarly flawed by mercaptan. May soften and open up with time. Drink '88–'90.

ALLANMERE

Location:
Allandale Road, Allandale via Pokolbin, 2321;
12 km north of Cessnock.
(049) 30 7387.

Winemaker:
Newton Potter.

1985 Production:
500 cases.

Principal Wines:
A limited range of traditional Hunter Valley varietal table wines, comprising Semillon, Shiraz and Cabernet Sauvignon.

Distribution:
Exclusively cellar-door sales and mailing list; cellar-door sales 10 a.m. to 5 p.m. 7 days. Mailing-list enquiries to PO Box 327, Maitland, 2320.

Overall Quality:
Not yet rated.

Vintage Rating 1982–85:
Not relevant; first vintage 1984.

Grape Varieties

Albillo: An incorrect name for the grape variety chenin blanc.

Aleatico: A grape of the muscat family from Italy and grown in Australia chiefly in the Mudgee region. Produces red or fortified wine.

Alicante Bouschet (or **Bouchet**): A French hybrid red grape grown extensively in France and, to a lesser degree, California. High-yielding but inferior quality grapes are produced. Limited plantings in Australia, chiefly north-east Victoria.

Alvarelhao: A Portuguese grape variety once propagated in tiny quantities in southern New South Wales and northern Victoria. Has little or no future.

Aubun: An extremely rare red-grape variety from the Mediterranean region of France; a few vines still exist at Bests Great Western Vineyards.

Aucerto: Incorrect name for montils.

Barbera: The principal red-wine grape of Italy, grown in tiny quantities in Australia, chiefly in Mudgee but also in the Murrumbidgee Irrigation Area. Noted for its high acidity and pH.

Bastardo: A red-grape variety from Spain, incorrectly called cabernet gros in South Australia. Of minor importance.

Biancone: A white grape of Corsica; the highest-yielding variety in commercial propagation in Australia, regularly achieving 30 tonnes per hectare in the relatively small plantings in South Australia's Riverland area.

Blanquette: Synonym for clairette.

Blue Imperial: Synonym for cinsaut.

Bonvedro: A red grape of Portugal, grown principally in South Australia with a little in New South Wales and Victoria. Produces a relatively light-bodied wine; not an important variety.

Bourboulenc: A white-grape variety from the Mediterranean region of France, included in the Busby importation of 1832 but now restricted to a few wines in central and northern Victoria. Unlikely ever to be of significance in Australia.

Brown frontignac: Incorrect name for muscat à petits grains.

Brown muscat: Incorrect name for muscat à petits grains.

Cabernet: In Australia, simply an abbreviation for cabernet sauvignon; also used to denote the cabernet family (see below).

Cabernet franc: An important red-grape variety in Bordeaux and the Loire Valley in France; also extensively propagated in Italy. Until recently, little attention was paid to the variety in Australia but it is now assuming greater importance for top-quality reds. Produces a wine similar to but slightly softer than cabernet sauvignon.

Cabernet gros: Incorrect name for bastardo.

Cabernet sauvignon: The great red grape of Bordeaux and, with pinot noir, one of the two most noble red varieties in the world. It has become the most important top-quality red-wine grape in Australia only during the last two decades; prior to that time it was grown in small quantities.

Carignan, Carignane: A grape variety of Spanish origin but very widely propagated in the south of France to produce *vin ordinaire*. Also extensively grown in California for similar purposes. Some South Australian plantings of an unidentified grape are incorrectly called carignane; the grape is not commercially propagated in Australia.

Chardonnay: The greatest white grape of France (Burgundy and Champagne), grown extensively throughout the world and in particular in California. All but unknown in Australia before 1970, it has since had a meteoric rise. As elsewhere, it provides rich table wines and fine sparkling wines.

Chasselas: The principal white-wine grape of Switzerland, and also extensively propagated in France and Italy. In Europe and in Australia it is used both for wine-making and as a table grape. In the last century it was called sweet-water; the principal area of propagation in Australia is at Great Western in Victoria.

Chenin blanc: The principal white grape of the Loire Valley in France, grown in relatively small quantities in Western Australia, South Australia and Victoria and for long incorrectly identified variously as semillon and albillo. Seldom produces wines of the same character as in the Loire Valley, but the plantings have recently shown a modest increase. Can produce great botrytised wines.

Cinsaut: A red-grape variety from the Mediterranean region of France. Frequently called blue imperial in north-east Victoria, black prince at Great Western and confused with oeillade in South Australia. Produces agreeable soft wines with good colour but low in tannin.

Clairette: A once very important white-grape variety in the south of

France, grown in relatively small quantities in Australia where it is often called blanquette (particularly in the Hunter Valley). A difficult wine to make and of no great merit.

Clare riesling: Incorrect name for crouchen.

Colombard: A white grape extensively grown in France, used both for table-winemaking and also in the production of brandy. Extensively propagated in California where it is known as French colombard. Has been planted extensively in Australia's warm irrigated regions because of its excellent acid-retention capacity. Used both in blends and in varietal white wines.

Crouchen: A white grape originally from France but now propagated only in South Africa and Australia. The substantial plantings in this country have been consistently incorrectly identified for a century, being called Clare riesling in the Clare Valley, semillon in the Barossa Valley, and firstly Clare riesling and then semillon in South Australia's Riverland, before being finally identified as crouchen. A relatively high-yielding variety, producing wines of modest quality; of declining importance.

Dolcetto: A red grape from Piedmont in Italy, grown in tiny quantities in South Australia and Victoria. Many of the old classic Saltram reds contained small quantities of the variety.

Doradillo: An extremely important white grape in Australia but of little significance elsewhere, which was brought to Australia by James Busby from Spain. Grown principally in the Riverland areas for distillation into brandy and for the production of sherry.

Durif: A variety first propagated in the Rhone Valley only a century ago, and called petite sirah in California. Grown in tiny amounts in Australia, notably in north-eastern Victoria by Morris.

Esparte: Synonymn for mataro.

Farana: A white grape from the Mediterranean region grown in tiny quantities in the Barossa Valley, where it was previously confused with trebbiano.

Fetayaska: A white grape grown in tiny quantities in north-east Victoria and South Australia to make a white table wine of no great significance.

Folle blanche: A still important white-grape variety used in the production of brandy in France. The supposed Australian plantings have now been identified as ondenc.

Frontignac: Incorrect name for muscat à petits grains.

Furmint: The white grape used to make the famous Hungarian tokay. Introduced into Australia by James Busby; a few wines exist at Great Western and one or two boutique wineries have experimental plantings.

Gamay: Gamay is the red grape which produces beaujolais in France; it is also grown extensively in the Loire Valley. Two attempts to introduce the variety into Australia from California have failed. The first introduction turned out to be pinot noir, the second valdigue. Still grown only in tiny quantities; it seems inevitable that further attempts to propagate it in the future will be made.

Gewurztraminer: Synonym for traminer.

Glory of Australia: A black grape from the Burgundy region of France, from which it disappeared after phylloxera; frequently mentioned in the nineteenth-century accounts of the vineyards of Geelong. A few vines survive at Great Western. Also called liverdun, la gloire, but correctly called troyen.

Gouais: A minor white-grape variety from the centre of France, extensively propagated in Victoria in the nineteenth century but now largely disappeared except from areas around Rutherglen.

Graciano: A red variety of importance in Spain's Rioja area. Called morrastel in France, but unrelated to the variety once called thus in South Australia (which is in fact mataro). Grown in small quantities in north-eastern Victoria. Produces strongly coloured wines, rich in tannin and extract, which age well.

Hárslevelü: A white grape of Hungary used in making Hungarian tokay. Tiny plantings in Australia.

Hermitage: An incorrect name for shiraz.

Hunter River riesling: Incorrect name for semillon.

Irvine's white: Incorrect name for ondenc.

Jacquez: An American variety thought to be a naturally occurring hybrid between the species *Vitis aestivalis* and *Vitis vinifera*. Small quantities grown in the Murrumbidgee Irrigation Area and the Hunter Valley where it is usually called troia. It has a strong, unusual flavour less unpleasant than those of the species *Vitis labrusca*.

Malbec: A red-grape variety grown chiefly in and around Bordeaux and also in the Loire Valley where it is known as cot. Grown on a vast scale in Argentina and in a minor way throughout Australia. Has been confused with dolcetto and tinta amarella. Ideal for blending with cabernet sauvignon which it soften and fills out.

Mammolo: A red-grape variety once of minor importance in Tuscany, Italy; a few vines exist in Mudgee, and there have apparently been some other isolated recent plantings. The wine is said to have an aroma resembling the scent of violets.

Marsanne: A white-grape variety of declining importance in the Rhône Valley of France, grown in relatively small quantities in the Goulburn Valley, north-east Victoria and the Hunter Valley. Once famous in the Yarra Valley, where tiny plantings also still exist.

Mataro: A red grape of major importance in Spain, where it is called morastell or monastrell. Once one of Australia's most important red grapes in terms of production, but now declining. Called balzac at Corowa and esparte at Great Western. Yields well and produces a neutrally flavoured but astringent wine which is best blended with other varieties.

Melon: A white grape which originated in Burgundy but is now propagated principally in the Loire Valley, where it is known as muscadet. Significant plantings in California are called pinot blanc. Only small quantities are propagated in Australia, chiefly in South Australia.

Merlot: One of the most important red-grape varieties in the Bordeaux region, dominant in St Emilion and Pomerol. A relatively recent arrival in California, and even more recent in Australia, where the small commercial plantings to date have been disappointing from a viticultural viewpoint. Poor fruiting has caused some experimental plantings to be abandoned. However, others are persevering and plantings are on the increase.

Meunier: A red grape almost invariably known under its synonym pinot meunier in Australia. Also called Miller's burgundy at Great Western. A naturally occurring derivative of pinot noir and grown principally in France in Champagne. The upsurge in interest in sparkling wine in Australia may see an increase in the presently small and isolated plantings, chiefly in Victoria.

Miller's burgundy: Incorrect name for meunier.

Monbadon: A white variety of declining importance in Bordeaux and Cognac; grown on a small scale in the Corowa–Wahgunyah area of north-eastern Victoria.

Mondeuse: A red grape of minor importance in the east of France, grown chiefly by Brown Brothers at Milawa in north-eastern Victoria. Introduced to Australia at the suggestion of Francois de Castella in the aftermath of phylloxera. Produces a very strong, tannic wine ideal for blending with softer varieties.

Montils: A white grape grown in small quantities in Cognac. Small plantings in the Hunter Valley where it is also known as aucerot; the aucerot of north-eastern Victoria is a separate and, as yet, unidentified variety. Produces a wine with low pH and high acidity, and would appear to have at least as much potential as colombard, but little commercial interest has so far been demonstrated.

Moschata paradisa: A white-grape variety grown in tiny quantities in Mudgee, but so far its overseas source has not been identified. Australia's most unusual grape.

Müller-Thurgau: A cross, bred by Dr Müller in 1882 and put into commercial propagation in 1920 in Germany; now that country's most important grape. Originally thought to be a riesling–silvaner cross, but now believed to be a cross of two riesling grapes. Propagated in limited quantities in Australia; produces a fairly uninteresting wine. The most important white grape in New Zealand, where it is generally known as riesling sylvaner.

Muscadelle: The white grape which is the third and least important component of the wines of Sauternes. Grown across Australia, and usually known as tokay. The largest plantings are in South Australia, but in north-east Victoria extremely ripe, raisined grapes are used to make the famous fortified tokay of that region. The grape is not used for this purpose anywhere else in the world.

Muscadet: Synonym for melon.

Muscat à petits grains: A grape variety grown over much of Europe and which is called by a wide variety of names both there and in Australia, not surprising given that it appears in three colour variants—white, rosé and red. The coloured forms mutate readily from one to the other, while chimeras, in which the genetic make-up of the skin differs from that of the flesh, also exist. It is grown principally in South Australia and New South Wales and Victoria (most frequently called white, red or brown frontignac). The white variety is common in South Australia, the red in north-eastern Victoria, where it is known as brown muscat (or brown frontignac) and used to make the great fortified wines of that region. The white variant is used to make table wine of very high flavour, often used in small percentages with other more noble varieties such as rhine riesling.

Muscat gordo blanco: A white-grape variety, originating in Spain but grown in many countries. A very important variety in Australia for winemaking, drying and table-grape use. Widely called muscat of Alexandria, it is a high-yielding multi-purpose grape. For winemaking it is used for fortified sweet wines such as cream sherry and also in cask and flagon wines, often in combination with sultana.

Muscat of Alexandria: Synonym for muscat gordo blanco.

Oeillade: Incorrect name for cinsaut.

Ondenc: An obscure white grape from France, travelling both there and in Australia under a confusingly large number of names. Probably brought to this country by James Busby as piquepoule, but then became known as sercial in South Australia and Irvine's wine in Victoria at Great Western. In France it is used for brandy-making; in Australia for sparkling wine (because of its neutrality), chiefly by Seppelt at Great Western and Drumborg.

Orange muscat: A highly aromatic white-grape variety, also known in France as muscat fleur d'orange; grown chiefly in north-eastern Victoria.

Palomino: A white grape from Spain providing virtually all the raw material for sherry. Grown on a very large scale in South Africa and an important variety in Australia. Very similar to pedro ximinez. Used chiefly for fortified wine in Australia, and in particular dry sherry.

Pedro ximinez: Another Spanish variety used to produce both dry and sweet fortified wines. Extensively propagated in Argentina and important in Australia (although decreasing). Grown chiefly in the Riverland areas, it is used in the making of sherry, but also to provide flagon and cask white wine.

Peloursin: An ancient grape variety from the east of France but of little or no commercial significance. Survives in Australia and California interplanted with durif, which it resembles.

Petit meslier: An extremely obscure, although still permitted, white-grape variety in Champagne in France; a few vines survive amongst ondenc plantings at Great Western.

Petit verdot: A minor red grape of Bordeaux of declining importance in that region. The once significant Hunter Valley plantings have disappeared since 1930, but a few tiny plantings have since been established elsewhere in Australia by those seeking to emulate the great wines of Bordeaux.

Petite sirah: Incorrect name for durif used throughout America.

Pinot blanc: The true pinot blanc is a white variant of pinot noir, seemingly grown only in Alsace, Germany and Italy. Varieties grown elsewhere and called pinot blanc are variously chardonnay, chenin blanc or melon.

Pinot chardonnay: Incorrect name for chardonnay.

Pinot de la Loire: French synonym for chenin blanc.

Pinot gris: Another colour variant of pinot noir similar to pinot blanc. Grown in Alsace, Germany (where is is called rulander) and northern Italy.

Pinot meunier: Synonym for meunier.

Pinot noir: The classic red grape of Burgundy, grown in practically every country in the world but only producing wine of real quality in cool climates. Plantings in Australia are expected to increase substantially with increasing use of the variety for sparkling wine.

Piquepoule noir: A minor red-grape variety from the Chateauneuf-du-Pape region of France, surviving as a few vines at Great Western.

Rhine riesling: Simply known as riesling in its native Germany, where it is the most highly regarded white grape. Grown extensively around the world; known as white riesling or Johannisberg riesling in California and by a host of names in other countries. While it has fallen from public favour in Australia, it still remains the most important high-quality white grape. The widespread advent of botrytis has meant that both dry and very sweet wines of excellent quality can be made from it.

Riesling:
(i) Preferred for rhine riesling.
(ii) A dry white wine which may or may not be made from or contain a percentage of rhine riesling in it.

Rkatitseli: A Russian white grape propagated chiefly in the Murrumbidgee Irrigation Area by McWilliam's and others.

Roussanne: A white grape grown in the Rhône Valley and usually blended with marsanne. Also a minor component of some (red) Chateauneuf-du-Pape wines. Experimental plantings at Yeringberg in Yarra Valley.

Rubired: An American-bred red hybrid producing wines of startlingly intense colour and very useful for blending in small quantities for this purpose. Propagated on a limited scale in Australia.

Ruby cabernet: Another red hybrid bred by Professor Olmo at the University of California. Grown on a very limited scale in Australia.

Rulander: German synonym for pinot gris.

Semillon: The major white grape of Bordeaux and the second most widely grown in the whole of France. Outside France it is propagated chiefly in the southern hemisphere, particularly in Chile. Has been confused with chenin blanc in Western Australia and crouchen in South Australia; Barnawartha pinot of north-eastern Victoria is semillon. The classic white grape of the Hunter Valley; produces wines which are extremely long-lived and often need five or 10 years to reach their peak. Now also matured in new oak to produce a different style, and increasingly used for the production of sauterne-style wines in South Australia.

Sercial: Incorrect name for ondenc.

Shepherds riesling: An incorrect (and no longer used) name for semillon.

Shiraz: A red grape coming from the Hermitage area of the Rhône Valley, the origins of which are obscure and hotly debated. Frequently called hermitage in Australia (particularly in New South Wales and Victoria). For long the mainstay of the Australian red-wine industry, and still the most widely propagated red grape. The fact it can produce wines of the very highest quality is frequently forgotten; a very versatile variety which can do well in all climates and soil types. Also useful for blending with cabernet sauvignon.

Silvaner, Sylvaner: A vigorous, high-yielding white grape extensively grown in Germany, producing rather neutral-flavoured wines. Even in cool-climate areas such as Drumborg and Keppoch it produces an unexciting wine. The modest plantings are not likely to increase.

Souzão: A minor red grape grown in the Douro Valley of Portugal.

Sultana: A white grape which originated in Asia Minor or the Middle East, and which is principally used both in Australia and elsewhere as a table grape. In California, where it is known as Thompson's seedless, it is grown on a very large scale and significant quantities are used for white-winemaking. In Australia it is produced primarily for drying, but a considerable amount is used in winemaking and some for table-grape purposes. It produces a very neutral wine with quite good acidity.

Sylvaner: See **Silvaner**.

Syrah: Synonym for shiraz.

Tarrango: A red hybrid grape bred by the CSIRO. Chiefly used in the production of nouveau-style reds by Brown Bros and others; has considerable promise.

Tempranillo: The most highly regarded of the red-grape varieties grown in Spain's Rioja, and known as valdepenas in California. A small planting by that name in the Upper Hunter Valley is presumably tempranillo. The wine matures extremely quickly.

Terret noir: A grape grown in the Languedoc area of France. Appearing in three colour combinations—white, grey and black. A small planting of the latter type exists in the Barossa Valley.

Thompson's seedless: American synonym for sultana.

Tinta amarella: A red grape widely grown in the Douro Valley of Portugal and used in vintage port. There is a small amount in South Australia, where the variety is known as portugal. It has from time to time been confused with malbec.

Tinta Cão: A red grape grown in the Douro Valley in Portugal and important in the making of vintage port. Only experimental plantings in Australia.

Tokai friulano: A white grape closely related to sauvignon blanc and grown extensively in the Friuli-Venezia-Giulia region of north Italy. Grown on a large scale in Argentina where it is called sauvignon. Isolated vines exist in Mudgee, the Goulburn Valley and Great Western, sometimes in surprisingly large numbers. The wine has a definite bouquet and a slight bitterness, as its sauvignon blanc heritage would suggest.

Tokay: See **Muscadelle**.

Touriga: The most important red grape in the Douro Valley in Portugal, used extensively in vintage port. Small plantings have been grown for many years in the Corowa region, and there have been small recent plantings on the floor of the Barossa Valley. It is used to make high-quality vintage port, and a modest increase in plantings can be expected.

Traminer: An ancient white-grape variety derived from the primitive wild grapes of Europe. The main European plantings are in Alsace and Germany, and also northern Italy. Produces a highly aromatic wine which can quickly become overbearing and over-blown. Contrary to popular belief, there is no viticultural or other distinction between traminer and gewurztraminer, although the latter is supposedly more spicy in aroma and taste.

Trebbiano: The leading white grape of Italy, and now dominant in the Cognac region of France where it is known as St Emilion, although the official French name is ugni blanc. It is known by both these names in Australia and also (incorrectly) as white shiraz or white hermitage. It is grown in virtually all Australian wine regions, bearing well to produce a neutral and rather hard table wine and an excellent distillation base for brandy.

Ugni blanc: French synonym for trebbiano.

Valdepenas: California synonym for tempranillo.

Verdelho: A white grape from Portugal, grown on the island of Madeira where it is used to make fortified wine, and in small quantities in the Douro Valley. The Australian plantings of under 100 hectares are divided between Western Australia, South Australia and New South Wales. Produces a very distinctive full-bodied table wine, and can also be used to make fortified wine.

Viognier: A white grape grown chiefly at the northern end of the Rhône Valley to produce distinctive and highly flavoured although relatively quick-maturing wine. Experimental plantings in Australia show some promise.

White frontignac: Synonym for muscat à petits grains.

White hermitage: Incorrect name for trebbiano.

Zinfandel: A grape variety grown chiefly in California, but may be related to the widely propagated primitivo variety of Italy. Grown in small quantities in Australia, chiefly in Western Australia and South Australia. Can produce a wine deep in colour and rich in soft, spicy flavour.

Wine-producing Regions

NEW SOUTH WALES

1. Lower Hunter Valley
2. Upper Hunter Valley
3. Mudgee
4. Murrumbidgee Irrigation Area

VICTORIA

6. Bendigo and District
7. Central Goulburn Valley
8. East Gippsland
9. Geelong
10. Great Western and District
11. Macedon
12. Mornington Peninsula
13. Murray River
14. North-East Victoria
15. North Goulburn River
16. Pyrenees
17. Southern and Central Victoria
18. Yarra Valley

SOUTH AUSTRALIA

19. Adelaide Hills
20. Adelaide Metropolitan Area / Adelaide Plains
21. Barossa Valley
22. Clare Valley
23. Coonawarra
24. Langhorne Creek
25. Padthaway / Keppoch
26. Riverland
27. Southern Vales

WESTERN AUSTRALIA

28. Lower Great Southern Area
29. Margaret River
30. South-West Coastal Plain
31. Swan Valley

32. **CANBERRA DISTRICT**

33. **QUEENSLAND**

34. **TASMANIA**

Introduction

This book is written as a companion to my *Australian Wine Compendium*. The *Compendium* covers the history of the wine regions and the wineries which populate those regions; it gives a detailed description of the vineyards; and it tells you much about the winemakers and their winemaking philosophies.

Here I cover rather different ground. On the one hand there are all the hard facts: precise addresses; telephone numbers; where, when and how the wines may be purchased; up-to-date (1985 vintage) production details; and current prices. The page reference at the beginning of each entry indicates where in *The Australian Wine Compendium* I discuss that particular winery. A wine-glass symbol at the beginning of an entry indicates a winery that has started producing since *The Australian Wine Compendium* was prepared.

Then there is a one-line overview of the general quality of the wines produced by each winery, a rating which I have given. It is followed by a relative rating of the last four vintages ('82–'85 inclusive), and then a one-line listing of outstanding prior vintages. These vintage rankings are those of the winemaker and, even if I disagree with them, I have left them unaltered.

Finally, and most obviously, follow my tasting notes of wines. Up to this point the book is self-explanatory, but I believe the tasting notes require explanation and—if you wish—justification.

Wine Selection

Firstly, except where specifically indicated, the wines were tasted (and the notes made) between May and September 1985, specifically for the purposes of this book. I in fact tasted many more wines (over 2500 in all), but for a variety of reasons have not included all the notes. The primary reason for exclusion was the limits necessarily imposed by the size of this book. Thus the (somewhat arbitrary) maximum number of wines for any one winery is six, while that for small or less important wineries is significantly lower.

I also tasted a substantial number of 1985 wines, but have only included notes on these where I was confident they were already showing a reliable indication of the final quality and style of the wine. This excluded all red wines and almost all wood-matured white wines (notably chardonnay, sauvignon blanc and semillon), although by the end of August an increasing number of wines were in finished condition.

I have tried to select wines which are most likely to reflect favourably the quality and style of the winery—in other words, those wines which I would be most likely to choose to drink from the output of the winery concerned. This was a matter of delicate judgment, because I did not wish to provide an unrealistic view of quality. So even in the better wineries, one or two less than perfect wines have been reviewed.

Finally, I have endeavoured to restrict the notes to wines which are likely to be available for sale in late 1985–early 1986. With some of the more fashionable small wineries this may prove a vain hope—although the "sold out" sign is an increasingly rare phenomenon, it is still not extinct.

Tasting Jargon

There are as many schools of thought about the language of tasting notes as there are wine-lovers (or critics). At the one extreme there are those who poke fun at the inevitably odd language of even the most restrained tasting note, reaching the ultimate in asking "how can a wine have a nose?" At the other end there are those who argue that if the taster is restricted to a prescribed series of defined technical terms, tasting notes will be of very limited use. They will be able to convey certain basic impressions, but will fail utterly to come to grips with the myriad differing sensations and tastes which one constantly comes face to face with in the world of wine.

The very reason that so much is written about wine is its endless complexity and subtlety. It is trite in the extreme to observe that no two wines are precisely the same; more significantly, one can find the most unexpected flavours and sensations in a high-quality wine, let alone one which exhibits a winemaking fault.

So the liberals say that if a wine smells of truffles, wood violets, salami, hazelnuts (or whatever) you should say so; if its texture seems voluptuous (in other words, generous, rounded, fleshy and soft) you should likewise say so. Above all else, the initial impression should be captured and recorded. It is often the most accurate: repeated visits to the glass tend to blur the impact of the initial sensation. All agree it is impossible to measure a taste or a colour scientifically or objectively. It is all a matter of comparison, of imagery.

Those who are most prone to criticise the language of tasting notes are those who have never attempted the exercise of writing them in the first place.

The Fallibility of Tasting Notes

In any event, I believe the limitations of tasting notes go far deeper than the clothing of language which surrounds them.

First and foremost, they are one person's views at a given time of the highly subjective impact of the taste of a wine. They have no universal or immutable validity. No matter how skilled the taster nor how perfect the tasting conditions, there will inevitably be *some* difference in two successive tasting notes by the same taster of the same wine completed (say) at an interval of one week. Most probably, there will be what seems to the untutored eye a substantial difference.

The wine has not changed in this time, but its effect on the taster has. There are an infinite number of variables which interface with the tasting process. Is the tasting conducted in the morning, afternoon or night? Is the taster tired or alert? Has he (or she) eaten within the previous hour or two? Is the wine tasted as part of a comparative line-up, or on its own? Was there any prior knowledge of the wine (district, water, grape variety or vintage)? Was the tasting conducted with others present? If so, was there any discussion about the wine?

Let me explain a little more about just a few of these factors, all of which are quite clearly important and all of which will impact on the tasting note which is ultimately produced.

I have absolutely no doubt that the comparative tasting is the most reliable method of tasting wines, and of putting them into perspective. The opposite extreme is the tasting of a wine drawn from a barrel in the dim recesses of a winery you know and love by a winemaker you respect. It is nearly certain you will think the wine is magnificent.

Tasted in a comparative line-up in the cold light of the following day, in the glare of the colour-corrected neon lights of a winemaker's laboratory, it is very probable you will detect a shortcoming, if not a positive fault (possibly remediable), in the wine which so impressed you the day before.

There can be no better example of this than the elementary procedure of the three-way trial which should be—but unhappily frequently is not—part of a winemaker's repertoire. Young red (and sometimes white) wines frequently suffer from hydrogen sulphide problems. At high levels the fault is readily detectable, but in small concentrations it can be very difficult to tell whether the wine is simply showing the after-effects of fermentation or whether indeed it has hydrogen sulphide. (I should add that, if untreated, hydrogen sulphide ultimately produces mercaptan.)

Hydrogen sulphide is readily removed by the addition of small quantities of copper. So one or two of the three glasses are treated (the taster does not know if it is one or two) and the three glasses then placed in random order (marked on their under-base, if needs be).

Even the slightest contamination is immediately detectable to the skilled taster once the comparison is available. Yet this technique works as well as it does because the three wines are of basically identical composition and style.

Once wines of differing parentage, age and weight are placed next to each other, the picture becomes more confused. A light-bodied, fragrant and delicate red which follows a blockbuster—a strong cabernet high in tannin and from a warm vintage—may easily be lost or unfairly downpointed. So the comparative system, while still the best, is not foolproof. At the very least, it requires considerable skills on the part of the taster.

Another factor worth looking at in a little more detail is the question of whether the taster knows anything of the origin of the wine. An English wine writer once observed that a quick glance at the label is worth 20 years in the wine trade.

Closer to home I have seen the following exercise practised with devastating results. Each guest at a dinner party (or wine-tasting) is asked to bring a bottle of his or her favourite wine. All of the bottles are then lined up, and each person lists the wines in expected order of preference. The wines are then masked, and each is tasted and assessed without knowledge of the identity. Once again each taster ranks the wine (this time by glass number) in order of preference. It is not uncommon to find the initial "consensus" order reversed by the blind tasting. Certainly it is rare to find that any one taster's two lists correspond to any marked degree.

Indeed, even the most skilled taster cannot help but be influenced by knowledge of the label. It is for this reason that wherever practicable (and for logistical reasons it is not always possible) I conduct "blind" comparative tastings.

When to Drink

There is no doubt that the most difficult task for someone learning about wine is to foresee what is likely to happen to a particular wine in the years to come. I am asked the "cellaring potential" question more frequently than any other. So I have attempted to forestall those questions by providing a "drink '86–'89" type of guide. The most obvious feature of this guide is that (with a few exceptions) it does not say "drink '86". More particularly, it does not say "drink 14 July 1986". Contrary to widespread belief, there is no particular point in the development of a wine which either human or computer can identify as the perfect moment for consumption.

The reason is simple enough; the process of wine development is a leisurely one. Obviously, the life span (and development potential) of a beaujolais nouveau will be decidedly shorter and more rapid than that of a great cabernet. But such exceptions to one side, at any given point in the maturity (or drink) span I have given, someone is going to regard the wine as at its most perfect, someone not.

The development of wine in bottle is an extremely complex one; while many of the chemical changes are far better understood and recorded than in years gone by, their relevance to the flavour and style of the wine is still hotly debated and imperfectly understood.

The overall result of cellaring, however, is not in dispute: from the day the wine is put into the bottle there is an inexorable progression as the wine loses primary fruit aroma and flavour, and in its place—and up to a certain point—gains in complexity.

How one relates to the wine during this initial development phase is an intensely personal (and subjective) matter. Some look to fruit freshness, life and lift of a young wine; others to the more mellow and rounded depths of complexity of the same wine three, 10, or 15 years later.

The spans I have given in the tasting notes are deliberately conservative, particularly at their outer end. There is no doubt that a significant number of the wines will still be in first-class condition 10 or 20 years after the end of the span I have stipulated. On the other hand, many Australian wines made in the 1960s and the first half of the 1970s which promised so much when young are now found wanting. This is due to two things: firstly, an inherent lack of fruit durability in the wine; and, secondly, to changes in winemaking techniques and styles which have since altered the public's perception of just what is desirable in a top-quality red wine.

In other words, in the mid-1960s there were virtually no straight cabernet sauvignons available on the market; by mid-1975 they had started to appear in numbers, but most were made from grapes grown in warm climates, and the cabernet flavour tended to be chocolatey and somewhat burnt; in the latter part of the 1970s the first of the herbaceous/cool climate cabernets started to appear in quantity; and finally, by 1985 the pendulum had swung back somewhat from the ultra-green/grassy unripe cabernet flavour to a fuller and more modulated flavour profile. Thus it is that a perfectly cellared bottle of 1973 Cabernet Sauvignon, which has done everything its maker could have expected or hoped of it, and which (when first released) was highly regarded, will now seem passé and old-fashioned.

In fact, the overwhelming number of Australian reds have really failed to live up to expectations, even if one discounts the impact of the style change. For all of these reasons I have been conservative in stipulating the outer limit of the cellaring span; from this time onwards you would be well advised to keep a close watch on the development of the wine. It may continue to develop complexity and richness for decades, and you will have chosen well.

A brief word on cellaring white wines. So far, at least, Australian white wines have defied conventional wisdom. All but a handful of Australian chardonnays have bloomed all too briefly; luscious when young, they tend to become tired and flabby in the third or fourth year after vintage. On the other hand, well-made semillon and a considerable number of the traditional rhine rieslings (particularly those from the Eden and Clare Valleys) can improve in bottle for as long as many red wines. A quick visit to a Lindeman's Classic Wine Stockist and the purchase of a 1968 Hunter River Riesling (in other words, Semillon) or a 1973 Leo Buring White Label Rhine Riesling will prove the point.

The one word of warning here is that one should carefully inspect the bottle. The quality of Australian bottles, and the quality of the corks used by the majority of the major wine companies, leave a very great deal to be desired. Whereas a 15-year-old French wine is likely to be at the same level in the bottle as the day it was filled, that of an Australian wine will have receded down the neck and probably part-way down the shoulders of the bottle. Ullage, as it is known, is the chief problem confronting those who wish to have and enjoy fully mature Australian wine. It is not too much to say that the major Australian winemakers should be condemned for their penny-pinching and short-sighted views about wine bottles and the corks which go into them.

Points Score and Quality Grading

You will see that I have given my appreciation of the overall quality of each winery's wines, and have also given points for each wine tasted. The overall quality assessment is based not simply on the currently available wines (and hence those reviewed in this book), but rather on all of the wines I have tasted over the years from the winery concerned. Hence there may be some inconsistency between the points awarded and the overall assessment, most particularly where the current vintage wines are for one reason or another not up to the usual standard of the winery.

I have adopted five classifications: exceptional, very good, good, adequate, and poor. In a few instances I have used the "not rated" classification, where my first-hand experience of the wine is either limited or non-existent. (This occurs particularly in the case of ethnic wineries selling principally in bulk to local populations, such as in the Murrumbidgee Irrigation Area of New South Wales or the Swan Valley of Western Australia.)

It may well seem that a disproportionately large number of assessments fall in the good to very good range. I make no apology for this. The fact of the matter is that the overall standard of winemaking in Australia is extremely high, and is arguably the best of any major wine-producing country. Increased competition and increased awareness and understanding of wine quality has led to the disappearance of most of the lesser quality wineries, or to the restriction of their markets to local clientele, with sales based purely on price.

In much the same way, the points awarded to the wines tend to fall within the 15.4 to 17.4 range, relatively few wines falling either side of this. Traditional Australian point score systems move in half points, but I have long felt that this was too restrictive. I have accordingly used one-fifth of a point movements. I was sorely tempted to use a 100 point system, and indeed the system I have adopted is something of a compromise; obviously enough, multiplying the points given by five will result in a 100-point ranking, with all points being in whole numbers. One of these days I may well take the plunge.

This apart, the points conform to the Australian show system; in other words, wines awarded between 15.6 and 16.8 points inclusive would receive a bronze medal; those awarded between 17 and 18.4 points inclusive would receive a silver medal; and those awarded 18.6 points and over would receive a gold medal.

In this system, almost all of the points fall between 12 and 19. Any wine awarded 14 points or less is suffering from a major wine fault, and 12 or less, from a multiplicity of faults to the point where the wine is truly undrinkable (or at least, decidedly unpleasant to drink). Any wine awarded 19 or more points is, obviously enough, quite magnificent.

The limitation of this system is the degree of significance in the difference between 16.2 and 16.4, a difference which is easy to gloss over. Even more important is the difference between 15.4 and 15.6; between 16.8 and 17; and between 18.4 and 18.6. These points will be chosen with the utmost of care, placing a wine just within or just outside a particular medal.

The statistically minded reader will quickly come to the conclusion that the points given in this book for the wines would result in a far greater number of medals than one would normally expect in a wine show. There are two reasons for this. Firstly, in a wine show there are three judges, and the average of the points is taken. This has a lowest common denominator effect.

Secondly, I am, overall, more interested in style than in the technical perfection of a wine. Show judges who come from the industry as full-time winemakers tend to be far more critical of faults, and to down-point wines accordingly. My personal feeling is that many of these so-called faults—a slight level of volatility is a particular example—are not faults at all so far as the average consumer is concerned, and indeed may add to his or her enjoyment of the wine. More generally, I happen to like wine, and would far rather err on the side of generosity.

Prices

There is inevitably a time lag between the time a book such as this is written and the time it is published. I asked winemakers to use a crystal ball—a piece of equipment not usually found in a winery—to estimate their likely prices in January 1986. Some had success, others did not; thus the cellar-door prices may in some instances be five or 10 per cent lower than those actually prevailing in 1986.

Recommended retail prices are, by and large, a snare and a delusion. The only question is: are they 30 per cent, 50 per cent or 100 per cent higher than what I loosely term the real price? This real price varies from day to day, from store to store, rather like prices of products in countries suffering from hyper-inflation.

If you are at the right place at the right time, there will be no cause for complaint. But in the medium term—and certainly in the longer term—it is a marketing system which is fundamentally at odds with the realisation of Australia's potential to produce great white and red wine for sale at home and abroad.

New South Wales

Lower Hunter Valley

1985 Vintage

Adequate and evenly distributed late-winter, spring and early summer rainfall gave the Hunter Valley one of its best leadups to vintage for many years. Unlike 1984, the rain did not continue, and mild, dry conditions extended from the end of December until the third week of February. What might have been a perfect vintage was spoilt for some by a hailstorm on 28 January which cut a swathe through some vineyards and caused a fruit loss of up to 30 per cent. The only other problem was a certain amount of stress on unirrigated vineyards which also led to a marginal crop reduction.

Despite these seemingly inevitable vicissitudes, the vintage was one of the largest in recent years (though not quite so big as 1984); it commenced throughout the district in the last week of January. The 50 millimetres of rain which fell at the end of February caused few problems. The fruit was harvested in exceptional condition, free from any mould and disease. Overall the wines have considerably more weight and flavour than those of 1984, semillon in particular holding out the promise of great quality if allowed to mature in bottle. Many vignerons rate the '85 semillon in front of the very good '83 vintage. The chardonnays are very full-bodied, and promise to develop very early; some lack finesse and delicacy.

The red wines all have far better flavour, depth and balance than those of 1984, with pinot noir the best for many, many years.

The Changes

Tamalee has gone into liquidation, largely unlamented. Dr Lance Allen seemed confident that he would have sold Tamburlaine before the end of 1985, while Sydney restaurateur Oliver Shaul has sold the vineyard from which George Hunter Estate wines are made. He is, however, confident that he will be able to continue to buy grapes from the vineyard and, if necessary, supplement these with grapes purchased elsewhere in the Valley, so the label will continue.

On the credit side, as it were, two new wineries have released their first wines in the second half of 1985: Chateau Pato and Allanmere.

ALLANDALE

pp. 21–3

Location:
Allandale Road, Pokolbin via Maitland, 2321;
5 km north of Cessnock.
(049) 90 4526.

Winemaker:
Edward Jouault.

1985 Production:
7500 dozen (65% white, 35% red).

Principal Wines:
Varietal releases identified both by variety and (frequently) vineyard source. Principal labels are Semillon, Chardonnay, Shiraz, Pinot Noir and Cabernet Sauvignon.

Distribution:
Principally cellar-door sales and mailing list. Cellar-door sales 9 a.m. to 5 p.m. Monday to Saturday, noon to 5 p.m. Sunday. Mailing list (regular newsletters) as above. Wholesale distribution; Sydney, The Oak Barrel; Melbourne, Classic Wine Brokers.

Prices:
$6 to $9.90 cellar door.

Overall Quality:
Whites very good, sometimes exceptional; reds variable.

Vintage Rating 1982–85:
White: '85, '84, '83, '82.
Red: '83, '85, '84, '82.

Outstanding Prior Vintages:
'79 and '80.

Tasting Notes:

1984 HUNTER VALLEY SEMILLON (LEONARD VINEYARD) [18] *Colour:* light to medium yellow-green. *Bouquet:* quite rich, with excellent oak integration and balance; a touch of oak spice with strong aromatic fruit. *Palate:* attractive wine, medium to full in weight, with smooth, spicy integrated oak, and good acid. Drink '86–'90.

1984 CHARDONNAY (DAWSON VINEYARD) [17.6] *Colour:* medium yellow-green. *Bouquet:* attractive counterplay between citric/toasty oak and fruit aromas, with good balance; overall quite full fruit. *Palate:* as yet of medium weight, with a slight hollowness in the mid-palate, which will fill out as the wine ages. A fine and elegant chardonnay in the lighter style. Drink '86–'88.

1984 CHARDONNAY (TREVENA VINEYARD) [18.2] *Colour:* strong yellow-green. *Bouquet:* complex and rich with a touch of honeyed, buttery aromas and also a fraction of volatile lift (which does not mar the wine). *Palate:* considerable grip and style, with pleasantly assertive citric/grapefruit flavours and considerable length to the finish. Drink '86–'89.

1984 HUNTER VALLEY GEWURTZTRAMINER [15.4] *Colour:* pale but bright yellow-green. *Bouquet:* clean, but rather light and featureless. *Palate:* a pleasant, light, fresh commercial style of no great consequence. Drink '85.

1983 CABERNET SAUVIGNON (LEONARD VINEYARD) [15] *Colour:* medium to full red-purple. *Bouquet:* solid, but a touch of mercaptan closes off the fruit. *Palate:* strong fruit, similarly flawed by mercaptan. May soften and open up with time. Drink '88–'90.

ALLANMERE

Location:
Allandale Road, Allandale via Pokolbin, 2321;
12 km north of Cessnock.
(049) 30 7387.

Winemaker:
Newton Potter.

1985 Production:
500 cases.

Principal Wines:
A limited range of traditional Hunter Valley varietal table wines, comprising Semillon, Shiraz and Cabernet Sauvignon.

Distribution:
Exclusively cellar-door sales and mailing list; cellar-door sales 10 a.m. to 5 p.m. 7 days. Mailing-list enquiries to PO Box 327, Maitland, 2320.

Overall Quality:
Not yet rated.

Vintage Rating 1982–85:
Not relevant; first vintage 1984.

AUDREY WILKINSON

pp. 23–4

Location:
De Beyers Road, Pokolbin, 2321;
10 km west of Cessnock.
(049) 98 7517.

Winemaker:
Trevor Drayton (contract).

1985 Production:
3800 cases.

Principal Wines:
Hunter River Riesling, Chablis, Chardonnay, Traminer, Hermitage and Cabernet Sauvignon. Occasional other blended releases.

Distribution:
Principally cellar-door sales and mailing list. Cellar-door sales 10 a.m. to 4 p.m. Monday to Saturday, noon to 4 p.m. Sunday. Mailing-list enquiries to Box 314, GPO, Sydney. Limited Sydney retail, restaurant and club distribution.

Prices:
$5.33 to $9.90 cellar door.

Overall Quality:
Adequate.

Vintage Rating 1982–85:
'85, '84 (no '83s made).

Outstanding Prior Vintages:
'79.

Tasting Notes:

1985 TRAMINER [15.4] *Colour:* light yellow. *Bouquet:* clean and light with just a touch of spice but no marked varietal character. *Palate:* a fresh, well-made wine, without excessive residual sugar although overall with a clear commercial orientation. Drink '86.

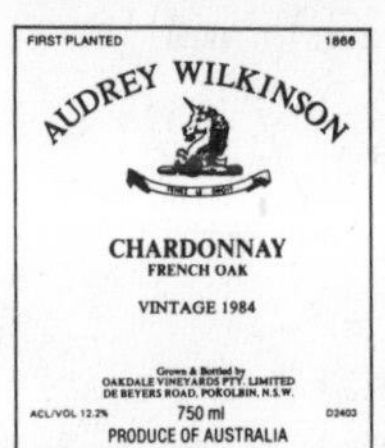

1984 FRENCH OAK CHARDONNAY [15.2] *Colour:* pale straw-yellow. *Bouquet:* some fruit; a little yeast-derived lift, but lacking fruit complexity. *Palate:* that volatility returns to help lift the flavour; lacks richness but commercially acceptable. Drink '86–'87.

1980 PINOT MALBEC SHIRAZ CABERNET [15.6] *Colour:* tawny red. *Bouquet:* smooth and clean, with a nice touch of light, ripe berry aromas. *Palate:* some smoky regional flavours; very light in body but with some fruit complexity. Drink '85–'87.

BELBOURIE

p. 24

Location:
Branxton Road, Rothbury via Branxton, 2330;
24 km north of Cessnock.
(049) 38 1343.

Winemaker:
James H. Roberts.

1985 Production:
Not for publication.

Principal Wines:
A range of unconventionally made and labelled table wines, with the carbonic maceration process being used both for whites and reds. Many of the wines do not conform to any known style. Labels include Semillon, Montils Shiraz, Hermitage and Cabernet Hermitage.

Distribution:
Chiefly cellar door and through club mailing list with well-presented brochures.

Prices:
$7.50 to $10.

Overall Quality:
By normal judging standards, poor.

Tasting Notes:

1984 SEMILLON [10] *Colour:* deep straw-yellow. *Bouquet:* curious sherry/straw aromas, almost certainly deriving from carbonic maceration. *Palate:* aggressive aldehydic flavours and a biting finish.

1984 MONTILS SHIRAZ [14] *Colour:* light to medium straw-yellow. *Bouquet:* green stalky/aldehyde aromas. *Palate:* much better than bouquet; attractive cinnamon spice flavours, fleshing out some rather green malic/apple flavours. (An unusual white wine made from a blend of montils and trebbiano.)

1983 HERMITAGE [12.8] *Colour:* medium red, with some purple hints. *Bouquet:* solid, slightly medicinal aromas with spice/cherry/plum characters all pointing to carbonic maceration. *Palate:* assertive and rather thick, with an aggressive finish.

1983 CABERNET HERMITAGE [15.4] *Colour:* medium to full red. *Bouquet:* clean, strong grassy cabernet varietal aroma. *Palate:* again cabernet sauvignon dominates the blend; full-flavoured and quite deep, with cabernet varietal character again coming through very clearly. Drink '86–'89.

BROKENWOOD

pp. 24–6

Location:
McDonalds Road, Pokolbin, 2321;
11 km north-west of Cessnock.
(049) 98 7559.

Winemaker:
Iain Riggs.

1985 Production:
7700 cases.

Principal Wines:
Varietal releases comprise Semillon, Chardonnay, Pinot Noir, Cabernet Hermitage and Cabernet Sauvignon. Special Graveyard Vineyard releases; also Hunter/Coonawarra Cabernet Sauvignon and Cabernet Hermitage.

Distribution:
Substantial cellar-door and mailing-list sales. Also fine wine retailers. Cellar-door sales 10 a.m. to 5 p.m. 7 days. Mailing list, regular newsletters. Wholesale distributors: Sydney, Tucker & Co; Melbourne, Rutherglen Wine Company; Adelaide, Classic Wine Merchants; Hobart, Tasmanian Fine Wine Distributors.

Prices:
$10 to $11 retail.

Overall Quality:
Very good; often exceptional.

Vintage Rating 1982–85:
White: '83, '84, '85, '82.
Red: '83, '85, '82, '84.

Outstanding Prior Vintages:
'75, '79.

Tasting Notes:
1984 SEMILLON WOOD MATURED [18.2] *Colour:* full, bright yellow. *Bouquet:* excellent oak, well-integrated and not excessive, given the relatively light fruit; some peachy overtones. *Palate:* again, immaculate oak handling a feature of the wine, perfectly fleshing out the light-to-medium-weight fruit, with attractive citric/grassy flavours. Drink '86–'91.

1984 CHARDONNAY (GRAVEYARD VINEYARD) [18] *Colour:* very full yellow, partly oak-derived. *Bouquet:* very big, with a touch of volatile lift which does not flaw the wine. Oak held well in restraint. *Palate:* rich and surprisingly generous for the year; solid mid-palate fruit with well-integrated oak, and overall unusual depth and length. A forward style. Drink '86–'88.

1984 CABERNET SAUVIGNON HUNTER / COONAWARRA) [17.6] *Colour:* excellent bright red-purple. *Bouquet:* very clean, of medium-weight fruit and clear, red berry aromas. *Palate:* a very well-balanced and constructed wine; fresh mid-palate fruit and gentle tannin on the finish, probably at its best while the fresh fruit flavours remain. Drink '87–'90.

1983 CABERNET HERMITAGE (HUNTER/COONAWARRA) [17.8] *Colour:* medium red-purple. *Bouquet:* very clean, with some pleasantly lifted fruit. *Palate:* again the excellent balance which marks all of the Brokenwood wines, very clean, berry/cherry flavours on the mid-palate, and soft but perceptible tannin on the finish. Drink '87–'91.

CHATEAU FRANCOIS

p. 27

Location:
Off Broke Road, Pokolbin, 2321;
13 km north-west of Cessnock.
(049) 98 7548 (weekends) or (02) 32 3816 (a/h).

Winemaker:
Don Francois.

1985 Production:
1000 cases.

Principal Wines:
Varietal releases comprising Semillon, Chardonnay, Pinot Noir and Shiraz. Pinot Noir and Shiraz frequently blended.

Distribution:
Principally mailing list, to Box N197, Grosvenor Street, Sydney. Cellar-door sales and tastings by appointment on weekends.

Prices:
$6 to $8 cellar door.

Overall Quality:
Whites: good with age; reds good.

Vintage Rating 1982–85:
'85, '83, '82, '84.

Outstanding Prior Vintages:
'73, '75, '79.

Tasting Notes:

1984 POKOLBIN SEMILLON [16.2] *Colour:* medium yellow-green. *Bouquet:* quite full, with a trace of solids fermentation characters, but not excessively marred. *Palate:* some lemony fruit; fairly obvious solids fermentation characteristics. Demands time. Drink '88–'92.

1983 POKOLBIN SEMILLON [16.8] *Colour:* bright, strong yellow-green. *Bouquet:* trace of solids character; starting to develop richness, with a faint hint of honey. *Palate:* a well-made, full-flavoured wine in traditional, old-fashioned style; good mid-palate fruit, will improve. Drink '86–'90.

1983 POKOLBIN SHIRAZ PINOT NOIR [16.4] *Colour:* light red, losing purples rapidly and starting to move into tawny shades. *Bouquet:* light; some leafy/strawberry aromas from pinot, but really more regional than varietal. *Palate:* some nice, light, fragrant fruit flavours; an attractive, early drinking light red. Drink '85–'88.

CHATEAU PATO

Location:
Thompson's Road, Pokolbin, 2321;
11 km north-west of Cessnock.
(049) 98 7634.

Winemaker:
David Paterson.

1985 Production:
125 cases.

Principal Wines:
A so far limited range of wines, with only Gewurztraminer and Hermitage yet made and marketed. Malbec and Pinot Noir are planned for future releases.

Distribution:
Exclusively mailing list and by direct sale to selected restaurants. No cellar-door sales. Mailing-list enquiries as above.

Prices:
$6 to $8 per bottle mailing list.

Overall Quality:
Red wines good; white wines still experimental.

Vintage Rating 1982–85:
Not relevant; 1984 first vintage.

Tasting Notes:

1985 GEWURZTRAMINER [15.4] *Colour:* medium straw-yellow, with a trace of pinking. *Bouquet:* of light to medium weight, smooth but with little or no varietal character. *Palate:* a clean wine, showing surprising technology; palate fleshed out by residual sugar, but again lacking varietal distinction. Certainly a very commercial wine. Drink '86–'87.

1984 HERMITAGE [17.8] *Colour:* strong red-purple of medium depth. *Bouquet:* quite full, with very rich small oak influence, with that characteristic edge which Portuguese oak imparts; overall clean and robust. *Palate:* a lively and fresh wine with an excellent pepper/spice varietal accent; some lively berry flavours, and the Portuguese oak has added an extra dimension to the texture. A great success. Drink '88–'92.

DAWSON ESTATE

p. 28

Location:
Londons Road, Nulkaba, 2325;
5 km north of Cessnock.
(049) 90 2904.

Winemakers:
Made under contract variously by Ralph Fowler, Ed Jouault (1984) and David Lowe (1985).

1985 Production:
3500 cases.

Principal Wines:
Exclusively Chardonnay (200 cases Traminer released through cellar door each year).

Distribution:
Principally cellar-door sales and mailing list. Cellar-door sales 9 a.m. to 5 p.m. 7 days. Mailing list as above. Limited restaurant and club distribution Sydney; retail sales through Camperdown Cellars.

Prices:
$9.60 cellar door.

Overall Quality:
Considerable variation, from adequate to exceptional.

Vintage Rating 1982–85:
'83, '85, '84, '82.

Outstanding Prior Vintages:
'80, '81.

Tasting Notes:

1984 CHARDONNAY [17.6]
Colour: **full yellow, with considerable development.** ***Bouquet:*** **warm, rich and buttery, with a whisper of complexing sulphide.** ***Palate:*** **finer and more elegant than the bouquet would suggest; of medium weight with both fruit and oak flavours in a lemony/citric mould. Drink '86–'88.**

DRAYTON'S BELLEVUE

pp. 28–9

Location:
Oakey Creek Road, Cessnock, 2321;
7 km west of Cessnock.
(049) 98 7513.

Winemakers:
Reg and Trevor Drayton.

1985 Production:
Not stated.

Principal Wines:

Main varietal releases are of Semillon, Chardonnay, Rhine Riesling, Traminer, Shiraz and Cabernet Sauvignon, some additionally identified by vineyard names and others by bin number. Also occasional brand name releases, e.g. Jagerwein.

Distribution:
Substantial cellar-door sales 9 a.m. to 5 p.m. Monday to Saturday. Retail distribution through Cinzano & Company.

Prices:
$5.50 to $9 recommended retail; less cellar door.

Overall Quality:
Extremely variable in recent years; poor to good.

Vintage Rating 1982–85:
'83, '85, '84, '82.

Outstanding Prior Vintages:
'75, '79.

Tasting Notes:

1984 HUNTER VALLEY SEMILLON [11] ***Colour:*** **water white.** ***Bouquet:*** **dank, poor and smelly.** ***Palate:*** **thin, watery and acidic. A poor wine.**

1984 JAGERWEIN [15] ***Colour:*** **touch of straw.** ***Bouquet:*** **soft, slightly sweet; cosmetic overtones.** ***Palate:*** **sweet and slightly cloying but in commercial moselle mould. Drink '85.**

1983 IVANHOE SHIRAZ PRESSINGS BIN 5555 [16.8]
Colour: **bright, purple red of medium depth.** ***Bouquet:*** **smooth and clear, not aggressive or assertive but with good fruit depth.** ***Palate:*** **medium to full weight, with attractive cherry flavours. Well-made; good cellaring potential, though pressings tannin not obvious. Drink '85–'89.**

1981 CABERNET HERMITAGE BIN 8180 [15.6]
Colour: **tawny red.** ***Bouquet:*** **some tar/earthy/sweaty saddle aromas, distinctly regional.** ***Palate:*** **quite aged, leathery/regional fruit flavours, in traditional Hunter Valley mould. Drink '85–'88.**

EVANS FAMILY

pp. 29–30

Location:
Off Palmers Lane, Pokolbin, 2321;
12 km north-north-west of Pokolbin.
(02) 27 4413.

Winemakers:
David Lowe (consultant), Len Evans.

1985 Production:
1450 cases.

Principal Wines:
Chardonnay wines only estate release; Pinot Noir planned. Botrytised Rhine Riesling releases ex Coonawarra, made at Petaluma.

Distribution:
Chiefly mailing list and Sydney restaurants. Len Evans Wines principal retail outlet.

Prices:
$12.70 retail.

Overall Quality:
Consistently very good.

Vintage Rating 1982–85:
'85, '83, '82, 84.

Tasting Notes:

1985 CHARDONNAY *Colour:* medium yellow. *Bouquet:* good fruit and, early in its life, outstanding oak pick-up, with spicy/citric aromas intermingling. *Palate:* excellent overall style and flavour, showing great potential. (Tasted from cask June 1985.)

1984 CHARDONNAY [17.6] *Colour:* medium yellow-green. *Bouquet:* pleasant, slightly bready aroma but with good fruit and oak balance and a hint of butter aromas developing. *Palate:* while not a big wine, has more weight than the bouquet suggests; clear chardonnay varietal flavour with gently honeyed flavours and excellently balanced and integrated oak. Drink '86–'88.

GEORGE HUNTER ESTATE

p. 30

Location:
Formerly Wilderness Road, Allandale (property sold mid-1985).

Winemakers:
Variously Edward Jouault and McWilliams (under contract).

1985 Production:
750 cases (250 cases of each wine).

Principal Wines:
Three wines only sold: Chablis Chenin Blanc, Semillon and Chardonnay.

Distribution:
Through Oliver Shaul restaurants (Summit, Circles on the Square, Central Park Bar & Grill) and other Sydney restaurants. Limited quantities through Camperdown Cellars, Sydney.

Prices:
$4.50 to $8 retail.

Overall Quality:
Good, occasionally very good.

Vintage Rating 1982–85:
'83, '84, '85, '82.

Tasting Notes:

1985 CHARDONNAY Good fruit, excellent acid; some toasty flavours already developing; good potential. (Tasted from cask late May 1985.)

1985 PINOT CHARDONNAY [15] *Colour:* bright green-yellow. *Bouquet:* rather hard and green malic aromas with some solids fermentation character. *Palate:* better, but at this stage lacks fruit. May develop. Drink after '88.

1984 HUNTER RIVER SEMILLON [16.8] *Colour:* medium yellow with green tinges. *Bouquet:* clean fruit of light to medium weight with lemony oak aromas; quite stylish. *Palate:* lemony Nevers oak still to integrate and soften. Quite pleasant fruit flavours, with improvement in front of it. Drink '86–'90.

1983 CHARDONNAY [18.2] *Colour:* full yellow, with a touch of gold. *Bouquet:* attractive, peachy fruit aromas with a touch of charred oak; complex and full. *Palate:* first-class wine; lovely fruit/oak balance; clearly expressed varietal character and good acid. Should be a long-lived chardonnay. Drink '86–'90.

1982 CHABLIS CHENIN BLANC [16.4] *Colour:* bright yellow. *Bouquet:* soft, slightly dull, cardboardy aroma, but some fruit underneath. *Palate:* much better; soft, round and quite rich, with a clean finish. Not a chablis, but who cares? Drink '85–'87.

HUNGERFORD HILL

pp. 30–2

Location:
Corner McDonalds Road and Broke Road,
Pokolbin, 2321;
11 km north-west of Cessnock.
(049) 98 7666.

Winemaker:
Ralph Fowler.

1985 Production:
30,000 cases.

Principal Wines:
Top of range is "Collection Series", comprising Coonawarra Rhine Riesling, Coonawarra Cabernet Sauvignon, Pokolbin Chardonnay, Pokolbin Shiraz. Varietal releases follow, chiefly sold cellar door.

Distribution:
National retail distribution. Also cellar-door sales at first-class Pokolbin Wine Village, 9 a.m. to 5 p.m., 7 days. Pokolbin Wine Village offers wide range of restaurant, tasting and barbecue facilities for whole family; none better in Australia. Special releases also available only at cellar door.

Prices:
$9.50 to $10.50 retail.

Overall Quality:
Good to very good.

Vintage Rating 1982–85:
White: '83, '84, '85, '82.
Red: '83, '85, '84, '82.

Outstanding Prior Vintages:
'79.

Tasting Notes:

1984 POKOLBIN COLLECTION CHARDONNAY [17.8] *Colour:* medium full yellow, already into buttercup fullness. *Bouquet:* considerable fruit richness with some buttery characteristics and good oak. Bigger and richer than many of the whites of the year. *Palate:* attractive, rich, buttery chardonnay with abundant mouth-feel and overall flavour. A considerable success. Drink '86–'88.

1984 POKOLBIN VERDELHO [16.8] *Colour:* medium yellow-green. *Bouquet:* clean, with some soft, slightly tropical fruit aromas. *Palate:* quite distinctive fruit, with a hint of spice; good weight and that extra dimension of weight and tongue-feel of verdelho. Available cellar door only. Drink '86–'89.

1982 POKOLBIN COLLECTION CABERNET MERLOT [18.6] *Colour:* very good red purple. *Bouquet:* exceptional complexity, with clean, berry aromas intermingling with cedar oak and a touch of leafy astringency. *Palate:* Most attractive, sweet, blackcurrant/cassis flavours; intense yet not cloying, and finishing with good acid. A quite lovely wine. Drink '86–'90.

1980 POKOLBIN COLLECTION SHIRAZ [15] *Colour:* tawny red of medium depth. *Bouquet:* quite firm with strong regional/tarry aromas. *Palate:* excessively regional, marred by mercaptan, although some may like the style. Drink '85–'87.

KINDRED'S LOCHLEVEN ESTATE

p. 33

Location:
Palmers Lane, Pokolbin, 2321;
13 km north-north-west of Cessnock.

Winemakers:
Various, including Rothbury, Tyrrell, Jouault and Saltram.

1985 Production:
Nil; all grapes sold.

Principal Wines:
Range of varietal wines of many vintages (1976 to 1982) available cellar door.

Distribution:
Cellar door only, Sundays 10 a.m. to 4 p.m.

Prices:
$3 to $6 cellar door.

Overall Quality:
Extremely variable according to vintage. (The tasting notes are for the best wines.)

Tasting Notes:

1982 ***SEMILLON*** **[16.8]** ***Colour:*** **medium full green-yellow.** ***Bouquet:*** **toasty/honeyed aromas, rich and full.** ***Palate:*** **medium to full weight; good mid-palate fruit, developing some honey; lingering finish. Drink '85–'89.**

1982 ***TRAMINER*** **[17.6]** ***Colour:*** **medium yellow-green.** ***Bouquet:*** **excellent varietal spice/lime, and not heavy.** ***Palate:*** **rich mid-palate, full of flavour, yet not hard or tannic. Excellent winemaking. Drink '86.**

1980 ***CABERNET SAUVIGNON*** **[15.2]** ***Colour:*** **tawny red.** ***Bouquet:*** **clear, light fruit.** ***Palate:*** **light weight, with soft cabernet varietal flavour. Drink '85–'86.**

LAKE'S FOLLY

pp. 33–5.

Location:
Broke Road, Pokolbin, 2321;
8 km north of Cessnock.
(049) 87 7507.

Winemaker:
Stephen Lake.

1985 Production:
4500 cases.

Principal Wines:
Chardonnay and Cabernet Sauvignon the two great labels; also Folly Red (a cabernet shiraz blend).

Distribution:
Principally mailing list; also cellar-door sales 10 a.m. to 4 p.m. weekends, weekdays by appointment. Limited fine wine retail distribution and clubs. Some exports.

Prices:
$8.75 (Cabernet Sauvignon); $10 (Chardonnay) cellar door.

Overall Quality:
Very good.

Vintage Rating 1982–85:
Chardonnay: '85, '83, '82, '84.
Cabernet Sauvignon: '85, '83, '84, '82.

Outstanding Prior Vintages:
'81.

Tasting Notes:

1984 ***CHARDONNAY*** **[16]** ***Colour:*** **superb, bright green-yellow.** ***Bouquet:*** **distinct lift to fruit aroma; oak not obtrusive.** ***Palate:*** **a very "lifted" style, with a recurrent suspicion of volatility; the wine's zest will appeal to many but, quite frankly, not to me. Drink '87–'90.**

1984 ***CABERNET SAUVIGNON*** **[17.2]** ***Colour:*** **very light red-purple, which promises to develop early.** ***Bouquet:*** **excellent oak handling with light, charred oak aromas and a touch of spice; some light berry aromas.** ***Palate:*** **a light, fresh and crisp wine, destined to drink well early, but also to mature early. Drink '87–'91.**

1983 ***CABERNET SAUVIGNON*** **[17]** ***Colour:*** **bright, light to medium red with some purple hues lingering.** ***Bouquet:*** **complex, with some definite regional overtones.** ***Palate:*** **an elegant wine with good acid and a long finish but very regional; the district characters will build further as the wine ages. Definitely a wine for devotees of the Lake's Folly style. Drink '87–'92.**

LINDEMANS

pp. 35–43

Location:
McDonalds Road, Pokolbin, 2321;
9 km north-west of Cessnock.
(049) 98 7501.

Winemaker:
Karl Stockhausen.

1985 Production:
Approximately 40,000 cases.

Principal Wines:
Reserve bin range (with annually changing bin numbers) of Riesling, Chablis, White Burgundy and Burgundy (the last made from shiraz, the others from semillon). Also varietal releases, chiefly Chardonnay. Old vintages under classic release program.

Distribution:
National retail distribution, cellar-door sales 9 a.m. to 5 p.m. Monday to Friday and 10 a.m. to 5 p.m. Saturday. Winery tours.

Prices:
$2.90 to $40 cellar door.

Overall Quality:
Good to very good; old vintages exceptional.

Vintage Rating 1982–85:
White: '83, '82, '84, '85.
Red: '83, '82, '84, '85.

Outstanding Prior Vintages:
'65, '68, '70, '79.

Tasting Notes:

1984 CHABLIS RESERVE BIN 6475 [16.4] *Colour:* light to medium green-yellow. *Bouquet:* light, firm and crisp with a faint suggestion of mercaptan. *Palate:* light, crisp and lemony; oak playing no part in the wines; fair fruit, but no real excitement at this stage. May develop. Drink '86–'91.

1984 WHITE BURGUNDY RESERVE BIN 6470 [17.2] *Colour:* light to medium green-yellow. *Bouquet:* much fuller and softer, with a touch of buttery fruit, although still of light to medium weight. *Palate:* softer wine with some sweet buttery fruit developing, and the evidence of the verdelho used in the blend quite apparent. A wine of good mouth feel and obvious potential. Drink '87–'93.

1982 RESERVE BIN BURGUNDY BIN 7400 [16.6] *Colour:* clear red of light to medium depth. *Bouquet:* clean, quite crisp, with light oak and no particular regional identity. *Palate:* a fairly fresh and crisp wine with good acid; some straw/hay flavours on the mid-to-back palate. A light, well-balanced commercial wine. Drink '86–'89.

1970 BURGUNDY RESERVE BIN 4000 [18] *Colour:* light to medium brick-red with distinct tawny hues. *Bouquet:* soft, velvety and typically earthy regional style of charm and complexity. *Palate:* round, velvety, with very complex vegetative fruit flavours and soft tannin on the finish. Drink '85–'88.

1968 HUNTER RIVER RIESLING RESERVE BIN 3455 [19] *Colour:* deep buttercup yellow, still tinged with green. *Bouquet:* magnificent honey/nut aroma of fully mature semillon. *Palate:* rich, smooth and extremely full, with the texture one would expect from oak, although it played no part in shaping the wine. Butter and honey on toast is the best description. Good acid gives the wine length and youth. Drink '85–'90.

LITTLE'S

pp. 43–4

Location:
Lot 3, Palmers Lane, Pokolbin, 2321;
12 km north of Cessnock.
(049) 98 7626.

Winemaker:
Ian Little.

1985 Production:
3000 cases.

Principal Wines:
Varietal releases comprising Semillon, Chardonnay, Traminer, Shiraz, Pinot Noir and Cabernet Sauvignon.

Distribution:
Principally cellar-door sales and mailing list; cellar-door sales 10 a.m. to 5 p.m. 7 days. Limited wholesale through The Incredible Wine Company.

Prices:
$5.67 to $9.58 recommended retail.

Overall Quality:
Good to very good.

Vintage Rating 1984–85:
'85, '84 (first vintage).

Tasting Notes:
1985 HONEYTREE SEMILLON [17.6] *Colour:* light to medium yellow-green. *Bouquet:* rich tropical/passionfruit/honeyed aromas, unusual and striking. *Palate:* excellent flavour in tropical fruit spectrum; plenty of weight, but lively, with good balance. Drink '87–'89.

1985 TRAMINER [16.8] *Colour:* bright, light yellow-green. *Bouquet:* clear, light and fresh; faintest touch of varietal spice. *Palate:* plenty of weight, though strong reliance on residual sugar. Commercial style. Drink '86.

1984 CHARDONNAY (OAK MATURED) [17] *Colour:* medium yellow; green tinges. *Bouquet:* marked oak influence, with some peachy fruit aromas. *Palate:* rich, with some sweetness on mid palate; fruit flavours maximised by very careful winemaking. Drink '86–'87.

MARSH ESTATE

p. 46

Location:
Deasey Road, Pokolbin, 2321;
13 km north-west of Pokolbin.
(049) 98 7587.

Winemaker:
Peter Marsh.

1985 Production:
6200 cases.

Principal Wines:
Varietal wines comprise Semillon, Chardonnay, Traminer, Hermitage Vat S & Vat R, Cabernet Shiraz, Cabernet Sauvignon Vat N. Also Vintage Port.

Distribution:
Entirely cellar door and mailing list. Cellar-door sales 10 a.m. to 4 p.m. Monday to Friday, 10 a.m. to 5 p.m. Saturday and public holidays, noon to 5 p.m. Sunday. Mailing list to PO Box 164, Beecroft 2119.

Prices:
$5.50 to $8 cellar door.

Overall Quality:
Adequate; some good wines.

Vintage Rating 1982–85:
'83, '85, '84, '82.

Tasting Notes:
1984 POKOLBIN TRAMINER [15.8] *Colour:* pale straw-green. *Bouquet:* odd cosmetic aromas, some spice. *Palate:* big, soft, spicy traminer, not too sweet; just a fraction broad. Drink '86.

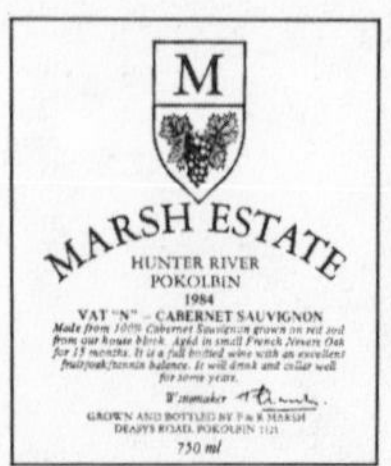

1984 CABERNET SAUVIGNON VAT N [16.4] *Colour:* dark red, though already very advanced. *Bouquet:* clear, quite firm and some depth. *Palate:* a big, ripe flavoursome wine with gentle tannin on finish. Regional rather than varietal, but no off-flavours. Drink '87–'90.

1981 HERMITAGE VAT S [16] *Colour:* dark tawny red. *Bouquet:* very rich, old style wine with some mercaptan. *Palate:* big, soft, velvety, ripe wine with high alcohol. Drink '85–'93.

McWILLIAM'S MOUNT PLEASANT

pp. 44–6

Location:
Marrowbone Road, Pokolbin, 2321;
7 km west of Cessnock.
(049) 98 7505.

Winemaker:
Phillip Ryan.

1985 Production:
Not for publication; substantial.

Principal Wines:
Under Mt Pleasant badge, Elizabeth Riesling, Philip Hermitage, Cabernet Hermitage, Pinot Hermitage and occasional special releases including Vintage Port; varietal releases including Chardonnay, Cabernet Sauvignon and Pinot Hermitage; occasional vineyard releases e.g. Rosehill Hermitage, O.P. and O.H. Hermitage.

Distribution:
National retail through own distribution channels. 10 a.m. to 4 p.m. Monday to Friday, offering special releases not available elsewhere.

Prices:
$9.80 recommended retail, but frequently savagely discounted.

Overall Quality:
White wines good; reds variable and in particular style; poor to very good.

Vintage Rating 1982–85:
White: '85, '82, '83, '84.
Red: '83, '85, '82, '84.

Tasting Notes:

1981 MT PLEASANT ELIZABETH RIESLING [16.4] *Colour:* medium to full yellow. *Bouquet:* touch of toast but still remarkably closed and rather hard. *Palate:* much better, with good mid-palate fruit, although a touch of hardness on finish. Will be very long-lived. Drink '85–'91.

1977 MT PLEASANT VINTAGE PORT [18.8] *Colour:* medium purple-red. *Bouquet:* deep and rich berry aromas, with complex brandy-spirit aroma. *Palate:* rich, deep, softly tannic, with rounded berry ripeness and again complex brandy spirit. Drink '85–'92.

1975 MT PLEASANT CABERNET SAUVIGNON [16] *Colour:* medium to full red with a tawny rim. *Bouquet:* strong regional/vineyard aroma; slightly tarry, with strong fruit underneath. *Palate:* enormous regional/vineyard flavours; little or nothing to do with cabernet in the classic sense; an absolutely unmistakable wine, almost impossible to judge by normal standards. Drink '85–'92.

MILLSTONE VINEYARD

p. 47

Location:
Talga Road, Allandale, 2321;
20 km north-east of Cessnock.
(049) 30 7317.

Winemaker:
Peter Dobinson.

1985 Production:
1350 cases.

Principal Wines:

Varietal releases comprise Sauvignon Blanc, Semillon, Shiraz, Cabernet Sauvignon and Ruby Cabernet, all made by a modified carbonic maceration process.

Distribution:
Exclusively cellar door and mailing list. Cellar-door sales Friday to Sunday 10 a.m. to 4 p.m. Mailing list as above.

Prices:
$7.50 to $8 per bottle.

Overall Quality:
Wines do not fall into normal judging criteria because of winemaking methods.

Vintage Rating 1982–85:
'83, '85, '82, '84.

Tasting Notes:

1984 CHARDONNAY [15.2] *Colour:* full straw-yellow. *Bouquet:* a big wine, with the spice aroma (though little fruit to go with it) typical of carbonic maceration wines; most unusual overall effect. *Palate:* similarly unusual; dip in mid-palate before firm (but not fruity) finish. Drink '88 onwards.

1985 SHIRAZ NOUVEAU [15.6] *Colour:* light to medium red-purple. *Bouquet:* aromatic with strong meaty/gamy maceration aromas. *Palate:* fresh, with good acid, although again mid-palate fruit somewhat lacking. Drink '85–'86.

1983 CABERNET SAUVIGNON [16.2] *Colour:* blackish purple. *Bouquet:* a touch of spice allied with sweet berry aromas; muted maceration effect. *Palate:* soft fruit; the most successful (and for that matter most conventional) of the wines. Drink '86–'88.

MOUNT VIEW WINES

p. 47

Location:
Mount View Road, Mount View, 2325;
9 km west of Cessnock.
(049) 90 3307.

Winemaker:
Harry Tulloch.

1985 Production:
Approximately 2700 cases.

Principal Wines:
Varietal releases of several vintages comprising Semillon, Semillon-Verdelho, Verdelho, Traminer, Late-Picked Traminer, Shiraz, Cabernet Shiraz, Shiraz Port and Liqueur Muscat.

Distribution:
Cellar-door sales and mailing list. Open 9 a.m. to noon Monday to Friday, 9 a.m. to 5 p.m. weekends and holidays. Mailing list enquiries to PO Box 220, Cessnock, 2325.

Prices:
$6.50 to $8.50 cellar door.

Overall Quality:
Good.

Vintage Rating 1982–85:
'85, '82, '83, '84.

Outstanding Prior Vintages:
'79.

Tasting Notes:

1984 VERDELHO [16.8] *Colour:* medium yellow-green. *Bouquet:* considerable depth of honey/melon fruit aromas. *Palate:* plenty of character and flavour, complexed by a touch of grassiness. Drink '86–'90.

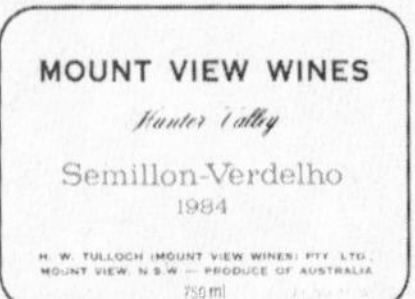

1984 SEMILLON VERDELHO [16] *Colour:* light straw. *Bouquet:* clean but a little bland, with just a hint of honey/malt. *Palate:* pleasant, round, fruit flavours, but without the depth of the straight verdelho. Drink '86–'88.

1983 CABERNET HERMITAGE [16.4] *Colour:* dark red, with some tawny hues on the rim. *Bouquet:* big, soft, earthy and ripe: an old-style bouquet. *Palate:* follows on logically; earthy/velvety ripe, soft fruit. Drink '86–'91.

OAKVALE WINES

p. 49

Location:
Broke Road, Pokolbin, 2321;
11 km north-west of Cessnock.

Winemaker:
John Elliott.

Principal Wines:
Belford Private Bin Semillon (riesling), Oakvale Chardonnay Semillon, Oakvale Chardonnay, Belford Shiraz, Oakvale Private Bin Shiraz and Hunter Valley Cabernet Sauvignon.

Distribution:
Almost exclusively cellar door and mail order. Cellar-door sales 9 a.m. to 5 p.m. Friday, Saturday.

Prices:
$6.99 to $8 per bottle cellar door.

Overall Quality:
Poor.

Tasting Notes:

1984 BELFORD PRIVATE BIN HUNTER RIVER RHINE RIESLING [9.4] *Colour:* pale with a straw tinge. *Bouquet:* rather heavy and coarse, with some oxidative characters, and also strong solids fermentation aromas. *Palate:* very heavy with some unpleasant off-flavours.

1983 PRIVATE BIN HUNTER VALLEY HERMITAGE [9] *Colour:* excellent, deep red-purple. *Bouquet:* curious fish-oil mercaptan aromas overlying concentrated and deep fruit. *Palate:* utterly destroyed by mercaptan.

PETERSONS

p. 50

Location:
Mount View Road, Mount View, 2325;
9 km west of Cessnock.
(049) 90 1704.

Winemaker:
Gary Reed.

1985 Production:
5000 cases.

Principal Wines:
A limited range of high-quality table wines and the occasional fortified wine, including Semillon, Chardonnay Semillon, Chardonnay, Traminer, Pinot Noir, Hermitage, Cabernet Hermitage, Cabernet Sauvignon, Sauternes and Vintage Port.

Distribution:
Exclusively cellar-door sales and mailing list; cellar-door sales 9 a.m. to 5 p.m. Monday to Saturday, open to 5 p.m. Sunday. Mailing list PO Box 182, Cessnock, 2325.

Prices:
$7 to $9.80 cellar door.

Overall Quality:
Exceptional.

Vintage Rating 1982–85:
'85, '83, '84, '82.

Tasting Notes:

1985 CHARDONNAY [18.2] *Colour:* medium yellow with a touch of oak-derived straw. *Bouquet:* clean, with most attractive, complex, charred oak aromas, intermingling with generous and clearly defined varietal chardonnay in the peachy spectrum. *Palate:* an excellent wine; rich, peachy mid-palate fruit, and good length to finish. Very much in the class of the previous outstanding wines from this vineyard. Drink '87–'90.

1984 CHARDONNAY [17.6] *Colour:* full yellow, again tinged with straw. *Bouquet:* very elegant oak handling; lifted and stylish, although quite advanced. *Palate:* excellent oak handling again a feature of the wine, with good complexity and attractive buttery fruit on the back palate. Drink '85–'87.

1984 SAUTERNES [18.4] *Colour:* medium full yellow-orange. *Bouquet:* pungent, rich and complex with strong suggestions of botrytis; remarkably structured aroma. *Palate:* magnificent flavour with good acid on the finish, and that touch of volatile lift essential to prevent the wine from cloying. A great Hunter sauternes. Drink '86–'92.

1984 HERMITAGE [17.8] *Colour:* very good red-purple. *Bouquet:* clean and fresh with a touch of cherry and excellent fruit/oak balance. *Palate:* offers greater complexity than the bouquet suggests; very good mid-palate fruit, and a long, firm finish. Drink '87–'93.

THE ROBSON VINEYARD

pp. 51–2

Location:
Mount View Road, Mount View, 2325;
9 km west of Cessnock.
(049) 90 3670.

Winemaker:
Murray Robson.

1985 Production:
5075 cases.

Principal Wines:
Chardonnay, Traditional Semillon, Early Harvest Semillon, Oak-Matured Semillon, Traminer, Sauvignon Blanc, Cabernet Sauvignon, Pinot Noir, Malbec, Hermitage, Cabernet-Merlot, Muscat and Cabernet Port.

Distribution:
Cellar-door sales, mailing list, selected fine wine retailers in all eastern states and restaurants. Cellar-door sales 9 a.m. to 5 p.m. Monday to Saturday, noon to 5 p.m. Sunday. Outstanding regular mailing list bulletins (address as above).

Prices:
$8 to $12 cellar door.

Overall Quality:
White wines good; red wines frequently exceptional.

Vintage Rating 1982–85:
White: '85, '83, '84, '82.
Red: '83, '85, '84, '82.

Outstanding Prior Vintages:
'78 & '79

Tasting Notes:

1985 EARLY HARVEST SEMILLON [16.6] *Colour:* **pale straw-yellow.** *Bouquet:* **clean, relatively soft; fresh with well-protected fruit flavour.** *Palate:* **clean; attractive soft fruit; a light-bodied, early drinking style. Drink '85–'86.**

1985 TRADITIONAL SEMILLON [17.2] *Colour:* **medium green-yellow.** *Bouquet:* **had already developed some toasty aromas (perhaps still settling down after fermentation) in June '85.** *Palate:* **clean; very attractive, round, rich fruit; no solids fermentation characters whatsoever. Excellent potential. Drink '88–'93.**

1985 MALBEC [17] *Colour:* **light purple-red.** *Bouquet:* **soft spicy fruit aromas with a touch of plum.** *Palate:* **vibrant spice/plum fruit flavours; a great success. Early maturing style. Drink '86–'87.**

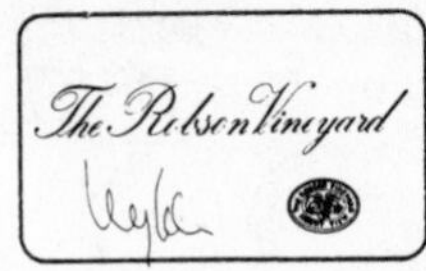

1984 HERMITAGE [16.8] *Colour:* **developing quickly, already losing its purple hues, and of medium depth.** *Bouquet:* **fragrant with soft, almost squashy, berry fruit aromas.** *Palate:* **unusual aniseed/herbal flavours (perhaps from oak) underlie fruit. Drink '88–'91.**

1984 CABERNET SAUVIGNON [17.2] *Colour:* **very light red, with just a touch of purple.** *Bouquet:* **clean, but light and just a hint of minty fruit and oak.** *Palate:* **fragrant, light minty/blackberry fruit flavours. Drink '86–'88.**

THE ROTHBURY ESTATE

pp. 52–8

Location:
Broke Road, Pokolbin, 2321;
10 km north of Cessnock.
(049) 98 7555.

Winemaker:
David Lowe.

1985 Production:
80,000 cases.

Principal Wines:

A multi-tiered system of quality releases. At the top are Black Label Shareholder and Individual Paddock wines, identified additionally by variety and vineyard. Next come the White Label Individual Vineyard wines, followed by the Rothbury Estate varietal white and red wines, then the "Slash Label" varietal releases and finally SDW (soft dry white) and SDR (soft dry or blended red). Also occasional "Len Evans" releases for commercial markets.

Distribution:
Principally cellar door and through The Rothbury Estate Society. Members receive monthly bulletins, special wine offers. Unequalled tasting facilities in splendid winery. Open 7 days 9.30 a.m. to 4.30 p.m. (Sunday 11 a.m. to 4 p.m.).

Prices:
$5.50 to $7 members' mailing list.

Overall Quality:
White wines very good, many older vintages exceptional. Red wines (particularly younger vintages) very good.

Vintage Rating 1982–85:
White: '84, '85, '83, '82.
Red: '85, '83, '82, '84.

Outstanding Prior Vintages:
White: '72, '74, '79.
Red: '73, '75, '79.

Tasting Notes:

1985 ROTHBURY ESTATE MARSANNE [17.6] *Colour:* medium yellow-green. *Bouquet:* stylish, spicy, charred oak aromas. *Palate:* attractive oak again dominant, but has the fruit to balance it and will develop well. Very much in the Mitchelton style. Drink '86–'88.

1984 BLACK LABEL WOOD MATURED SEMILLON [17.8] *Colour:* medium to full yellow, reflecting oak maturation. *Bouquet:* lemony oak aromas obvious but not excessive; good fruit will balance the oak in time. *Palate:* good structure although not a big, fleshy wine. Very well-made. Drink '87–'92.

1984 LEN EVANS SEMILLON CHARDONNAY [17.8] *Colour:* medium yellow-green. *Bouquet:* lifted, aromatic, fresh, peachy aromas. *Palate:* flavoury, rich, peachy fruit to a round and soft mid-palate with surprising depth. A lovely forward style. Drink '85–'87.

1984 BLACK LABEL CHARDONNAY [18] *Colour:* bright yellow of medium depth. *Bouquet:* clean, well-made wine of light-to-medium weight, with well-balanced and integrated oak; has developed good characters and will go further. *Palate:* relatively light-weight, but very well-balanced, with some melon/peach fruit flavours. Drink '86–'88.

1983 WHITE LABEL HOMESTEAD HILL HERMITAGE [17.4] *Colour:* medium red-purple. *Bouquet:* some small-oak-barrel influence apparent adds complexity; nice berry aromas in a pleasantly ripe and well-balanced bouquet. *Palate:* fresh, smooth berry flavours followed by a hint of new oak and a flick of spice. Drink '87–'91.

1983 BLACK LABEL I.P. HERMITAGE (ROTHBURY VINEYARD) [17.6] *Colour:* dark, deep red-purple. *Bouquet:* medium to full, a strong wine with marked ripe fruit aromas. *Palate:* dense and strong, the biggest Rothbury red since 1975. Persistent tannin on finish adds further cellaring potential. Drink '88–'95.

ROTHVALE

pp. 58–9

Location:
Broke Road, Fordwich;
35 km north-west of Cessnock.

Winemaker:
Murray Tyrrell (contract).

1985 Production:
1000 cases approximately.

Principal Wines:
Semillon and Chardonnay.

Distribution:
Mailing list c/- Peter Meier, P.O. Box 218, Cessnock, 2325. Also available Casuarina Restaurant.

Outstanding Prior Vintages:
Not applicable, first vintage 1983.

SAXONVALE

pp. 59–61

Location:
Fordwich Estate, Broke Road, Broke, 2330;
(065) 79 1009.

Winemaker:
Alasdair Sutherland.

1985 Production:
More than 50,000 cases.

Principal Wines:
Bin 1 Limousin Oak Chardonnay (Buff Label) is flag-bearer. Then follow Gewurtztraminer, Hunter Fumé, Limited Release White Burgundy, Semillon (Buff Label), Rhine Riesling, Cabernet Sauvignon and IVP Shiraz. Next are Sauvignon Blanc, Bin 2 Chardonnay, Hermitage and Cabernet Shiraz (all Black Label). Finally follow Hunter Chablis, Traminer Riesling and White Burgundy.

Distribution:
National retail through own distribution network. Cellar-door sales 10 a.m. to 5 p.m. 7 days.

Prices:
$4.30 to $12.65 recommended retail; subject to normal levels of discounting.

Overall Quality:
Good red wines, very good white wines.

Vintage Rating 1982–85:
'85, '83, '82, '84.

Outstanding Prior Vintages:
'80 & '81 (latter red wines).

Tasting Notes:

1985 SEMILLON Very considerable fruit aroma and depth on both bouquet and palate. A rich wine with a touch of fruit/alcohol sweetness. Tasted ex-tank. Potentially very good indeed.

1985 LIMOUSIN OAK CHARDONNAY BIN 1 Pungent grapefruit aromas intermingling with strong charred oak characters in bouquet, and full, lemony/zesty palate. Incomplete barrel sample, but the wine appears likely to be exceptional.

1984 LIMOUSIN OAK CHARDONNAY BIN 1 [16.6] _Colour:_ bright green-yellow. _Bouquet:_ citric/grapefruit aromas with some charred oak characters, but not particularly deep. _Palate:_ well enough made, but the fruit is unquestionably light and the oak is a major contributor to flavour. Not in the class of previous years (or probably the '85). Drink '86–'87.

1983 SEMILLON [17.2] _Colour:_ medium yellow, still tinged with green. _Bouquet:_ very rich, attractive wine with complex toasty/grapefruit aromas, of considerable weight and already fairly developed. _Palate:_ soft fruit, with a slightly lighter mid-palate than the bouquet would suggest, and attractive regional honey/toast flavours. Drink '86–'88.

1983 BLACK LABEL HERMITAGE [16.6] _Colour:_ dark, dense red. _Bouquet:_ huge wine, with highly aromatic minty/herbaceous characters. _Palate:_ a big wine with some charred oak characters, substantial tannin and again curious plum/spice/herbaceous flavours reminiscent of some new generation Coonawarra reds. Drink '86–'90.

1983 BLACK LABEL CABERNET SAUVIGNON [16.4] _Colour:_ dark red, quite developed, but showing no brown tinges. _Bouquet:_ a big wine with leafy/minty, ripe fruit aromas, a little short on elegance. _Palate:_ a big, almost thick wine with strong, sweet, minty flavours almost verging on passionfruit. Soft finish. Drink '86–'89.

SIMON WHITLAM

p. 61

Location:
Wollombi Brook Vineyard, Broke, 2330;
on outskirts of town. (Vineyard only).

Winemaker:
Arrowfield Wines (contract).

1985 Production:
3060 cases.

Principal Wines:
Semillon, Late Harvest Semillon, Chardonnay and Cabernet Sauvignon.

Distribution:
Chiefly mailing list; enquiries to Simon Whitlam & Co., 21 Kingston Road, Camperdown, 2050, (02) 51 5735. Retail sales through Camperdown Cellars and associated stores.

Prices:
$11 to $13.50 recommended retail. Mailing list prices substantially less ranging between $79.50 and $96 per dozen.

Overall Quality:
Good.

Tasting Notes:

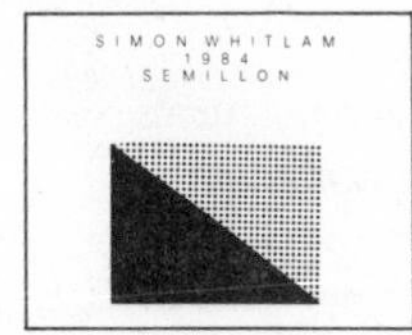

1984 SEMILLON [16.8] *Colour:* medium to full yellow. *Bouquet:* clean; some honey/toast characters developing, also a suggestion of fresh hay; a fairly firm, old-fashioned style. *Palate:* clean and fresh; very light fruit, but has the structure and acid to develop over the short term. Drink '85–'89.

SUTHERLAND WINES

p. 62

Location:
Deasey Road, Pokolbin, 2321;
14 km north-west of Cessnock.
(049) 98 7650.

Winemaker:
Neil Sutherland.

1985 Production:
3000 cases.

Principal Wines:
Varietal white and red table wines. Labels comprise Chenin Blanc, Semillon, Chardonnay, Shiraz, Pinot Noir and Cabernet Sauvignon.

Distribution:
Principally cellar-door sales and mailing list. Cellar-door sales 10 a.m. to 5 p.m. Monday to Saturday, Sunday 11 a.m. to 5 p.m. Mailing list as above. Sydney distribution through The Oak Barrel.

Prices:
$7.50 to $9.50 mailing list.

Overall Quality:
Very good.

Vintage Rating 1983–85:
White: '85, '83, '84.
Red: '83, '85, '84.

Outstanding Prior Vintages:
Not applicable; 1983 first vintage.

Tasting Notes:

1984 SEMILLON [17.2] *Colour:* medium green-yellow. *Bouquet:* highly aromatic and pungent grapefruit aromas, not regional and at least partly yeast-induced. *Palate:* big, slightly squashy fruit flavours, again with a strong yeast influence. Overall considerable, albeit idiosyncratic, flavour. Drink '85–'88.

1984 OAK MATURED SEMILLON [17] *Colour:* medium yellow, quite full. *Bouquet:* full; oak of neutral variety and well-balanced with the fruit. *Palate:* overall of medium depth, but very good oak balance and integration; lacks a little in fruit richness and sparkle. Drink '86–'90.

1984 CHARDONNAY [17.8] *Colour:* medium yellow-green. *Bouquet:* strong grapefruit aromas, partly yeast induced but with good varietal fruit also evident. *Palate:* lively citric/grapefruit flavours with abundant character and good balance; should settle down well. Drink '86–'90.

1984 CHENIN BLANC [16.6] *Colour:* light to medium yellow. *Bouquet:* slightly grassy aroma with some reductive characters, indicating a high degree of protection during the winemaking process. *Palate:* a crisp wine with good acid grip, very different in style to the other Sutherland whites, and certainly a commercial proposition. Drink '86.

1984 SHIRAZ [16.8] *Colour:* medium red-purple. *Bouquet:* solid with some charred oak aromas, but lacking varietal lift. *Palate:* provides more than the bouquet promises, with some varietal spice and overall crispness and life. Should develop well. Drink '87–'90.

TAMBURLAINE WINES

p. 63

Location:
McDonalds Road, Pokolbin, 2321;
10 km north-west of Cessnock.
(049) 98 7570.

Winemaker:
Dr Lance Allen (to 1985).

1985 Production:
2000 cases.

Principal Wines:

Semillon, Chardonnay, Shiraz and Cabernet Sauvignon.

Distribution:
Almost exclusively cellar-door sales 9 a.m. to 4.30 p.m. Monday to Saturday and noon to 4.30 p.m. Sunday. It is almost certain Tamburlaine will be sold prior to the 1986 vintage and distribution arrangements may well be different in the future.

Prices:
$6.50 to $11 cellar door.

Overall Quality:
Variable; some wines very good, others not.

Vintage Rating 1982–85:
White: '85, '84, '82, '83.
Red: '83, '85, '82, '84.

Outstanding Prior Vintages:
'75, '79.

Tasting Notes:

1983 POKOLBIN SEMILLON OAK MATURED [17] *Colour:* full yellow. *Bouquet:* a very strong, robust wine with some slight evidence of solids fermentation; oak merely incidental. *Palate:* a very big, old-fashioned wine of enormous depth and strength; a touch of honeyed fruit already building; will be a long-lived wine despite its advanced colour. The white-wine equivalent to the red wine of Bailey's. Drink '86–'91.

1982 WILLS HILL SEMILLON [16.6] *Colour:* glowing buttercup yellow. *Bouquet:* a big, deep and strong wine, still building fruit aroma. *Palate:* firm and robust, with a slight bitterness on the back-palate, but masses of flavour and still very fresh. Drink '86–'89.

1983 SHIRAZ VAT 10 [16.2] *Colour:* dense purple, quite extraordinary for the district. *Bouquet:* a very big, distinctly regional aroma, slightly astringent and leathery, but with plenty of fruit. *Palate:* a very big wine, dipping somewhat in the mid-palate in the face of astringent tannin on the finish. It may fill out, but then again, it may not. Drink '88–'92.

1983 CABERNET SAUVIGNON [16.4] *Colour:* full purple-red. *Bouquet:* smooth, deep and clean, but nonetheless regional rather than varietal. *Palate:* a wine of great strength in terms of structure but not so much in terms of flavour; again a slight hollowness in the mid-palate accentuated by persistent tannin. A wine which it is extremely difficult to predict the future for. Drink '87–'91.

TERRACE VALE

p. 64

Location:
Deasey Road, Pokolbin, 2321;
13 km north-west of Cessnock.
(049) 98 7517.

Winemaker:
Alain le Prince.

1985 Production:
7500 cases.

Principal Wines:
Varietal white and red table wines (and a vintage port) released under a combination varietal/bin number system. Semillon Bin 1, Semillon Bin 1A, Chardonnay Bin 2, Gewurtztraminer Bin 3, Semillon Chardonnay Bin 12, Hermitage Bins 6 and 6A, Cabernet/Hermitage Bin 76, Pinot Noir and Vintage Port.

Distribution:
Principally cellar-door sales and mailing list. Cellar-door sales 10 a.m. to 4 p.m. 7 days; mailing list as above. Sydney distribution through Carol Anne Classic Wines.

Prices:
$5.50 to $7.50 cellar door.

Overall Quality:
Adequate at best.

Vintage Rating 1982–85:
White: '85, '84, '83, '82.
Red: '83, '85, '84, '82.

Outstanding Prior Vintages:
'79.

Tasting Notes:

1984 SEMILLON BIN 1A [15] *Colour:* **full straw yellow.** *Bouquet:* **strong, chalky, solids ferment characters.** *Palate:* **lighter than bouquet would suggest, crisp and clean almost into a chablis style. Should develop quite well with age. Drink '88–'92.**

1984 CHARDONNAY, FRENCH OAK MATURED [15.4] *Colour:* **pale straw green.** *Bouquet:* **clean, exhibiting less solids character than most of the Terrace Vale wines, with some lift, although not particularly varietal.** *Palate:* **certainly one of the best Terrace Vale whites for some years; some fruit richness helped by a touch of residual sugar. Drink '86–'88.**

1983 HERMITAGE BIN 6 [15.8] *Colour:* **dark red purple.** *Bouquet:* **some mercaptan evident in a rich wine.** *Palate:* **very rich, ripe fruit, with strong and persistent tannin adding yet further strength to an uncompromisingly big wine. If mercaptan does not build, could be a real surprise. Drink '88–'93.**

TULLOCH

pp. 64–8

Location:
De Beyers Road, Pokolbin, 2321;
10 km north-west of Cessnock.
(049) 98 7503.

Winemaker:
Pat Auld.

1985 Production:
500 tonnes (the equivalent of 37,500 cases).

Principal Wines:

Traditional Hunter white and red table wines released in two principal quality grades, with the top wines enjoying the same label but overprinted "Private Bin". This once-simple division has been thoroughly obscured in recent years by numerous label re-designs and also by the introduction of a range of "Selected Vintage" premium varietals headed by chardonnay. Even greater confusion has arisen from the intermittent appearance of Glen Elgin on certain of the labels, Glen Elgin being the home vineyard surrounding the winery. Labels include Semillon Verdelho, Glen Elgin Verdelho, Glen Elgin Private Bin Hunter River Riesling (the old name for semillon), Private Bin Hunter Valley Riesling, Hermitage, Private Bin Dry Red Hermitage and Cabernet Sauvignon.

Distribution:
National retail through Allied Vintners, now part of the Penfolds Group. Cellar-door sales 9 a.m. to 5 p.m. Monday to Saturday. No mailing list.

Prices:
Recommended retail $7 to $11 but bearing little or no relation to reality. In the first half of 1985 back vintages of Tulloch wines were selling for less than $2 a bottle retail in Melbourne, something which can only be deplored (unless one is the purchaser).

Overall Quality:
Good; occasional wines very good, and one or two exceptional.

Vintage Rating 1982–85:
White: '83, '84, '85, '82.
Red: '83, '85, '82, '84.

Outstanding Prior Vintages:
'65 (red), '74 (white) and many others.

Tasting Notes:

1984 PRIVATE BIN HUNTER VALLEY RIESLING [16.4] *Colour:* **bright yellow-green.** *Bouquet:* **firm, closed and rather light fruit, but with the potential for development.** *Palate:* **light, crisp and firm wine, still slightly hard on the finish, and will unquestionably benefit from bottle age. Drink '85–'91.**

1983 SEMILLON VERDELHO [16.8] *Colour:* **medium to full yellow-green.** *Bouquet:* **solid, slightly coarse malty/chalky aromas.** *Palate:* **infinitely better than the bouquet promises; rich, clean and round mid-palate fruit, with a bone dry finish. Will develop well. Drink '86–'89.**

1982 GLEN ELGIN VERDELHO [16.6] *Colour:* **pale straw-yellow.** *Bouquet:* **some camphor/mothball aromas; curiously enough, not unpleasant.** *Palate:* **a very fresh wine of medium to full weight with good acid; a fraction one-dimensional, but once again will improve in bottle. Drink '85–'90.**

1982 SELECTED VINTAGE HERMITAGE [16.8] *Colour:* **medium red-purple, holding its hue very well.** *Bouquet:* **clean, solid and rather undeveloped with low aromatics.** *Palate:* **clean; a solid wine, lacking a little lift, but with years in front of it; a nice soft finish. Drink '86–'92.**

1980 GLEN ELGIN PRIVATE BIN HUNTER RIVER RIESLING [18.2] *Colour:* **deep yellow.** *Bouquet:* **classic toasty/honeyed aromas, highly aromatic, though not especially deep.** *Palate:* **beautifully flavoured and balanced; gently honeyed and some nutty flavours; a long, soft finish. In the mould of great Hunter Valley whites, though with far more delicacy than one usually encounters. Drink '85–'89.**

TYRRELL'S WINES

pp. 68–74

Location:
Broke Road, Pokolbin, 2321;
12 km north-west of Cessnock.
(049) 98 7509.

Winemakers:
Murray Tyrrell (principal), Mike de Garis.

1985 Production:
Just under 2000 tonnes (equivalent to 150,000 cases).

Principal Wines:
A very large range, headed by the "Vat" wines: whites comprise Semillon Vats 1, 15, 18 and 30; Chardonnay Vats 47 and 63 and other white varietals Vats 3, 16 and 31. Also Rhine Riesling, Verdelho Traminer. Red Vats 5, 7, 8, 9, 10, 11, 12A and 70, together with Pinot Noir and Pinot Hermitage. Then follow top commercial varietal white and red releases under Old Winery Label and HVD Label, and finally the traditional range, including White Burgundy and Long Flat Red. Also top-quality *méthode champenoise* wines from pinot noir, chardonnay and semillon.

Distribution:
Vat wines sold only cellar door and by excellent mailing list with very well-presented brochures (two major mailings each year). Old Winery and traditional releases through national distribution plus substantial exports. Cellar-door sales 9 a.m. to 5 p.m. Monday to Saturday.

Prices:
Vary widely; Vat wines $6 to $10 cellar-door; Old Winery $8 to $10 recommended retail.

Overall Quality:
Very good; some wines exceptional (particularly Vat 1 Semillon & Vat 47 Chardonnay).

Vintage Rating 1982–85:
Whites: '85, '83, '84, '82.
Reds: '85, '84, '83, '82.

Outstanding Prior Vintages:
Whites: '79, '74, '68, '73.
Reds: '75, '65, '67, '80.

Tasting Notes:

1985 VAT 1 RIESLING [17.4] *Colour:* bright yellow-green. *Bouquet:* of medium to full weight, with good fruit depth though aromatics yet to build. *Palate:* a substantial and generous wine with round, medium to full palate and a solid finish. Of markedly different style to more recent Vat 1 wines. Drink '87–'92.

1984 HVD SEMILLON [16.6] *Colour:* light to medium yellow-green, with a touch of straw. *Bouquet:* clean and solid, slow developing and as yet rather neutral and lacking aroma. *Palate:* old-style, traditional Hunter semillon with some straw characters, and unquestionably needing time in bottle. (The '83 is now superb.) Drink '88–'94.

1984 OLD WINERY PINOT CHARDONNAY [18.4] *Colour:* glowing, medium full green-yellow. *Bouquet:* very complex and full, with ripe buttery-honeyed fruit; some grapefruit also intermingling with excellent oak. *Palate:* rich and rounded extremely complex and beautifully integrated fruit and oak; some fruit sweetness; an outstanding commercial chardonnay, although in mid '85 probably close to its best. Drink '85–'87.

1984 CHARDONNAY VAT 47 [18.2] *Colour:* surprisingly full yellow. *Bouquet:* solid, buttery fruit and oak with a slight lift to the fruit character, although full varietal aroma still to build. *Palate:* that touch of lift is again evident; oak handling particularly successful; above average weight for the year. Drink '86–'90.

1984 VAT 11 HERMITAGE [17.4] *Colour:* medium red-purple. *Bouquet:* complex and potentially regionally distinctive bouquet, with an added dimension of weight over the other "Winemaker Selection" vats of the same year. *Palate:* attractive rich fruit, gently ripe with some cherry flavours and very soft tannins adding a dimension. To my taste, the top hermitage Vat of the vintage. Drink '87–'93.

1983 PINOT NOIR METHODE CHAMPENOISE [16.8] *Colour:* uncompromising salmon-pink. *Bouquet:* very strong, aggressive pinot in radically different style to the marvellous 1982 vintage of the same wine. *Palate:* strong pinot flavour, and, as the bouquet suggests, rather aggressive. A wine which seems to have been taken off yeast lees far too young and needed at least two more years before disgorgement and sale. Bottle age may help. Drink '88–'91.

WOLLUNDRY

pp. 74–5

Location:
Palmers Lane, Pokolbin, 2321;
12 km north of Cessnock.
(049) 98 7572.

Winemaker:
Ron Hansen.

1985 Production:
300 cases.

Principal Wines:
Substantial stocks of Semillon and Shiraz, covering most vintages back to 1977 at winery. Also limited quantities of younger vintages of Chardonnay, Traminer, Blanquette, Cabernet Sauvignon, Light Sweet Semillon, Late Harvest Semillon, Sauternes and Vintage Port.

Distribution:
Exclusively cellar door and mailing list, cellar-door sales 10 a.m. to 5 p.m. 7 days. Mailing list as above.

Prices:
$5 to $8 cellar door.

Overall Quality:
Older vintages very variable and mostly poor; '84 and '85, good.

Vintage Rating 1982–85:
'85, '84, '83, '82.

Outstanding Prior Vintages:
'79

Tasting Notes:

1984 SEMILLON [16.8] *Colour:* light to medium yellow-green. *Bouquet:* clean and soft, well-made and with fresh, well-protected fruit aromas. *Palate:* lively, crisp and clean, with light to medium fruit and good overall balance. Drink '86–'89.

1984 CHARDONNAY [17.2] *Colour:* light to medium yellow-green. *Bouquet:* clean, with some attractive peachy varietal aroma and overall good weight and style. *Palate:* most attractive crisp peach/grapefruit flavours; very well made. Drink '85–'87.

WYNDHAM ESTATE

pp. 75–8

Location:
Dalwood via Branxton 2335;
6 km east of town.
(049) 38 1311.

Winemakers:
Jon Reynolds (Chief); Neil McGuigan.

1985 Production:
Approximately 300,000 cases.

Principal Wines:
A substantial range of white and red table wines under three brands. Chief Wyndham Estate labels are Chablis Superior, Graves Exceptional, Bin 222 Chardonnay, Oak Cask Chardonnay, Wood Matured Semillon, Gewurztraminer, Bin TR2 Black Label Traminer Riesling, Cabernet Sauvignon Bin 444, Burgundy Bin 555, Pinot Noir and Homestead Ridge. Hunter Estate labels include Fumé Blanc, Blanc de Blanc, Gewurztraminer, Chardonnay, White Burgundy, Première Chardonnay, Sauternes, Pinot Noir and Cabernet Sauvignon. Richmond Grove labels include Chablis Oak Matured, French Oak Chardonnay, White Bordeaux, Semillon Chardonnay, Chardonnay Special Release, Cabernet Merlot, Ruby Cabernet, Hermitage Claret and Cabernet Sauvignon.

Distribution:
Extensive Australian and export sales. Eastern states self-distributed; Perth, Regional Vineyard Distributors; Adelaide, R. G. Clampett & Co; Brisbane, Condon & Co. Cellar-door sales 9. a.m. to 5 p.m. 7 days; lavish tasting facilities in historic surroundings.

Prices:
$5.95 to $8.25 recommended retail; Wyndham is critical of discounting, but still subject to it.

Overall Quality:
Good, particularly given volume and price.

Vintage Rating 1982–85:
White: '85, '83, '82, '84.
Red: '83, '85, '82, '84.

Outstanding Prior Vintages:
White: '81.
Red: '78 & '79.

Tasting Notes:

1984 WYNDHAM ESTATE SEMILLON SAUVIGNON BLANC [16.4] *Colour:* bright and lively, pale green-yellow. *Bouquet:* plenty of aromatic fruit characters, although no discernible varietal stamp. *Palate:* pleasant and well-balanced, with some grassy sauvignon blanc characters evident, allied with a touch of toast. A good commercial wine. Drink '85–'87.

1980 WYNDHAM ESTATE CABERNET SAUVIGNON BIN 444 [18] *Colour:* medium to full red-purple, outstanding for a 5-year-old Hunter Valley red. *Bouquet:* very clean with excellent fruit/oak balance; smooth cherry aromas with a cedary oak overlay. *Palate:* a lively, attractive wine with crystal-clear, sweet, berry flavours, lively acid and soft tannin. An exceptionally good wine for a totally commercial label. Drink '85–'89.

1982 HUNTER ESTATE PINOT NOIR [15.8] *Colour:* medium red, good for pinot noir. *Bouquet:* clean, with some depth to fruit balanced by gently sweet oak and just a suspicion of sappy pinot noir varietal aroma. *Palate:* some pleasant sweet fruit flavours of medium depth; not at all varietal but a pleasant, medium-weight red. Drink '85–'87.

1979 HUNTER ESTATE CABERNET SAUVIGNON [16] *Colour:* dark red, tinged with purple. *Bouquet:* a big, solid wine lacking lift and sparkle, however. *Palate:* ripe, full sweet fruit with soft tannin on the finish. A red wine which could come from anywhere, but which certainly has a depth of flavour and which has aged remarkably well. Drink '85–'88.

1984 RICHMOND GROVE FUME BLANC [16.6] *Colour:* bright green-yellow of medium depth. *Bouquet:* a touch of slightly oily oak and rather nondescript fruit, but nonetheless seems to hang together in the end with good weight. *Palate:* much better than the bouquet; good mid-palate fruit with a touch of grassy/gooseberry flavours and a firm finish. Drink '85–'88.

RICHMOND GROVE SEMILLON CHARDONNAY BRUT [16.2] *Colour:* bright medium green-yellow. *Bouquet:* clean with an odd combination of slightly green fruit intermingling with riper vanillin aromas. *Palate:* fairly firm, with good balance and acidity; a fresh style, but with noticeable green characters to the fruit. Drink '85–'86.

Upper Hunter Valley

1985 Vintage

Not surprisingly, the growing season in the Upper Hunter was similar to that of the Lower: adequate winter and spring rains, followed by mild, dry growing conditions, set the scene for a very good vintage. But, as with the Lower Hunter, nature seemed intent on taking with one hand what it gave with the other. Instead of the late-January hailstorm of the Lower Hunter, the Upper Hunter was visited in late October by one of its rare frosts, which caused substantial damage in some vineyards, with consequent crop loss.

A short burst of extreme heat in mid-January saw vintage commence on January 18, but the heat did not last, and the remainder of vintage continued in abnormally cool and relatively dry conditions. Indeed, botrytised semillon and botrytised chardonnay were not harvested until early April, an exceptionally late finish for this district.

The sauvignon blanc, rhine riesling and traminer are rated as the best ever produced in the Upper Hunter; rather surprisingly, semillon and chardonnay are not outstanding, and considered to be on a par with the wines of 1984.

The best reds were shiraz, merlot and pinot noir, producing well-balanced and intensely flavoured wines of considerable elegance.

The Changes

No wineries have gone, nor are there any new faces. However, as in so much of Australia, the wine styles are changing in response to substantial alterations to vineyard plantings. Increasing quantities of chardonnay and pinot noir are being made in the Upper Hunter, while merlot is starting to come into commercial production for blending with cabernet sauvignon.

ARROWFIELD

pp. 84–5

Location:
Highway 213, Jerry's Plains, 2330;
20 km south-east of Denman.
(065) 76 4041.

Winemaker:
Simon Gilbert.

1985 Production:
More than 10,000 cases.

Principal Wines:

Range now restricted to eight varietal white table wines and one red table wine: Chardonnay, Semillon, Chardonnay Semillon and Fumé Blanc (all oak-matured); Rhine Riesling, Traminer and Traminer Riesling; and Cabernet Sauvignon.

Distribution:
National retail distribution. Cellar door 9 a.m. to 5 p.m. Monday to Saturday, noon to 5 p.m. Sunday.

Prices:
Recommended retail of limited relevance; $5.80 to $11.50 (the latter for Show Reserve Chardonnay).

Overall Quality:
Good.

Vintage Rating 1982–85:
'82, '85, '84, '83.

Tasting Notes:

1985 HUNTER VALLEY SEMILLON [17.2] *Colour:* **bright green of light to medium depth.** *Bouquet:* **fresh, round and soft, already showing good fruit weight and, somewhat surprisingly, a touch of honey.** *Palate:* **a very clean, well-balanced wine with excellent mid-palate weight and lively, crisp acid on the finish. Should develop very well, but fairly quickly. Drink '87–'89.**

1985 HUNTER VALLEY/COWRA TRAMINER [16.6] *Colour:* **medium green-yellow.** *Bouquet:* **full and clean, with marked though soft varietal character; gentle aromatic spice which avoids oiliness.** *Palate:* **a light, clean and well-made wine, with a touch of spice, but at the end of the day, somewhat innocuous—a fault of the variety, not the winemaker. Drink '86.**

1985 COWRA PINOT NOIR [16.8] *Colour:* **excellent purple red of medium depth.** *Bouquet:* **very clean; of light to medium weight, with a faint touch of sweet strawberry fruit, but not particularly varietal.** *Palate:* **quite firm, middle-of-the-road Australian light red; has good weight and mouth-feel. Drink '87–'88.**

1985 FUME BLANC [17.6] *Colour:* **very light, pale green-yellow.** *Bouquet:* **strong and complex, with some warm, sweaty, ripe fruit aromas, with lingering after-effects of fermentation.** *Palate:* **fresh; quite marked though light varietal flavours; again that slightly sweaty character, and in the particular regional style. Drink '86–'87 but a wine certain to improve.**

CALLATOOTA ESTATE

p. 85

Location:
Wybong Road, Wybong, 2333;
15 km north-east of Denman and 25 km north-west of Muswellbrook.
(065) 47 8149.

Winemakers:
John and Andrew Cruickshank.

1985 Production:
3200 cases.

Principal Wines:
Exclusively cabernet sauvignon vineyard and production. Wines produced are Rosé, Cabernet Sauvignon Vat I and Cabernet Sauvignon Vat II.

Distribution:
Principally cellar door and mailing list. Cellar-door sales 9 a.m. to 5 p.m. winter, 9 a.m. to 6 p.m. summer, 7 days. Mailing-list enquiries to 504 Pacific Highway, St Leonards, NSW, 2065. Limited retail distribution Sydney and Canberra.

Prices:
$7 per bottle or $70 per case cellar door.

Overall Quality:
Somewhat variable. Rosé usually adequate to good.

Vintage Rating 1982–85:
'83, '85, '82, '84.

Tasting Notes:

ROSE (NON VINTAGE) [16] *Colour:* **light to medium tawny-red.** *Bouquet:* **light with some complexity and obvious signs of bottle age, though no oxidation.** *Palate:* **attractive light, but developed, grassy cabernet varietal character. Drink '86.**

1983 CABERNET SAUVIGNON VAT II [14.8] *Colour:* **medium red with tawny rim.** *Bouquet:* **curious musty/biscuity aroma with distinct signs of deterioration.** *Palate:* **some fruit remaining but slightly acetic, all suggestive of problems with oak casks. Drink '86.**

DENMAN ESTATE WINES

pp. 85–6

Location:
Denman Road, Muswellbrook, 2333;
12 km south-west of town.
(065) 47 2473.

1985 Production:
250 tonnes.

Principal Wines:
Approximately 1500 cases bottled and sold under Denman Estate label; balance of production sold in bulk to other Hunter producers.

Distribution:
Cellar-door sales 9 a.m. to 5 p.m. Monday to Friday, weekends by appointment. Limited retail distribution through selected outlets in Sydney and Australian Capital Territory.

HORDERNS WYBONG ESTATE

pp. 86–7

Location:
Yarraman Road, Wybong, Muswellbrook, 2323.
(065) 47 8127.

Winemaker:
John Hordern.

1985 Production:
4000 cases.

Principal Wines:

Limited range of wines, though offering a spread of vintages up to six years old. Labels include Semillon, Semillon Winemaker's Selection, Wood Aged Chardonnay, Riesling Spatlese, Sauternes, Bengala Shiraz and Vintage Port.

Distribution:
Principally cellar-door sales and mailing list. Cellar-door sales 9 a.m. to 4 p.m. 7 days.

Prices:
$5.50 to $8.50 cellar door.

Overall Quality:
Variable: adequate to good; some older white vintages very good.

Vintage Rating 1982–85:
'85, '82, '84, '83.

Outstanding Prior Vintages:
White: '73, '79.
Red: '75, '79.

Tasting Notes:

1984 HUNTER VALLEY SEMILLON [16.2] *Colour:* medium straw-yellow. *Bouquet:* surprisingly deep and quite complex, with some straw/malty solids aromas underlying fruit richness. *Palate:* very marked tropical fruit, then some of the straw/malt flavours of the bouquet. An unusual and highly individual wine. Drink '86–'89.

1980 WINEMAKER'S PERSONAL SELECTION SEMILLON [15.4] *Colour:* full yellow-green. *Bouquet:* big, old-fashioned wine with strong solids fermentation characters and some malic greenness. *Palate:* still fairly hard and ungenerous, but will probably develop further with more bottle age. Drink '87–'92.

1979 SEMILLON (WOOD-AGED) [17.4] *Colour:* full yellow-green, bright and strong. *Bouquet:* quite rich and smooth, with no obvious oak aroma, but lots of fruit complexity. *Palate:* an attractive, well-balanced wine with rich fruit, and a long, soft, fruity finish. Drink '86–'90.

1979 HUNTER VALLEY SHIRAZ [15.6] *Colour:* brick red with a tawny rim. *Bouquet:* marked bottle development, quite fragrant but with strong leafy/leathery regional aromas. *Palate:* an old wine, retaining some ethereal fragrances but tiring rapidly. Probably now past its best. Drink immediately.

QUELDINBURG

pp. 87–8

Location:
New England Highway, Muswellbrook, 2333.
(065) 43 2939.

Winemaker:
Kevin Sobels.

1985 Production:
Nil; change in policy; grapes sold.

Principal Wines:
Limited range of varietal table wines released under Pinot Riesling, Chablis Traminer, Rhine Riesling and Semillon labels.

Distribution:
Almost exclusively cellar door. Cellar-door sales 9 a.m. to 5 p.m. Monday to Saturday, noon to 5 p.m. Sunday.

Prices:
$5.50 to $5.99 cellar door.

Overall Quality:
Poor.

Vintage Rating 1982–85:
White: '84, '83, '82.
Red: '83, '84, '82.

Tasting Notes:

1984 CHABLIS [15] *Colour:* light to medium yellow-green. *Bouquet:* clean, lacking any particular varietal character, and of light to medium weight. *Palate:* a somewhat pedestrian wine, lacking any real distinction, but free from any major fault. Drink '85.

1984 PINOT RIESLING [9.2] *Colour:* distinct pinking evident. *Bouquet:* fairly coarse, with obvious signs of oxidation. *Palate:* an unattractive wine suffering from a substantial number of winemaking faults, chiefly oxidation.

1983 CABERNET SAUVIGNON [11] *Colour:* medium to full purple-red. *Bouquet:* dominated by mercaptan, with barely distinguishable fruit underneath. *Palate:* similarly destroyed by mercaptan. (All three wines tasted November '84.)

ROSEMOUNT ESTATE

pp. 88–91

Location:
Rosemount Road, Denman, 2328;
8 km west of town.
(065) 47 2410.

Winemaker:
Phillip Shaw.

1985 Production:
Not for publication.

Principal Wines:

A wide range of sparkling, white and red table wines variously identified by area (Hunter Valley or Coonawarra), vineyard (e.g. Roxburgh), variety (with special emphasis on Oak Matured Chardonnay) and headed in terms of quality by Roxburgh and Show Reserve wines.

Distribution:
Nationally distributed by own sales force.

Prices:
$6.50 to $8.50 recommended retail for standard releases; Show Reserve releases $12 to $17.15 recommended retail.

Overall Quality:
Very good. Top Chardonnays exceptional.

Vintage Rating 1982–85:
'85, '83, '84, '82.

Tasting Notes:

1985 FUME BLANC [17.8] *Colour:* bright light to medium green-yellow. *Bouquet:* pungent, aromatic sauvignon blanc in softer/riper mould, but distinctly varietal and with plenty of weight. *Palate:* very strong varietal flavour in the grassy/gooseberry spectrum; an excellently made wine. Drink '86–'88.

1985 CHARDONNAY [17] *Colour:* light to medium green-yellow. *Bouquet:* light toasty/charred oak aromas, with good fruit balance. *Palate:* rich and full, with a strong impression of sweetness which may be at least partially alcohol-derived rather than from residual sugar. Abundant flavour. Drink '86–'87.

1984 ROXBURGH SHOW CHARDONNAY [19] *Colour:* rich, buttercup yellow. *Bouquet:* immense aroma, with superb charred oak providing an exceedingly complex and rich wine. *Palate:* marvellously full flavour, though not quite as extravagant as the bouquet would suggest. Certainly in the peaches and cream style; within its terms of reference, simply cannot be faulted. Drink '86–'87.

1982 SEMILLON SAUTERNES [17] *Colour:* deep gold. *Bouquet:* voluminous, complex, vanillin aromas with some attractive volatile lift, but botrytis not obvious. *Palate:* a luscious, old-style Australian sweet white with a very long cellaring future. Drink '86–'92.

1984 PINOT NOIR [17.2] *Colour:* medium red, developing quickly. *Bouquet:* good oak handling adds complexity; overall there is a touch of Burgundian sappiness. *Palate:* plenty of flavour and style; nice grip to fruit. An impressive pinot from this district. Drink '86–'88.

1983 ROXBURGH CABERNET SAUVIGNON [17.8] *Colour:* medium full red-purple. *Bouquet:* a big, full, strong wine with a touch of mint and well-integrated oak. *Palate:* ripe, soft, sweet berry flavours tending to blackcurrant, together with positive charred oak flavours. Drink '87–'91.

VERONA VINEYARD

p. 91

Location:
New England Highway, Muswellbrook, 2333; on northern outskirts of town.
(065) 43 1055.
And at McDonalds Road, Pokolbin, 2321.
(049) 98 7668.

Winemaker:
Keith Yore.

1985 Production:
Very restricted; most grapes sold.

Principal Wines:

Four white varietal releases: Chardonnay, Traminer, Semillon, Rhine Riesling; top releases under "Estate Grown Premium" label.

Distribution:
Principally cellar door and mailing list. Cellar-door sales 10 a.m. to 5 p.m. Monday to Saturday, noon to 5 p.m. Sunday. Mailing list PO Box 217, Muswellbrook, 2333. Limited distribution through Hunter Valley Wine Society and Australian Wine Club and limited Melbourne distribution.

Prices:
$6 cellar door.

Overall Quality:
Extremely variable; some wines poor, some good.

Vintage Rating 1982–85:
'83, '85, '82, '84.

Outstanding Prior Vintages:
'75, '79, '81.

Tasting Notes:

1983 PREMIUM RHINE RIESLING [16] *Colour:* good yellow-green. *Bouquet:* quite full and clean, with some soft lime characters. *Palate:* clean, fairly soft fruit but with positive rhine riesling character and overall a well-flavoured, well-made wine. Drink '85–'86.

1981 PREMIUM CHARDONNAY [15.4] *Colour:* medium to full yellow, quite bright. *Bouquet:* clean, with some lemony/citric aromas, possibly oak-derived. *Palate:* lemony flavours again apparent with a touch of camphor, but the wine lacks richness. Probably over-protected either by sulphur (or possibly sorbate) as a young wine and still developing character. Drink '87–'89.

1979 PREMIUM CHARDONNAY [17] *Colour:* medium full yellow-green. *Bouquet:* quite firm and full, with remarkable freshness and gentle complexity. *Palate:* fresh, honeyed, buttery fruit flavours with little or no oak influence, and showing very attractive bottle-developed characters. Drink '86–'88.

Mudgee

1985 Vintage

After three years of severe drought extending from 1981 through to the end of 1983, excellent winter and early spring rains brought smiles to the faces of the district's beleaguered vignerons. But the frosts which had some impact on the Upper Hunter were devastating in Mudgee, some vineyards losing up to 80 per cent of their entire crop.

Then, as if this were not enough, the rainfall disappeared, and warm windy weather further reduced crop levels in unirrigated vineyards. At the end of the season, little more than half the usual crop was produced across the district.

Those vineyards which were not frost-affected and which had irrigation have produced some very good wines. Chardonnay, semillon and sauvignon blanc are the best of the white wines, with ample depth of flavour and very good varietal character.

All of the district's main red wines—pinot noir, shiraz and cabernet sauvignon—are generously proportioned, with the usual intense colour and big, clean fruit flavour.

The Changes

A number of the smaller vineyards and wineries are finding the going extremely difficult. Bramhall Wines, Mudgee Wines and Hill of Gold are all either overtly on the market or would be available for sale if someone were to make a reasonable offer.

Augustine and Burnbrae have both been reorganised; John Rozentals is winemaker at Augustine while Burnbrae has been purchased and re-invigorated, with winemaking now taking place at Thistle Hill.

Settlers Creek, too, is about to emerge from the shadows and should be actively marketed during 1986. Perhaps the greatest encouragement to vignerons in the district will come from the ever-improving quality of the wines from Montrose and (under its new Montrose-ownership) Craigmoor.

AMBERTON

pp. 98–9

Location:
Lowe's Peak Vineyard, Henry Lawson Drive, Mudgee, 2850;
8 km north of township, (2 km past Lawson Memorial).
(063) 73 3910.

Winemaker:
David Thompson.

1985 Production:
3000 cases.

Principal Wines:
Varietal white and red table wines; labels include Semillon Classique, Sauvignon Blanc, Traminer, Traminer Riesling, Chardonnay, Shiraz and Cabernet Sauvignon.

Distribution:
Both retail and cellar-door sales/mailing list. Cellar-door sales 10 a.m. to 4.30 p.m. Monday to Saturday, 11 a.m. to 4 p.m. Sunday. Mailing list as above. Wholesale distribution to fine wine retailers and restaurants through Haviland Wine Co., Sydney, and Wayne Leicht Wine Brokers.

Prices:
$5.95 to $8.95 recommended retail.

Overall Quality:
Very good.

Vintage Rating 1982–85:
'84, '85, '82, '83.

Outstanding Prior Vintages:
'81 Cabernet Sauvignon, '82 Chardonnay.

Tasting Notes:

1985 TRAMINER [17] *Colour:* pale straw. *Bouquet:* clean, fragrant and gently spicy. *Palate:* excellent mid-palate fruit weight, with gentle varietal spice and overall near-perfect balance and acidity. Drink '86.

1984 LOWES PEAK SAUVIGNON BLANC [17.8] *Colour:* medium full yellow-green. *Bouquet:* clean, lifted fruit, though varietal character not particularly obvious. *Palate:* much more to it than the bouquet suggests; a cunningly wrought wine with very good palate-feel and a long finish which avoids phenolic hardness. Drink '85–'87.

1984 CHARDONNAY [17.6] *Colour:* medium full yellow. *Bouquet:* smooth, quite rich with complex honey/malt/straw aromas and well-controlled oak. *Palate:* really comes into its own, with full-flavoured grapefruit/melon flavours and a long, soft finish. Drink '86–'88.

1984 CABERNET SAUVIGNON [18] *Colour:* medium purple-red. *Bouquet:* clean, with sweet cherry/red berry fruit aromas, backed by charred oak. *Palate:* lively, a touch of spice goes with sweet berry/blackcurrant fruit flavours on the mid-palate, then spicy oak comes again on the finish. Drink '88–'93.

1984 SHIRAZ [17.6] *Colour:* dense purple-red. *Bouquet:* clean, firm and solid wine, but not particularly varietal. *Palate:* very smooth, with clean sweet berry flavours and just a hint of spice on the back-palate. Drink '87–'90.

AUGUSTINE

p. 99

Location:
Airport Road, Mudgee, 2850;
7 km north-east of township.
(063) 72 3880.

Winemaker:
John Rozentals.

1985 Production:
1500 cases (reduced by frost).

Principal Wines:
Chablis, Moselle, Traminer, Chardonnay, Frontignan Rosé, Pinot Noir, Cabernet Shiraz, Cabernet Port and Liqueur Frontignan.

Distribution:
Exclusively cellar-door sales and mailing list. Cellar-door sales 11 a.m. to 4.30 p.m. Monday to Saturday, noon to 4.30 p.m. Sunday.

Prices:
$5.50 to $7.50 per bottle cellar door.

Overall Quality:
Adequate, but with the potential to improve.

Vintage Rating 1982–85:
Not applicable; change in winemaker and ownership.

Tasting Notes:

1985 TRAMINER [15.6] *Colour:* pale bright straw. *Bouquet:* quite clean, with a touch of spicy varietal character. *Palate:* marked residual sugar the dominant feature, making the wine unashamedly commercial, but well enough handled for all that. Drink '86.

1985 PINOT NOIR Quite good sappy, varietal aroma and good early/mid-palate flavour; peculiar off-character on finish, but tasted from cask very early in its life, and may well grow out of whatever problem was affecting it.

BOTOBOLAR

pp. 99–100

Location:
Botobolar Lane, Mudgee, 2850;
18 km north-east of town.
(063) 73 3840.

Winemaker:
Gil Wahlquist.

1985 Production:
3750 cases.

Principal Wines:
A diverse range of labels and styles including Crouchen, Marsanne, Vineyard White, Budgee Budgee, Chardonnay, Vincentia Sauternes, Shiraz, St Gilbert, Cabernet Sauvignon, Vintage Muscat and Cooyal Port.

Distribution:
Virtually exclusively cellar door and mailing list. (Isolated retail distribution including Oak Barrel, Sydney.)

Prices:
$3.50 to $6.60 cellar door.

Overall Quality:
Reliable; good to very good.

Vintage Rating 1982–85:
White: '84, '85, '82, '83.
Red: '85, '84, '82, '83.

Outstanding Prior Vintages:
White: '79.
Red: '77, '79.

Tasting Notes:

1984 MARSANNE [17.4] *Colour:* medium straw-yellow. *Bouquet:* smooth with a touch of honeysuckle; clean and well-made. *Palate:* big honeysuckle fruit flavour, very varietal and very interesting. An outstanding example of the grape flavour not obscured by oak. Drink '86–'88

1984 CHARDONNAY [16.6] *Colour:* bright yellow-green. *Bouquet:* lifted limey, almost essency, aroma. *Palate:* strong, rich tropical fruit flavours, unusual but quite attractive. A well-made wine. Drink '86–'88.

1984 BUDGEE BUDGEE [16.8] *Colour:* bright medium to full yellow. *Bouquet:* huge, aromatic lychee fragrances. *Palate:* a spectacularly flavoured spice/lychee wine crammed full of grapy muscat flavour. Drink '86.

1982 ST GILBERT [18] *Colour:* medium red, retaining just a hint of purple. *Bouquet:* complex cedar aromas; stylish, indeed outstanding. *Palate:* finely structured and flavoured wine, with cedar/tobacco characters excellently balanced against good fruit. Drink '86–'90.

1980 SHIRAZ [17.4] *Colour:* dark red. *Bouquet:* big, soft, ripe berry aromas with a counter-balance of attractive oak. *Palate:* excellent, full-flavoured, sweet, berry/black cherry flavours augmented by a touch of sweet oak and then soft tannin on the finish. Drink '85–'88.

BURNBRAE

p. 100

Location:
Hargraves Road, Eurunderee via Mudgee, 2850; 10 km south-west of Mudgee.
(063) 73 3853.

Winemakers:
Paul Tuminello (red wines) and Ian MacRae (white wines).

1985 Production:
2000 cases.

Principal Wines:
Chardonnay, Semillon, Cabernet Sauvignon/Shiraz, Cabernet Sauvignon, Shiraz, Cabernet Vintage Port and Vintage Port.

Distribution:
Virtually exclusively cellar-door sales and mailing list. Cellar-door sales 9 a.m. to 5 p.m. 7 days.

Prices:
$6.50 to $9 cellar door.

Vintage Rating 1982–85:
'85, '82, '84, '83.

Outstanding Prior Vintages:
'77, '79.

Tasting Notes:

1984 SEMILLON [16.2] *Colour:* pale bright green-yellow. *Bouquet:* complex with some green herbaceous characters and a hint of yeastiness lingering. *Palate:* good structure; a firm wine which will age well, but which shows the same very slightly off-character evident on the bouquet. Drink '87–'89.

1984 CHARDONNAY [16.6] *Colour:* bright yellow-green. *Bouquet:* some grassy/citric/grapefruit aromas. *Palate:* a lemony, crisp wine which presently lacks generosity and needs time to fill out. Drink '87–'88.

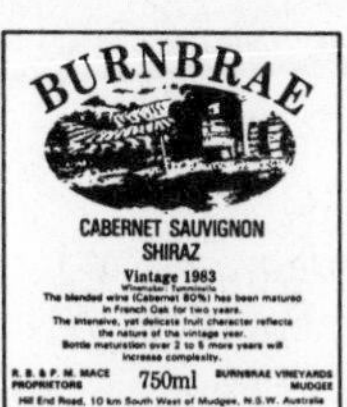

1983 CABERNET SHIRAZ [17.8] *Colour:* dense, impenetrable purple-red. *Bouquet:* a very big wine, slightly extractive, though high in aroma and richness. *Palate:* big, ripe cassis/berry flavours; richly textured with soft tannin. Drink '88–'93.

1981 CABERNET SAUVIGNON VINTAGE PORT [18.2] *Colour:* dense purple-red. *Bouquet:* fine, strong concentrated aroma with great depth and strength. *Palate:* lovely dark chocolate flavours, rich and long; clean spirit and a touch of soft tannin to add complexity. Drink '86–'92.

CRAIGMOOR

pp. 100–2

Location:
Craigmoor Road, Mudgee, 2850;
5 km north of town.
(063) 72 208.

Winemaker:
Carlo Corino.

1985 Production:
12,000 cases.

Principal Wines:
Chablis, Semillon Chardonnay, Spatlese Rhine Riesling, Traminer, Traminer Rhine Riesling, Late-Picked Semillon, Pinot Noir, Cabernet Shiraz and Cabernet Sauvignon.

Distribution:
National wholesale distribution through Taylor Ferguson providing good retail representation. Also cellar-door sales through historic winery and restaurant complex 10 a.m. to 4 p.m. Monday to Saturday, noon to 5 p.m. Sunday.

Prices:
Retail prices in $6 to $8.40 range, with exception of Botrytis Semillon at $10.50.

Overall Quality:
Very good, bordering on exceptional.

Vintage Rating 1984-85:
'84, '85.

Outstanding Prior Vintages:
Not relevant because of change in ownership after '83 vintage.

Tasting Notes:

1984 CHABLIS [18] *Colour:* medium yellow-green. *Bouquet:* very good balance between fruit and oak; clean, abundant aroma, yet not heavy; an extremely attractive style. *Palate:* fresh, clean and light on the tongue—authentic labelling. A very well constructed wine. Drink '85–'86.

1984 SEMILLON CHARDONNAY [18] *Colour:* bright green-yellow. *Bouquet:* spicy nutmeg oak the initial impression, followed by fresh, round fruit aromas. *Palate:* a stylish wine, with plenty of weight on the back palate and a tightly knit amalgam of grapefruit/grassy fruit flavours. Drink '86–'89.

1984 CHARDONNAY [18.2] *Colour:* bright yellow-green. *Bouquet:* skilfully-integrated spicy/lemony oak together with pungently aromatic grapefruit aroma. *Palate:* a long, clean and lingering wine with good balance, and marked grapefruit/citric fruit and oak flavours intermingling. Drink '86–'89.

1984 CABERNET SAUVIGNON [17.8] *Colour:* strong red-purple. *Bouquet:* deep and strong, richly flavoured cabernet/blackcurrant aromas with a touch of smoky oak. *Palate:* good berry flavours feature of a very long-flavoured wine. Drink '88–93.

1984 CABERNET SHIRAZ [18.4] *Colour:* medium to full red-purple. *Bouquet:* firm and clean with a touch of grassy cabernet and although very solid, not heavy or extractive. *Palate:* even better than the bouquet promises, with a lovely touch of herbaceous cabernet, plus generous shiraz, rounded off with beautifully handled spicy oak. A totally seductive wine. Drink '88–'92.

HILL OF GOLD

p. 102

Location:
Henry Lawson Drive, Mudgee, 2850;
9 km north of town.
(063) 73 3933.

Winemaker:
Peter Edwards.

1985 Production:
2000 cases.

Principal Wines:
Specialises in Pinot Noir; also releases Cabernet Sauvignon, Gamay Beaujolais, Merlot and Cabernet Port.

Distribution:
Chiefly cellar door and mailing list. Cellar-door sales 8 a.m. to 6 p.m. 7 days. Mailing list as above. Limited local and Sydney retail distribution.

Prices:
$3.50 to $6 per bottle cellar door.

Overall Quality:
Poor, due to problems with acetic oak casks. Several good ports available.

Tasting Notes:

1984 GAMAY BEAUJOLAIS [14.8] *Colour:* light red-purple, a little dull. *Bouquet:* strong meaty/spicy carbonic maceration aromas. *Palate:* light and with some freshness, lacking fruit richness on the mid-palate, but nonetheless an authentic maceration style. (Not, however, made from the Gamay grape.) Drink '85.

1984 MERLOT [15.4] *Colour:* blackish red. *Bouquet:* cigar box, together with some grassy varietal fruit aromas. *Palate:* quite good, solid construction, with some sweet, berry flavours, although a little one-dimensional. Drink '86–'88.

1983 PINOT NOIR [13.6] *Colour:* red of medium depth and quite good hue. *Bouquet:* a suggestion of varietal aroma is quickly lost in volatility. *Palate:* like most of the older wines from Hill of Gold, and particularly the pinots, utterly spoilt by volatility.

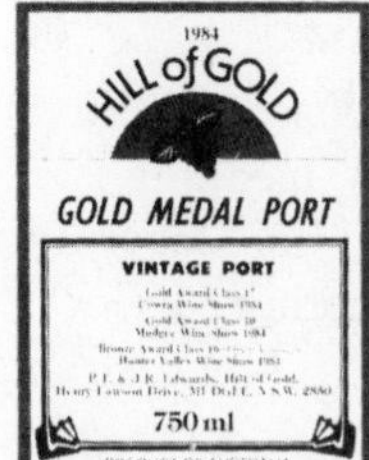

1984 GOLD MEDAL PORT [17.2] *Colour:* medium to full purple-red. *Bouquet:* complex and unusual tea-leaf aroma, with distinct lift and fresh earth from spirit. *Palate:* softly complex, round and soft; not too sweet, and good spirit character. Drink '87–'89.

HUNTINGTON ESTATE

pp. 102–4

Location:
Cassilis Road, Mudgee, 2850;
10 km north-east of town.
(063) 73 3825.

Winemaker:
Bob Roberts.

1985 Production:
Not stated; estimated 10,000 cases.

Principal Wines:
An unusually wide range. White table wine labels include Semillon Medium Dry, Semillon, Chardonnay Medium Dry, Chardonnay Wood Aged Dry, Sweet White Blend. Light reds include Rosé Dry, Rosé Wood Aged, Rosé Medium Dry and Barton Range Beaujolais style. Red table wines labelled by variety and progressively changing Bin Number with FB (full-bodied) or MB (medium-bodied) prefix; they include Shiraz, Shiraz Cabernet Sauvignon, Cabernet Sauvignon, Cabernet Merlot and Pinot Noir.

Distribution:
Largely by cellar-door sales and regular mailing list. Cellar-door sales 9 a.m. to 5 p.m. Monday to Saturday, Sunday 10 a.m. to 5 p.m. Mailing list PO Box 188, Mudgee, 2850.

Prices:
$4.98 to $7.80 per bottle (less 15% per case) cellar door.

Overall Quality:
Exceptional.

Vintage Rating 1982–85:
'84, '85, '82, '83.

Outstanding Prior Vintages:
'74, '79.

Tasting Notes:

1984 SEMILLON MEDIUM DRY [18.2] *Colour:* pale straw-yellow. *Bouquet:* clean and aromatic, with grassy overtones of Sauvignon Blanc. *Palate:* very similar to bouquet, with authoritative grassy/gooseberry flavours, yet with full weight and balance. Drink '86–'90.

1983 PINOT NOIR SHIRAZ [18] *Colour:* medium full red-purple. *Bouquet:* considerable richness from both fruit and oak; not obviously varietal, but balanced and attractive. *Palate:* lovely, gentle, velvety structure, with a spectrum of sweet berry flavours; wood well-balanced; an outstanding success. Drink '86–'89.

1982 CABERNET SAUVIGNON BIN FB 13 [17.8] *Colour:* medium red, still holding some purple hues. *Bouquet:* lively, elegant leafy/leathery aromas. *Palate:* relatively light by Huntington standards, and particularly so given the FB Bin rating. Scores well because of its elegant lively flavour and lingering finish. Drink '86–'90.

1981 CABERNET MERLOT BIN FB 12 [17] *Colour:* medium to full red with just a touch of purple. *Bouquet:* strong leathery/cedar aromas with a suspicion of mercaptan. *Palate:* much better than the bouquet suggests with strong, tightly knit fruit and oak; a long-lived, robust style. Drink '88–'94.

1979 SHIRAZ BIN FB 16 [17.4] *Colour:* outstanding medium to full red-purple. *Bouquet:* full and clean; a ripe style with masses of fruit aroma. *Palate:* full, sweet and smooth berry flavours, yet avoids heaviness; soft tannin rounds off the finish; has aged beautifully but will go on from here. Drink '86–'91.

MANSFIELD WINES

p. 104

Location:
Eurunderee Lane, Mudgee,.2850;
7 km north of town.
(063) 73 3871.

Winemaker:
Peter Mansfield.

1985 Production:
400 cases from Mudgee fruit; balance purchased from other makers in other areas.

Principal Wines:
Limited range of generic styles and Cudgee Special.

Distribution:
Exclusively cellar-door sales 9 a.m. to 6 p.m. Monday to Saturday, 11 a.m. to 6 p.m. Sunday.

Overall Quality:
Not rated.

MIRAMAR

pp. 104–5

Location:
Henry Lawson Drive, Mudgee, 2850;
12 km north of town.
(063) 73 3874.

Winemaker:
Ian MacRae.

Principal Wines:

Selected range of white and red table wines and an occasional vintage port. Labels include Semillon, Semillon Chardonnay, Chardonnay, Wood Aged Semillon, Traminer Rhine Riesling, Rhine Riesling, Eurunderee Moselle, Eurunderee Rosé, Mudgee Shiraz, Miramar Shiraz, Cabernet Sauvignon and Vintage Port.

Distribution:
Principally cellar door and mailing list. Cellar-door sales 9 a.m. to 5 p.m. 7 days. Mailing list as above. Limited New South Wales retail and restaurant distribution.

Prices:
$5 to $9 cellar door.

Overall Quality:
Very good; some years (such as '84) exceptional.

Vintage Rating 1982–85:
White: '84, '85, '82, '83.
Red: '84, '85, '83 (no '82 reds).

Outstanding Prior Vintages:
'79.

Tasting Notes:

1984 SEMILLON [18.4] *Colour:* **bright, light to medium yellow-green.** *Bouquet:* **strong, pungent grassy fruit with a delicate backdrop of a light touch of spicy oak.** *Palate:* **a marvellously zesty and lively crisp wine; again that touch of grass is evident; long, lingering finish. Drink '86–'90.**

1984 SEMILLON CHARDONNAY [18.2] *Colour:* **vibrant, glowing green-yellow, pale but bright.** *Bouquet:* **very fresh, with evidence of extremely careful fermentation and still needing time; semillon dominant with a touch of herbaceousness.** *Palate:* **a crisp, clean wine, with a little bit of extra weight on the back palate from the chardonnay; very well-balanced and again a long finish. Drink '86–'89.**

1984 CHARDONNAY [18.2] *Colour:* **bright yellow-green.** *Bouquet:* **a touch of honeyed toast married with melon/grapefruit aromas results in an extremely complex bouquet.** *Palate:* **lively, fresh grapefruit characters with very good acid and quite obvious barrel ferment characters; should develop superbly. Drink '86–'89.**

1984 RHINE RIESLING **A complete aberration; hard, stripped and simply not pleasant.**

1984 CABERNET SAUVIGNON [18.4] *Colour:* **medium purple-red.** *Bouquet:* **fine, elegant with very pronounced herbaceous/leafy cabernet aroma.** *Palate:* **fine, elegant and long-flavoured wine with some mulberry fruit; excellent structure, augmented by soft tannin. Drink '89–'94.**

MONTROSE

pp. 105–6

Location:
Henry Lawson Drive, Mudgee, 2850;
8 km north of town.
(063) 73 3853.

Winemaker:
Carlo Corino.

1985 Production:
16,500 cases.

Principal Wines:

Sparkling and white and red varietal table wines including several uncommon varieties. Labels include Semillon, Chardonnay, Traminer, Rhine Riesling, Auslese Rhine Riesling, Bemosa Sauternes, Shiraz, Barbera/Nebbiolo and Cabernet Sauvignon.

Distribution:
Extensive retail distribution. Also cellar-door sales and mailing list. Cellar-door sales 9 a.m. to 4 p.m. Monday to Friday, 11 a.m. to 4 p.m. Saturday, noon to 4 p.m. Sunday. Mailing list as above.

Prices:
$5.80 to $8.25 recommended retail.

Overall Quality:
Very good; '84 and '85 promise to be exceptional.

Vintage Rating 1982–85:
White: '84, '82, '85, '83.
Red: '82, '84, '85, '83.

Outstanding Prior Vintages:
'77.

1984 WOOD MATURED SEMILLON [17.8] *Colour:* full yellow with oak-derived depth. *Bouquet:* rich and strong spicy/nutmeg limousin oak aromas, beautifully handled. *Palate:* spicy/clove flavours from oak, but intense fruit to provide balance; a long finish to a highly individual wine. Drink '86–'90.

1984 STONEY CREEK CHARDONNAY [18.6] *Colour:* bright green-yellow. *Bouquet:* spicy nutmeg oak presently dominates (but does not obscure) good fruit. *Palate:* first impression is of spicy nutmeg oak then rich grapefruit/peach fruit. A big, but not heavy, wine with an outstanding future. Drink '87–'90.

1984 POETS CORNER CHARDONNAY [18.2] *Colour:* bright green-yellow. *Bouquet:* extremely rich; complex and harmonious balance between fine fruit and oak. *Palate:* lighter and more elegant than Stoney Creek, and will be ready sooner. Drink '86–'89.

1983 SAUTERNES [18.4] *Colour:* medium full buttercup yellow. *Bouquet:* superbly complex with strong lifted aroma and true sauternes overtones. *Palate:* spicy oak with extremely complex fruit flavours possessing both life and lift; a lingering finish. A worthy successor to the outstanding 1980 vintage. Drink '87–'93.

1983 CABERNET SAUVIGNON [16.6] *Colour:* medium full red-purple. *Bouquet:* complex leathery/cedar aromas with a suspicion of mercaptan. *Palate:* quite sweet fruit, with plummy flavours on the ripe side. Drink '86–'89.

1982 BARBERA NEBBIOLO [17.2] *Colour:* medium red. *Bouquet:* complex fragrances of cedar, tobacco and spice. *Palate:* similar flavours evident, together with well-structured firm fruit providing backbone, and then just a touch of wood-derived spice on the finish. Drink '86–'89.

MUDGEE WINES

p. 106

Location:
Henry Lawson Drive, Mudgee, 2850;
5 km north of town.
(063) 72 2258.

Winemaker:
Jennifer Meek.

1985 Production:
375 cases (frost-ravaged, normally much more).

Principal Wines:
Premium releases headed by Pinot Noir, Chardonnay and Cabernet Sauvignon; also Dry White, Shiraz, Cabernet Shiraz and Muscat.

Distribution:
Cellar-door sales 9 a.m. to 5 p.m. Monday to Saturday, noon to 4 p.m. Sunday.

Overall Quality:
Erratic and frequently poor.

Vintage Rating 1982–85:
'85, '82 (no wine made 1983 or 1984).

Outstanding Prior Vintages:
'79.

PIETER VAN GENT

p. 106

Location:
Black Springs Road, Mudgee, 2850;
9 km north-east of town.
(063) 73 3807.

Winemaker:
Pieter Van Gent.

1985 Production:
Not for publication.

Principal Wines:
Limited range with special interest in chardonnay and fortified wines. Labels offer Chardonnay, Dry Frontignan, Shiraz, Angelic White, Pipeclay Port, Pipeclay Muscat, Pipeclay Vermouth.

Distribution:
Virtually exclusively cellar door and mailing list; some exports. Cellar-door sales 10 a.m. to 5 p.m. Monday to Saturday; noon to 4 p.m. Sunday. Mailing list enquiries Box 222, Mudgee, 2850.

Prices:
$6 to $7.

Overall Quality:
Poor.

PLATT'S

pp. 106–7

Location:
Mudgee Road, Gulgong, 2852;
5 km from Gulgong, 20 km from Mudgee.
(063) 74 1700.

Winemaker:
Barry Platt.

1985 Production:
2000 cases.

Principal Wines:
Will eventually concentrate on Chardonnay and Sauvignon Blanc. Initial releases offer Mudgee Chardonnay, Gulgong Chardonnay, Mudgee Semillon, Hunter Valley Semillon, Mudgee Traminer Late Harvest, Mudgee Traminer Dry, Mudgee Pinot Noir, Mudgee Shiraz and Mudgee Cabernet Sauvignon.

Distribution:
Present limited production sold exclusively by cellar-door sales and mailing list. Cellar-door sales 9 a.m. to 5 p.m. 7 days. Mailing list to Box 200, Gulgong, 2852.

Prices:
$6.50 to $8 per bottle cellar door.

Overall Quality:
Good.

Vintage Rating 1983–85:
'84, '85, '83.

Outstanding Prior Vintages:
Not applicable: 1983 first release.

Tasting Notes:

1984 MUDGEE SEMILLON [16.4] *Colour:* **medium yellow-green, with a touch of straw.** *Bouquet:* **rather closed and heavy, with some obvious solids ferment characters.** *Palate:* **firm, clean, old-fashioned slow-developing style. Drink '88–'91.**

1984 MUDGEE TRAMINER (LATE HARVEST) [16.4] *Colour:* **pale straw.** *Bouquet:* **clean and smooth with no solids fermentation characters, although equally little varietal spice.** *Palate:* **a very well-made highly commercial wine with marked residual sugar although, as with the bouquet, not particularly varietal. Drink '86.**

1983 MUDGEE PINOT NOIR [17] *Colour:* **strong purple-red of medium depth.** *Bouquet:* **full strong and stylistic powdery aroma.** *Palate:* **strong, ripe, strawberry flavours; well-made (with a reservation about the after-taste) and will live for many years. Drink '86–'90.**

1984 CABERNET SAUVIGNON [16.2] *Colour:* **medium full red, developing very quickly.** *Bouquet:* **some powdery oak aromas; surprisingly soft and ripe.** *Palate:* **distinct lift to berry fruit flavours on the mid-palate, followed by soft tannin on the finish. Not typical of the vintage. Drink '86–'89.**

Murrumbidgee Irrigation Area

1985 Vintage

Obviously enough, districts which rely as heavily on irrigation as does the MIA experience far less vintage variation than other regions. Climatic conditions are nonetheless important, particularly with the growing popularity of the botrytised sweet white wine styles pioneered by de Bortoli.

The region enjoyed a very cool and dry lead-up to vintage, with occasional hot days. Normal levels of irrigation were used, but so cool was the spring and early to mid-summer that difficulty was encountered in ripening some varieties to desired sugar levels.

Despite this, vintage commenced relatively early, although it finished far later than usual. Indeed, the last botrytised grapes were not picked until the end of June, a statistic which would surprise some of the cool-climate vignerons of Australia. The most successful white variety is sauvignon blanc, while the quality of the red wines is above average.

Vintage resulted in a record 98,000 tonnes of grapes, but this was nonetheless insufficient to meet total demand, and an additional 9000 tonnes were purchased from the Murray Valley in Victoria.

The Changes

Jolimont has moved its manufacturing base out of the district to Rutherglen (north-east Victoria), while the tiny Stanbridge Estate of Roger Hoare was on a winemaking vacation during the currency of Hoare's absence overseas on a Churchill Fellowship.

The principal changes in the district continue to revolve around increasing use of botrytised material, largely for late-harvest sweet styles, but with a dry, botrytised semillon also reported from the 1985 vintage.

CASELLA

p. 113

Location:
Farm 1471, Yenda, 2681.
(069) 68 1346.

1985 Production:
Between 150,000 and 200,000 litres.

Principal Wines:
Trebbiano, Semillon, Pedro Ximinez, Shiraz, Grenache and Cabernet Sauvignon, mostly sold in bulk to private customers for home bottling.

Overall Quality:
Not rated.

DE BORTOLI WINES

pp. 113–15

Location:
De Bortoli Road, Bilbul, 2680;
9 km east of Griffith.
(069) 62 1400 and (069) 63 4344.

Winemakers:
Darren and Deen De Bortoli.

1985 Production:
5,000,000 litres (the equivalent of more than 550,000 cases).

Principal Wines:

A large range of varietal table wines, both dry and sweet; sparkling wines and fortified wines sold in every type and size of container. More than 60 different wines are on sale at the winery. Since 1982 De Bortoli has produced some of Australia's greatest botrytised sweet table wines from semillon, recently extending to traminer and rhine riesling.

Distribution:
Extensive retail distribution, principally direct. Cellar-door sales 8 a.m. to 5.30 p.m. 7 days.

Prices:
From $2.30 to $30 (for '82 Botrytis Sauternes) recommended retail.

Overall Quality:
Good; sweet botrytised wines exceptional.

Vintage Rating 1982–85:
Botrytis whites: '84, '82, '85, '83.
White: '85, '84, '82, '83.
Red: '85, '84, '82, '83.

Tasting Notes:

1984 CHARDONNAY [15] *Colour:* light to medium yellow. *Bouquet:* clean; light fruit with no clearly marked varietal character; light oak in balance. *Palate:* again lacks fruit richness, and finishes a fraction hard. No winemaking fault. Drink '85–'86.

1984 TRAMINER BEERENAUSLESE [18.6] *Colour:* golden yellow of medium to full depth. *Bouquet:* immense lime botrytis aromas overlying typical tannic edge of traminer. *Palate:* magnificently handled wine; despite the masking effect of botrytis, varietal character still evident which gives a touch of firmness to go with the richness. Overall soft acid. Drink '86–'91.

1984 BEERENAUSLESE RIESLING [17.8] *Colour:* full golden/buttercup yellow. *Bouquet:* rich, lime/tropical fruit aromas, without excessive volatile lift. *Palate:* beautifully smooth and balanced wine, with a long finish in which acid offsets lusciousness to perfection. Drink '85–'89.

FRANCO'S WINES

pp. 115–16

Location:
Farm 161, Irrigation Way, Hanwood, 2680;
5 km south of Griffith.
(069) 62 1675.

1985 Production:
Approximately 6000 cases.

Principal Wines:
A wide range of generic table and fortified wines.

Distribution:
Almost exclusively cellar-door sales 8.30 a.m. to 5.30 p.m. Monday to Saturday.

Overall Quality:
Adequate given modest price.

LILLYPILLY ESTATE

pp. 116–17

Location:
Lillypilly Road, off Leeton–Yanco Road, Leeton, 2705;
2 km south-east of Leeton.
(069) 53 4069.

Winemaker:
Robert Fiumara.

1985 Production:
8000 dozen.

Principal Wines:

Tramillon (a blend of semillon and traminer), Fumé Blanc, Chardonnay, Rhine Riesling, Spatlese Semillon, Spatlese Lexia, Hermitage and Cabernet Shiraz.

Distribution:
Principally cellar-door sales and mailing list. Cellar-door sales 9 a.m. to 5 p.m. Monday to Saturday. Mailing list to Lillypilly Estate, PO Box 839, Leeton, 2705. Limited retail distribution; New South Wales distributors, The Incredible Wine Company Pty Limited.

Prices:
$4.70 to $5.95 cellar door.

Overall Quality:
Good.

Vintage Rating 1982–85:
White: '84, '85, '82, '83.
Red: '84, '82, '85, '83.

Tasting Notes:

1984 CHARDONNAY [15.8] *Colour:* bright medium yellow. *Bouquet:* soft and clean, with a touch of buttery varietal character, although not particularly rich. *Palate:* a full-flavoured but uncompromisingly sweet wine in which the residual sugar is too obvious for my palate. Drink '85 (and perhaps '86).

1984 FUME BLANC [16] *Colour:* light to medium yellow, still with a touch of green. *Bouquet:* quite complex toasty fruit with oak held well in restraint. *Palate:* quite rich with fair weight and palate feel; residual sugar is evident but not overdone. A trace of sauvignon varietal character lurks underneath. Drink '85–'86.

1984 SPATLESE LEXIA [17.6] *Colour:* bright light to medium green-yellow. *Bouquet:* very well-made, clean wine with spectacularly pungent, spicy/pastille frontignan aroma. *Palate:* very rich, marvellous grapy flavours, almost raisined. A unique Australian style. Drink '85–'87.

1984 SPATLESE SEMILLON [16.8] *Colour:* bright green-yellow. *Bouquet:* pungent, flowery tropical/frangipani aromas; very clean. *Palate:* a lively wine, full of somewhat unusual flavours again in the flower spectrum, running from frangipani to honeysuckle. Drink '86–'87.

McWILLIAM'S

pp. 117–18

Location:
Hanwood Winery, Winery Road, Hanwood, 2674; 1.5 km south of Hanwood.
(069) 62 1333.
Yenda Winery, Winery Road, Yenda, 2681; on eastern outskirts of town.
(069) 68 1001.
Beelbangera Winery, Winery Road, Beelbangera, 2686;
on eastern side of main Griffith–Yenda Road.
Robinvale Winery, Moore Street, Robinvale, 3549.
(050) 26 4004.

Winemakers:
Yenda: G. P. McWilliam, J. B. Jenkins, J. F. Brayne; Beelbangera: J. A. Martin and L. W. McWilliam; Robinvale: Max McWilliam and Jason Chester.

1985 Production:
In excess of 20,000,000 litres.

Principal Wines:
An immense range of wines made, both table and fortified. Principal brands are Bodega, Leeto, Hanwood, Max, Markview and Tavern. Hanwood white and red table wines and Hanwood Tawny Port are the most important premium wines in the 750 ml bottle range. BYO Gold Selection introduced mid-1985, providing bottled varietal and generic wines at rock-bottom prices; the quality is similar to flagon or cask wine. 1.5-litre, 2-litre and 4-litre flagons and casks also made and sold in vast quantities.

Distribution:
National retail at all levels, distributed by McWilliam's own sales force.

Prices:
$4.49 to $6.30 recommended retail; real price very substantially less.

Overall Quality:
Red wines adequate; white wines, particularly at price, good.

Vintage Rating 1982–85:
'84, '82, '85, '83.

Tasting Notes:

1982 HANWOOD CABERNET SAUVIGNON [15.8] *Colour:* **medium red with a touch of garnet.** *Bouquet:* **aged, sweet, smooth fruit with a touch of caramel; very light but some pleasant fragrances.** *Palate:* **pleasant, sweet, smooth berry flavours; for immediate consumption. Drink '85.**

1981 HANWOOD CABERNET MERLOT [14] *Colour:* **medium red with a touch of tawny on the rim.** *Bouquet:* **very light and very developed, with fruit rapidly diminishing and fading.** *Palate:* **a wine well past its best; first released in mid-1985, and should have been released (and consumed) two or three years ago.**

1972 HANWOOD CABERNET SAUVIGNON [14.2] *Colour:* **medium tawny.** *Bouquet:* **very aged, with an attractive touch of cigar box, bottle-developed characters, but fruit severely diminished.** *Palate:* **an aged, leathery wine, long past its best. (A re-release mid-1985.)**

MIRANDA WINES

p. 120

Location:
Farm 282, Irrigation Way, Griffith, 2680;
on south-eastern outskirts of town.
(069) 62 4033.

Winemakers:
Lou Miranda (production director), plus two qualified winemakers.

1985 Production:
Over 10,000,000 litres (including contract purchases).

Principal Wines:

The usual immense range of wines in every style, shape and size from white varietal table wines in 750 ml bottles to Golden Gate Spumante (for many years in Australia's 12 largest brand sales) to Coffee Marsala, Rum Port and others too numerous to mention.

Distribution:
National through own sales staff, with permanent representatives in Brisbane, Sydney and Newcastle. Cellar-door sales Monday to Saturday 8.30 a.m. to 5.30 p.m. through own liquor supermarket.

Prices:
$2 bottle, $4.55 4-litre cask (recommended retail).

Overall Quality:
Within its terms of reference, reliably good.

ORLANDO WICKHAM HILL

pp. 120–1

Location:
Harris Road, Griffith, 2680;
on south-eastern outskirts of township.
(069) 622 605.

1985 Production:
In excess of 5,000,000 litres.

Principal Wines:
Wickham Hill is the major source of base wine for Orlando's Coolabah cask and flagon range. Occasional releases of Semillon and Shiraz (both made from vines subject to specialised late pruning techniques) have been released for sale cellar door only.

RIVERINA WINES

p. 121

Location:
Farm 1, 305 Hillston Road, Tharbogang via Griffith, 2680;
6 km west of Griffith.
(069) 624 1222.

Winemaker:
Andrew Vasiljuk.

1985 Production:
Approximately 6,000,000 litres.

Principal Wines:
The full range of table wine, sparkling wine and fortified wine found throughout the district, chiefly marketed in bulk, with limited quantities marketed under the Riverina Wines and Ballingal Estates brands. Cellar-door sales 9 a.m. to 5.30 p.m. 7 days.

ROSSETTO'S WINES

p. 121

Farm 576, Beelbangera, 2686;
2 km south-east of Beelbangera.
(069) 63 5214.

Winemaker:
Peter Turley.

1985 Production:
Approximately 3,000,000 litres.

Principal Wines:
Premium white varietals marketed under Mount Bingar label, comprising French Traminer Riesling, Chardonnay, Traminer and White Frontignac; other white and red varietal table wines released under Beelgara brand; diverse range of fortified wines also made and marketed. Very substantial own brand and bulk sales.

Distribution:
Through cellar door, mail orders and retail through own direct-sales force. Cellar-door sales 9 a.m. to 5 p.m. Monday to Saturday.

Prices:
$1.70 to $2.60 recommended retail.

Overall Quality:
Adequate and occasionally good; certainly good value for money.

SAN BERNADINO

pp. 121–2

Location:
Farm 644, Leeton Road, Griffith, 2680;
on south-eastern outskirts of town.
(069) 62 4944.

Winemaker:
Brian Wilson.

1985 Production:
6,000,000 litres.

Principal Wines:

Perhaps the widest, and at times, most imaginative range of wine styles and labels in the entire MIA. The range of table, sparkling, flavoured, non-alcoholic and fortified wines are marketed under three main brand names: Woodridge for the premium varietal table wines; San Bernadino for the remainder of the table and fortified wines; and Castella for the non-alcoholic sparkling and still range.

Distribution:
Mainly through supermarkets and liquor chains, with limited fine wine retail distribution; sales both through own representatives and through distributors or agents in each state. Cellar-door sales 9 a.m. to 5.30 p.m. Monday to Saturday.

Prices:
Woodridge range have theoretical retail price of $6.20, but are likely to sell for far less.

Overall Quality:
Certainly adequate; from time to time releases of surprising quality have appeared under the San Bernadino and Woodridge labels.

Vintage Rating 1982–85:
White: '85, '83, '84, '82.
Red: '85, '84, '83, '82.

Tasting Notes:

1984 WOODRIDGE FUME BLANC [15.2] *Colour:* **medium to full yellow.** *Bouquet:* **extremely pronounced caramel/buttery aromas, and no recognisable sauvignon blanc varietal character.** *Palate:* **very developed buttery/butterscotch flavours, suggestive of some oxidation, but very full in weight. Drink '85–'86.**

1984 WOODRIDGE GEWURTZTRAMINER [15.8] *Colour:* **brilliant green-yellow.** *Bouquet:* **full and soft, with some tropical/lime fruit aromas, but no varietal spice.** *Palate:* **full, soft tropical fruit with some residual sugar balanced by good acid; non-varietal, but good total flavour and quite well-made. Drink '86.**

1984 WOODRIDGE CABERNET SAUVIGNON [14.8] *Colour:* **medium red-purple.** *Bouquet:* **soft, again a touch of coffee/caramel, suggestive of oxidation but not unattractive, together with some ripe berry aromas.** *Palate:* **soft, with obvious straw/oxidation characters and some ripe cherry flavours. Drink '86.**

STANBRIDGE ESTATE

p. 122

Location:
Farm 1773, Griffith–Leeton Highway, Stanbridge, 2705;
10 km west of Leeton.
(069) 955 1234.

Winemaker:
Roger Hoare.

1985 Production:
Nil; Roger Hoare on overseas study leave.

Principal Wines:
Limited range of white varietal table wines made in tiny quantities, centering on Chardonnay, Semillon, Rhine Riesling, Traminer and Sauvignon Blanc.

Distribution:
Only by cellar-door sales and limited mailing list (when wines available).

Overall Quality:
When wines available, good.

TOORAK WINES

pp. 122–3

Location:
Toorak Road, Leeton, 2705;
4 km west of township.
(069) 53 2523.

Winemaker:
Frank Bruno.

1985 Production:
700,000 litres.

Principal Wines:
A substantial range of table and fortified wines are produced, with significant sales in bulk, but also under the Toorak and Amesbury Estate labels.

Distribution:
By direct sale to retailers, cellar-door sales and by mail order. Cellar-door sales 8 a.m. to 5.30 p.m. Monday to Friday and 9 a.m. to 5.30 p.m. Saturday.

Prices:
$2.50 to $4.65 recommended retail.

Overall Quality:
Adequate and at times, good. A 1984 Late Harvest White Frontignac won a bronze medal in the Open Moselle Class at the 1985 Sydney Show.

WEST END WINES

p. 123

Location:
Farm 1283, Braynes Road, Griffith, 2680;
2 km west of township.
(069) 62 2868.

Winemaker:
William Calabria.

1985 Production:
Approximately 230,000 litres.

Principal Wines:
The usual catholic range of wines produced in the region, covering table wine, fortified wine, flavoured wine and sparkling wines, but made in smaller-than-usual quantities and, not infrequently, of better-than-average quality.

Distribution:
Exclusively cellar-door sales and mail orders. Cellar-door sales 8.30 a.m. to 5.30 p.m. Monday to Saturday, noon to 5 p.m. Sunday.

Prices:
$1.50 to $4 recommended retail.

Overall Quality:
Quite good.

Other Districts

1985 Vintage

The wineries covered in this chapter extend all the way from Inverell and the Hastings Valley in the north of the state to Tumbarumba in the extreme south; from Sydney metropolitan in the east to Wellington, Young, and Orange in the west. It is thus hardly surprising that conditions varied somewhat; if anything, the surprise lies in the consistent pattern which followed throughout much of the state.

All of the western and southern vineyards suffered devastating frosts. At Wellington yields were down by as much as 70 per cent in some locations, and 50 per cent overall. Cowra suffered likewise, the extensive vineyards there producing half their normal yield, while the hilltops region of Boorowa-Harden-Young was even more grossly affected. And at Tumbarumba, in the far south-west, only 10 per cent of the normal crop was harvested.

This mayhem was caused principally by spring frosts (and at Tumbarumba summer frosts, occurring on 23 November and 21 December) followed by near-drought conditions throughout the remainder of the growing season.

Inverell, the Sydney metropolitan area and the south coast at Nowra missed the frosts. The only problem came from December hailstorms at Inverell which halved the crop in some vineyards, and was, as I say, followed by excessively dry weather. In these last three districts, which normally suffer rot and mould conditions due to the frequent showers and high humidity which prevail in January and February, vignerons were more than pleased with the trouble-free vintage and with the excellent condition of the grapes.

Overall, the other districts of New South Wales moved strongly against the experience of the rest of Australia, in which crop levels were well above average. It is nigh on impossible to generalise about wine styles, except to say that in most districts the red wines in particular show exceptional intensity of colour and depth of flavour, no doubt caused by the much lower than normal crop levels and a degree of vine stress.

The Changes

The viticultural map has grown extensively with the establishment of two further outposts, Cassegrain Wines' Hastings Valley Winery at Port Macquarie, and Tumbarumba Champagne Estates.

It came as a considerable surprise to find that back in 1867 there were several vineyards and wineries in the Hastings Valley, and that the most famous of them—Douglas Vale—continued in production until 1919, reaching a peak of 1600 cases in 1877. Cassegrain Vineyards, owned by the Cassegrain family, and with John Cassegrain, a Roseworthy graduate who worked for Murray Tyrrell for 10 years, at the helm, is certain to be more than a mere tourist curio.

At the other end of the state Ian Cowell's Tumbarumba Champagne Estates have come into production, only to be acquired immediately by Rosemount. Given the obliteration of the vintage, Ian Cowell must be happy with his decision to go with the strength.

Elsewhere in the state wineries are in incubation, notably John Swanson's Midas Tree at Orange (not yet in production and hence rating no entry), but in the hilltops region Geoff Carter has just opened the doors for business at his Cartobe Vineyard.

I still do not believe we will see the rate or extent of development that is occurring in other states—notably Victoria—but New South Wales covers a vast area, and the potential from a viticultural viewpoint (although not necessarily from a marketing viewpoint) is infinite.

BARWANG

p. 125

Location:
Barwang Road, Young, 2594;
23 km south-east of Young.
(063) 82 2689.

Winemaker:
Peter Robertson.

1985 Production:
Approximately 1200 cases.

Principal Wines:
Range about to be increased; presently limited to Semillon, Late Harvest Semillon, Rhine Riesling, Shiraz, Cabernet Sauvignon and Cabernet Shiraz.

Distribution:
Exclusively cellar door and mailing list. Cellar-door sales 9 a.m. to 5 p.m. Monday to Saturday, 11 a.m. to 5 p.m. Sunday.

Prices:
$4 to $6 cellar door; 1982 Selectively Late Picked Semillon $14 (cellar door).

Overall Quality:
Variable; from poor to good; recent vintages show marked improvement.

Vintage Rating 1982–85:
White Dry: '82, '85, '84, '83.
White Sweet: '82, '85, '83, '84.
Red: '84, '82, '85, '83

Outstanding Prior Vintages:
'80 (Late Harvest Semillon).

Tasting Notes:

1984 SEMILLON [15.8] *Colour:* **medium yellow, tinged with straw.** *Bouquet:* **some evidence of solids fermentation, but fruit (and a touch of honey) is present.** *Palate:* **a wine of surprising richness with honey/malt flavours and a fairly soft finish. Should develop well in bottle. Drink '87–'90.**

1984 LATE PICKED SEMILLON [17.6] *Colour:* **full yellow orange.** *Bouquet:* **immense, raisined apricot/peach aromas.** *Palate:* **soft and rich, with dried apricot flavours; mouth-filling, softly lingering finish. Drink '85–'88.**

1984 SHIRAZ [16] *Colour:* **light to medium red-purple.** *Bouquet:* **clean; light but firm fruit with some cherry aromas.** *Palate:* **distinctly light-bodied, but attractive cherry flavours on the mid-palate; low tannin, and a wine which will probably be at its best while retaining fresh fruit character. Drink '85–'87.**

1984 CABERNET SAUVIGNON [16.2] *Colour:* **light to medium red-purple.** *Bouquet:* **Crystal clear varietal definition in leafy herbaceous mould; very clean.** *Palate:* **very light-bodied, with conspicuous absence of mid-palate weight; nonetheless, beautiful varietal character and a light, crisp finish. Some added new oak treatment might have helped. Drink '86–'88.**

BRIDGEFARM WINES

pp. 125–8

Location:
Lot 3, Macarthur Road, Camden, 2570;
adjacent to the long Macarthur Bridge.
(046) 668 337.

Winemaker:
Dr Sue Hanckel.

1985 Production:
10,000 cases.

Principal Wines:
Chardonnay most important commercial release; Shiraz due for release at a later date.

Distribution:
Cellar-door sales 9 a.m. to 5 p.m. Friday to Sunday; restaurant and limited retail distribution through Carol Ann Classic Wines in Sydney.

Prices:
$9 cellar door.

Overall Quality:
Good.

Vintage Rating 1983–85:
White: '83, '85, '84.

Tasting Notes:

1983 CHARDONNAY **[16.8]** ***Colour:*** **brilliant yellow-green.** ***Bouquet:*** **clean, fresh, light fruit with some varietal character but no oak evident.** ***Palate:*** **of medium weight, with pleasant mid-palate fruit and a soft, clean finish; a little simple and one-dimensional, with no oak apparent. Drink '85–'86.**

CARTOBE VINEYARD

Location:
Young Road, Boorowa, 2586;
5 km west of township, and 3 km from main Cowra Road.
(063) 85 3128.

Winemaker:
Geoff Carter.

1985 Production:
Approximately 450 cases (vastly reduced by drought).

Principal Wines:
Will eventually be sourced largely from own vineyards (planted principally to rhine riesling, with lesser quantities of chardonnay and pinot noir) and from other local growers providing sauvignon blanc and cabernet sauvignon. In the short to medium term, heavy reliance on Cowra chiefly for traminer to produce a moselle style. Wines produced in 1985 included Traminer, Rhine Riesling, Sauvignon Blanc, Auslese Rhine Riesling and Cabernet Sauvignon.

Distribution:
Principally cellar door and mailing list; cellar-door sales 9 a.m. to 5 p.m. Friday to Monday inclusive, school holidays and public holidays (other days by appointment); mailing list as above. Limited Queensland distribution through David Kruse; also some district restaurant listings.

Prices:
$9.50 to $9.90 cellar door.

Overall Quality:
Not rated.

CASSEGRAIN

Location:
Hastings Valley Winery, Pacific Highway, Port Macquarie, 2444;
7 km west of township.
(065) 851 0000.

Winemaker:
John Cassegrain.

1985 Production:
11,000 cases.

Principal Wines:
The releases to date come from a variety of sources, but will increasingly concentrate on wines made from grapes grown in the Hastings Valley, principally pinot noir and chardonnay, with sauvignon blanc, cabernet sauvignon and merlot under trial. Wines released both under simple varietal labels and also varietal labels which disclose the origin of the grapes, which to date have principally come from the Hunter Valley and Coonawarra. Wines include Pokolbin Chardonnay, Chardonnay (presumably a blend), Pokolbin Semillon, Clare Rhine Riesling, Rhine Riesling Traminer, Pokolbin Red Hermitage and Coonawarra Cabernet Sauvignon.

Distribution:
Cellar-door sales, mailing list and local distribution through North Coast retail outlets served direct from the winery. Cellar-door sales 9 a.m. to 5 p.m. 7 days. Mailing-list enquiries as above.

Prices:
$5.85 to $11.45 recommended retail; less cellar door.

Overall Quality:
Good.

Vintage Rating:
Not relevant because of varied sources and recent commencement of production.

Tasting Notes:

1984 CLARE RHINE RIESLING [16.8] *Colour:* medium to full yellow. *Bouquet:* a firm, slightly toasty aroma in typical Clare style, with none of the lime characters of other districts. *Palate:* a rich, gently toasty wine, with good mid-palate weight and a relatively soft finish. Not for long-term cellaring. Drink '86–'87.

1984 CHARDONNAY [16.6] *Colour:* deep yellow. *Bouquet:* rich and smooth, with good fruit-oak integration; weighty and stylish. *Palate:* very good flavour and style; the fruit is not particularly heavy, but has length and varietal character. Perhaps a little lacking on the mid-palate, but a good wine, and substantially better than the more expensive Pokolbin Chardonnay of the same year. Drink '85–'87.

1984 POKOLBIN HERMITAGE [16.2] *Colour:* red-purple of light to medium depth. *Bouquet:* a somewhat leafy, slightly astringent wine, with fruit a little subdued. *Palate:* a soft, light-bodied and fairly early developing style, balanced and fleshed out with a touch of light, sweet oak; clean and well-made with good acid on the finish. Drink '86–'88.

1984 COONAWARRA CABERNET SAUVIGNON [17.2] *Colour:* very good purple-red. *Bouquet:* aromatic and complex leafy/cedar/sweet berry characters. *Palate:* generous, soft fruit showing a nice amalgam of leafy/herbaceous flavours through to sweet berry; low tannin. Drink '87–'90.

COGNO BROTHERS

p. 128

Location:
Cobbitty Road, Cobbitty, 2570.
(046) 51 2281.

Winemaker:
Giovanni Cogno.

1985 Production:
100,000 litres.

Principal Wines:
A diverse range of Italian-accented wines including Frontignan Spatlese, Cobbitty Barbera, Lambrusco, Whisky Port, Liqueur Muscat and Mama Port.

Distribution:
Principally cellar door; limited retail and restaurant distribution. Cellar-door sales 8 a.m. to 6 p.m. Monday to Saturday, noon to 6 p.m. Sunday.

Overall Quality:
Not rated.

THE COLLEGE

pp. 131–2

Location:
Boorooma Street, North Wagga Wagga, 2650;
9 km north of town via the Olympic Way.
(069) 23 2435.

Winemaker:
Andrew Birks.

1985 Production:
7780 cases.

Principal Wines:

A wide range of varietal white and red table wines from an equally diverse number of areas, all of which vary from year to year. Labels clearly identify both.

Distribution:
Mixture of cellar door, mail order and retail sales. Cellar-door sales 9 a.m. to 5 p.m. Monday to Friday. Mailing list PO Box 588, Wagga Wagga 2650.

Prices:
$4.20 to $6.50 cellar door.

Overall Quality:
Somewhat variable; adequate to very good.

Vintage Rating 1982–85:
White: '85, '82, '83, '84.
Red: '82, '83, '85, '84.

Outstanding Prior Vintages:
'78, '80.

Tasting Notes:

1985 CHABLIS [15.8] *Colour:* very pale straw/green. *Bouquet:* clean, neutral fruit of medium weight, and quite smooth. *Palate:* crisp and clean, with firm fruit; quite dry and overall in chablis style; avoids early picked green fruit characters. (A blend of chardonnay, rhine riesling and pinot gris.) Drink '86–'87.

1984 CABERNET SAUVIGNON MERLOT [17] *Colour:* light to medium red-purple. *Bouquet:* very fresh, clean and vibrant fruit aromas with some structural complexity. *Palate:* fresh and clear, gently crisp herbaceous fruit; low tannin and good acid. (From own Booranga Vineyard.) Drink '86–'88.

1983 CHARDONNAY [13.8] *Colour:* light to medium yellow-green. *Bouquet:* very marked volatile acidity, presumably deriving from yeasts used during fermentation. *Palate:* volatility completely obscures the underlying fruit.

1982 COLOMBARD [16.6] *Colour:* medium full yellow. *Bouquet:* strong, pungently aromatic with slightly oily overtones, but very rich. *Palate:* flavoursome, with the suggestion of oak richness on the mid-palate (although presumably no oak in fact used); very good bottle development with some toasty flavours; typical, slightly oily acid on the finish. Drink '85–'87.

1981 COONAWARRA CABERNET SAUVIGNON [15.8] *Colour:* light to medium red. *Bouquet:* quite complex and aromatic; a gently ripe and fairly light wine with traces of gamy/meaty characters, and light oak. *Palate:* a light-bodied wine with soft cigar/plum flavours. Drink '85–'87.

1979 SEMILLON SAUTERNES STYLE [16.8] *Colour:* glowing yellow gold. *Bouquet:* full apricot/butterscotch aromas, but rather soft and lacking intensity. *Palate:* smooth, pleasant bottle-developed complexity; some butterscotch flavours again manifest themselves; quite good acid on finish. Drink '85–'88.

GILGAI

pp. 128–9

Location:
Tingha Road, Gilgai, 2360;
2 km south of Inverell.
(067) 23 1304.

Winemakers:
Keith and Charles Whish.

1985 Production:
Approximately 1500 cases.

Principal Wines:
Limited range of table and fortified wines. Varietal table wines released under Gilgai White or Gilgai Red labels, with variety (Cabernet Shiraz, Malbec, Semillon and Rhine Riesling) usually also specified.

Distribution:
Exclusively cellar door and mailing list. Cellar-door sales 10 a.m. to 6 p.m. Monday to Friday; noon to 6 p.m. Saturday. Mailing list PO Box 462, Inverell, 2360.

Prices:
$6 cellar door.

Overall Quality:
Variable.

GLENFINLASS

p. 129

Location:
Elysian Farm, Parkes Road, Wellington, 2820. (068) 45 2011.

Winemaker:
Brian Holmes.

1985 Production:
500 cases.

Principal Wines:
Tiny output of limited range; Shiraz, Cabernet Sauvignon and Sauvignon Blanc (the latter first released 1985).

Distribution:
Cellar door only; sales 10 a.m. to 5 p.m. Saturday or by appointment.

JASPER VALLEY

pp. 129–30

Location:
RMB 880 Croziers Road, Berry, 2535;
5 km south-east of town.
(044) 64 1596.

Winemaker:
Michael Kerr.

1985 Production:
Approximately 50 tonnes.

Principal Wines:
A wide range of wines including roadside-stall types. Labels offer White Burgundy, Riesling, Rhine Riesling, Traminer, Traminer Riesling, Moselle, Lambrusco, Summer Red, Cabernet Shiraz, Cabernet Sauvignon, Spumante, Passion Wine, Strawberry Wine and a full range of fortified wines.

Distribution:
Principally cellar door and mailing list; limited local retail distribution. Cellar-door sales Monday to Saturday 9.30 a.m. to 5.30 p.m., Sunday 10 a.m. to 5.30 p.m. Mailing list as above.

Prices:
$3.75 to $5.50 cellar door.

Overall Quality:
Adequate.

Tasting Notes:

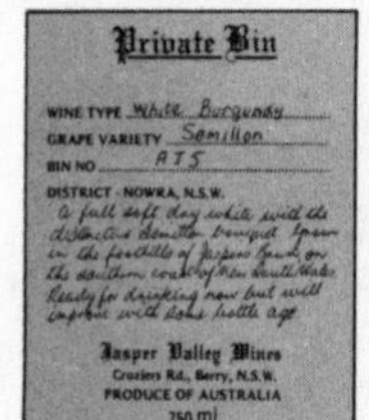

NV WHITE BURGUNDY BIN AJ5 [15.8] *Colour:* **full yellow with some straw/brown hints.** *Bouquet:* **full, soft but slightly cheesy and a little coarse.** *Palate:* **much better than the bouquet; full, soft and fleshy with some attractive, honeyed, buttery flavours in white burgundy style. Drink '85–'87.**

NV RIESLING [13.6] *Colour:* **light yellow-green.** *Bouquet:* **rather dull, with some solids fermentation characters; a little chalky.** *Palate:* **clean, innocuous and light fruit, varietally nondescript; a rather mawkish finish.**

1982 CABERNET SHIRAZ [15.4] *Colour:* **medium red-purple.** *Bouquet:* **clean, smooth and soft with gently ripe fruit and some caramel aromas.** *Palate:* **soft caramel/sweet fruit, lacking acid on the finish. Drink '85–'86.**

1982 CABERNET SAUVIGNON [14.4] *Colour:* **light to medium red-purple.** *Bouquet:* **soft, slightly mushy fruit, and evidence of some inferior oak.** *Palate:* **matchbox aromas largely obscure soft fruit.**

RICHMOND ESTATE

pp. 130–1

Location:
Gadds Lane, North Richmond, 2754;
off Kurmond Road, 3 km north-east of town.
(045) 73 1759.

Winemaker:
Ferdinand (Mick) Lesnick.

1985 Production:
Not stated.

Principal Wines:
Shiraz and Cabernet Sauvignon. Wide range of vintages available.

Distribution:
Virtually exclusively cellar door and mailing list. Cellar-door sales 8 a.m. to 6 p.m. seven days.

Prices:
$7 to $9 cellar door.

Overall Quality:
Good (though variable).

Vintage Rating 1982–85:
1985, 1983, 1982 (1984 not made).

Outstanding Prior Vintages:
1975, 1979, 1980.

Tasting Notes:
1983 CABERNET SAUVIGNON [12] *Colour:* medium red, some purple. *Bouquet:* volatile acidity plus curious meaty aromas. *Palate:* good fruit spoilt by volatile acidity from oak. Drink '86–'88.

1980 SHIRAZ [17.2] *Colour:* medium to full red. *Bouquet:* smooth, quite rich; some mint aromas; holding well. *Palate:* attractive rich ripe sweet fruit, touch of mint; very good structure and overall flavour. Drink '85–'89.

1979 SHIRAZ [17] *Colour:* excellent red, still holding touches of purple. *Bouquet:* clean, fresh and smooth. *Palate:* sweet, almost chewy fruit, with gentle tannin. Holding well though at its peak. Drink '85–'87.

TUMBARUMBA CHAMPAGNE ESTATES

Location:
Taradale Road, Tumbarumba, 2653;
3 km west of township.
(069) 48 2577.

Winemaker:
Ian Cowell.

1985 Production:
Between 20,000 and 30,000 cases of sparkling wine laid down under contract for other wineries.

Principal Wines:
Primarily a contract sparkling winemaker, but also produces limited quantities of *méthode champenoise* from estate and district grown grapes (pinot noir, chardonnay and pinot gris). The *méthode champenoise* is released under the Beaumont label, but following the acquisition of the Estates by Rosemount during 1985, it seems almost certain the Beaumont label will be replaced by Rosemount Tumbarumba. These sparkling wines will be a blend of Hunter Valley and Tumbarumba fruit, and are planned to appear at three quality and price levels: a vintage reserve, made from a traditional blend; a vintage chardonnay and a vintage pinot noir; a non-vintage sparkling blend.

Distribution:
Extensive national retail through Rosemount's distribution channels. Cellar-door sales 9 a.m. to 5 p.m. Monday to Saturday. Mailing list being considered.

Prices:
$9.

Overall Quality:
Very good.

Vintage Rating 1982–85:
'83, '84, '82, '85 (little '85, due to frost).

Tasting Notes:
NV BRUT [17.6] *Colour:* bright medium to full green-yellow. *Bouquet:* firm and clean, rather one-dimensional and has yet to build complexity. *Palate:* clean; very attractive mid-palate fruit, almost buttery, and seemingly with a strong chardonnay influence. Faintly sweet fruit flavours throughout contribute to a most interesting and very well-made sparkling wine. Drink now.

VICARY'S

p. 132

Location:
Northern Road, Luddenham, 2750;
20 km south of Penrith.
(047) 73 4161.

Winemaker:
Chris Niccol.

1985 Production:
1800 cases (normally 4500 cases).

Principal Wines:
A full range of wines available cellar door, including fortified and flavoured wines no doubt made elsewhere. Varietal table wines include Semillon, Rhine Riesling, Chablis, Fumé Blanc, Chardonnay, Traminer Riesling, Gewurtztraminer, Spatlese Riesling and Shiraz. Generic wines also available in both bottle and flagon. Premium table wines made from grapes grown in other regions, typically the Hunter Valley and Mudgee.

Distribution:
Exclusively cellar door and mailing list. Cellar-door sales Tuesday to Friday 9 a.m. to 6 p.m., weekends noon to 6 p.m. Mailing list as above.

Prices:
$2.99 to $6.95 cellar door.

Overall Quality:
Variable; wines adequate to good.

Vintage Rating 1982–85:
White: '84, '83, '85, '82.
Red: '85, '84, '83, '82.

Tasting Notes:

1984 CHARDONNAY [15.4] *Colour:* medium yellow-green. *Bouquet:* a trace of mercaptan tends to hold back fruit; lacks weight and lusciousness. *Palate:* a light, well-made commercial wine but lacking fruit character and in particular varietal flavour. Drink '86–'87.

1984 FUME BLANC [15] *Colour:* bright light green-yellow. *Bouquet:* distinct mercaptan and rather marked solids fermentation aromas; smelly. *Palate:* some sauvignon blanc flavour, and quite good back-palate, with clean, crisp acid on the finish. A much better wine than the bouquet would suggest. Drink '86.

Victoria

Bendigo and District

1985 Vintage

The growing season was both very cool and very dry. In parts of this widespread district, the season was the coolest ever, with only one very hot day in the lead-up to the commencement of vintage. Nonetheless, there still proved to be adequate warmth to allow all varieties to reach full maturity, the major difficulties coming from inadequate moisture for the unirrigated vineyards, which were still suffering the after-effects of the severe 1983 drought.

Harvest commenced between two to three weeks late, hastened at the end by a week of warm weather immediately prior to vintage. Those vineyards with drip irrigation produced grapes of good to outstanding quality; some of the dry-land vineyards were not so successful.

The white wines have good balance and fruit character, and are similar in structure to the elegant 1984 wines. The red wines are deeply coloured and richly flavoured, with none of the heaviness or jamminess encountered in warmer years. It is almost certain that less of the district mint character than usual will manifest itself, and that instead the cabernets in particular will show more grassy/herbaceous flavours.

The Changes

The major change has been the sale during the year by the doyen of the region, Stuart Anderson, of Balgownie to Mildara. The two trophies won by Heathcote Winery at the Royal Melbourne Show in August 1985 will no doubt also help the morale of the numerous small wineries in the district, proving it has the capacity to make high-quality white wines as well as its long-recognised ability to make some of Victoria's best reds.

BALGOWNIE

pp. 142–4

Location:
Hermitage Road, Maiden Gully, 3551;
8 km west of Bendigo off Calder Highway.
(054) 49 6222.

Winemaker:
Stuart Anderson.

1985 Production:
5000 cases.

Principal Wines:

Chardonnay, Rhine Riesling, Cabernet Sauvignon, Pinot Noir and Hermitage under Balgownie Estate label made from 100% Balgownie grapes. Premier cuvée range blended wines from other regions.

Distribution:
Until 1985, principally mailing list and cellar-door sales, with limited retail distribution through fine wine merchants in capital cities. Subsequent acquisition by Mildara may well see greater availability. Cellar-door sales 10 a.m. to 5 p.m. Monday to Saturday; mailing-list enquiries to c/- Maiden Gully, Vic. 3551.

Prices:
$7 to $12 cellar door.

Overall Quality:
Usually, though not invariably, exceptional.

Vintage Rating 1982–85:
White: '85, '84, '82 (none made '83).
Red: '84, '85, '82, '83 (Cabernet Sauvignon only '83).

Outstanding Prior Vintages:
'73, '76, '80.

Tasting Notes:

1984 *CHARDONNAY* [17.8] *Colour:* yellow-gold, with a tinge of straw. *Bouquet:* complex and firm; a touch of burgundian sulphide, and some solids fermentation character. *Palate:* comes alive; rich, lemony/nutmeg oak with long, firm fruit and a lingering finish. Drink '87–'91.

1984 *PINOT NOIR* [18.4] *Colour:* light to medium red. *Bouquet:* great grip and style, very Burgundian, with superb oak handling. *Palate:* marvellous lingering flavours, light bodied yet intense, with grip and structure. Drink '86–'89.

1984 *CABERNET SAUVIGNON* [18] *Colour:* medium to full red-purple. *Bouquet:* a robust but clean wine with marked varietal aroma. *Palate:* bell-clear herbaceous cabernet fruit, yet rich and smooth, with excellent oak. Drink '88–'93.

BLANCHE BARKLY WINES

p. 144

Location:
Rheola Road, Kingower, 3517;
on western outskirts of Kingower.
(054) 43 3664.

Winemakers:
David and Alvin Reimers.

1985 Production:
1100 cases.

Principal Wines:

Only red wines made, including Hermitage Nouveau, Mary Eileen Hermitage, Johanne Cabernet Sauvignon, Alexander Cabernet Sauvignon and George Henry Cabernet Sauvignon.

Distribution:
Almost exclusively cellar-door sales and mailing list. Cellar-door sales 9 a.m. to 5 p.m. Monday to Saturday. Mailing list RMB 348, Kingower, 3517.

Prices:
$7 to $9 cellar door.

Overall Quality:
Good to very good.

Vintage Rating 1982–85:
'85, '84, '82, '83.

Outstanding Prior Vintages:
'76, '77, '80.

Tasting Notes:

1984 *HERMITAGE NOUVEAU* [17.4] *Colour:* vibrant pink-red. *Bouquet:* arresting barrel ferment aromas, smoky and complex. *Palate:* a lively, spicy wine with strong smoky oak characters; the only possible description is a pink fume. (Tasted November '84.) Drink '85.

1983 *JOHANNE CABERNET SAUVIGNON* [17.2] *Colour:* very good purple-red. *Bouquet:* given the impact of the drought year, amazingly fine and elegant with clean, grassy varietal aroma. *Palate:* clean, fine and elegant, with delicate astringency and none of the expected mid-Victorian eucalypt/mint characters. An outstanding success for the year. Drink '87–'92.

CHATEAU DORE

p. 145

Location:
Mandurang, 3551;
8 km south of Bendigo.
(054) 39 5278.

Winemaker:
Ivan Grose.

Principal Wines:
Rhine Riesling, Chardonnay, Shiraz and Cabernet Sauvignon.

Distribution:
Almost exclusively cellar-door sales 10.30 a.m. to 4.30 p.m. Tuesday to Saturday, open Sunday by appointment.

CHATEAU LE AMON

p. 145

Location:
140 km post, Calder Highway, Bendigo, 3550;
10 km south-west of town.
(054) 47 7995.

Winemakers:
Philip and Ian Leamon.

1985 Production:
Approximately 5000 cases.

Principal Wines:
Semillon/Rhine Riesling, Dry Red Beaujolais style, Marong Shiraz, Cabernet Sauvignon.

Distribution:
Substantial cellar-door sales and mail orders, but also significant retail distributions throughout capital cities, direct ex vineyard. Cellar-door sales 10 a.m. to 5 p.m. weekdays (but closed Thursdays except during school holidays), 9 a.m. to 6 p.m. Saturday and noon to 6 p.m. Sunday. Mailing-list enquiries to PO Box 487, Bendigo, 3550.

Prices:
$5.30 to $8.35 cellar door.

Overall Quality:
Very good and not infrequently exceptional.

Vintage Rating 1982–85:
'83, '84, '82 ('85 not yet rated).

Outstanding Prior Vintages:
1980.

Tasting Notes:

1984 SEMILLON RHINE RIESLING [16.6] *Colour:* pale green-straw. *Bouquet:* soft, gently aromatic fruit; clean and very well-made, simply lacking varietal richness. *Palate:* crisp and lively, with good, clean fruit but, seemingly inevitably, varietally nondescript. Drink '85–'88.

1984 DRY RED BEAUJOLAIS STYLE [16.8] *Colour:* light red-purple, showing some spritz. *Bouquet:* fresh, with most attractive background hints of pepper spice. *Palate:* while light and fresh, showing a wide spectrum of flavours through from pepper spice to regional mint; a most interesting wine. Drink '85–'86.

1984 MARONG SHIRAZ [17.4] *Colour:* vibrant purple. *Bouquet:* of medium weight, clean, very light oak and a hint of varietal pepper spice. *Palate:* light and fresh, beautifully made with vibrant spicy/fruit flavours and very low tannin. Drink '86–'87.

1983 CABERNET SAUVIGNON [18.8] *Colour:* outstanding purple of medium to full depth. *Bouquet:* a beautifully rich and complex wine with perfect fruit/oak balance. *Palate:* near perfect cabernet fruit flavour, with some blackcurrant flavours, but neither minty at the one extreme nor herbaceous at the other. Literally a definition of perfectly ripened cabernet. Oak handling again immaculate, as is the balance of the wine, aided by gentle tannin astringency on the finish. Drink '87–'95.

HARCOURT VALLEY VINEYARDS

pp. 145–6

Location:
118 km post, Calder Highway, Harcourt, 3453.
(054) 74 2223.

Winemaker:
Ray Broughton.

1985 Production:
670 cases.

Principal Wines:
Chardonnay, Rhine Riesling, Cabernet Sauvignon, Pinot Noir and Hermitage.

Distribution:
Exclusively cellar-door sales and mailing list.

Prices:
$7.50 to $8 cellar door.

Overall Quality:
Whites variable; reds good.

Vintage Rating 1982–85:
White: '84, '82 (no '83, and '85 not yet rated).
Red: '83, '84, '82 ('85 not yet rated).

Tasting Notes:

1984 CHARDONNAY [14.6] *Colour:* deep straw-yellow. *Bouquet:* fruit diminished by evident oxidation. *Palate:* some fruit weight, but basically oxidised and a rather bitter finish. Drink '86.

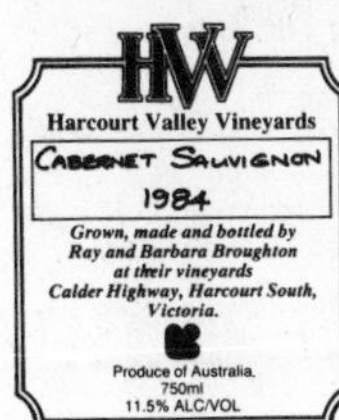

1984 CABERNET SAUVIGNON [17.6] *Colour:* medium full purple-red. *Bouquet:* clean, very good oak handling, with fresh minty/berry aromas. *Palate:* an excellent wine with strong regional mint flavours, then balancing acid which prevents the flavour cloying and invests style. Drink '88–'92.

HEATHCOTE WINERY

pp. 146–7

Location:
183–185 High Street, Heathcote, 3523.
(054) 33 2595.

Winemaker:
Elaine Tudhope.

1985 Production:
3000 cases.

Principal Wines:
Chardonnay, Chenin Blanc, Traminer, Blanc de Blanc, Shiraz, Pinot Noir.

Distribution:
Principally cellar-door sales and mailing list; limited capital city fine wine retail distribution. Cellar-door sales 10 a.m. to 6 p.m. 7 days, but advisable to telephone during the week.

Prices:
$6.90 to $9 cellar door.

Overall Quality:
Very good.

Vintage Rating 1982–85:
White: '84, '85, '83, '82.
Red: '84, '82, '85, '83.

Tasting Notes:

1984 CHARDONNAY [18.4] *Colour:* bright yellow-green. *Bouquet:* marvellously aromatic, pungent grapefruit aromas, with some yeast-derived richness still to dissipate. *Palate:* rich, slightly chewy oak, then long, soft, lingering grapefruit flavours. Overall very richly flavoured. Drink '86–'88.

1984 PINOT NOIR [16.6] *Colour:* light to medium purple-red. *Bouquet:* very clean and fresh with some mint/peppermint aromas. *Palate:* fairly light, with some attractive pinot/strawberry mid-palate flavours before merging again into the peppermint flavours evident in the bouquet. Drink '86–'87.

JASPER HILL

p. 147

Location:
Drummonds Lane, Heathcote, 3523;
6 km north of Heathcote.
(054) 33 2528.

Winemaker:
Ron Laughton.

1985 Production:
1100 cases.

Principal Wines:
Georgias Paddock Riesling, Georgias Paddock Shiraz, Emilys Paddock Shiraz/Cabernet Franc, Emilys Paddock Shiraz. Beautiful and innovative packaging a feature of the wines.

Distribution:
Principally cellar door and mailing list; limited fine wine retail Sydney and Melbourne. Cellar-door sales 10 a.m. to 6 p.m. weekends, weekdays by appointment. Mailing-list enquiries to PO Box 110, Heathcote, Vic. 3523.

Prices:
$7 to $10 retail (less cellar door).

Overall Quality:
Some variability but reds good, some very good.

Vintage Rating 1982–85:
White: '85, '84 (latter first vintage).
Red: '84, '85, '82, '83.

Tasting Notes:

1985 GEORGIAS PADDOCK RIESLING [16] *Colour:* medium yellow, straw-tinged. *Bouquet:* clean, chunky fruit aromas with a touch of lime; well-made, and no solids fermentation characters. *Palate:* full-flavoured though not too heavy, indeed bordering on elegance; crisp acid on finish. Simply lacks intensity. Drink '87–'89.

1984 GEORGIAS PADDOCK SHIRAZ [16.6] *Colour:* dark purple-red. *Bouquet:* very solid, slightly stalky/extractive aromas, with firm fruit. *Palate:* abundant flavour, though much less dense than the '83s; a touch of regional mint on the mid-palate and then again a rather stalky finish. Drink '87–'92.

1984 EMILYS PADDOCK SHIRAZ/CABERNET FRANC [16.8] *Colour:* dark purple. *Bouquet:* smooth; some slightly dull oak aromas; firm, tightly knit fruit. *Palate:* attractive, youthful fruit with good structure; will build flavour complexity on the existing depth and texture. Drink '87–'93.

1983 EMILYS PADDOCK SHIRAZ [17] *Colour:* dense purple-red. *Bouquet:* dense and concentrated, high in alcohol and with a complex spectrum of aromas, ranging from gravel to meat. *Palate:* a veritable monster, with huge minty/sweet fruit with strong, astringent tannin on the finish. Will be extremely long-lived. Drink '88–'94.

1983 GEORGIAS PADDOCK SHIRAZ [17.4] *Colour:* dense, impenetrable purple. *Bouquet:* dense and solid, rich and deep, yet against all the probabilities, not jammy. *Palate:* rich and full, with an almost viscous and quite extraordinary texture, full of minty flavours, yet fairly low in tannin and not extractive. Very much the product of a low-yielding vintage. Drink '88–'94.

MALMSBURY ESTATE

p. 147

Location:
Calder Highway, Malmsbury, 3446.
(054) 23 2267.

Winemaker:
Roger Aldridge.

Principal Wines:
Cabernet Sauvignon, Shiraz, Pinot Noir, Merlot.

Distribution:
Largely cellar-door sales and mailing list. Limited retail distribution through Duke and Moorefield, Melbourne.

MOUNT IDA

pp. 147–8

Location:
147 High Street, Heathcote, 3523.

Winemaker:
John Ellis (contract).

1985 Production:
1300 cases.

Principal Wines:
Rhine Riesling, Shiraz and Cabernet Shiraz.

Distribution:
Limited fine wine retail sales in Melbourne (wholesale through Wayne Leicht) and Sydney (wholesale through David Haviland & Co.).

Prices:
$5.50 to $10.50 recommended retail.

Overall Quality:
Very good.

Vintage Rating 1982–85:
'82, '84, '85 (?), '83.

Outstanding Prior Vintages:
'81.

Tasting Notes:

1984 RIESLING [17.4] *Colour:* very pale green-yellow. *Bouquet:* very light, with a touch of bottling SO_2 and grassy notes to fruit. *Palate:* ultra-fresh, clean, crisp wine, very well-made, and showing none of the fatness typical of the district. Drink '85–'86.

1983 SHIRAZ [17.8] *Colour:* vibrant purple-red of medium to full depth. *Bouquet:* very big, with rich, ripe fruit balanced by strong vanillin American oak; little or no mint evident. *Palate:* clearly accented, dark cherry flavours, textured by soft but persistent tannin throughout, and vanillin/coconut/oak flavours. Very much a Heathcote style. Drink '87–'92.

1982 SHIRAZ CABERNET [17.6] *Colour:* strong purple-red. *Bouquet:* full, smooth and minty, very clean and very well-made. *Palate:* smooth wine with modulated mint characters, a light touch of oak and low tannin. Drink '85–'88.

1982 SHIRAZ [18.4] *Colour:* dense purple-red. *Bouquet:* intense essence-of-peppermint characters, with extraordinary depth. *Palate:* a voluptuously sweet and richly minty wine; the ultimate expression of mid-Victorian style. Drink '86–'94.

PASSING CLOUDS

p. 148

Location:
Kurting Road, Kingower, 3517;
in township.
(054) 38 8257.

Winemaker:
Graeme Leith.

1985 Production:
Approximately 3000 cases.

Principal Wines:
Red table wines only produced; Pinot Noir, Shiraz, Shiraz Cabernet and Cabernet Sauvignon.

Distribution:
Principally cellar-door sales and mailing list; cellar-door sales 10 a.m. to 6 p.m. 7 days but by appointment; telephone first. Mailing list as above. Limited fine wine retail distribution through 5 Melbourne wine merchants (Victorian Wine Centre, Richmond Hill Cellars, Toc H, Nicks and Templestowe Cellars); Aberfeldy Cellars, Hobart; Vintage Cellars, Adelaide; and Farmer Bros, Canberra.

Prices:
$8 cellar door.

Overall Quality:
Exceptional.

Vintage Rating 1982–85:
'85 (?), '82, '84, '83.

Tasting Notes:

1984 SHIRAZ CABERNET [18.8] *Colour:* medium red-purple. *Bouquet:* fine and fragrant with gentle mint, a touch of herbaceous cabernet, a whisper of spice; spotlessly clean and of great elegance. *Palate:* magnificent amalgam of flavours; vibrantly fresh, gentle mint, balanced by some herbaceous cabernet flavours; a glorious wine. (Due for release May '86.) Drink '87–'92.

1984 CABERNET SAUVIGNON [18.4] *Colour:* excellent purple-red of medium depth. *Bouquet:* strong, crystal clear, herbaceous cabernet aroma; not thin or green, and with real overtones of bordeaux. *Palate:* strong, herbaceous cabernet but plenty of weight, not stalky or skinny; long clean finish. Superb winemaking, but also the product of a very cool vintage. Drink '87–'91.

1983/1984 PINK LABEL [18] *Colour:* medium purple-red. *Bouquet:* in typical fashion, spotlessly clean; just a hint of mint; good fruit depth; a very civilised wine. *Palate:* distinct touch of shiraz spice; clean, very good balance and length; also mint aromas and flavours but held well in restraint. (A blend of estate-grown drought-year shiraz and cabernet sauvignon blended with shiraz and cabernet sauvignon from Carisbrook, Heathcote and Harcourt, from the '84 and '83 vintages.) Drink '86–'90.

ROMANY RYE

p. 148

Location:
Metcalfe Pool Road, Redesdale, 3444;
9 km north of town.
(054) 25 3135.

Winemaker:
Rod Hourigan.

1985 Production:
Over 4000 cases.

Principal Wines:
Dry White, Shiraz, Cabernet Sauvignon.

Distribution:
Principally cellar door and mailing list. Cellar-door sales 10 a.m. to 6 p.m. Monday to Saturday, Sunday noon to 6 p.m. Mailing-list enquiries to RSD Redesdale, 3444.

Prices:
$6.50 to $8 recommended retail.

Overall Quality:
Adequate.

Tasting Notes:

1984 DRY WHITE [15.8] *Colour:* light to medium yellow-green. *Bouquet:* clean, soft, well-made wine without fault, although no great varietal character. *Palate:* clean, soft, bland wine; easy drinking commercial style. Drink '85.

1981 SHIRAZ MALBEC [15.6] *Colour:* light to medium red. *Bouquet:* quite fragrant; touch of leather but also sweet berry aromas. *Palate:* in radically different style to '80 vintage; crisp, light fruit and a touch of bottle-developed cigar box. Drink '86–'87.

1980 HERMITAGE CABERNET GRENACHE [15.4] *Colour:* full red-purple. *Bouquet:* a very big, very robust wine with full fruit marred by a trace of tarry/leathery mercaptan. *Palate:* a ripe, aggressive, textured wine with huge, old-fashioned fruit and equally forbidding tannin. Drink '85–'88.

WATER WHEEL VINEYARDS

pp. 148–9

Location:
Bridgewater-on-Loddon, 1 km north of the town of Bridgewater, 3516.
(054) 37 3000.

Winemaker:
David Von Saldern.

1985 Production:
4000 cases.

Principal Wines:
Rhine Riesling, Chardonnay, Chardonnay Private Bin, Estate Blanc, Rosé, Hermitage, Hermitage Reserve Bin, Cabernet Franc, Cabernet Sauvignon Private Bin 46 and Vintage Port.

Distribution:
Cellar-door sales, mailing list and limited Victorian and retail distribution. Distributed direct in Victoria and through The Incredible Wine Company in New South Wales. Cellar-door sales 9 a.m. to noon and 1 p.m. to 5 p.m. Monday to Saturday.

Prices:
$7.80 to $9 recommended retail; less cellar door.

Overall Quality:
Has been poor, with mercaptan a major problem, but quality is now improving.

Vintage Rating 1982–85:
White: '84, '85, '82, '83.
Red: '85(?), '84, '83, '82.

Tasting Notes:

1984 ESTATE BLANC [15.4] *Colour:* quite deep yellow-green. *Bouquet:* full, slightly broad fruit, with spicy/nutmeg aromas. *Palate:* a very full-flavoured, quite sweet commercial wine, a cross between a moselle and a white burgundy. Drink '85–'86.

1984 RHINE RIESLING [16] *Colour:* bright green-yellow. *Bouquet:* clean and fresh, with good riesling/lime aromas. *Palate:* a solid wine, full-flavoured and slightly broad; again obvious residual sugar. Drink '85–'87.

1983 CABERNET SAUVIGNON PRIVATE BIN 46 [15.8] *Colour:* medium full red-purple. *Bouquet:* quite complex; some lifted aromas and only a faint trace of leathery mercaptan. *Palate:* light to medium weight, with some berry flavours and a touch of volatile lift. Drink '85–'87.

YELLOWGLEN

pp. 149–50

Location:
White's Road, Smythesdale, 3551;
off Glenelg Highway, south-west of Ballarat.
(053) 42 8617.

Winemaker:
Dominique Landragin.

1985 Production:
6500 cases.

Principal Wines:
Méthode champenoise specialist, with base wines almost entirely composed of Chardonnay, Pinot Noir and Pinot Meunier in various blends.

Distribution:
Extensive fine wine and retail distribution, particularly given still-limited production.

Prices:
$12 to $18 recommended retail.

Overall Quality:
Good.

Vintage Rating 1982–85:
'84, '85, '82, '83.

Outstanding Prior Vintages:
'80.

Tasting Notes:

1983 CUVEE VICTORIA [16.8] *Colour:* some straw with the faintest blush of pink. *Bouquet:* a very strong, robust aroma with some oxidation. *Palate:* a very big, solid wine, with abundant flavour and some of the typically creamy characters of Yellowglen, but one which might conceivably have benefited from more time in bottle prior to disgorgement. Drink '85–'88.

1983 CHARDONNAY METHODE CHAMPENOISE [17] *Colour:* full straw-yellow with fairly large bead. *Bouquet:* very full and buttery with some autolysed yeast characters evident. *Palate:* a mouth-filling, soft, buttery/creamy wine, showing considerable development. Drink '85–'87.

ZUBER ESTATE

p. 150

Location:
Northern Highway, Heathcote, 3523;
1 km north of town.
(054) 33 2142.

Winemaker:
A. Zuber.

1985 Production:
Very limited.

Principal Wines:
Shiraz and Cabernet Sauvignon.

Distribution:
Cellar-door sales and mailing list. Cellar-door sales 9 a.m. to 5 p.m. Monday to Saturday and Sunday noon to 6 p.m.

Overall Quality:
Not rated.

Tasting Notes:
1984 PINK CLIFFS SHIRAZ [13.2] *Colour:* medium red-purple. *Bouquet:* strong mint/medicinal aromas, most unusual and not attractive. *Palate:* soft medicinal/spice flavours, almost certainly indicating the use of carbonic maceration.

Central Goulburn Valley

1985 Vintage

A wet and relatively mild winter led on to a dry and cool to warm spring and summer. Apart from minor problems of sunburn in vineyards which defoliated due to lack of moisture, grapes throughout the district matured well, free from disease and in very good condition.

As in much of eastern Australia, vignerons were surprised by the above-average yield, particularly given the dry conditions throughout spring and summer. Only cabernet sauvignon failed to produce above-average quantities.

The resultant wines range from normal to above-average quality. The white wines are already showing very good flavour and structure, with Mitchelton winning a trophy at the Melbourne Show with its 1985 Rhine Riesling. The red wines are certainly very well-balanced, with ample weight, but have no special concentration of colour or flavour.

The Changes

The district has been extremely stable, with the newer wineries all continuing to attract favourable attention. One of the older and in many ways less fashionable wineries, Osicka's, also surprised many observers with the excellence of its red wine (1981 Cabernet Sauvignon) featured at the main banquet for the 1985 Victorian Exhibition of Winemakers.

CHATEAU TAHBILK

pp. 155–6

Location:
Tabilk, 3607;
off western side of Goulburn Valley highway,
8 km south-west of Nagambie.
(057) 94 2388.

Winemaker:
Alister Purbrick.

1985 Production:
40,000 cases.

Principal Wines:

Top-quality white varietal wines released under gold label (Rhine Riesling, Semillon, Chardonnay and Marsanne); less expensive white varietals under "traditional" label. Red wines are Cabernet Sauvignon and Shiraz, together with yearly release of a Private Bin red (usually but not invariably Cabernet Sauvignon) and usually six years old.

Distribution:
National retail distribution through Rhine Castle Wines Pty Ltd (all states). Cellar-door sales in one of Australia's most beautiful wineries, 9 a.m. to 5 p.m. Monday to Saturday, noon to 5 p.m. Sunday and all public holidays except Christmas Day and Good Friday. Mailing list also available. Address as above.

Prices:
$5.86 to $10.06 recommended retail.

Overall Quality:
Particularly having regard to price, very good.

Vintage Rating 1982–85:
White: '84, '85, '82, '83.
Red: '84, '82, '85, '83.

Outstanding Prior Vintages:
White: '80, '79, '75.
Red: '81, '71, '68.

Tasting Notes:

1984 GOLD LABEL RHINE RIESLING [16.8] *Colour:* full yellow-green. *Bouquet:* pronounced flowery aroma with hints of tropical fruit. *Palate:* very rich and softly pungent, with some lime flavours and an ever-so-slightly oily finish. Drink '85–'87.

1984 GOLD LABEL SEMILLON [16.6] *Colour:* strong yellow-green. *Bouquet:* a firm, strong and clean wine with some grassy overtones. *Palate:* reflects the bouquet in every way; firm, with some herbaceous flavours and a clear promise of bottle development. Drink '86–'89.

1984 GOLD LABEL CHARDONNAY [17] *Colour:* hints of straw, no doubt oak-derived. *Bouquet:* a most attractive aroma in the modern idiom, with clean and soft spicy/nutmeg oak aromas. *Palate:* once again, the very well-handled spicy oak is the wine's main attraction, with some light chardonnay fruit underneath. Drink '85–'87.

1982 SHIRAZ [17] *Colour:* dense red-purple. *Bouquet:* very clean, potent wine with deep fruit and high alcohol; mint/steradent aromas. *Palate:* very rich, full-bodied wine with some mint on the mid-palate, then typical pronounced tannin building on the mid-palate and following through to the back palate. Drink '87–'92.

1980 SHIRAZ [17.4] *Colour:* excellent red of medium to full depth. *Bouquet:* solid, almost dense, with a touch of fresh earth; in traditional style but complete and satisfying. *Palate:* a touch of regional mint flavour adds flesh to the mid-palate; the tannin is soft and in balance; a mouth-filling wine. Drink '86–'91.

1978 CABERNET SAUVIGNON BIN 65 [16.6] *Colour:* strong red with a touch of garnet developing on the rim. *Bouquet:* extremely complex aromas with gumleaf/mint/leather intermingling. *Palate:* ripe, complex fruit on the fore- and mid-palate, then a touch of leather followed by mouth-gripping tannin on the finish; a very typical Tahbilk wine. One has to be very patient indeed for that tannin to soften. Drink '88–'94.

HENKE

p. 157

Location:
Henke Lane, Yarck, 3719;
off Goulburn Highway, south of Seymour.
(057) 97 6277.

Winemaker:
Tim Miller.

1985 Production:
Not stated, but relatively small.

Principal Wines:
Shiraz, Shiraz Cabernet and Cabernet Sauvignon.

Distribution:
Principally cellar door; limited retail distribution Melbourne through Victorian Wine Centre and Gatehouse Cellars.

Prices:
$6.95 retail.

Overall Quality:
Good.

Tasting Notes:

1982 SHIRAZ [16.4] *Colour:* strong, deep purple, still with red tints. *Bouquet:* strong, perfumed minty aromas to deep fruit. *Palate:* the ultimate regional manifestation of peppermint flavours, almost toothpaste-like. Strong, rather abrasive tannin on the finish. Drink '87–'92.

1982 SHIRAZ CABERNET [17] *Colour:* good purple-red. *Bouquet:* clean, minty, regional fruit aromas with an underlying touch of gravel. *Palate:* strong regional peppermint fruit on the fore- and mid-palate, with textured tannin in much better balance than shiraz, though still marked; a long-lived style. Drink '88–'93.

1981 SHIRAZ CABERNET [17.4] *Colour:* outstanding medium to full purple. *Bouquet:* clean and stylish, very regional but also extremely well-made. *Palate:* a lovely wine, with fleshy/minty mid-palate flavours and gentle tannin rounding off a long, soft finish. Drink '85–'91.

LONGLEAT

p. 157

Location:
Cemetery Lane, Murchison, 3610;
2 km south of town.
(058) 26 2294.

Winemaker:
Alister Purbrick (consultant).

1985 Production:
1800 cases.

Principal Wines:

Under Longleat label (estate-grown), two wines released: Semillon-Rhine Riesling, Shiraz-Cabernet. Under Murchison label, wines made in other regions also offered, including Coonawarra Rhine Riesling and Cabernet Sauvignon, Nagambie Spatlese Rhine Riesling, McLaren Vale Vintage Port, Rutherglen Liqueur Muscat and Champagne.

Distribution:
Principally cellar-door sales and mailing list. Cellar-door sales 9 a.m. to 5 p.m. Monday to Saturday and 12.30 p.m. to 5 p.m. Sunday. Open most public holidays. Mailing-list enquiries to Murchison Vineyard Company Pty Ltd, Box 25, Murchison, 3610. Limited Victorian distribution through Nick Walko.

Prices:
$5.50 to $6.95 cellar door.

Overall Quality:
Good.

Vintage Rating 1982–85:
White: '85, '84 (first vintage).
Red: '83, '84, '85, '82.

Tasting Notes:

1983 CABERNET SHIRAZ [16.6] *Colour:* medium full purple-red. *Bouquet:* a big, complex wine with abundant fruit; structured, and indicating tannin. *Palate:* complex and rich mint fruit on the fore-palate; tannin commences to build on the mid-palate and overwhelms on the back. Certainly needs time. Drink '89–93.

1982 CABERNET SHIRAZ [17] *Colour:* outstanding, deep red-purple. *Bouquet:* firm; some lift to a complex bouquet with some gravel/earth aromas, but also ample fruit. *Palate:* very complex, rich wine; a touch of ripe caramel fruit; persistent but soft tannin. Excellent mid-palate flavour. Drink '88–'92.

MITCHELTON

pp. 157–60

Location:
Mitchellstown via Nagambie, 3608;
due west of Tabilk off Goulburn Valley Highway.
(057) 94 2388.

Winemakers:
Don Lewis and David Traeger.

1985 Production:
750,000 litres.

Principal Wines:
The substantial range of white and red table wines (the only products of the winery) come under three labels. At the top end of the quality range is the Mitchelton "Winemaker's Selection" label made from grapes grown in other quality areas of Australia (particularly Coonawarra but also Mount Barker in Western Australia) including Rhine Riesling, Botrytis-Affected Rhine Riesling and Cabernet Sauvignon; of equal quality are the Mitchelton label wines made entirely from grapes grown at Mitchelton and including Rhine Riesling, Marsanne (wood-matured), Chardonnay (wood-matured), Semillon (wood-matured) and Cabernet Sauvignon; at the bottom end of the premium-quality range is the Thomas Mitchell label, with wines made from Victorian-grown grapes and including Thomas Mitchell Cabernet Sauvignon and Thomas Mitchell Chablis. Show stocks of older vintages marketed as Classic Release Wines with special label.

Distribution:
Extensive eastern states retail distribution through affiliated distribution networks. Cellar-door sales from a spectacular modern winery with a host of other attractions too numerous to list exhaustively but including walk-through aviary, 55 m high observation tower and Riverbank Grill open Sundays and public holidays. Cellar-door sales 9 a.m. to 5 p.m. Monday to Saturday and Sunday noon to 5 p.m. Very active mailing list with highly informative, regular brochures. Address as above.

Prices:
$5.85 to $13.95 recommended retail.

Overall Quality:
Consistently very good.

Vintage Rating 1982–85:
White: '85, '84, '82, '83.
Red: '84, '85, '83, '82.

Outstanding Prior Vintages:
'78, '79 (Cabernet Sauvignon), '80 (Marsanne and Cabernet Sauvignon), '81 (Rhine Riesling).

Tasting Notes:

1984 THOMAS MITCHELL CHABLIS WOOD MATURED [16.2] *Colour:* pale straw-green. *Bouquet:* of medium full weight, with slightly oily oak aromas, otherwise clean but somewhat common. *Palate:* light, gently spicy oak is the main contributor to flavour; a fair food wine and within the expanded concept of what is regarded as Chablis these days. Drink '85–'87.

1984 RHINE RIESLING [17] *Colour:* bright green-yellow of medium depth. *Bouquet:* rich aromatic pineapple, very full and with a touch of butterscotch/toast. *Palate:* very full, ripe tropical/lime/pineapple flavours; a very long, soft finish. Drink '85–'88.

1983 MARSANNE [16.8] *Colour:* medium yellow with some oak-derived straw. *Bouquet:* very much more chalky/honey varietal aroma than in previous releases, and commensurately less oak. *Palate:* firm, marked varietal marsanne; some chalky/malty flavours. Quite a departure in style. Should develop well given further bottle maturation. Drink '86–'88.

1982 THOMAS MITCHELL CABERNET SAUVIGNON [16] *Colour:* medium red-purple. *Bouquet:* smooth, very light fruit and a little cedary oak. *Palate:* of light to medium weight, with gentle fruit backed by similar cedary oak flavours to those appearing in the bouquet. Well-made but fully mature. Drink '85–'86.

1982 CABERNET SAUVIGNON [16.8] *Colour:* excellent red-purple of medium to full depth. *Bouquet:* quite firm though aromatic, with good depth and excellent fruit/oak balance. *Palate:* gently leafy fruit flavours, smooth, with low tannin and gentle oak. Again basically ready now. Drink '85–'87.

1980 CLASSIC RELEASE MARSANNE [18] *Colour:* bright yellow of medium depth. *Bouquet:* harmonious fruit/oak integration, with the two merging imperceptibly into each other, although the lemony oak is undoubtedly dominant. *Palate:* has matured beautifully; excellent balance and structure; once again difficult to tell where the fruit stops and the oak starts, and it is the lemony oak which makes the major contribution to the now quite lovely flavour. At its peak. Drink '85–'87.

OSICKA'S VINEYARD

p. 160

Location:
Graytown, 3608;
off Heathcote–Nagambie Road, 24 km west of Nagambie.
(057) 94 9235.

Winemaker:
Paul Osicka.

1985 Production:
Approximately 7000 cases.

Principal Wines:
Limited quantities of white wines made; principal wines Cabernet Shiraz, Cabernet Malbec Shiraz, Cabernet Sauvignon and Vintage Port.

Distribution:
Principally cellar-door sales and by mail order. Limited retail distribution through The Oak Barrel, Sydney, and Flinders Trading, Melbourne. Cellar-door sales 9 a.m. to 5.30 p.m. Monday to Saturday.

Prices:
$6.80 to $7.95 (table wines), $9.80 (fortified wines) cellar door.

Overall Quality:
White wines adequate; red wines and Vintage Port often very good.

Vintage Rating 1982–85:
'85, '84, '82, '83.

Outstanding Prior Vintages:
'76, '78.

Tasting Notes:
1982 SHIRAZ [16.6] *Colour:* red-purple of medium depth. *Bouquet:* firm, of medium weight, and slightly leathery. Lacks varietal spice and fruit richness. *Palate:* much better than the bouquet suggests; smooth, with good mid-palate fruit and a clean, well-balanced finish. Drink '85–'88.

1982 CABERNET SAUVIGNON [17.2] *Colour:* very good red-purple, bright and clear. *Bouquet:* clean, gently minty fruit of medium to full depth; quite stylish. *Palate:* good berry fruit flavours with soft but persistent tannin providing structural complexity. As with most Osicka red wines, oak does not play a role in building flavour. Drink '86–'90.

SEYMOUR VINEYARDS

pp. 160–1

Location:
1 Emily Street, Seymour, 3660.
(057) 92 1372.

Winemaker:
Maurice Bourne.

1985 Production:
Not stated.

Principal Wines:
A diverse range of white and red varietal table wines, reflecting the large number of grape types propagated in the two vineyards (also often specified on the label, and being Northwood Vineyard and Chinaman's Garden).

Distribution:
Chiefly cellar door and mailing list. Cellar-door sales 9 a.m. to 5.30 p.m. Monday to Saturday and public holidays; Sunday noon to 6 p.m. Limited retail distribution in Sydney and Melbourne (Victorian Wine Centre).

Prices:
$6.50 to $11.50.

Overall Quality:
Extremely variable, from poor to good.

Tasting Notes:
1982 RHINE RIESLING [16.8] *Colour:* distinct straw-yellow. *Bouquet:* rich, indeed potent, bottle-developed camphor aromas. *Palate:* full lime/camphor flavours, though starting to crack up a little; slightly salty finish. (A gold medal winner 1983 Victorian Wines Show.) Drink '85–'86.

WALKERSHIRE WINES

p. 161

Location:
Rushworth Road, Bailieston, 3608;
14 km east of Nagambie.
(057) 94 2726.

Winemaker:
John Walker.

1985 Production:
Less than 1000 cases.

Principal Wines:

Shiraz, Cabernet Shiraz and Cabernet Sauvignon.

Distribution:
Principally cellar-door sales and mailing list. Cellar-door sales 9 a.m. to 6 p.m. Monday to Saturday, 10 a.m. to 6 p.m. Sunday. Mailing-list enquiries to PO Box 74, Nagambie, 3608. Melbourne retail sales through Moorfield Vintners.

Prices:
$9.50 to $12.

Overall Quality:
Very high.

Vintage Rating 1982–85:
'83, '85, '82, '84.

Tasting Notes:

1983 CABERNET SHIRAZ [18.4] *Colour:* strong, bright purple-red of medium to full depth. *Bouquet:* very clean, with good fruit oak balance and most attractive perfumed aroma; whilst full, no excessive extraction or jamminess, or excessive drought effects. *Palate:* a superbly fashioned wine with near-perfect fruit/oak balance; concentrated and yet not heavy; a triumph for a difficult vintage. Only 150 cases made. Released January 1986. Drink '88–'94.

1982 CABERNET SAUVIGNON [17.2] *Colour:* medium to full red, quite dense. *Bouquet:* a very big, tightly-structured wine, but with attractive, wood-developed aromatics. *Palate:* complex and powerful; minty fruit on the fore-palate, then tannin on the finish, and finally a slightly biscuit/mousy after-taste which slightly flaws an otherwise very high-quality wine. Spent three years in Nevers oak. Drink '86–'91.

East Gippsland

1985 Vintage

The last soaking winter rains in East Gippsland fell in 1976, and the winter of 1984 did not really change the pattern. Only September recorded average rainfall, and though hopes flickered briefly, the rain then disappeared until vintage-time.

Although the summer was very cool, the very low crops on the vines (no more than 50 per cent of normal) ripened at the usual time, their development hastened by the stress on the vines. Not surprisingly, alcohols did not reach normal levels, and most grapes were harvested at between 11 and 11.5 baume, a full degree down on average.

Chardonnay and cabernet sauvignon show good fruit flavours, but the wines will lack the strength and depth of a more equable vintage.

The Changes

This immensely far-flung region, remote from markets and tourist trade, struggles on. The district badly needs one substantial winery to generate the volume to allow effective promotion and some penetration of capital city retailing.

Parish Wines–Briagolong Estate will market its wines in 1986 for the first time.

GOLVINDA

p. 164

Location:
RMB 4635, Lindenow Road, Lindenow South, via Bairnsdale, 3865;
20 km west of Bairnsdale.
(051) 57 1480.

Winemaker:
Robert Guy.

Principal Wines:

Rhine Riesling, Semillon, Chenin Blanc, Cabernet Sauvignon and Shiraz.

Distribution:
Almost exclusively cellar-door sales and mail orders. Cellar-door sales Monday to Saturday 9 a.m. to 6 p.m.; Sundays by appointment. Closed Anzac Day and Good Friday.

Prices:
$6 to $7.

Overall Quality:
Good.

Tasting Notes:
1982 CABERNET SAUVIGNON [17.6] *Colour:* **excellent, youthful purple of medium depth.** *Bouquet:* **very clean, round, sweet, berry flavours; touch of sweet, vanillin oak.** *Palate:* **a technically perfectly made wine, suggesting a surprising degree of sophistication. Opulent cassis/cherry flavours, and spotlessly clean. Relatively warm in style, and soft. Drink '86–'90.**

LULGRA

p. 164

Location:
RMB 137, Lakes Entrance–Bairnsdale Road, 3909;
4 km west of Lakes Entrance.

Winemaker:
Andrew Smith (future).

Principal Wines:
Sauvignon Blanc, Rhine Riesling and Cabernet Sauvignon.

Distribution:
As at mid-1985, very uncertain. Vineyard and winery sold by previous owners (Pauline and Dacre Stubbs) to Herbert and Andrew Smith. Andrew Smith, having recently left school, is commencing the Riverina Winemaking Course.

Overall Quality:
Variable, but Sauvignon Blanc in particular has shown great promise.

McALLISTER VINEYARDS

p. 164

Location:
Golden Beach Road, Longford, 3851;
9 km from Longford.

Winemaker:
Peter Edwards.

Principal Wines:
A single red wine made from the classic bordeaux blend of cabernet sauvignon, cabernet franc, petite verdot and merlot.

Distribution:
Exclusively cellar-door sales. No mailing list.

NICHOLSON RIVER WINERY

p. 164

Location:
Liddell's Road, Nicholson, 3882;
14 km from Bairnsdale.
(051) 56 8241.

Winemaker:
Ken Eckersley.

1985 Production:
150 cases.

Principal Wines:
Chardonnay, Semillon, Cabernet Sauvignon and Pinot Noir.

Distribution:
Exclusively cellar-door sales, mailing list and local restaurants. Cellar-door sales by appointment only; mailing-list enquiries to PO Box 664, Bairnsdale, 3875.

Prices:
$9 cellar door.

Overall Quality:
Red wines good, with potential to improve even further; white wines adequate at best.

Tasting Notes:

1984 CHARDONNAY [15.2] *Colour:* full yellow, tinged with orange/straw. *Bouquet:* strong, malty/ honey solids fermentation aromas. *Palate:* a replica of the bouquet; strong, malty, solids flavours, indicating barrel fermentation of unclarified juice. A touch of oxidation present. Certainly needs time before it becomes approachable. Drink '88–'91.

1984 PINOT NOIR [17] *Colour:* very good purple-red of medium depth. *Bouquet:* clean, with good pinot varietal character in the sweeter spectrum, with plum-like characters. *Palate:* fresh, gentle plum/spice flavour, but with very good structure and balance. Oak nicely handled; a well-made and complete Pinot Noir. Drink '86–'89.

1984 CABERNET SAUVIGNON [16.6] *Colour:* purple-red of medium depth. *Bouquet:* full, gently ripe, sweet redcurrant/berry aromas. *Palate:* full-textured, with slightly powdery oak and a trace of oxidation; firm acid on the finish. Drink '87–'91.

PARISH WINES—BRIAGOLONG ESTATE

Location:
118 Boisdale Street, Maffra, 3860;
due east of Bairnsdale.
(051) 47 2322.

Winemaker:
Dr Gordon McIntosh.

1985 Production:
Approximately 100 cases.

Principal Wines:
Chardonnay and Pinot Noir. Wines have been made since 1981 but only in experimental quantities throughout most of the vintages until 1983.

Distribution:
When offered for sale, will be exclusively mailing list.

Overall Quality:
Variable; wines made in a very distinctive style.

Tasting Notes:

1985 CHARDONNAY [16.4] *Colour:* light to medium straw-yellow. *Bouquet:* distinct apricot/peach fruit aromas, with a touch of solids fermentation character. *Palate:* similar peach/apricot flavours; a slightly tart acid finish. Drink '87–'89.

1984 CHARDONNAY [16] *Colour:* light to medium yellow-green. *Bouquet:* the most burgundian chardonnay I have ever encountered in Australia, with sulphide, fibre and sinew. *Palate:* very austere, very French, and in utterly individual style. Will be extremely long-lived. Drink '88–'93.

1984 PINOT NOIR [17.4] *Colour:* strong red-purple. *Bouquet:* smooth, clean and well-balanced, with a touch of mint, good fruit depth although varietal aroma not particularly marked. *Palate:* of somewhat surprising intensity and weight; strawberry/mint flavour; very good structure and length. A wine with considerable future. Drink '87–'90.

Geelong

1985 Vintage

After reasonable winter rain, windy and damp (but not really wet) conditions during spring caused problems at flowering, and guaranteed that the abundant 1984 harvest would not be repeated. Wind at flowering is one of the district's major problems. A very cool and dry summer retarded ripening and gradually worsened into drought, placing considerable stress on unirrigated vineyards. Bird damage was also extensive throughout the district.

As in much of central and southern Victoria, moist and humid conditions arrived with vintage, although provided an adequate spray regime had been undertaken, these conditions assisted crop quality by relieving vine stress.

Not surprisingly, yields were substantially down on 1984, although not much below normal levels. White wines are of average quality, well-balanced and with the usual good varietal characteristics. Overall the red wines hold out greater promise, with the finesse and elegance one would expect from a very cool growing season.

The Changes

No new faces arrived on the scene, nor did any old ones depart.

BANNOCKBURN

pp. 169–70

Location:
Midland Highway, Bannockburn, 3331.
(052) 81 1363.

Winemaker:
Garry Farr.

1985 Production:
3500 cases.

Principal Wines:
Chardonnay, Rhine Riesling, Sauvignon Blanc, Pinot Noir, Cabernet Sauvignon and Shiraz.

Distribution:
By mailing list, wholesale through Chas Cole Cellars Pty Ltd, Geelong, and retail through Bannockburn Cellars, 150 Pakington Street, Geelong West. No cellar-door sales. Mailing-list enquiries to Bannockburn Vineyards, PO Bannockburn, 3331.

Prices:
$84 to $125 per dozen.

Overall Quality:
Good; occasional very good wines.

Vintage Rating 1982–85:
White: '85, '84, '83, '82.
Red: '84, '85, '83, '82.

Outstanding Prior Vintages:
'80.

Tasting Notes:

1983 CHARDONNAY [16.6] *Colour:* light to medium green-yellow. *Bouquet:* very complex; burgundian sulphide aromas dominate but do not unduly detract from the wine. *Palate:* less complex and rather cleaner, with light to medium fruit with some cool-climate citrus mid-palate flavours and good length. Drink '85–'87.

1983 PINOT NOIR [15.8] *Colour:* very good red-purple of medium depth. *Bouquet:* sweet caramel/vanillin American oak dominant. *Palate:* caramel/vanillin oak flavours utterly dominate fruit; pleasant enough, but little to do with pinot noir. Drink '85–'88.

1982 PINOT NOIR [16.4] *Colour:* light to medium red. *Bouquet:* distinct caramel/coffee aromas are the main feature. *Palate:* somewhat unexpectedly, fruit weight is much better, with light but clean pinot strawberry flavours on the mid-palate and good acid on the finish. Drink '85–'88.

1982 SHIRAZ [18] *Colour:* very good red-purple. *Bouquet:* full and smooth; very clean, with excellent fruit/oak balance and integration and overall complexity. *Palate:* abundant, perfectly ripe fruit flavours with very good balance and gentle tannin on the finish. A lovely wine. Drink '85–'92.

1981 CABERNET SAUVIGNON [16.4] *Colour:* medium red. *Bouquet:* some leathery bottle-developed aromas with sweet fruit lurking under a suspicion of mercaptan. *Palate:* fine, lifted fruit, much better than the bouquet would suggest; some bottle-developed elegance. Drink '85–'88.

CLYDE PARK

p. 170

Location:
Midland Highway, Bannockburn, 3331.
(vineyard only).

Winemaker:
Garry Farr.

1985 Production:
440 cases.

Principal Wines:
Chardonnay and Pinot Noir.

Distribution:
Direct to restaurants; no mailing list or cellar-door sales.

Prices:
Not applicable.

Overall Quality:
Too early to judge.

Vintage Rating 1983–85:
White: '85, '84, '83.
Red: '84, '85, '83.

Tasting Notes:

1984 CHARDONNAY [14.8] *Colour:* bright green-yellow. *Bouquet:* strong oak with curious oily/marzipan aromas and some volatile lift. *Palate:* marked marzipan-almond meal flavours; most unusual and non-varietal. Drink '86.

1983 PINOT NOIR [16.8] *Colour:* medium to full red-purple. *Bouquet:* a touch of caramel/coffee oak; solid and clean, and of medium to full weight. *Palate:* full though non-varietal, flavoury/minty fruit and oak. Drink '85–'88.

HICKINBOTHAM

pp. 170–2

Location:
Staughton Vale Road, Anakie, 3221;
3 km north of Anakie.
(052) 84 1256.

Winemakers:
The Hickinbotham family; Stephen Hickinbotham has primary responsibility.

1985 Production:
7100 cases.

Principal Wines:
An explicit labelling system which eschews the use of generic or European-influenced names is used for the white and red table wines produced from a diverse range of grape varieties and sources. 90% of grapes are estate-grown, but purchases from Tasmania, Mornington Peninsula and East Gippsland have spread the net far and wide for a small winery. Also large-volume seller Cab Mac employs purchased grapes. Labels include Anakie Late May Riesling, Anakie Semillon, Anakie Early June Riesling, Botrytis Cinerea and Anakie Cabernet Shiraz.

Distribution:
Cellar-door sales, mailing list and retail distribution through Taylor Ferguson (eastern states and Western Australia) and Classic Wines (South Australia). Also some exports. Cellar-door sales 10 a.m. to 5 p.m. Tuesday to Sunday and public holidays. Mailing-list enquiries to Hickinbotham Winemakers, 120 Warragul Road, Burwood, 3125.

Prices:
$8.50 to $13.50 recommended retail.

Overall Quality:
Very good; Cab Mac (within its terms of reference) usually exceptional.

Vintage Rating 1982–85:
White: '84, '82, '85, '83.
Red: '84, '83, '85, '82.

Outstanding Prior Vintages:
'78, '76.

Tasting Notes:

1985 CAB MAC [16.8] ***Colour:*** **light to medium purple-red.** ***Bouquet:*** **marked, complex, carbonic maceration aromas, with an amalgam of cinnamon/spice/meat.** ***Palate:*** **much bigger and more complex than preceding vintages; very strong gamy/meaty flavours and some spice. In my view too much of a good thing and does not match the clarity and brilliance of the earlier releases. Drink '86.**

1984 ANAKIE LATE MAY RIESLING [16.8] ***Colour:*** **full yellow, tinged with straw.** ***Bouquet:*** **very rich, intensely perfumed, flowery botrytis aromas.** ***Palate:*** **similar, very flowery fruit flavours; fermented almost completely dry, and in the result is somewhat hard on the finish. Would have been pointed much higher were it not for that finish. Drink '85–'87.**

1983 ANAKIE CHARDONNAY [17] ***Colour:*** **medium full yellow.** ***Bouquet:*** **marked Burgundian characters with a touch of sulphide, and considerable weight and robustness.** ***Palate:*** **very rich, ripe melon/fig flavours on the mid-palate and a somewhat phenolic finish. Drink '85–'89.**

1983 ANAKIE CABERNET [18.2] ***Colour:*** **strong, deep purple-red.** ***Bouquet:*** **very rich and very ripe with complex, scented cassis/berry aromas and a touch of straw.** ***Palate:*** **a deeply flavoured wine with good varietal character manifesting itself in cherry flavours on the mid-palate; excellent grape tannins on the finish round off the wine. Drink '86–'92.**

IDYLL VINEYARD

pp. 172–3

Location:
Ballan Road, Moorabool, 3221;
7 km west of North Geelong.
(052) 76 1280.

Winemaker:
Darryl Sefton.

1985 Production:
Approximately 4500 cases.

Principal Wines:

Gewurztraminer, Gewurztraminer Wood-matured, Idyll Blush, Cabernet Shiraz.

Distribution:
Cellar-door sales, mailing list and limited fine wine retail distribution in capital cities; significant exports to Europe and the United Kingdom. Cellar-door sales September 1 to January 31—10 a.m. to 5 p.m. Monday to Saturday and noon to 5 p.m. Sunday. February 1 to August 31—10 a.m. to 5 p.m. Tuesday to Saturday. Mailing-list enquiries as above.

Prices:
$5.50 to $9.50 recommended retail.

Overall Quality:
Gewurztraminer and Idyll Blush variable;
Cabernet Shiraz very good.

Vintage Rating 1982–85:
White: '84, '83, '82.
Red: '82, '84, '83 ('85 not rated).

Outstanding Prior Vintages:
'80, '76, '75, '71.

Tasting Notes:

1984 GEWURTZTRAMINER WOOD-MATURED [17.6] *Colour:* medium yellow with straw tinges. *Bouquet:* full, with softly spicy rich aroma of fully ripe fruit; very good varietal character, yet not oily or harsh. *Palate:* a very successful wine, in which oak adds a dimension to the flavour and structure but does not overwhelm; nutmeg spice flavours from oak entirely harmonious with fruit. Drink '86–'89.

1984 GEWURTZTRAMINER [17.4] *Colour:* medium yellow-green. *Bouquet:* smooth, with some spicy varietal characters evident, and of medium to full weight. *Palate:* attractive, soft fleshy/spicy flavours; well-balanced; together with the wood-matured wine of the same vintage, by far the best traminer to so far come from the vineyard. Drink '86–'88.

1984 IDYLL BLUSH A wine made in a particular style which I actively dislike.

1982 CABERNET SHIRAZ [17] *Colour:* medium full red. *Bouquet:* rich and deep, with complex fruit/oak integration; clean, and a slight lift which seems to be the hallmark of the winery. *Palate:* some minty fruit flavours on the fore- and mid-palate, and again that slightly lifted finish. If it is volatility, it is well within the parameters of the style; overall a wine of considerable weight and cellaring potential. Drink '86–'92.

MOUNT DUNEED

p. 173

Location:
Feehans Road, Mt Duneed, 3221; off right-hand side of Torquay Road, 10 km past Geelong.
(052) 64 1281.

Winemakers:
Ken and Peter Caldwell.

Principal Wines:

Semillon, Sauvignon Blanc, Cabernet Blend and Shiraz. Specialties are late-harvest styles. Some wines made from grapes purchased in other regions; such wines clearly identified.

Distribution:
Principally cellar-door sales 10 a.m. to 6 p.m. Tuesday to Saturday and public holidays. Limited retail distribution through Victorian Wine Centre.

Prices:
$4 to $8.60.

Overall Quality:
Some very good late-harvest styles have been made; other wines less exciting.

Tasting Notes:

1982 BEVERFORD CROUCHEN [15.6] *Colour:* pale straw-green. *Bouquet:* soft, broad, full tropical fruit; holding remarkably well. *Palate:* a well-made wine with marked pastille/tropical, fruit flavours. Drink '85–'86.

1982 REBENBERG CABERNET SAUVIGNON [14.6] *Colour:* medium to full red. *Bouquet:* a big, firm robust wine with some sweet, deep berry aromas, a touch of gravel, and then distinct volatile lift. *Palate:* a big wine spoilt by wood-derived volatility.

PRINCE ALBERT

pp. 173–4

Location:
Lemins Road, Waurn Ponds, 3221;
10 km south-west of Geelong.
(052) 22 1766.

Winemakers:
Bruce Hyett and Neil Everist.

1985 Production:
500 cases.

Principal Wines:
Only one wine made: Pinot Noir.

Distribution:
Principally cellar-door sales and mailing list, together with local restaurants. Sydney retail distribution through Carol Anne Classic Wines; ACT, Farmer Bros; Melbourne, Crittendens. Cellar-door sales 9 a.m. to 5 p.m. while wine available (usually only throughout October).

Prices:
$8 cellar door.

Overall Quality:
Has tended to be somewhat variable, but on the whole, good.

Vintage Rating 1982–85:
'83, '84, '85, '82.

Outstanding Prior Vintages:
'78.

Tasting Notes:

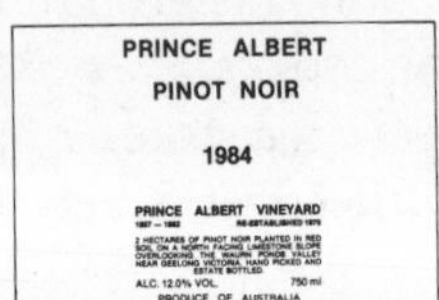

1984 PINOT NOIR [16.8] *Colour:* light vibrant purple-red. *Bouquet:* clean; shortly after bottling in mid-1985 rather closed and with subdued aromatics; light touch of vanillin oak. *Palate:* some authentic pinot fruit flavours with a touch of sappiness and, although light-bodied, has good fruit structure. For short-term cellaring. Drink '86–'89.

TARCOOLA

p. 174

Location:
Maude Road, Lethbridge, 3332;
5 km north-east of Lethbridge on the Moorabool River.
(052) 81 9245.

Winemaker:
Alastair Scott.

1985 Production:
Approximately 2000 cases.

Principal Wines:

Rhine Riesling, Muller Thurgau, Shiraz and Cabernet Sauvignon. All wines, both white and red, offered with substantial bottle age.

Distribution:
Principally cellar-door sales and mailing list; very limited Melbourne retail distribution.

Prices:
$6.50 to $8 ex cellar door.

Overall Quality:
Adequate to good.

Tasting Notes:

1982 RHINE RIESLING [16.2] *Colour:* medium yellow-green. *Bouquet:* clean; of medium to full weight and showing no small-winemaker problems; attractive lime aromas. *Palate:* a generously flavoured, fairly big wine with the lime flavours of the bouquet repeating themselves, and a slightly peppery finish. Drink '85–'87.

1981 SHIRAZ [17] *Colour:* medium to full red-purple. *Bouquet:* quite fragrant and complex cedar/tea-leaf overtones to fruit. *Palate:* has developed quite beautifully in bottle with good balance and smoothly rich mid-palate fruit. Has the structure to go on for a long time. Drink '85–'90.

Great Western and District

1985 Vintage

The year was one which kept winemakers guessing until the very end. Excellent winter and spring rains produced an abundant crop in near-perfect growing conditions which continued well into the new year. The cool and very dry summer which dominated central and southern Victoria then started to have a marked impact, severely stressing some varieties (mainly in unirrigated vineyards), with sugar levels rising rapidly and acid levels falling even more quickly.

After a brief burst of hot weather at the end of March, cool conditions returned—with quite substantial rain. The coolness and rain together operated to save a number of threatened vineyards. Nonetheless, the vintage was not an easy one, both because of variable weather and because of uneven ripeness of grapes in some vineyards.

Irrigated vineyards produced grapes in outstanding condition, and overall the white wines are very promising. There is excellent varietal definition, and abundant flavour. The red wines are surprisingly big and generous in flavour, but look unlikely to produce long-lived wines.

The Changes

There have been no new arrivals on the scene during 1985, but some of the new small vineyards have achieved considerable success during the year both in the marketplace and in the show ring. Foremost among these are Mount Chalambar Estate, Mount Langhi Ghiran and Cathcart Ridge Estate. Cathcart Ridge, in particular, came to the fore by winning the Wine Press Club Trophy for the Best Victorian Wine at the 1985 Royal Melbourne Wine Show. The number of wineries in the district is still not great, but there is no question that the Great Western region is capable of producing excellent wines of all styles, particularly reds.

BEST'S

pp. 179–81

Location:
Great Western, 3377;
2 km off Western Highway at 219 km post, just north of Great Western.
(053) 56 2250.

Winemakers:
Viv Thomson and Trevor Mast.

1985 Production:
Estimated 15,000 cases.

Principal Wines:
Chardonnay, Rhine Riesling, Golden Chasselas, Gewurztraminer, Ondenc, Pinot Meunier, Hermitage Bin No. 0, and Cabernet Sauvignon.

Distribution:
Cellar-door sales, mailing list and reasonable capital city fine wine retail distribution. Wholesale distributors Flinders Wines, Melbourne and Walcie Pty Limited, Sydney. Cellar-door sales 9 a.m. to 5 p.m. Monday to Friday, and 9 a.m. to 4 p.m. Saturday and public holidays. Closed Sunday, Christmas Day and Anzac Day. Mailing-list enquiries as above.

Prices:
$7.70 to $11 recommended retail; significantly less cellar door.

Overall Quality:
Whites variable but can be very good; reds reliably good.

Vintage Rating 1982–85:
White: '84, '85, '82, '83.
Red: '84, '82, '85, '83.

Outstanding Prior Vintages:
White: '79.
Red: '64, '66, '67, '76 and '80.

Tasting Notes:

1984 GREAT WESTERN RHINE RIESLING [14.8] *Colour:* **medium yellow-green.** *Bouquet:* **rather heavy and slightly phenolic, with some unusual cosmetic overtones.** *Palate:* **a rather big riesling, tending to heaviness, and with marked residual sugar. Drink '86.**

1984 CHENIN BLANC [15.2] *Colour:* **light to medium yellow-green.** *Bouquet:* **voluminous toasty oak aromas, and the suggestion of some mercaptan.** *Palate:* **lively, with fruit and oak well-balanced and just a touch of fruit sweetness. Reasonable short-term cellaring. Drink '85–'87.**

1984 CHARDONNAY BIN No. 0 [17] *Colour:* **excellent full green-yellow.** *Bouquet:* **very pronounced lift to rich, ripe fruit, backed by a touch of smoky oak.** *Palate:* **lively, lifted, melon/grapefruit flavours in a wine which may have a touch of volatility, but which is a pleasure to drink nonetheless. Drink '86–'88.**

1982 HERMITAGE BIN No. 0 [17] *Colour:* **very good, bright, purple-red of medium depth.** *Bouquet:* **smooth berry aromas, with excellent fruit/oak integration.** *Palate:* **a deliciously fresh wine, with gentle cherry fruit flavours, light oak and low tannin, all in perfect balance. Drink '85–'89.**

BOROKA

p. 181

Location:
Pomonal Road, Halls Gap, 3381;
5 km from Halls Gap towards Ararat.
(053) 56 4252.

Winemaker:
Bernie Breen.

1985 Production:
670 cases.

Principal Wines:
Sauvignon Blanc, Boroka Provençale (a light, dry-oaked red made from a blend of shiraz, trebbiano and ondenc), Shiraz and Vintage Port.

Distribution:
Principally cellar-door sales and mailing list, with very limited retail distribution. Cellar-door sales 9 a.m. to 5 p.m. Monday to Saturday and Sunday 1 p.m. to 5 p.m. Mailing-list enquiries to RMB 2072 via Stawell, 3380.

Prices:
$4.50 to $6.50 cellar door.

Overall Quality:
Variable: adequate to good.

Vintage Rating 1982–85:
White: '85, '82, '84, '83.
Red: '84, '85, '82, '83.

Tasting Notes:

1985 SAUVIGNON BLANC [14.8] *Colour:* light to medium yellow-green. *Bouquet:* clean, light, slightly smoky sauvignon blanc aroma. *Palate:* fresh and crisp, but very light fruit, lacking flesh. Drink '85.

1985 BOROKA PROVENÇALE [16.4] *Colour:* light red, slightly dull. *Bouquet:* crisp and clean, with a trace of smoky oak. *Palate:* most attractive light red, with sweet mid-palate fruit flavours (though no sugar) and good balance. Drink '85.

CATHCART RIDGE

p. 181

Location:
Byron Road, Cathcart via Ararat, 3377;
5 km from Ararat along Moyston Road.
(053) 52 4082.

Winemaker:
Dr Graeme Bertuch.

1985 Production:
1000 cases.

Principal Wines:
Shiraz, together with a tiny quantity of Sparkling Riesling.

Distribution:
Principally mailing list and through Richmond Hill Cellars, Melbourne.

Prices:
$7.50 to $8 recommended retail.

Overall Quality:
Good.

Vintage Rating 1982–85:
'83, '85, '84, '82.

Tasting Notes:

1984 SHIRAZ [18] *Colour:* medium to full red-purple. *Bouquet:* firm and clean, gently astringent, and much more elegant than the '83. *Palate:* while the bouquet is somewhat closed, the wine comes alive on the palate with lovely, gently sweet cherry/berry flavours and a touch of clove on a long finish. Gold medal and trophy winner Melbourne Show 1985. Drink '87–'90.

1983 SHIRAZ [16.2] *Colour:* dense, impenetrable purple. *Bouquet:* an immensely strong and robust wine, with earthy/gravel aromas and a touch of leathery mercaptan. *Palate:* an immense wine, dense and concentrated, yet surprisingly low in tannin and with good fruit depth. Faulted principally by the touch of mercaptan which comes again on the palate. Will be extraordinarily long-lived. Drink '89–'96.

1982 SHIRAZ [15.8] *Colour:* strong purple-red of medium depth. *Bouquet:* medium to full in weight with very good fruit/oak balance, and again a touch of leather/meat mercaptan-derived aroma. *Palate:* smooth, solid and deep, with concentration, although not to anything like the extent of the '83. A trace of lift on the finish, and again some evidences of mercaptan underneath the fruit. Drink '86–'92.

DONOVIEW

pp. 181–2

Location:
Pomonal Road, Stawell, 3380;
5 km south-west of Stawell.
(053) 58 2727.

Winemaker:
Chris Peters.

1985 Production:
Very small; less than 500 cases.

Principal Wines:
Crouchen Shiraz and Shiraz Cabernet Sauvignon (non-vintage).

Distribution:
Principally cellar-door sales and mailing list; also Victorian Wine Centre and selected restaurants. Cellar-door sales 10 a.m. to 5 p.m. Monday to Saturday. Mailing-list enquiries to RMB 2017, Stawell, 3380.

Prices:
$6.50 to $7.75 recommended retail.

Overall Quality:
Adequate to good.

Tasting Notes:
N.V. SHIRAZ CABERNET SAUVIGNON [15.2] *Colour:* medium red-purple. *Bouquet:* clean; quite smooth; a trace of mint and of medium fruit depth. *Palate:* tannin commences to build early, leading to a hollow mid-palate and a rather dry finish. May soften with further age. Drink '87–'89.

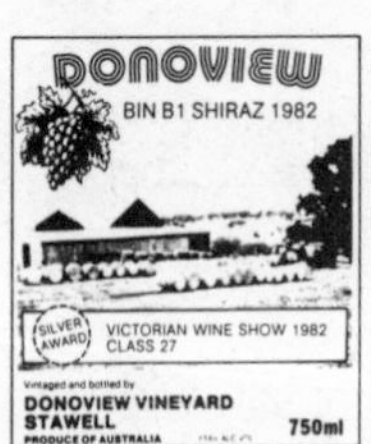

1982 SHIRAZ BIN B1 [16.4] *Colour:* bright medium to full red-purple. *Bouquet:* complex and quite fragrant with some varietal, sweaty saddle aromas which are not unpleasant. *Palate:* smooth with some complex cigar box/meaty mercaptan characters; curiously, as with the bouquet, these are not at all offensive. A quite elegant wine, with soft tannin. Drink '85–'89.

MONTARA

p. 182

Location:
Chalambar Road, Ararat, 3377;
3 km from Ararat on Hamilton Road.
(053) 52 3868.

Winemaker:
Michael McRae.

1985 Production:
Approximately 6000 cases.

Principal Wines:
Ondenc, Chasselas, Rhine Riesling, Pinot Noir, Shiraz, Cabernet Sauvignon and Vintage Port.

Distribution:
Principally cellar door and mailing list; limited Melbourne distribution through J. H. Long Wine Brokers. Cellar-door sales 9.30 a.m. to 5 p.m. Monday to Saturday. Mailing-list enquiries as above.

Prices:
$5.50 to $8.50 cellar door.

Overall Quality:
Good to very good, particularly Pinot Noir.

Vintage Rating 1982–85:
White: '85, '82, '84, '83.
Red: '84, '82, '85, '83.

Outstanding Prior Vintages:
'80.

Tasting Notes:
1984 ONDENC [17.6] *Colour:* green-yellow. *Bouquet:* marked vanillin/spicy oak aromas with green/citric fruit underneath. *Palate:* an extremely well-made wine of most attractive commercial style; spicy vanillin oak, with fleshy, rounded fruit aided by a touch of residual sugar. Drink '85–'87.

1984 PINOT NOIR [18.4] *Colour:* medium red. *Bouquet:* outstanding strawberry varietal aromas, backed by a touch of spice; striking and most attractive. *Palate:* very rich fruit with almost mead-like clove/nutmeg spice flavours. A first-class Australian pinot noir. Drink '86–'89.

1982 CABERNET SAUVIGNON [16.8] *Colour:* medium to full red. *Bouquet:* solid and firm, with some herbaceous fruit but also a trace of mercaptan-derived astringency. *Palate:* good varietal character but again some slightly bitter/charred flavours apparent, probably mercaptan sourced, but possibly from oak. Drink '85–'88.

MOUNT CHALAMBAR

p. 182

Location:
Off Tatyoon Road, Ararat, 3377;
3 km from town. (Vineyard only.)
(053) 52 3768.

Winemaker:
Trevor Mast.

1985 Production:
1800 cases.

Principal Wines:
Rhine Riesling and Méthode Champenoise Chardonnay.

Distribution:
By mailing list and wholesale through I. H. Baker & Co. (to retailers and restaurants). No cellar-door sales. Mailing list to Box 301, Ararat, 3377.

Prices:
$8.30 to $10.80.

Overall Quality:
Very good.

Vintage Rating 1984–85:
'84, '85.

Tasting Notes:

1984 RHINE RIESLING [18] *Colour:* strong green-yellow. *Bouquet:* voluminous, aromatic, spicy lime characters, with strong germanic overtones. *Palate:* a marvellously flavoursome wine, strong and rich, yet avoiding the phenolic hardness on the finish which so often afflicts otherwise generous wines. Drink '85–'88.

MOUNT LANGI GHIRAN

pp. 182–3

Location:
Vine Road, off Buangor–Ararat Road, Buangor, 3375;
16 km from Ararat towards Melbourne.
(053) 54 3207.

Winemaker:
Trevor Mast (consultant).

1985 Production:
2500 dozen.

Principal Wines:
Rhine Riesling, Hermitage and Cabernet Sauvignon.

Distribution:
Cellar-door sales, mailing list and through I. H. Baker & Co. to selected retailers and restaurants.

Prices:
$8 to $10 recommended retail.

Overall Quality:
Variable: from adequate to very good.

Outstanding Prior Vintages:
White: '85, '84 (no '83 or '82).
Red: '84, '83, '85, '82.

Tasting Notes:

1984 RHINE RIESLING [15.4] *Colour:* pale straw-yellow. *Bouquet:* slightly coarse, with distinct solids fermentation characters. *Palate:* fine, almost lemony fruit flavours, partially obscured by chalky/harsh structure from solids fermentations. May improve in bottle. Drink '86–'88.

1982 HERMITAGE [15.8] *Colour:* red-purple of medium depth. *Bouquet:* quite solid, with a touch of leather/caramel aroma, but not a power-house. *Palate:* fresh and clean; a little light on the mid-palate, and a gently astringent finish. Drink '85–'87.

1982 CABERNET SAUVIGNON [17.2] *Colour:* medium to full red-purple. *Bouquet:* a very big, clean aroma with textured vanilla bean/spice oak and sweet fruit. *Palate:* a very big wine with spicy, Portuguese-like oak married with rich and ripe fruit; enormous texture and structure. Drink '86–'91.

SEPPELT GREAT WESTERN

pp. 183–6

Location:
Moyston Road, Ararat, 3377;
off Western Highway 16 km north-west of Ararat.
(053) 56 2202.

Winemakers:
Ian McKenzie (chief), Warren Randall (sparkling).

1985 Production:
Approximately 690,000 litres of Great Western wine and 600,000 litres Barooga wine.

Principal Wines:
Seppelts Great Western Sparkling and Méthode Champenoise wines are still Australia's best-known examples of the style, even if market leadership is from time to time contested by other brands. Some fine varietal white and red table wines also come from Great Western, notably Black Label Hermitage and Black Label Cabernet Sauvignon. Increasing plantings of Chardonnay will see more of this variety sourced from the Great Western vineyard in the future.

Distribution:
National retail through all types of wine outlets.

Prices:
Recommended retail prices subject to intermittent severe discounting; most wines sell in $6 to $9.50 range.

Overall Quality:
Very good.

Vintage Rating 1982–85:
White: '84, '82, '83, '85.
Red: '84, '82, '83, '85.

Outstanding Prior Vintages:
'80 (red), '81 (white).

Tasting Notes:

VICTORIAN 150TH ANNIVERSARY BRUT CHAMPAGNE [17] *Colour:* pale straw-yellow. *Bouquet:* complex toasty/bready/cheesy aromas of considerable substance. *Palate:* quite fresh and crisp, with pleasant mid-palate weight showing some apparent chardonnay influence; clean and smooth. Drink '86.

1983 CUVEE DE PRESTIGE [17.6] *Colour:* deep straw-yellow. *Bouquet:* a big, very complex and solid wine with a touch of marmite yeast aroma. *Palate:* as the bouquet promises, very complex fruit structure with some smoky overtones to the fore-palate, and an excellent round finish. Drink '86–'88.

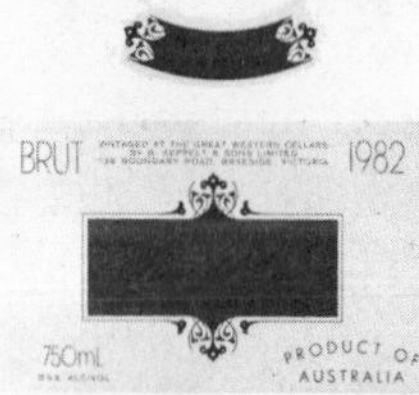

1982 FLEUR DE LYS [16.2] *Colour:* deep yellow-bronze, surprisingly dark. *Bouquet:* big, slightly biscuity aroma, not particularly expressive or aromatic, and a suspicion of oxidation. *Palate:* very big, buttery, slightly caramelised fruit flavours. Not in the class of the '81 Fleur De Lys. Drink '86.

1982 SHOW RHINE RIESLING [17] *Colour:* yellow-green of medium depth. *Bouquet:* very full, tropical/scented aroma, grapy and almost into muscat richness. *Palate:* very full, rich wine with a trace of phenolic heaviness; a good food wine. Drink '85–'86.

1981 CHARDONNAY CHAMPAGNE [17] *Colour:* medium full buttercup-yellow. *Bouquet:* big, smooth and soft, gently buttery aromas of medium complexity. *Palate:* round and soft, buttery fruit with some developed camphor/vanillin characters; overall ripe and soft. Drink '85–'86.

1981 VICTORIAN HERMITAGE [16.4] *Colour:* red-purple. *Bouquet:* a somewhat old-fashioned style; clean, fairly ripe and very smooth. *Palate:* full and soft; oak somewhat pedestrian, and the wine lacks final complexity. Drink '85–'88.

Macedon

1985 Vintage

Good winter/spring rains set the 1985 vintage off in style, with a number of the vineyards still suffering the after-effects of the 1983 drought. Wind, both at flowering and fruit set and throughout the growing season, is a problem in much of the Macedon region in most years, and 1985 was no exception.

As elsewhere, the summer was very cool, but the conditions overall were infinitely more favourable than they were in 1984. In that vintage real problems were encountered in satisfactorily ripening the fruit; no such problems were experienced in 1985.

The red wines should be outstanding, with far greater depth of flavour and colour; and overall, the vintage has been the best since 1980.

The Changes

The region is still developing, with a large number of small vineyards which will come into production over the next few years. It is more than probable that much of the fruit from these vineyards will end up in sparkling wine, the likely purchaser being the giant French champagne house Moet et Chandon, which seems likely to establish its winery and tourist facilities within the Macedon region—and 1986 will see whether or not this in fact transpires. If it does, it will give tremendous strength to viticulture in the region, although it may well have the effect of limiting the number of small wineries which might otherwise have been established.

COPE-WILLIAMS

pp. 189–90

Location:
Glenfern Road, Romsey, 3434;
3 km north-west of township.
(054) 29 5428.

Winemaker:
Gordon Cope-Williams.

1985 Production:
900 cases.

Principal Wines:
Chardonnay, Méthode Champenoise, Pinot Noir and Cabernets (the last a cabernet-dominant blend). Estate plantings are only now coming into production, and prior vintages have been supplemented by wine purchased from Tisdall.

Distribution:
Limited fine wine retail distribution planned but still to be finalised. Cellar-door sales noon to 5 p.m. Saturday and Sunday. Mailing-list address as above.

Prices:
$5.50 to $9.50 recommended retail.

Overall Quality:
Promises to be good.

Vintage Rating 1982–85:
White: '85, '83, '84, '82.
Red: '85, '83, '82, '84.

Tasting Notes:
1985 CHARDONNAY [16.8] *Colour:* light to medium yellow-green. *Bouquet:* very clean with pronounced lemony oak; a stylish wine, although there is some volatility apparent. *Palate:* fresh, light and fruity with very good acidity and again a trace of volatile lift. Very much a chablis style. Drink '87–'89.

1984 RHINE RIESLING/CHARDONNAY [16.2] *Colour:* brilliant green-yellow. *Bouquet:* clean; of medium weight, with quite pronounced lime aromas. *Palate:* a very well-made wine with lime flavours from the rhine riesling and a touch of yeasty/toasty flavour from the chardonnay. (A blend of Tisdall Rhine Riesling and Romsey Chardonnay.) Drink '86.

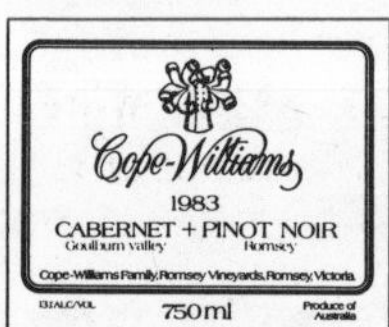

1983 CABERNET PINOT NOIR [16.4] *Colour:* light to medium purple-red. *Bouquet:* soft; fairly light fruit with some smoky oak aromas. *Palate:* quite fine, fresh, cherry-flavoured fruit; gentle acid and low tannin; a good commercial wine. (A blend of Tisdall Cabernet Sauvignon and Romsey Pinot Noir.) Drink '86–'87.

CRAIGLEE VINEYARD

p. 190

Location:
Sunbury Road, Sunbury, 3429;
on southern outskirts of Sunbury town,
35 minutes' drive from Melbourne GPO.
(03) 744 1160.

Winemaker:
Pat Carmody.

1985 Production:
2000 cases.

Principal Wines:
Only two wines produced: Chardonnay and Craiglee Red (the latter a blend of shiraz and cabernet sauvignon, with shiraz dominant).

Distribution:
Principally cellar-door sales and mailing list; also fine wine retail distribution Melbourne and Sydney. Cellar-door sales 10 a.m. to 5 p.m. Tuesday to Saturday, and noon to 5 p.m. Sunday.

Prices:
$8.50 to $12 recommended retail; less cellar door, mailing list.

Overall Quality:
Good to very good.

Vintage Rating 1982–85:
White: '83, '84, '85, '82.
Red: '83, '85, '84, '82.

Outstanding Prior Vintages:
'80 (Hermitage).

Tasting Notes:
1984 CHARDONNAY [16.4] *Colour:* pale yellow. *Bouquet:* very light in aroma, but clean and showing all the signs of good winemaking. *Palate:* a clean and very well-made wine; it simply lacks fruit depth and varietal character. May well benefit from a year or two in bottle. Drink '86–'87.

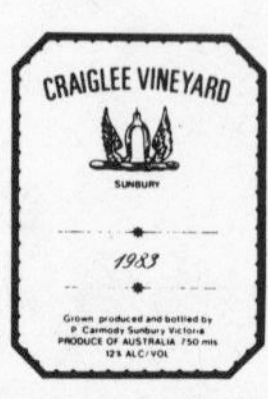

1983 CRAIGLEE (RED) [18.2] *Colour:* vibrant fuchsia-purple. *Bouquet:* most attractive smoky oak, marked varietal spice and considerable finesse and delicacy. *Palate:* a beautifully flavoured and balanced wine, with strong crushed pepper/spice flavours throughout; crisp and fresh, yet neither light nor skinny. Cool climate shiraz at its very best. Drink '86–'89.

FLYNN AND WILLIAMS

pp. 190–1

Location:
Flynns Lane, Kyneton, on outskirts of town.
(054) 22 2427.

Winemakers:
John Flynn and Laurie Williams.

1985 Production:
500 cases.

Principal Wines:
Gewurztraminer and Cabernet Sauvignon. Until 1984 wines principally made from vineyard owned by the partners at Heathcote. No '83 wine was produced, and Heathcote vineyard sold in that year, 1984 and subsequent production coming from two new vineyards established in Kyneton region.

Distribution:
Principally direct sales from vineyard to fine wine retailers and restaurants. Cellar-door sales at any time by appointment; no mailing list.

Prices:
No wines for sale mid-1985.

Overall Quality:
Very good, if not exceptional.

Vintage Rating 1982–85:
Not relevant because of change in vineyards.

Tasting Notes:

1982 *CABERNET SAUVIGNON* [18.8] *Colour:* strong purple-red. *Bouquet:* rich, deep and complex with outstanding fruit/oak balance and integration. *Palate:* sweet fruit together with rich vanillin oak flavours; very sophisticated wine-making and oak handling to produce a magnificently lush, soft and full wine. (Tasted January '85.) Drink '87–'94.

GOONAWARRA

p. 191

Location:
Sunbury Road, Sunbury, 3429;
on southern outskirts of town.

Winemaker:
John Barnier.

1985 Production:
Negligible.

Principal Wines:
Chardonnay, Semillon and Cabernet Franc.

Distribution:
Cellar-door sales and mailing list.

Prices:
No wine presently available.

Overall Quality:
Too early to assess.

Tasting Notes:
1984 COWRA SEMILLON **A relatively well-made wine; while light in fruit weight and varietal character, suggests that the future Goonawarra wines will be well-handled.**

KNIGHT GRANITE HILLS

pp. 191–2

Location:
RSD 83, Baynton via Kyneton, 3444;
on Lancefield–Mia Mia Road, 24 km south of Heathcote.
(054) 23 7264.

Winemaker:
Lew Knight.

1985 Production:
Approximately 7500 cases.

Principal Wines:

Rhine Riesling, Shiraz and Cabernet Sauvignon.

Distribution:
Substantial cellar-door and mailing-list sales; Victorian retail through Flinders Wholesale and New South Wales through David Bainbridge, providing reasonable fine wine retail sales. Cellar-door sales 10 a.m. to 6 p.m. Monday to Saturday, 1 p.m. to 6 p.m. Sunday.

Prices:
$8.60 to $9.30 recommended retail.

Overall Quality:
Very good.

Vintage Rating 1982–85:
White: '84, '82, '85(?), '83.
Red: '82, '85, '84, '83.

Outstanding Prior Vintages:
'81.

Tasting Notes:

1984 RHINE RIESLING [17.8] *Colour:* bright green-yellow. *Bouquet:* full, aromatic lime/tropical fruit, rich and clean. *Palate:* excellent riesling flavours, unmodified by either yeast or botrytis; residual sugar well-handled and balanced against crisp acid; a firm, long finish. Drink '86–'89.

1984 SEMILLON CROUCHEN [16.8] *Colour:* straw-yellow. *Bouquet:* a big, soft and full wine, slightly broad; well-handled spicy oak. *Palate:* a rich fore-palate, with similar spicy oak to that apparent in the bouquet; mid- and back-palate surprisingly light and delicate, with good acid. An interesting wine. Drink '86–'87.

1983 CABERNET SAUVIGNON [16.2] *Colour:* light to medium red-purple. *Bouquet:* of light to medium weight, smooth fruit with a touch of cedar/cigar/old oak pencil shavings, suggesting the wine was left in cask for too long. *Palate:* a touch of pepper to the fruit, but flawed by distinct old oak pencil shavings flavours. Well behind the '82 in quality. Drink '86–'88.

1983 SHIRAZ [16.8] *Colour:* light to medium red-purple. *Bouquet:* clean and fragrant, lively pepper/spice aromas. *Palate:* very light, early maturing style, with slightly dusty, peppery varietal shiraz, and again just a suggestion of a slightly dull oak. A good wine but pales into insignificance against the spectacular '82 vintage. Drink '86–'89.

VIRGIN HILLS

pp. 192–4

Location:
Salisbury Road, Lauriston West via Kyneton, 3444; 24 km east of Kyneton.
(054) 23 9169.

Winemaker:
Mark Sheppard.

1985 Production:
900 cases red; 100 cases white (1985 first production).

Principal Wines:
Only one wine so far commercially released, simply called Virgin Hills. No other description, varietal or generic, is provided on the label. It is in fact a cabernet-dominant blend, with the cabernet content increasing substantially from 1982, and now accounting for approximately 75% of the blend, with the remainder made up by shiraz and a little malbec.

Distribution:
All sold ex-vineyard by mailing list and by direct sale to fine wine retailers in Sydney and Melbourne. Mailing-list enquiries to PO Kyneton, 3444.

Prices:
$12.50 retail.

Overall Quality:
Exceptional.

Vintage Rating 1982–85:
'85, '82, '83, '84.

Outstanding Prior Vintages:
'74, '76, '79.

Tasting Notes:

1983 VIRGIN HILLS [18.2] *Colour:* medium full red-purple. *Bouquet:* excellent fruit/oak balance; oak softer and more spicy than in previous years; considerable fruit depth. *Palate:* medium to full in weight, with very good ripe cassis/berry flavours on the mid-palate and persistent, lingering tannin on the mid- and back-palate. Good acidity. Very much in the distinguished line of wines from the vineyard. Drink '88–'96.

Mornington Peninsula

1985 Vintage

As with Macedon, wind and rain in late spring, and hence during flowering, are a major viticultural problem in the region, and they significantly reduced the 1985 harvest. An abnormally dry (and very cool) summer further reduced yields, although quality at no stage looked in doubt.

Vintage commenced in mid-April and continued, on and off, in very cool and showery weather. Apart from minor outbreaks of botrytis in rhine riesling, all of the grapes were harvested in very good condition.

White wines are uniformly regarded as outstanding, and potentially the best in the last five years. The red wines, like the whites, show outstanding varietal character; a few vignerons still believe the '84s could prove superior, but most favour this vintage. Certainly it is an outstanding year.

The Changes

There are still only five vineyards offering wine for sale on a commercial basis, with a sixth (Balnarring) due to come on stream in 1986. However, there are numerous plantings scattered throughout the district which will come into bearing over the next few years. Some of these enterprises inevitably will result in wineries; others will be content to sell their grapes for the undoubtedly high prices which the premium fruit of the region will command.

If adequate means can be found to protect its vineyards from wind-effect, Mornington looks certain to become an important quality-winegrowing area. Its proximity to the market of Melbourne must inevitably help this endeavour.

DROMANA ESTATE VINEYARDS

p. 197

Location:
Cnr Harrisons Road and Bittern Dromana Road, Dromana, 3936;
3 km inland from Dromana.
(059) 87 3275.

Winemaker:
Nat White (contract).

1985 Production:
Approximately 530 cases.

Principal Wines:
Chardonnay, Pinot Noir and Cabernet Sauvignon, all of which are made at Main Ridge Estate by Nat White.

Distribution:
Simply by mailing list, with limited fine wine retail and restaurant distribution. All wines sold through Main Ridge Estate under its vigneron's licence; mailing-list enquiries, however, to Dromana Estate Vineyards, PO Box 332, Mornington, 3931.

Prices:
$9.50 per bottle mailing list.

Overall Quality:
Good to very good.

Vintage Rating 1984–85:
'85, '84.

Tasting Notes:

1984 CABERNET SAUVIGNON [17] *Colour:* medium purple-red. *Bouquet:* intense cool climate, herbaceous/green capsicum aroma; spotlessly clean; reminiscent of some Tasmanian cabernets, but with a little more weight. *Palate:* light to medium weight, crystal-clear fruit flavours, with just a trace of tannin and marked, crisp acid on the finish. Simply lacks mid-palate flesh. Drink '87–'90.

ELGEE PARK

pp. 197–8

Location:
Wallaces Road, Merricks North, 3926.
(059) 89 7338.

Winemakers:
Oenotec Pty Limited (consultant);
Henk Vandenham (manager).

1985 Production:
600 cases.

Principal Wines:
Rhine Riesling, Chardonnay and Cabernet Sauvignon (the latter with cabernet franc and merlot in the blend).

Distribution:
Exclusively through mailing list. Postal address: Junction Road, Merricks North, 3926. No cellar-door sales.

Prices:
$8.50 to $12.50.

Overall Quality:
Very good.

Vintage Rating 1982–85:
White: '85, '84, '83, '82.
Red: '84, '85, '83, '82.

Outstanding Prior Vintages:
'80.

Tasting Notes:
1985 RHINE RIESLING [18] *Colour:* bright green-yellow. *Bouquet:* brilliantly clean, gently aromatic/floral riesling aroma without extraneous flavours. *Palate:* crisp and very clean, with excellent mid-palate weight and varietal definition; long, crisp finish again dominated by fruit, and without phenolics. Drink '86–'89.

1984 CHARDONNAY [17.8] *Colour:* bright, light to medium yellow with just a touch of oak-derived straw. *Bouquet:* oak still to integrate fully, although it will undoubtedly do so as it is smooth rather than raw; good fruit-weight, with aromas in grapefruit spectrum. *Palate:* a stylish wine which needs time; very good acid to "cool" fruit flavours and fairly firm oak. Drink '87–'90.

1983 CABERNET SAUVIGNON [17.6] *Colour:* vibrant crimson-purple of medium depth. *Bouquet:* clean, light cherry/berry aromas. *Palate:* most attractive, fresh cherry fruit with a touch of spice and very low tannin; good length even though, in typical regional style, the wine is only of light to medium body. Drink '87–'91.

MAIN RIDGE ESTATE

p. 198

Location:
Lot 48, William Road, Red Hill, 3937;
(Melway Map 190 C4).
190 C4).
(059) 89 2686.

Winemaker:
Nat White.

1985 Production:
225 cases.

Principal Wines:
An eclectic, if not esoteric, range of varietal table wines including Pinot Meunier, Gewurztraminer, Chardonnay, Pinot Noir and Cabernet Sauvignon.

Distribution:
Mailing-list enquiries to PO Box 40, Red Hill South, 3937. Limited restaurant and fine wine retail distribution, chiefly in Melbourne.

Prices:
$8 to $12 recommended retail (mailing list $6.50 to $8.50).

Overall Quality:
Consistently very good, with high probability of some exceptional wines from time to time.

Vintage Rating 1982–85:
White: '85, '83, '82, '84.
Red: '85, '84, '83, '82.

Outstanding Prior Vintages:
'80.

Tasting Notes:
1984 GEWURTZTRAMINER [17] *Colour:* yellow with a few orange tints. *Bouquet:* soft lychee/pastille aromas; clean, with good fruit-weight, and not oily. *Palate:* round, soft and gently fruity; low tannin and good overall varietal character. Drink '86–'87.

1984 CHARDONNAY [17.6] *Colour:* bright light to medium yellow, with a few straw tinges. *Bouquet:* quite firm fruit backed by spicy oak and a trace of volatile lift. *Palate:* very well-handled, spicy-clove oak is the initial impression; good mouth-feel and weight on the mid-palate, with a long, soft finish. Has fruit intensity, and again, very well-made. Drink '86–'89.

1984 PINOT MEUNIER [18] *Colour:* very light tawny-red. *Bouquet:* extremely light, but extraordinarily fragrant, sappy pinot and spicy oak aromas intermingling; very striking. *Palate:* similarly fragrant and fresh; light, but lively spicy/sappy fruit and oak flavours. To be drunk while the vibrant life is present. Drink '85–'86.

1983 PINOT NOIR [17.8] *Colour:* medium red, with a touch of purple. *Bouquet:* clean; of medium weight with some sweet strawberry fruit. *Palate:* follows on logically from the bouquet, with similar rich and sweet strawberry fruit flavours in a ripe pinot noir style; excellent weight and flavour, and very clear varietal definition. Drink '85–'89.

MERRICKS

pp. 198–9

Location:
62 Thompsons Lane, Merricks, 3916;
(near Balnarring).
(059) 89 8352.

Winemaker:
Hickinbotham Winemakers (contract).

1985 Production:
150 cases.

Principal Wines:

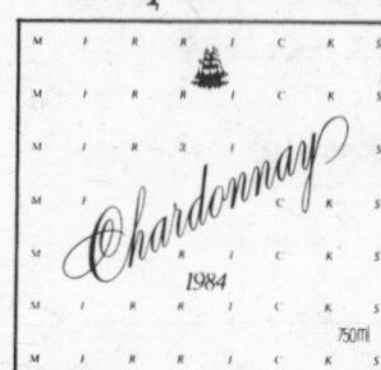

Chardonnay and Cabernet Sauvignon. Principally through Gatehouse Cellars, Melbourne; for mailing-list enquiries, apply to Merricks Winery, 62 Thompsons Lane, Merricks.

Prices:
$12 recommended retail.

Overall Quality:
On evidence of '84 Cabernet Sauvignon, exceptional.

Vintage Rating 1982–85:
White: '85, '83, '84, '82.
Red: '84, '85, '83, '82.

Tasting Notes:
1984 CABERNET SAUVIGNON [18.4] *Colour:* vibrant cherry-purple. *Bouquet:* intense and highly aromatic berry/herbaceous fruit, fresh and clean. *Palate:* similar intense, fresh, capsicum/berry fruit flavours; good mid-palate flavours; crisp, low tannin finish. Drink '87–'92.

MERRICKS ESTATE

p. 199

Location:
Thompsons Lane, Merricks, 3916;
(near Balnarring).
(059) 89 8416.

Winemaker:
George Kefford.

1985 Production:
150 cases.

Principal Wines:
Given tiny production, a wide range including Chardonnay, Rhine Riesling, Pinot Noir, Shiraz and Cabernet Sauvignon.

Distribution:
Principally mailing-list and cellar-door sales; cellar-door sales weekends by appointment; telephone first. Limited restaurant distribution.

Prices:
$9.50 cellar door.

Overall Quality:
Very good; Shiraz exhilarating.

Vintage Rating 1983–85:
White: '85, '84, '83.
Red: '84, '85, '83.

Tasting Notes:

1984 RHINE RIESLING [16.8] *Colour:* light to medium yellow-green. *Bouquet:* a surprisingly full and broad wine with quite rich lime characters and just a touch of caramel, possibly due to oxidation. *Palate:* abundant flavour, again surprisingly rich for a very cool year. Clean fermentation characters, although again there is a trace of the oxidation evident in the bouquet. Nonetheless, an impressive small winery white wine. Drink '86–'89.

1984 SHIRAZ [19] *Colour:* full, deep, purple-red. *Bouquet:* magnificently perfumed aromatic pepper spice varietal fruit, intense and lingering. *Palate:* outstanding, lively peppery/spice flavours, which literally dance in the mouth; of medium to full weight overall, and with a long finish. A superb Australian shiraz. Drink '86–'93.

1984 CABERNET SAUVIGNON [17.6] *Colour:* medium full purple-red. *Bouquet:* intense grassy/herbaceous aromas, slightly dusty. *Palate:* strong herbaceous/pepper/cigar flavours; clearly articulated varietal characters; overall of medium weight and soft tannin finish. A very good wine by any standards. Drink '87–'91.

Murray River

1985 Vintage

Building on the natural benefits of a very wet winter, one of the coolest growing seasons ever recorded produced crops of excellent quality. The long, dry and mild summer ensured the grapes ripened without any disease problems whatsoever, and of course the absence of rainfall caused no problems, given the district's total reliance on irrigation.

The white wines are rated as the best ever to come from the region, with sauvignon blanc quite outstanding. Chardonnay, colombard and rhine riesling are also particularly successful. Among the reds, cabernet sauvignon, ruby cabernet and shiraz grapes were particularly successful, producing soft and full-flavoured wines.

The Changes

The area is an extremely buoyant one, with a number of major, relatively new wineries, and other longer-established wineries enjoying continued growth. The district remains first and foremost a bulk producer, with much of the wine being sold to major wine companies in other regions for use in casks and flagons. Not only are the wineries by and large new and highly efficient, but the benefits of a major replanting program in the late 1970s are now being felt as the new vineyards are coming into full bearing. These are producing large quantities of sauvignon blanc and chardonnay, much of which finds its way not into casks but into bottles selling in the mid-sector of the market.

The north-west Murray may not be a particularly fashionable area, but it is one of the few winegrowing districts to provide an above-average return to the wineries operating within it. It came as no surprise when Mitchelton acquired Woorinen Wine Estates from its receiver in the second half of 1985. Woorinen's problems came strictly from marketing, not winemaking.

ALAMBIE WINES

pp. 203–4

Location:
Nangiloc Road, Nangiloc, 3494.
(050 29 1546.

Winemaker:
David Martin.

1985 Production:
Approximately 2000 tonnes, or 1,500,000 litres.

Principal Wines:
All wines, exclusively made from estate-grown grapes, are sold in bulk to other winemakers, packagers and re-users.

BEST'S ST ANDREWS

p. 204

Location:
St Andrews Vineyard, Lake Boga, 3584.
(050) 37 2154.

Winemakers:
Viv Thomson and Trevor Mast.

1985 Production:
Approximately 300 tonnes.

Principal Wines:
A number of table wines, both white and red, are produced; not all are released under the Best's labels. By far the most important estate release is Best's St Andrews Cabernet Sauvignon. Other regular releases are Shiraz and Rhine Riesling.

Distribution:
Retail distribution as for Best's Great Western. Cellar-door sales 9 a.m. to 5 p.m. Monday to Friday and 9 a.m. to 4 p.m. Saturday and public holidays.

Prices:
$5.30 to $6.70 recommended retail.

Overall Quality:
St Andrews Cabernet Sauvignon is usually good, offering above-average value for money. White wines extremely variable.

Vintage Rating 1982–85:
'84, '85, '82, '83.

Tasting Notes:

1984 RHINE RIESLING [11] *Colour:* very pale, almost watery in appearance. *Bouquet:* unattractive, rather smelly "armpit" characters with little or no fruit evident. *Palate:* relies totally upon residual sugar for the modest level of flavour.

1983 SHIRAZ [15] *Colour:* bright red-purple, but some grassy spritz evident. *Bouquet:* rather ripe, dull and somewhat old-fashioned fruit. *Palate:* full, if not downright solid, but cloys slightly, lacking backbone and acid lift. Redeemed principally by the abundance of fruit flavour. Drink '85–'86.

1983 CABERNET SAUVIGNON [16.2] *Colour:* red-purple of medium depth. *Bouquet:* solid, fairly ripe fruit with some raw unintegrated oak aromas. *Palate:* falls into compartments; initial impression of aggressive, unintegrated oak, followed by most attractive cherry/berry fruit flavours underneath. If the wine comes together, and it may well do so, would be most attractive. Certainly the fruit quality is there. Drink '87–'89.

BONNONEE WINES

p. 204

Location:
Campbell Avenue, Irymple, 3498;
10 km from Mildura.
(050) 24 5843.

Winemakers:
Neville Hudson and Graham Goddard.

1985 Production:
4,000,000 litres.

Principal Wines:
By far the greatest part of the production is sold either as clarified grape juice or as wine in bulk to other winemakers and re-packagers. A small percentage is estate-bottled and released under a series of labels. Premium-quality table wines are released under the Fitzpatrick Estate label, comprising Chardonnay, Rhine Riesling, Traminer, Rhine Riesling Traminer, Ruby Cabernet and Barbera, and Cabernet Sauvignon. Moselle, Sandalong Dry White and Belara Light Red are released under the Bonnonee Wines label, while spumante and flavoured sparkling wines are released under the Mildura Vineyards label. Non-alcoholic wines are also made and released under the Golden Lexia and Sparkling Golden Lexia labels. (Highly commended.) There is, in addition, the usual range of fortified wines and bulk wines sold in 20-litre casks.

Distribution:
Principally cellar door and mailing list; cellar-door sales 10 a.m. to 6 p.m. Monday to Saturday and most public holidays. Mailing-list enquiries to Box 695, Irymple, 3498.

Prices:
$4.10 to $6.50 cellar door for Fitzpatrick Estate. Other wines $2.80 to $3.30 cellar door.

Overall Quality:
Fitzpatrick Estate wines offer consistently good value for money.

Vintage Rating 1982–85:
White: '84, '85, '83, '82.
Red: '85, '82, '83, '84.

Outstanding Prior Vintages:
'79.

Tasting Notes:

1984 CHARDONNAY [15] *Colour:* **full yellow.** *Bouquet:* **fairly light fruit with somewhat raw and unintegrated oak.** *Palate:* **very light fruit, with very recognisable varietal character, and just a little oak to flesh out the palate. Drink '85–'86.**

1984 RHINE RIESLING TRAMINER [16.6] *Colour:* **strong yellow-green.** *Bouquet:* **soft, slightly sweet fruit and with considerable richness; clean.** *Palate:* **light residual sugar, well-backed by pleasing fruit flavours, without either variety dominating; a very good commercial wine. Drink '85–'86.**

1984 TRAMINER [16.2] *Colour:* **full yellow-green.** *Bouquet:* **clean, gently spicy with pronounced but not aggressive varietal character.** *Palate:* **light fruit, with very gentle spice; quite dry. Drink '85–'86.**

1982 RUBY CABERNET AND BARBERA [15.6] *Colour:* **light to medium red-purple.** *Bouquet:* **soft, fairly non-descript fruit with some slight old-oak characters.** *Palate:* **much better than the bouquet suggests; soft, clean and pleasant wine, with good balance, although one is hard pressed to describe any particular fruit character or flavour. Drink '85–'86.**

BULLERS BEVERFORD

p. 205

Location:
Murray Valley Highway, Beverford, 3590;
14 km north of Swan Hill.
(050) 37 6305.

Winemakers:
The Buller family.

1985 Production:
About 1300 tonnes of grapes crushed; a little over 50% is for distillation to make fortifying spirit.

Principal Wines:
A full range of generic and varietal table wines, principally white but also red, offered in bottle and in 10-litre and 20-litre soft-pack casks. Likewise, a range of fortified wines including sherries of all styles. Most of the tawny and vintage ports are made at Rutherglen. White table wines include Rhine Riesling, Spatlese Muscat Blanc, Colombard, Chenin Blanc, Chablis, Sylvaner, Spatlese Lexia, White Burgundy, Riesling and Moselle; red wines include Cabernet Shiraz, Cabernet Malbec and Cabernet Sauvignon.

Distribution:
Substantial cellar-door and mailing-list sales, with cellar-door sales both at Rutherglen and Beverford. Cellar-door sales 9 a.m. to 5 p.m. Monday to Saturday; open Sundays long weekends only. Mailing-list enquiries to PO Box 28, Rutherglen, 3685. Victorian distribution through Melbourne office (telephone no. 570 1717).

Prices:
Recommended retail: table wines $2.75 to $5.75; fortified wines $3.75 to $14.25.

Overall Quality:
Adequate to good; the very good wines come from Rutherglen.

Vintage Rating 1982–85:
'85, '84, '82, '83.

Tasting Notes:

1984 WHITE BURGUNDY [14.4] *Colour:* **light to medium yellow-green.** *Bouquet:* **slightly chalky aroma with fruit diminished by some evident solids fermentation characters; little or no oak influence.** *Palate:* **a fresh, light and crisp wine, with fairly pronounced acid and some bottling SO_2 still lingering. Drink '86.**

1984 SPATLESE LEXIA [16.2] *Colour:* **light to medium yellow-green.** *Bouquet:* **perfumed muscat varietal aroma; of light to medium weight, but well-handled.** *Palate:* **fresh, lively and grapy, with clearly marked but not over-blown varietal character and balanced by good acid. Drink '86.**

CAPOGRECO WINES

p. 205

Location:
Riverside Avenue, Mildura, 3500;
between 17th and 18th Streets.
(050) 23 3060.

Winemaker:
Bruno Capogreco.

1985 Production:
Approximately 200 tonnes (the equivalent of 15,000 cases).

Principal Wines:
A range of table, fortified, dessert and flavoured wines (including vermouths), all made in the Italian style and without the addition of preservatives, marketed in 750 ml bottles and in 2-litre flagons. Premium table wines include Rhine Riesling, Moselle, Cabernet Sauvignon, Barbera, Shiraz Mataro, Claret and Rosé Light Red. Herb-infused dessert wine Rosso Dolce particularly good.

Distribution:
Exclusively cellar-door sales and mail order; no bulk sales. Cellar-door sales 10 a.m. to 6 p.m. Monday to Saturday and most public holidays. Mailing-list enquiries to PO Box 7, Cabarita via Merbein, 3505.

Prices:
$3 to $4.50 cellar door.

Overall Quality:
Some table wines poor due to lack of preservatives and cask oxidation. Rosso Dolce good.

Tasting Notes:

1980 RHINE RIESLING [11.4] *Colour:* **yellow-brown.** *Bouquet:* **very oaky, dry and with marked oxidation.** *Palate:* **aged kerosene rhine riesling characters largely submerged in oak.**

ROSSO DOLCE [16] *Colour:* **dark brownish-red.** *Bouquet:* **pungent herbal/fruit aromas with clean fortifying spirit.** *Palate:* **rich, herbal and sweet, somewhere between a sweet vermouth and a marsala. Excellent as a mixing base for a punch, or with mineral water. Drink now.**

LINDEMANS' KARADOC

pp. 205–6

Location:
Nangiloc Road, Karadoc, off Calder Highway;
27 km east of Mildura.
(050) 24 0303.

Winemakers:
A substantial but anonymous team.

1985 Production:
45,000 tonnes.

Principal Wines:
Karadoc is the principal production point for all of Lindemans' cask and flagon range of wines, for Ben Ean Moselle and for Leo Buring Liebfrauwine (these two wines being two of Australia's largest brand sellers). In 1982 the Matthew Lang range of wines produced at Karadoc was first released, representing selected parcels of the best quality wine made from Victorian-grown grapes in the Karadoc region. The range comprises Rhine Riesling, Chardonnay, Fumé Blanc and Cabernet Sauvignon.

Distribution:
National retail through Lindemans' own distribution channels. Cellar-door sales (and winery tours) 9 a.m. to 5 p.m. Monday to Friday and Saturday 9 a.m. to noon. Winery tours on weekdays on the hour.

Prices:
$7.20 recommended retail but real price very substantially less.

Overall Quality:
Consistently good, indeed very good, given price.

Vintage Rating 1982–85:
No material variation.

Tasting Notes:

1985 CHARDONNAY CHABLIS [15.6] *Colour:* light to medium yellow-green. *Bouquet:* rather lemony oak and some distinct "armpit" fermentation characters lingering and needing to settle down. *Palate:* lemony citrus oak, a little raw and unintegrated as at August, 1985, and a slightly oily finish. Will undoubtedly improve in bottle. Drink '86–'88.

1983 RHINE RIESLING [16.6] *Colour:* medium yellow. *Bouquet:* rich and full, with quite remarkable rhine riesling aroma; some bottle-developed toastiness. *Palate:* again unusual depth of flavour and varietal character for Riverland rhine riesling; the marked residual sugar seems unnecessary and to detract from the intrinsic merit of the wine. Drink '85–'86.

1983 CABERNET SAUVIGNON [18.2] *Colour:* vibrant purple-red. *Bouquet:* very rich cassis/berry aromas; spotlessly clean and beautifully made. *Palate:* marvellously rich cassis/raspberry fruit flavours, with life and lift. As an early drinking red, they don't come much better than this. Drink '85–'86.

1982 FUME BLANC [17.2] *Colour:* bright yellow of medium depth. *Bouquet:* very good fruit/oak integration and balance, with plenty of richness, but little or no varietal character evident. *Palate:* a round, soft and gently fruity wine, with good mid-palate weight; excellent winemaking, although it says little about sauvignon blanc. Drink '85–'87.

MURRAY VALLEY WINES

p. 212

Location:
15th Street, Mildura, 3500;
within precincts of town.
(050) 23 1500.

Winemaker:
George Kalamastrakis.

1985 Production:
Not stated.

Principal Wines:
A range of Greek-influenced wines, some made in traditional Greek style, including Riesling Hock, Moselle, Retsina, Claret and Kokinella. Specialist in various fortified and flavoured wines.

Distribution:
Cellar door, mailing list and substantial bulk trade with Melbourne Greek community.

Prices:
$2.70 to $3 per bottle cellar door.

Overall Quality:
Not rated.

MILDARA

pp. 207–12

Location:
Wentworth Road, Merbein, 3505;
11 km west of Mildura.
(050) 25 2303.

Winemakers:
Jack Schultz and Tony Murphy.

1985 Production:
18,000 tonnes.

Principal Wines:
Until recently, production largely devoted to fortified wines and sherries including Supreme Dry Sherry, George Dry Sherry, Chestnut Teal together with lower-priced Rio Vista range of dry, medium-dry, cream and sweet sherry; also substantial brandy production, with Mildara Supreme Pot Still Brandy heading the range. More recently, 'Flower Series' varietal table wines have become of importance; Church Hill Chardonnay and Cabernet Sauvignon and Merlot major brand sellers.

Distribution:
National retail through all types of outlets.

Prices:
Flower Series $5.30 recommended retail, but real price far lower; sherries and brandies vary substantially according to quality grade.

Overall Quality:
Sherry and Brandy very good; Flower Series good value for money.

Vintage Rating 1982–85:
White: '85, '82, '84, '83.

Tasting Notes:

1985 CHURCH HILL CHARDONNAY [15.4] *Colour:* **light to medium yellow-green.** *Bouquet:* **soft, slightly cheesy, and relatively little fruit.** *Palate:* **soft and light, well-made and balanced; lacks mid-palate weight and certainly lacks varietal character, but pleasant, easy drinking. Drink '86.**

1982 CABERNET SAUVIGNON AND MERLOT [16.8] *Colour:* **light to medium red-purple.** *Bouquet:* **fresh, gently fragrant fruit, light but very clean.** *Palate:* **fresh, gently astringent with clean berry flavours and a crisp finish. An outstanding commercial wine. Drink '85–'87.**

1981 BIN 47 CABERNET SHIRAZ [17.6] *Colour:* **medium red, with obvious signs of development.** *Bouquet:* **smooth and quite full, with a most attractive touch of peppery spice.** *Palate:* **a generously flavoured wine with excellent peppery shiraz fruit and good balance; not heavy but of ample weight. By far the best Yellow Label Cabernet Shiraz since the early 1960s. Drink '85–'91.**

ROBINVALE WINES

p. 213

Location:
Sea Lake Road, Robinvale, 3549;
5 km south of Robinvale.
(050) 26 3955.

Winemaker:
William Caracatsanoudis.

1985 Production:
Approximately 100 tonnes (the equivalent of 7500 cases).

Principal Wines:
A wide range of table wines, sparkling wine, fortified wine, flavoured wine and non-alcoholic wines is made; many of the wines have Greek emphasis.

Distribution:
Chiefly cellar-door sales and mail order; cellar-door sales 9 a.m. to 6 p.m. Monday to Saturday. Melbourne distribution through Flinders Trading.

Overall Quality:
Not rated.

North-East Victoria

1985 Vintage

1985—or, to be more accurate, 1984–85—was a season in which the vignerons of the north-east had a little bit of everything. A wet winter and ideal flowering conditions set the vines off on a magnificent start, but five months of near-drought commenced in mid-October. The summer was then cool except for a short burst of heat-wave conditions in January which burnt part of the crop. The extremely cool conditions both before and after the heat wave prevented the development of desirable sugar levels.

And, as if this were not enough, torrential rains at the end of March brought picking to a halt, with local flooding adding to the problems. Within days the weather had cleared, and an unusually warm spell in late April brought some relief and allowed the vintage to conclude by mid-May—far later than usual.

Overall yields were down and, not surprisingly, quality was average at best. The fortified wines are not luscious, although the fruit flavour is good; dry whites were probably the most successful, with fair acid and good flavour; and the red wines are softer and lighter than normal.

The Changes

North-east Victoria continues to face an identity crisis. The solutions are numerous, probably all too numerous: to continue to specialise in fortified wines and full-bodied reds; to diversify into white table wines and into new-style reds using existing vineyards; or to take to the high country of the Great Dividing Range to produce cool-climate wines.

There is no absolute choice; but to sit and do nothing seems the least rewarding course. One or two of the old wineries are doing just that, and seem certain to fade away. Others, such as Pfeiffer, John Gehrig Wines and Jolimont (the last the only new face for 1985) will take their place, and next year Harry Tinson will start to market wines from his own small weekend estate. Baileys wish him to stay on as winemaker, but one senses the lure of what, for some, might seem a gentlemanly retirement, but which, in truth, will simply be an exchange of one kind of hard work for another.

ALL SAINTS

pp. 219–20

Location:
All Saints Road, Wahgunyah, 3687;
4 km north-east of Wahgunyah.
(060) 33 1218.

Winemaker:
George Sutherland Smith.

1985 Production:
550,000 litres, the equivalent of 60,000 cases.

Principal Wines:

A large range of table and fortified wines is produced. The table wines employ both generic and varietal labelling; marsanne has long been a vineyard specialty in the white varietal table wines and more recently chardonnay has made its appearance. Traditional white wine range comes out under the Lyre Bird Label, and comprises Riesling, White Burgundy, Chablis, Semillon, Rhine Riesling, Traminer and Spatlese Frontignac. Red table wines centre on Shiraz and Cabernet Sauvignon (in various combinations); all the red wines are released with considerable bottle age. The full range of fortified wines covering all of the north-east Victorian styles is also available.

Distribution:
Significant retail and restaurant distribution in Melbourne and Sydney through own wholesale company; also important cellar-door sales through historic and visually superb winery 9 a.m. to 5 p.m. Monday to Saturday, noon to 5 p.m. Sunday. Mail orders to All Saints Vineyard, Wahgunyah, 3687.

Prices:
$7.50 to $10 recommended retail; old fortified wines more expensive.

Overall Quality:
Adequate at best.

Vintage Rating 1982–85:
No rating supplied.

Outstanding Prior Vintages:
None specified.

Tasting Notes:

1984 CHARDONNAY [14.8] *Colour:* medium yellow-green. *Bouquet:* clean, light fruit with no solids characters but distinct volatile lift. *Palate:* light, with some lemony oak and again some volatile lift, but little or no identifiable chardonnay varietal character. Drink '86.

1982 MARSANNE [14.4] *Colour:* light to medium green. *Bouquet:* very light, slightly chalky and basically thin. *Palate:* curious coconut/oily oak flavours, not successful, and lacking fruit. At least the wine is dry, and not propped up by residual sugar. Drink '86.

1981 PINOT [13.6] *Colour:* very light red with tawny hues. *Bouquet:* very light, slightly aldehydic, with some mercaptan-derived leathery characters. *Palate:* very thin and sour, either slightly corked or from old, mouldy oak. (A blend of pinot meunier, pinot noir and shiraz.)

1981 CABERNET SAUVIGNON [14.2] *Colour:* very light tawny red, washed out. *Bouquet:* thin, tired with little fruit and some mercaptan evident. *Palate:* much cleaner than the bouquet, but very light and lacking fruit. Drink '86.

1975 GEORGES PRIVATE STOCK CABERNET SAUVIGNON [15.8] *Colour:* medium to full red, holding well. *Bouquet:* a ripe, rather old-fashioned style with good fruit weight and obvious, slightly medicinal, bottle-developed aromas. *Palate:* a full but rather one-dimensional traditional Australian red in which oak has played no part and which is largely sustained by its high alcohol. Drink '85–'88.

FINE OLD TAWNY PORT [16.4] *Colour:* tawny, with some youthful reds showing. *Bouquet:* sweet and appreciably fruity; clean spirit, but lacks rancio complexity. *Palate:* sweet caramel/fruity flavours of medium weight; a pleasant, commercial tawny port. Drink now.

BAILEYS

pp. 220–2

Location:
Cnr Taminick Gap Road and Upper Taminick Road, Glenrowan, 3675;
6 km north-west of Glenrowan.
(057) 66 2392.

Winemaker:
Harry Tinson.

1985 Production:
Approximately 12,000 cases, plus bulk sales.

Principal Wines:

One of the two greatest fortified wine producers in the north-east, but producing a range of table wines including Chablis, Colombard, Rhine Riesling, Auslese Rhine Riesling, Late Harvest Lexia, Hermitage, Hermitage Classic Selection, HJT Hermitage, Cabernet Sauvignon, HJT Cabernet Sauvignon and Cabernet Hermitage. Incomparable fortified Muscat and Tokay released under three labels: Founder Series, being the basic wines; Gold Label (not always available); and HJT Liqueur Muscat and HJT Tokay (on strict allocation).

Distribution:
Substantial cellar-door and mailing-list sales; also extensive wholesale distribution through Emerald Wines, Melbourne; P. F. Caon and Co., Adelaide; Regional Vineyard Distributors, Perth; and to Sydney and elsewhere through own distribution network. Cellar-door sales 9 a.m. to 5 p.m. Monday to Friday, 10 a.m. to 5 p.m. Saturday. Mailing-list enquiries to RMB 4160, Glenrowan, 3675.

Prices:
Table wines $4.80 to $9 recommended retail; fortified wines $9 to $29 recommended retail.

Overall Quality:
White and red table wines good; fortified wines exceptional.

Vintage Rating 1982–85:
'85, '82, '84, '83.

Outstanding Prior Vintages:
'78.

Tasting Notes:

1984 RHINE RIESLING [15.8] *Colour:* light to medium yellow-green. *Bouquet:* clean and quite sweet with an almost pastille-like character. *Palate:* very strong lime/pastille flavours, with a curious acid/salty prickle on the fore-palate and obvious mid-palate residual sugar. Drink '86.

1983 LATE HARVEST LEXIA [17.6] *Colour:* full yellow. *Bouquet:* intense, pungent, spicy/grapy, rich muscat aromas. *Palate:* enormously rich and highly flavoured to the point where it almost seems as if it were lightly fortified (which it is not). A great by-the-glass dessert wine. Drink '85–'88.

1982 CABERNET SAUVIGNON BIN 35 [16.6] *Colour:* medium to full red-purple. *Bouquet:* big, clean, very ripe wine with distinct volatile lift, perhaps partly due to alcohol. *Palate:* a strongly structured wine with full, sweet, chewy berry flavours on the mid-palate, followed by persistent tannin on the mid- and back-palate. A huge wine. Drink '86–'91.

FOUNDER'S LIQUEUR MUSCAT [18.4] *Colour:* medium brown, with olive rim; no reds at all; obvious wood age. *Bouquet:* very rich, with a touch of caramel sweetness; smooth spirit; complex higher alcohols. *Palate:* very rich and raisined with obvious age; complex structure, very weighty and absolutely extraordinary for a commercial release.

GOLD LABEL LIQUEUR MUSCAT [18.8] *Colour:* deep brown-green. *Bouquet:* even richer and deeper; the complexities are seemingly infinite, backed by some firm grip. *Palate:* almost explosively rich; very good acid balance to prevent the wine from cloying; by far the richest muscat generally available on the Australian market.

HJT LIQUEUR MUSCAT [19.2] *Colour:* dark brown-green. *Bouquet:* enormously concentrated and powerful, with extreme wood age and great depth. *Palate:* the ultimate muscat, if power, complexity and explosive intensity are the yardsticks. In a very different style to the top Morris muscat; you pay your money and you take your choice (if you can find the wine in the first place).

BOOTHS' TAMINICK

p. 222

Location:
Taminick via Glenrowan, 3675;
7 km north-east of Glenrowan.
(057) 66 2282.

Winemaker:
Cliff Booth.

Principal Wines:
Trebbiano, Shiraz and Cabernet Sauvignon.

Distribution:
All wine sold cellar door and by specialised mail order, particularly to corporate and Public Service wine clubs. Cellar-door sales Monday to Saturday 9 a.m. to 5 p.m.

Overall Quality:
Adequate to good.

BROWN BROTHERS

pp. 223–7

Location:
Milawa, 3678;
off main Glenrowan–Myrtleford Road,
16 km south-east of Wangaratta.
(057) 27 3400.

Winemaker:
John Brown Jnr.

1985 Production:
Approximately 200,000 cases of premium bottled wine, plus additional bulk production.

Principal Wines:
An extremely wide range of varietal table wines, released in a number of series. The basic wines are the traditional Milawa range (comprising 11 different white and red varietals); then follows the Special Limited Production (13 or 14 different varietals); then come the Individual Vineyard wines (Koombahla, Meadow Creek and, in the future, Whitfield); and finally the Classic Vintage releases, principally of red wines but also including Noble Riesling. All Classic Vintage releases have substantial bottle age; Noble Riesling 5 years and the red wines often up to 10 or more years.

Distribution:
Extensive cellar-door and mailing-list sales; regular mailing-list brochures and bulletins among the best in the country; very extensive retail distribution through own distribution network in Melbourne and Sydney. Also significant export sales. Cellar-door sales 9 a.m. to 5 p.m. Monday to Saturday. First-class tasting facilities. Mailing-list enquiries to Brown Brothers, Milawa, 3678.

Prices:
$6 to $10 recommended retail.

Overall Quality:
Consistently very good.

Vintage Rating 1982–85:
White: '85, '84, '82, '83.
Red: '85, '84, '82, '83.

Tasting Notes:

1984 SPECIAL LIMITED PRODUCTION SEMILLON [16.6] *Colour:* medium yellow-green with a touch of straw. *Bouquet:* quite pronounced lemony oak; light to medium fruit still developing weight and richness. *Palate:* light, crisp, slightly herbaceous fruit, and again fairly obvious oak which, while integrated, needs to soften. Drink '86–'88.

1984 CHARDONNAY [16.8] *Colour:* medium yellow-green, bright and lively. *Bouquet:* quite complex, with toasty oak, a touch of buttery varietal richness and just a suggestion of burgundian sulphide. *Palate:* quite complex, with some of the toasty flavours repeating themselves, mid-palate still to build depth and richness as at June, 1985. Drink '86–'88.

1982 KOOMBAHLA LATE HARVEST RHINE RIESLING [17.6] *Colour:* rich yellow-green. *Bouquet:* very full and soft, with rich lime/butterscotch aromas. *Palate:* a very generously flavoured wine, with lime and tropical fruit flavours balanced by excellent acid on finish which prevents the wine cloying. Drink '85–'88.

1982 KOOMBAHLA PINOT NOIR [17.2] *Colour:* medium red-purple. *Bouquet:* distinctive PK-peppermint aroma of a number of Victorian pinot noirs produced in cooler regions. *Palate:* strong, clean flavour with excellent structure; again the regional minty flavours assert themselves. Drink '85–'88.

1982 MEADOW CREEK CABERNET SHIRAZ [17] *Colour:* black to medium red-purple. *Bouquet:* highly aromatic with leafy/aniseed spice/floral aromas. *Palate:* intense, sweet cherry flavours, with some of the same floral characters of the bouquet, and also a hint of garden mint. An interesting, albeit somewhat unusual, fresh wine with good balance. Drink '85–'88.

BULLERS CALLIOPE

p. 227

Location:
Three Chain Road, Rutherglen, 3685; off Murray Valley Highway, 5 km west of Rutherglen.
(060) 32 9660.

Winemakers:
The Buller Family; Richard Senior, Richard Junior and Andrew.

1985 Production:
Approximately 3000 cases (Rutherglen).

Principal Wines:
Principally red table and fortified wines from the Calliope vineyard at Rutherglen (cheaper generic table wines, white varietal table wines and Cabernet Sauvignon come from Beverford Vineyard on the Murray River). Vineyard specialty is Calliope Vintage Port; also very good Liqueur Muscat and Liqueur Frontignac in somewhat lighter style than those of Bailey and Morris.

Distribution:
Principally cellar door and mailing list; cellar-door sales 9 a.m. to 5 p.m. Monday to Saturday, open Sundays long weekends only. Victorian distribution through Melbourne office (telephone number 570 1717); limited New South Wales distribution of top fortified wines through I. H. Baker.

Prices:
Table wines $2.75 to $5.75 recommended retail; fortified wines $3.75 to $14.25 recommended retail.

Overall Quality:
Table wines adequate to good; fortified wines good to very good.

Vintage Rating 1982–85:
Red: '85, '84, '82, (no '83 made—drought).

Tasting Notes:

1984 MONDEUSE SHIRAZ [16.8] *Colour:* light to medium red-purple. *Bouquet:* clean, with attractive spicy fruit of good weight and depth. *Palate:* a very well-made wine with good structure; spicy fruit on the mid-palate, followed by crisp acid and light tannin on the finish. (A blend of 80% mondeuse and 20% shiraz.) Drink '86–'89.

1982 SHIRAZ [14.8] *Colour:* very good medium to full red-purple. *Bouquet:* strong and potent, but distinctly stalky/astringent aromas. *Palate:* very firm wine in which stalky/bitter flavours take control. May conceivably soften in bottle. Drink '87–'89.

1982 VINTAGE PORT [17] *Colour:* medium red-purple. *Bouquet:* complex spirit, very stylish lighter style but not sweet, and with a touch of tobacco/cigar aroma. *Palate:* very complex, with unusual but attractive cigar box flavours, and again first-class pot-still spirit evident. Drink '85–'88.

CAMPBELLS

pp. 227–8

Location:
Murray Valley Highway, Rutherglen, 3685;
3 km west of Rutherglen.
(060) 32 9458.

Winemaker:
Colin Campbell.

1985 Production:
Approximately 10,000 cases.

Principal Wines:
Substantial range of table and fortified wines, with the table wine range recently expanded by the addition of a Chardonnay and a very distinguished Cabernets. The 8 white varietal and 4 red varietal wines are supplemented by re-releases of older vintage wines in restricted quantities. The fortified wines comprise Old Tokay, Tawny Port, Empire Port, Old Port, Liquid Gold, Vintage Port, Liqueur Muscat, Rutherglen Muscat (the oldest and most expensive) and Old Frontignac.

Distribution:
Cellar-door sales, mailing list and retail and restaurant distribution all significant. Wholesale distribution through Taylor Ferguson in all states other than Victoria; Victorian distribution direct ex-Campbells' Melbourne sales office. Cellar-door sales from 9 a.m. to 5 p.m. Monday to Saturday and noon to 5 p.m. Sunday. Mailing-list enquiries to PO Box 44, Rutherglen, 3685.

Prices:
Table wines $5.80 to $11.50 recommended retail; fortified wines $8.50 to $14.80 recommended retail.

Overall Quality:
Good to very good.

Vintage Rating 1982–85:
White: '82, '85, '83, '84.
Red: '85, '83, '82, '84.

Outstanding Prior Vintages:
'80.

Tasting Notes:

1984 CHARDONNAY [16.8] *Colour:* light to medium green-yellow. *Bouquet:* complex toasty oak with a faint medicinal aroma, together with fine lemony fruit. *Palate:* a wine which is remarkably fresh in the mouth with great life and very good acid balance; fruit is not particularly rich or heavy, and varietal character is only moderate. The wine scores because of its life and freshness. Drink '85–'87.

1983 CABERNETS [18.4] *Colour:* very good purple-red. *Bouquet:* quite outstanding; perfect fruit/oak balance and integration; smooth yet complex and rich, with a touch of minty fruit. *Palate:* very complex, round and softly sweet cherry fruit flavour and structure, complexed by vanillin/smoky oak. Good acid on the finish. (A blend of 50% ruby cabernet and 50% cabernet sauvignon, both gold medal winners as individual wines.) Drink '87–'92.

LIQUEUR MUSCAT [17.2] *Colour:* medium orange. *Bouquet:* fresh, lifted and lively grape aromas with clean spirit. *Palate:* fresh, but of surprising intensity; lively and grapy; very valid alternative to the profundities of the Bailey style.

RUTHERGLEN MUSCAT [17.8] *Colour:* medium orange, with just a hint of brown. *Bouquet:* of medium weight, complex and slightly powdery aroma with good fruit. *Palate:* fuller in weight than the Liqueur Muscat and rather more complex; still retaining freshness, with some butterscotch mid-palate flavours and a firm finish.

CHAMBERS ROSEWOOD

p. 229

Location:
Off Corowa–Rutherglen Road, Rutherglen, 3685; 2 km north-west of Rutherglen.
(060) 32 9641.

Winemaker:
Bill Chambers.

1985 Production:
Approximately 10,000 cases plus bulk wine.

Principal Wines:
An unusual array of table wines and some great fortified wines. Table wines include Rhine Riesling, Moselle-style Trebbiano, Riesling/Gouais, Spatlese/Rhine Riesling, Cabernet Shiraz, Cabernet/Blue Imperial/Alicante Bouchet and Lakeside Cabernet Sauvignon. Fortified wines include a range of old sherries including an excellent Flor Fino and even better Amontillado; Liqueur Muscat and Liqueur Tokay, Special Liqueur Muscat; intermittent releases of very old Tokay and Muscat of the highest possible quality.

Distribution:
Principally cellar-door sales and mail order. Cellar-door sales 9 a.m. to 5 p.m. Monday to Saturday. Mail orders to W. H. Chambers and Son, PO Box 8, Rutherglen, 3685. Retail distribution through Emerald Wines, Melbourne.

Prices:
$2.80 to $3.30 cellar door.

Overall Quality:
Table wines good, especially given price; fortified wines very good; old special fortified wines absolutely exceptional.

Vintage Rating 1982–85:
White: '85, '83, '84, '82.
Red: '84, '85, '82, '83.

Outstanding Prior Vintages:
'80.

Tasting Notes:

1984 CINSAUT ROSE [14.8] *Colour:* pale bright salmon-pink. *Bouquet:* soft and clean, with a faint touch of caramel spice, but not particularly fruity. *Palate:* fresh, a touch of sweetness, and quite good structure; fruit flavours deficient and a little stalky in character. Drink '85–'86.

1983 LAKESIDE CABERNET [15.4] *Colour:* light to medium red-purple. *Bouquet:* very light, soft berry aromas with some leathery astringency, not particularly pleasant. *Palate:* fuller and cleaner than the bouquet promises, with some ripe plum/berry fruit flavours. Low tannin. Drink '86.

1981 TREBBIANO [16.4] *Colour:* bright yellow-green. *Bouquet:* clean; considerable bottle developed aromas, slightly cheesy, but the fruit is still there and not drying out. *Palate:* rich, full, almost honeyed wine, which has developed surprisingly well in bottle. The only criticism is a slight dip in flavour on the back palate. Drink '85–'87.

1981 CABERNET SAUVIGNON [16.6] *Colour:* medium red. *Bouquet:* some distinct cigar box aromas; fruit light to the point of being ethereal. *Palate:* a clean, firm wine with some pleasant cigar/caramel overtones to mid-palate fruit, and soft tannin on the finish. Drink '85–'88.

LIQUEUR TOKAY [18.2] *Colour:* light to medium orange-brown. *Bouquet:* of medium weight, with clean spirit and clear tea-leaf/caramel varietal character. *Palate:* deceptively light on the mid-palate, gaining in intensity on the back palate and finish. Lingers in the mouth long after the wine is swallowed, with that unmistakable tokay tea-leaf flavour. At the opposite end of the spectrum to the wines of Bailey. Drink now.

FAIRFIELD

pp. 229–30

Location:
Murray Valley Highway, Browns Plains, via Rutherglen, 3685;
13 km east of Rutherglen.
(060) 32 9381.

Winemaker:
Stephen Morris.

1985 Production:
Very limited.

Principal Wines:
Small range of traditionally made wines.

Distribution:
Totally cellar-door sales 9 a.m. to 5 p.m. Monday to Saturday, from one of the most historic wineries in Victoria.

Overall Quality:
Not rated.

GAYFER'S CHILTERN

p. 230

Location:
Hume Highway, Chiltern, 3683;
between Springhurst and Chiltern at the 262 km post.
(057) 26 1265.

Winemaker:
Keith Gayfer.

Principal Wines:
Limited quantities of Trebbiano, Shiraz, Cabernet Sauvignon, Durif and Grenache.

Distribution:
Cellar-door sales and mail order. Cellar-door sales 9 a.m. to 5 p.m. Monday to Saturday. Mail order enquiries to PO Box 9, Chiltern, 3683. Limited retail distribution through Victorian Wine Centre.

Prices:
$7.50 recommended retail.

Overall Quality:
Poor to adequate.

Tasting Notes:

1979 DURIF [14] *Colour:* light to medium tawny-red. *Bouquet:* some bottle-developed complexity, but with distinct volatility evident and fruit now rather aged. *Palate:* similar aged fruit characteristics, with that volatility apparent in the bouquet again manifesting itself.

GEHRIG BROTHERS

p. 230

Location:
Cnr Murray Valley Highway and Howlong Road, Barnawartha, 3688; 6 km north of town.
(06) 26 7296.

Winemaker:
Bernard Gehrig.

1985 Production:
Not stated.

Principal Wines:
Rhine Riesling, Chardonnay, Cabernet Sauvignon, Pinot Noir and Shiraz.

Distribution:
Almost exclusively cellar-door sales 9 a.m. to 5 p.m. Monday to Saturday; retail through Victorian Wine Centre.

Prices:
$4.50 retail.

Overall Quality:
Poor.

Tasting Notes:
1982 PINOT CHARDONNAY [11.4] *Colour:* bright yellow-green. *Bouquet:* utterly dominated by sour mercaptan. *Palate:* searing, sour mercaptan totally obscures whatever fruit is there. Drink now.

1982 PINOT NOIR [15.6] *Colour:* pale amber. *Bouquet:* very light, and somewhat leathery but also intriguing sappy pinot varietal aroma. *Palate:* light, sweet tea-leaf fruit, but again that almost burgundian pinot flavour showing itself. A light but extremely interesting wine. Drink '86.

JOHN GEHRIG WINES

p. 230

(Formerly McKeone Cellars)

Location:
Oxley, 3678;
on Oxley to Milawa Road; 13 km south-east of Wangaratta.
(057) 27 3395.

Winemaker:
John Gehrig.

1985 Production:
3000 cases.

Principal Wines:
Rhine Riesling, Trebbiano, Spatlese Rhine Riesling, Chenin Blanc, Chardonnay, Pinot Noir, Merlot, Vintage Port and Tawny Port.

Distribution:
Principally cellar-door sales and mailing list; cellar-door sales 9 a.m. to 5 p.m. Monday to Saturday and 10 a.m. to 6 p.m. Sunday. Limited Melbourne distribution through John Bray Wine Brokers.

Overall Quality:
Adequate to good.

Vintage Rating 1982–85:
White: '82, '84, '83 ('85 not rated).
Red: '82, '84, '85, '83.

Tasting Notes:
1984 RHINE RIESLING [15.8] *Colour:* **medium yellow, with just a touch of green.** *Bouquet:* **a big, highly aromatic wine with traminer/muscat-like overtones.** *Palate:* **a big, soft and highly flavoured wine, not showing a great deal of rhine riesling varietal character, but very well-made for all that. Drink '86.**

1984 SPATLESE RHINE RIESLING [16] *Colour:* **medium green-yellow.** *Bouquet:* **clean and soft with gentle fruit; perhaps a fraction one-dimensional.** *Palate:* **clean, very well-made and balanced wine which simply lacks varietal definition, but again, very well made. Drink '86–'87.**

JOLIMONT

p. 116

Location:
Cnr Murray Valley Highway and Corowa Road, Rutherglen, 3685;
(planned opening 1986).

Winemaker:
Howard Anderson.

1985 Production:
290,000 litres (the equivalent of 32,000 cases).

Principal Wines:

1985 vintage wines consisted of 240,000 litres of Lachlan River Cabernet Sauvignon and Berrigan Semillon, both from New South Wales, and 50,000 litres of Rutherglen Shiraz. Vintages prior to 1984 came exclusively from Griffith, where the winery was located previously. Wines include Cabernet Sauvignon Nouveau, Berrigan Semillon (fermented and matured in oak) and Rutherglen Shiraz.

Distribution:
All Rutherglen wines will be sold cellar door. Other wines distributed through The Incredible Wine Company, Sydney and through Van Cooth & Co., Melbourne. Cellar-door sales hours not yet finalised. For all inquiries, write to PO Box 301, East Melbourne, 3002.
Telephone (03) 63 7826.

Prices:
Cabernet Nouveau $4.99.

Overall Quality:
Good.

Vintage Rating 1983–85:
Red: '85, '84, '83.

Tasting Notes:
1985 BERRIGAN SEMILLON [16] *Colour:* **pale yellow-green.** *Bouquet:* **somewhat raw, lemony oak, but good fruit underneath.** *Palate:* **has potential; good crisp fruit and adequate acid, with oak better-integrated than the bouquet would suggest. (Tasted mid-August 1985 Melbourne Show.) Drink '86–'87.**

JONES WINERY

pp. 230–1

Location:
Chiltern Road, Rutherglen, 3685;
2 km east of town.
(060) 32 9496.

Winemaker:
Les Jones.

Principal Wines:
White Hermitage, Rutherglen Pedro and Shiraz.

Distribution:
Exclusively cellar-door sales 9.30 a.m. to 5 p.m. Monday to Friday and 9 a.m. to noon Saturday.

Overall Quality:
Not rated.

MARKWOOD ESTATE

p. 231

Location:
Morris Lane, Markwood via Milawa, 3678;
6 km east of Milawa.
(057) 27 0361.

Winemaker:
F. J. (Rick) Morris.

1985 Production:
Approximately 1000 cases.

Principal Wines:
Chardonnay, Shiraz and Cabernet Sauvignon.

Distribution:
Exclusively cellar-door sales and mailing list. Cellar-door sales 9 a.m. to 5 p.m. Monday to Saturday. Mailing-list enquiries to RMB 84, Markwood via Milawa, 3678. Limited sales through Melbourne Regency Hotel.

Prices:
$8 per bottle cellar door.

Overall Quality:
Believed to be good.

Vintage Rating 1982–85:
White: '82, '85, '83, '84.
Red: '83, '85, '82, '84.

Outstanding Prior Vintages:
'75, '79.

MORRIS

pp. 231–3

Location:
Mia Mia Vineyard, Rutherglen, 3685;
15 km east of Rutherglen, 1.5 km off Murray Valley Highway.
(060) 26 7303.

Winemaker:
Mick Morris.

1985 Production:
Not available for publication.

Principal Wines:

In addition to producing some of north-east Victoria's greatest fortified wines (principally Muscat and Tokay), Morris also offers a full range of cask wines, medium-priced table wines, and premium varietal table wines including Traminer, Rhine Riesling, Semillon, Chardonnay, Durif, Cabernet Sauvignon, Malbec, Shiraz and Blue Imperial. The full range of fortified wines is headed by Liqueur Muscat and Liqueur Tokay, and at the top of the range are Old Premium Liqueur Muscat and Old Premium Liqueur Tokay.

Distribution:
Extensive retail distribution through own sales force in Victoria, New South Wales and Queensland. Cellar-door sales and mailing list also available; cellar-door sales 9 a.m. to 5 p.m. Monday to Saturday. Mailing list to Morris Wines Pty Ltd, Mia Mia Vineyards, Rutherglen, Victoria, 3685.

Prices:
Table wines $5.70 to $7.70 recommended retail; fortified wines $9.50 to $21.50.

Overall Quality:
Table wines good to very good; fortified wines exceptional.

Vintage Rating 1982–85:
'82, '85, '84, '83.

Outstanding Prior Vintages:
'80.

Tasting Notes:

1984 SEMILLON [17.8] *Colour:* light to medium yellow-green. *Bouquet:* strong, spicy nutmeg oak aromas, almost into chardonnay-weight. *Palate:* lively and spicy, with good fore-palate fruit weight and excellent acid finish. A very well-made, flavoursome and stylish wine. Drink '85–'88.

1984 CHARDONNAY [17.2] *Colour:* light to medium yellow-green. *Bouquet:* well-integrated fruit and oak, though uncompromisingly oaky. *Palate:* lively, zesty fruit with considerable flavour; oak adds a slightly oily texture, redeemed by cleansing finish. Drink '85–'87.

OLD PREMIUM TOKAY [18.6] *Colour:* medium to full dark brown, with no red tints whatsoever remaining. *Bouquet:* very clean and remarkably fresh, yet extremely complex, with classic varietal tea-leaf aroma. *Palate:* a generous wine, with cleansing spirit lift and obvious age, rich and luscious. As with all tokays, the texture and weight is less pronounced than with muscat, but the flavour is no less intense. Drink now.

OLD PREMIUM MUSCAT [18.6] *Colour:* dark red-brown, with an olive-green tinge on the rim. *Bouquet:* intense, raisined richness, with soft wood-aged spirit character. *Palate:* almost explosive in its richness and intensity, mouth-filling and lingering, yet never cloying. Drink now.

MOUNT PRIOR

p. 233

Location:
Cnr River Road and Popes Lane, Rutherglen, 3685; 12 km south-west of Rutherglen.
(060) 26 5591.

Winemaker:
Rick Kinsbrunner.

1985 Production:
4500 cases.

Principal Wines:
Gewurztraminer, Chardonnay, Shiraz, Cabernet Sauvignon, Durif and Carignane, together with several cheaper generic table wines and several fortified wines including Tawny Port, Vintage Port and Private Oak Reserve Tawny Port.

Distribution:
Principally cellar-door sales and occasional mailing list. Cellar-door sales 9 a.m. to 5 p.m. Monday to Saturday, 11 a.m. to 5 p.m. Sunday. Mailing-list enquiries to Mount Prior Vineyard, Howlong Road, Rutherglen, 3685.

Prices:
$3.50 to $16 cellar door.

Overall Quality:
Good; some very good.

Vintage Rating 1982–85:
White: '84, '85, '82, '83.
Red: '85, '82, '83, '84.

Tasting Notes:

1984 CHARDONNAY [17.4] *Colour:* deep yellow, tinged with straw. *Bouquet:* very rich, with aromas of dried apricots and tinned pineapple. *Palate:* an extremely rich wine, viscous on the palate, and suggestive of higher alcohol than the 12.7% disclosed on the label; some peach/apricot flavours mirror those of the bouquet. A huge chardonnay in a particular style. Drink '85–'87.

1984 GEWURTZTRAMINER [17] *Colour:* medium yellow, tinged with green. *Bouquet:* very full, very rich, highly perfumed aroma with hints of lychee and pineapple. Despite all of the richness, not oily. *Palate:* a very full-flavoured wine with rich fruit and some residual sugar; smooth and mouth-filling on the palate, then typical tannin/spice on the after-taste. For those who like traminer, great. Drink '85–'86.

1984 CARIGNANE [16.8] *Colour:* brilliant red, with some tints of purple. *Bouquet:* fragrant/floral cherry plum aromas, quite striking. *Palate:* light and vibrant cherry flavours on the fore-palate; a touch of hardness on the finish the only fault in a most unusual and attractive wine. Drink '86–'87.

1984 SHIRAZ [16.8] *Colour:* light to medium red-purple, suggesting it will develop quickly. *Bouquet:* scented, sweet floral fruit; incredibly aromatic, though non-varietal. *Palate:* essence of berries in strawberry/cherry/plum spectrum; a striking and unusual wine. Drink '85–'87.

1982 DURIF [16.4] *Colour:* medium to full red-purple. *Bouquet:* a big, solid wine, with some leathery astringency. *Palate:* rich and chewy, with some spice on the mid-palate, then again a touch of leather on the finish; overall very full-flavoured. Drink '86–'90.

1982 CABERNET SAUVIGNON [16] *Colour:* strong and deep red-purple, holding its hue very well. *Bouquet:* good cabernet varietal aroma, but marred by a touch of leafy/sour mercaptan. *Palate:* full, ripe fruit; soft but persistent tannin on the mid- to back-palate, but again a touch of mercaptan evident. Drink '85–'89.

PFEIFFER

pp. 233–4

Location:
Distillery Road, Wahgunyah, 3687;
midway between Corowa and Rutherglen, off Three Chain Road.
(060) 33 2805.

Winemaker:
Chris Pfeiffer.

1985 Production:
4500 cases.

Principal Wines:
White Burgundy, Rhine Riesling, Spatlese Frontignac, Shiraz Cabernet, Pinot Noir, Gamay, and Cabernet Sauvignon; Liqueur Muscat and Liqueur Tokay presently maturing for future release.

Distribution:
Almost exclusively cellar-door sales and mailing list. Cellar-door sales 9 a.m. to 5 p.m. Monday to Saturday, Sunday noon to 5 p.m. (on long weekends and school holidays only). Mailing-list enquiries to PO Box 35, Wahgunyah, 3687.

Prices:
$5.50 to $8 (table wines); $10.50 to $12.50 (fortified wines).

Overall Quality:
Good, with the potential to be even better.

Tasting Notes:

1985 PINOT NOIR [16.8] *Colour:* brilliant fuchsia-purple. *Bouquet:* clean, strong fruit with some strawberry aromas. *Palate:* a very well-made wine with strong, sweet fruit; some spicy carbonic maceration characters evident. Drink '87–'88.

1984 WHITE BURGUNDY [16.6] *Colour:* bright green-yellow. *Bouquet:* in mainstream of Australian white burgundy style, with considerable weight and some slightly cheesy aromas. *Palate:* a clean, well-made, big and solid wine which does not rely on residual sugar for its flavour, and which in addition is lifted by crisp acid on the finish. Careful winemaking is very evident. Drink '86–'88.

1984 RHINE RIESLING [16] *Colour:* medium green-yellow. *Bouquet:* pungent and floral with rich, if not heavy, tropical fruit aromas. *Palate:* a big, slightly broad, full-flavoured, early-drinking style of riesling; well-made but, for better or worse, the product of a warm climate. Drink '85–'86.

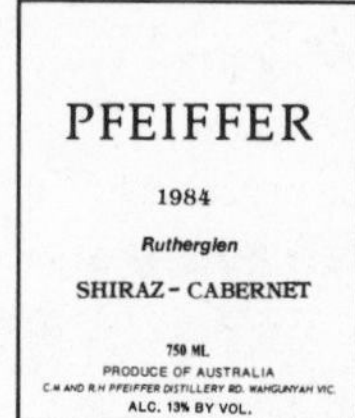

1984 SHIRAZ CABERNET [16.8] *Colour:* bright red-purple of medium depth. *Bouquet:* fresh, good fruit balance between delicate, leafy astringency of cabernet and smooth, sweet, berry aromas of shiraz. *Palate:* an attractive, fresh wine with good fruit; of light to medium body, and promises to be at its best while retaining all of its fresh fruit flavours. Crisp acid also adds to the attraction of the wine. Drink '86–'88.

ST LEONARDS

pp. 234–5

Location:
Wahgunyah, 3687;
5 km north-east of Corowa.
(060) 33 1004.

Winemaker:
John Brown Jnr (contract).

1985 Production:
9500 cases.

Principal Wines:

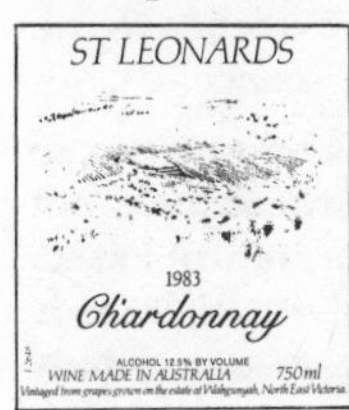

A diverse and always interesting range of table wines, invariably described by variety only, and all estate-grown. These include Chardonnay, Semillon, Gewurztraminer, Orange Muscat, Late Harvest Chenin Blanc, Late Harvest Sauvignon Blanc, Shiraz and Cabernet Sauvignon. Also limited range of fortified wines.

Distribution:
Principally mailing list through excellent and frequent bulletins, invariably full of information and frequently offering re-releases of back vintages. For enquiries write to Box 32, Wahgunyah, Victoria, 3687. Cellar-door sales Monday to Saturday 9 a.m. to 5.30 p.m.

Prices:
$6 to $9 cellar door.

Overall Quality:
Very good and frequently exceptional.

Tasting Notes:

1985 ORANGE MUSCAT [18] *Colour:* medium yellow-green. *Bouquet:* fragrant, spicy and very flowery orange blossom/frangipani aromas; quite spectacular. *Palate:* fresh, lively and fragrant grape flavours; a gloriously fruity wine, with good balance, only a trace of residual sugar and no phenolics on the finish. Drink '86.

1984 CHARDONNAY [18.8] *Colour:* glowing green-yellow. *Bouquet:* complex, charred/smoky oak aromas, excellent rich fruit in melon/grapefruit spectrum. *Palate:* richly opulent fruit/oak flavours; fruit of peach/melon/grapefruit flavours; the wine has outstanding mouth-feel and balance. Drink '86–'89.

1984 GEWURTZTRAMINER [17] *Colour:* straw-yellow with just a blush of pink. *Bouquet:* very clean, of medium weight, with restrained spicy varietal aroma, but unmistakably gewurztraminer. *Palate:* long, gently spicy fruit on the mid-palate; well-balanced and flavoured mid-palate, and a clean, soft finish. A very well-made wine. Drink '86.

1983 CABERNET SAUVIGNON [17.2] *Colour:* medium red-purple. *Bouquet:* very full, round and warm fruit flavours, with hints of dark chocolate. *Palate:* redolent with sweet red currant/raspberry flavours; of medium to full weight, very smooth; another lovely fruit wine, and the best red yet from St Leonards. Drink '86–'90.

1982 LATE BOTTLED PORT [18] *Colour:* medium to full red-purple. *Bouquet:* complex and fragrant, with tea-leaf aromas, fruit and spirit intermingling. *Palate:* very attractive, soft berry fruits on the mid-palate, followed by gentle tannin on the finish. Very good spirit; almost Portuguese in its elegance and delicacy, yet with abundant flavour. A great success. Drink '86–'89.

STANTON AND KILLEEN

pp. 235–6

Location:
Murray Valley Highway, Rutherglen, 3685;
3 km west of town.
(060) 32 9457.

Winemaker:
Chris Killeen.

1985 Production:
11,000 cases.

Principal Wines:

Red table and fortified wine specialists; top-quality table wines released under Moodemere label, including Cabernet Sauvignon, Cabernet Shiraz and Durif; fortified wines include Special Old Liqueur Muscat, Liqueur Muscat, Liqueur Tokay, Vintage Port, Liqueur Port and Old Tawny Port. A range of cheaper sherries is also produced.

Distribution:
Chiefly cellar-door sales and mailing list. Cellar-door sales 9 a.m. to 5 p.m. Monday to Saturday and noon to 4 p.m. Sunday. Mailing-list enquiries to PO Box 15, Rutherglen, 3685. Limited Sydney and Melbourne wholesale distribution through W. J. Seabrook and Co., Melbourne and The Oak Barrel, Sydney.

Prices:
Table wines $5.50 to $7.50 cellar door; fortified wines $6.60 to $15 ('75 Vintage Port).

Overall Quality:
Good, and frequently very good.

Vintage Rating 1982–85:
'83, '85, '84, '82.

Outstanding Prior Vintages:
'80.

Tasting Notes:

1982 DURIF [16] *Colour:* strong, deep purple-red. *Bouquet:* a very big, robust and complex aroma; ripe fruit, with some earthy/coffee characters. *Palate:* a very big, traditional north-east Victorian red, robust and gravelly; the tannin, however, is well under control. Drink '86–'90.

1982 MOODEMERE CABERNET SAUVIGNON [16.6] *Colour:* strong red-purple. *Bouquet:* full, quite aromatic and complex, with some leather/cigar characters almost certainly deriving from a trace of mercaptan, together with bright berry aromas. *Palate:* attractive ripe, high alcohol but smooth style, with lively cherry fruit flavours; despite the high alcohol, borders on elegance. Drink '85–'91.

1980 MOODEMERE SHIRAZ [17.4] *Colour:* medium red-purple. *Bouquet:* clean minty/sweet berry aromas of good weight. *Palate:* a highly flavoured wine, with strong, minty fruit flavours and a very crisp, clean, low tannin finish. Drink '85–'88.

1981 VINTAGE PORT [16.8] *Colour:* dense, dark red. *Bouquet:* full, rich and textured old-style "pie and peas" aroma with good spirit. *Palate:* richly textured, deep and satisfying wine, with soft tannin on the finish. Classic Australian vintage port style in total contrast to Portuguese. Will be exceedingly long-lived. Drink '86–'97.

1975 VINTAGE PORT [17.6] *Colour:* medium to full red. *Bouquet:* rich and textured, with a touch of aniseed, still going strong. *Palate:* softly rich, with almost no sign of age, with the fruit of great sweetness and character; again fine fortifying spirit used. (1985 re-release.) Drink '85–'92.

North Goulburn River

1985 Vintage

Overall, vintage conditions were similar to those of 1984. A cool, wet winter led into an excellent spring, with favourable weather during flowering. The summer was cool and dry, with particularly cold nights, but the grapes ripened well with the impact of the irrigation which is practised universally throughout the district.

A few days of hot weather in March brought a very large crop to maturity several weeks later than usual, but nonetheless earlier than the record late vintage of 1984. Given the abundant crop, fruit quality was good to excellent.

Vintage continued for an abnormally long time, with the late-harvest rhine riesling not being picked until the second week of June. Fruit flavours across the board are excellent, although the acid levels are not quite as high as those of 1984. By and large, the red wines are better than the whites, although the latter will produce very generously flavoured wines, which will develop quickly and offer much throughout 1986.

The Changes

The district is dominated by Tisdall; only Monichino offers a fully viable commercial alternative. Excelsior is no more, and Phillips' Goulburn Valley Winery continues to operate on a very small scale.

MONICHINO

p. 239

Location:
Berrys Road, Katunga, 3640;
8 km north of Numurkah.
(058) 64 6452.

Winemaker:
Carlo Monichino.

1985 Production:
81,900 litres (the equivalent of 9000 cases).

Principal Wines:
Premium varietal releases comprise Rhine Riesling, Sauvignon Blanc, Semillon, Chardonnay, Spatlese Frontignac, Malbec, Cabernet Sauvignon, Vintage Muscat and Liqueur Raisin. Also a range of generic table and fortified wines sold in bottle, flagon and in bulk containers.

Distribution:
Substantial cellar-door and mailing-list sales; cellar-door sales 9 a.m. to 6 p.m. Monday to Saturday and 10 a.m. to 6 p.m. Sunday and all public holidays except Good Friday. Mailing-list enquiries to PO Katunga, 3642. Limited Melbourne retail distribution through J. W. Bray Wine Brokers.

Prices:
Table wines $5 to $5.50 cellar door; fortified wines $9 cellar door.

Overall Quality:
Consistently good.

Vintage Rating 1982–85:
'85, '84, '82, '83.

Outstanding Prior Vintages:
'80.

Tasting Notes:

1985 SPATLESE FRONTIGNAC [16] *Colour:* a faint blush of pink evident. *Bouquet:* rich, softly fruity, with gentle spice; clean, fruit aromas throughout. *Palate:* full varietal fruit, spicy and flavoursome, with well-handled although certainly very obvious residual sugar. Attractive commercial style, the somewhat unconventional colour notwithstanding. Drink '86.

1985 SEMILLON SAUVIGNON BLANC [15.4] *Colour:* pale bright green-yellow. *Bouquet:* fermentation characters lingering mid-July, 1985 in a wine which again shows sophisticated winemaking technology. *Palate:* already developing some depth, with grassy fruit flavours, but a fraction oily on the finish. Will almost certainly come on in bottle. Drink '86–'87.

1984 CABERNET SAUVIGNON [16.8] *Colour:* light to medium red-purple. *Bouquet:* clean and fairly light, with gently astringent cabernet varietal aromas. *Palate:* fresh, with crisp and clearly marked berry cabernet varietal character; good oak handling does not overwhelm the fairly delicate fruit; clean soft finish. Drink '86–'88.

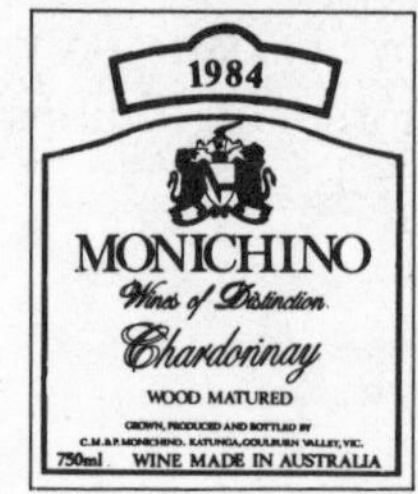

1984 CHARDONNAY [17.2] *Colour:* bright green-yellow. *Bouquet:* very complex buttery/nutty aromas together with peachy fruit. *Palate:* soft, round and ripe, gently peachy wine with surprising depth of flavour and nicely balanced soft oak. (The 1985 vintage seems certain to develop along similar tracks.) Drink '85–'87.

PHILLIPS' GOULBURN VALLEY WINERY

p. 240

Location:
52 Vaughan Street, Shepparton, 3630;
within commercial precincts of town.
(058) 21 2051.

Winemakers:
Contract: Peter Hayes, Brendan Darveniza.

1985 Production:
4000 litres (the equivalent of 450 cases).

Principal Wines:
Shiraz, Cabernet Merlot, Fortified Gewurztraminer and Shiraz Port.

Distribution:
Principally cellar-door sales 9 a.m. to 6 p.m. Monday to Saturday. Mailing-list enquiries as above. Melbourne retail through Don Phillips Cellars, 131 Lygon Street, East Brunswick.

Prices:
$4.50 to $5.75 cellar door.

Overall Quality:
Somewhat variable.

Tasting Notes:

1983 SHIRAZ [13.8] *Colour:* medium red-purple. *Bouquet:* rather heavy and coarse, with bitter, stalky aromas. *Palate:* very aggressive wine, rather bitter and harsh, and again those stalky characters are evident. May conceivably soften with further time in bottle.

SHIRAZ PORT [15.6] *Colour:* medium red-purple. *Bouquet:* solid, with clean fortifying spirit and quite good complexity and weight. *Palate:* very rich, soft, medicinal/friar's balsam flavours, but good flavour. Drink '85–'88.

TISDALL

pp. 240–2

Location:
Cornelia Creek Road, Echuca, 3625;
within township.
(054) 821911.

Winemaker:
Jeff Clarke.

1985 Production:
40,000 cases Tisdall Rosbercon wine, plus 20,000 cases Mount Helen, together with substantial bulk sales (in excess of 300,000 litres).

Principal Wines:
Wines are made from and released under two different vineyard labels. Premium table wines under the Mount Helen label are from the Mount Helen vineyard situated in the Strathbogie Ranges in Central Victoria; Tisdall Rosbercon wines under Tisdall Wines lable, coming from the Rosbercon vineyard at Echuca. In addition, there is a limited range under the Selected Series label of wine made from grapes purchased from other Victorian regions. Mount Helen vineyard wines comprise Rhine Riesling, Rhine Riesling Late Harvest, Chardonnay, Gewurtztraminer, Sauvignon Blanc Sauternes, Pinot Noir, Cabernet Merlot and Cabernet Sauvignon. Tisdall Rosbercon wines comprise Traminer Riesling, Chardonnay Riesling, Colombard, Chenin Blanc, White Burgundy, Sauvignon Blanc Semillon, Cabernet Primeur, Cabernet Merlot and Cabernet Sauvignon. Selected Series wines available cellar door only.

Distribution:
National retail through distributors in all states; also significant cellar-door and mailing-list sales. Cellar-door sales 10 a.m. to 5 p.m. Monday to Saturday and noon to 5 p.m. Sunday. Toll-free phone orders on (008) 03 4235 or order through PO Box 286, Echuca, 3564.

Prices:
$4.50 to $10.80 cellar door; recommended retail similar; cellar-door prices 10% less by the case.

Overall Quality:
Consistently very good, with Rosbercon wines often representing exceptional value for money.

Vintage Rating 1982–85:
White: '84, '85, '82, '83.
Red: '85, '84, '82, '83.

Outstanding Prior Vintages:
'80.

Tasting Notes:

1985 SELECTED SERIES CHARDONNAY **[16.8]** *Colour:* **medium yellow-green.** *Bouquet:* **somewhat dominant new oak, with fairly light fruit lurking underneath.** *Palate:* **complex spicy/vanillin oak to the fore, but smoother and more integrated than the bouquet suggests. Some buttery textures and flavours. Drink '86–'88.**

1984 MOUNT HELEN CHARDONNAY **[18.4]** *Colour:* **medium yellow-green.** *Bouquet:* **soft, of medium to full weight, gently complex, slightly buttery oak intermingling with grapefruit flavours.** *Palate:* **a lively, fresh wine with clear grapefruit/melon varietal flavours backed up by well-controlled nutmeg/spice oak flavours. Overall excellent length and weight, with good balancing acid. Drink '85–'88.**

1984 SELECTED SERIES SEMILLON **[17.6]** *Colour:* **medium yellow-green.** *Bouquet:* **complex, full and buttery oak and fruit aromas intermingle.** *Palate:* **a most attractive spicy/buttery rich wine in which oak is certainly the major contributor to flavour, but which is none the poorer for all that. Drink '86–'89.**

1984 MOUNT HELEN PINOT NOIR **[16.8]** *Colour:* **light to medium red-purple.** *Bouquet:* **light fruit with a trace of strawberry character, but charred vanillin oak is not a successful marriage.** *Palate:* **fresh, soft strawberry flavours, a little one-dimensional; lacks intensity and complexity. Drink '86–'87.**

1983 TISDALL CABERNET MERLOT **[17.6]** *Colour:* **medium purple-red.** *Bouquet:* **clean, with minty fruit and nicely balanced, light, fresh oak.** *Palate:* **soft, fresh, gently minty fruit with some light, sweet berry mid-palate flavours and a clean, low tannin finish. A consistently high-quality, early-drinking red wine. Drink '85–'86.**

1983 MOUNT HELEN CABERNET SAUVIGNON **[17.6]** *Colour:* **brilliant purple-red of medium depth.** *Bouquet:* **firm, with some charred oak aromas and a touch of astringency.** *Palate:* **an elegant wine, with light minty/blackcurrant fruit flavours on the mid-palate and a touch of soft tannin on the finish to give structure and authority. Drink '86–'90.**

Pyrenees

1985 Vintage

Although the Pyrenees is not an especially large district, climatic conditions vary considerably throughout. These variations were particularly evident in 1985.

Although all sub-regions shared good winter rains, the north-west area suffered from poor fruit-set. The reduced crops subsequently ripened rapidly, notwithstanding the cool conditions, with acid loss towards the end of vintage being quite alarming. In the remainder of the sub-regions vintage was two weeks later than normal; above-average yields of fruit, in very good condition, were picked.

Quality varies considerably; some very big, intense and full-flavoured reds were made in the north-westerly vineyards; in the remainder quality varied between adequate and good.

The Changes

There were no changes during the year to the commercial wineries, although a number made their first white wines (particularly from chardonnay) in commercial quantities. Once regarded as virtually exclusively a red-wine region, the Pyrenees is spreading its wings, benefiting in particular from the good results Taltarni has had with rhine riesling, sauvignon blanc and, more recently, chardonnay.

CHATEAU REMY

pp. 246–7

Location:
Vinoca Road, Avoca;
7 km west of Avoca.
(054) 65 3202.

Winemaker:
Christian Morlaes.

1985 Production:
Sparkling wine 20,000 cases.

Principal Wines:
Méthode champenoise sparkling wine from a blend of chardonnay and trebbiano is the winery specialty, released under Cuvée Speciale Brut label. Also cabernet-dominant red wine under spectacular Blue Pyrenees label.

Distribution:
National retail through own distribution network.

Prices:
$11.50 to $14.20 recommended retail.

Overall Quality:
Good, and improving all the time.

Vintage Rating 1982–85:
Not applicable to non-vintage sparkling wines.

Tasting Notes:
NV CUVEE SPECIALE BRUT [15.6] *Colour:* full yellow-green. *Bouquet:* full, if not somewhat heavy, showing some yeast development and bottle age but also lack of finesse in base material. *Palate:* a strongly flavoured and structured sparkling wine in which the rather common base material cannot be masked. Drink '86.

1982 BLUE PYRENEES ESTATE [17.6] *Colour:* medium red-purple. *Bouquet:* solid, verging on dense; clean, but lacking aromatics. *Palate:* offers much greater complexity than the bouquet suggests; very good oak handling adds a dimension to texture; substantial depth to well-balanced ripe fruit, without regional mint to distract. Drink '86–'91.

DALWHINNIE

pp. 247–8

Location:
Taltarni Road, Moonambel, 3478 (vineyard only).
(053) 31 3471; (053) 31 3533.

Winemaker:
Garry Farr (contract).

1985 Production:
1300 cases.

Principal Wines:

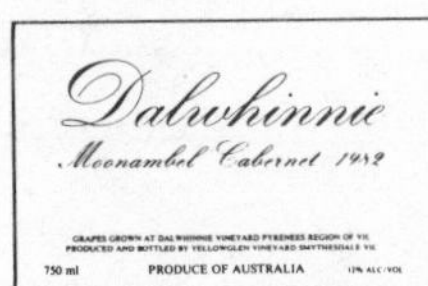

Chardonnay, Cabernet Sauvignon and Cabernet Shiraz.

Distribution:
By mailing list and direct sales to retailers, principally in Melbourne. Mailing-list enquiries to Dalwhinnie Wines, 22 Errard Street, Ballarat, 3350.

Prices:
$7 to $8 retail.

Overall Quality:
Occasional mercaptan problems, but most very good.

Vintage Rating 1982–85:
'84, '82, '83 ('85 not yet rated).

Outstanding Prior Vintages:
'80.

Tasting Notes:
1985 CABERNET SAUVIGNON [17] *Colour:* medium to full purple-red. *Bouquet:* very clean, and quite powerful, yet curiously closed, with little or no fruit aroma yet apparent; will undoubtedly build. *Palate:* a very clean wine, with fresh middle-of-the-road cabernet varietal flavours, and no district mint intruding. Well-modulated, with soft tannin on the mid-to-back palate. Drink '87–'91.

MOUNT AVOCA

p. 248

Location:
Moates Lane, Avoca, 3467;
6 km west of town.
(054) 65 3282.

Winemakers:
John Barry and Rodney Morrish.

1985 Production:
Approximately 3000 cases.

Principal Wines:
Riesling Trebbiano, Trebbiano, Semillon, Cabernet Sauvignon and Shiraz. All reds are kept in cask for three years before bottling.

Distribution:
Substantial cellar-door sales and mailing-list sales; wholesale distribution through Van Cooth & Co. Pty Limited. Cellar-door sales 10 a.m. to 5 p.m. Monday to Saturday, noon to 5 p.m. Sunday. Mailing-list enquiries to PO Box 60, Avoca, Victoria, 3467 (or telephone Melbourne (03) 419 8586).

Prices:
$6 to $9 retail.

Overall Quality:
Good to very good.

Vintage Rating 1982–85:
John Barry is not able to separate one vintage from the next; very even quality.

Tasting Notes:

1984 SEMILLON [17.6] *Colour:* medium yellow-green. *Bouquet:* very clean; pronounced but not excessive lemony oak well-integrated with medium-weight fruit. *Palate:* spicy/lemony German oak flavours well-married with fruit; a well-structured wine, with good acid and obvious cellaring potential. (Tasted January '85.) Drink '86–'89.

1984 TREBBIANO [16.4] *Colour:* medium yellow-green. *Bouquet:* some fruit, with traces of bottle-developed camphor/vanillin aromas. *Palate:* plenty of body and weight; again that touch of camphor and clean acid on the finish. Limited only by the ultimately ordinary nature of the grape variety. Drink '86–'90.

1981 CABERNET SAUVIGNON [17.4] *Colour:* still retaining red-purple hues. *Bouquet:* clean, some astringent/berry aromas, with the faintest hint of mid-Victorian mint. *Palate:* soft, sweet, berry flavours dominate; just a trace of mint; low tannin profile; a wine which combines substance and elegance. Drink '85–'88.

1982 CABERNET SAUVIGNON [17.4] *Colour:* medium to full, bright and clear purple-red. *Bouquet:* excellent unmodified cabernet varietal aroma (no regional mint) perfectly integrated with stylish oak; complex and attractive. *Palate:* very smooth feel and structure; sweet berry flavours on the mid-palate merging with gentle tannin on the back-palate and finish. A stylish wine. Drink '86–'91.

1981 SHIRAZ [16.6] *Colour:* medium red, with just a hint of purple. *Bouquet:* a quite fine wine, clean, but with little varietal accent to the aroma. *Palate:* soft and clean, with a touch of sweet, berry flavours; slightly one-dimensional and simple, but well-made. Drink '85–'87.

REDBANK

p. 249

Location:
Sunraysia Highway, Redbank, 3467;
3 km south of Redbank, opposite 200 km post.
(054) 67 7255.

Winemaker:
Neil Robb.

1985 Production:
2000 cases.

Principal Wines:

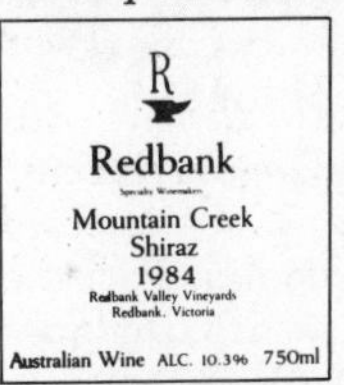

Sally's Paddock is principal estate-grown red wine; a number of other red wines, identified both by variety and by vineyard or sub-district, are also made each year from grapes purchased in and around the Pyrenees region. Recently the first white wine (Alexandra Kingsley Chardonnay) has made its appearance under the Redbank label.

Distribution:
Largely cellar door and mailing list; limited wholesale distribution through Rutherglen Wine Co., Melbourne and The Oak Barrel, Sydney. Cellar-door sales 9 a.m. to 5 p.m. Monday to Saturday, noon to 5 p.m. Sunday.

Prices:
$7.60 to $9.20 cellar door.

Overall Quality:
Chardonnay variable; reds very good, and sometimes exceptional.

Vintage Rating 1982–85:
White: '85, '84.
Red: '85, '83, '82, '84.

Outstanding Prior Vintages:
'76 and '80.

Tasting Notes:

1984 ALEXANDRA KINGSLEY CHARDONNAY [15.2] *Colour:* **medium yellow.** *Bouquet:* **strong, rather chalky structure, showing evidence of solids fermentation characters.** *Palate:* **honeyed/malty flavours, with a suggestion of some oxidation; demands time, but will always be out of the mainstream of Australian chardonnay. (Tasted January '85.) Drink '87–'90.**

1982 SALLY'S PADDOCK [18.4] *Colour:* **medium purple-red.** *Bouquet:* **marvellously fine and complex with cedary briary/berry aromas, with distinct overtones of Bordeaux.** *Palate:* **finely structured and elegant wine with soft, lingering acid on the finish; devoid of distracting mint flavours. First-class red. Drink '86–'91.**

1982 MARONG SHIRAZ [16.6] *Colour:* **strong purple-red.** *Bouquet:* **distinct volatile lift to deep fruit aroma.** *Palate:* **a flavoury, spicy wine but again with that somewhat intrusive volatile lift. Drink '85–'87.**

SUMMERFIELD

pp. 249–50

Location:
Moonambel, 3478;
on the western outskirts of town on Moonambel–Stawell Road.
(054) 67 2264.

Winemaker:
Craig Summerfield.

1985 Production:
1400 cases.

Principal Wines:
Champagne Méthode Champenoise (made from trebbiano), and Hermitage.

Distribution:
Principally cellar-door sales and mailing list; retail sales through Victorian Wine Centre, Melbourne. Cellar-door sales 9 a.m. to 6 p.m. Monday to Saturday; 1 p.m. to 6 p.m. Sunday. Mailing-list enquiries to Summerfield Vineyards, Moonambel, 3478.

Prices:
$8 cellar door.

Overall Quality:
Méthode Champenoise adequate; Hermitage good, sometimes very good.

Vintage Rating 1982–85:
White: '82, '84, '85, '83.
Red: '83, '85, '82, '84.

Outstanding Prior Vintages:
'79.

Tasting Notes:

NV CHAMPAGNE METHODE CHAMPENOISE [15.8] *Colour:* pale yellow-straw. *Bouquet:* strong bready/biscuity/wholemeal aromas, showing obvious yeast autolysis. *Palate:* a big, toasty, sparkling wine, with abundant, if not downright aggressive, flavour. Drink '86.

1983 HERMITAGE [17.4] *Colour:* dark red-purple. *Bouquet:* rich, dense and concentrated, with clean minty aromas. *Palate:* an extremely concentrated and deep wine with pronounced district mint flavour, but with overall excellent fruit weight and structure. Drink '86–'90.

TALTARNI

pp. 250–1

Location:
Taltarni Road, Moonambel, 3478;
5 km north-west of Moonambel.
(054) 67 2218.

Winemakers:
Dominique Portet and Greg Gallagher.

1985 Production:
Almost 40,000 cases.

Principal Wines:
Taltarni Brut, Brut Tache and Taltarni Royal (three *méthode champenoise* sparkling wines), Blanc Des Pyrénées Chablis style, Fumé Blanc, Rhine Riesling, French Syrah (the Taltarni newly adopted name for shiraz), Cabernet Sauvignon and Réserve Des Pyrénées (cabernet malbec blend).

Distribution:
Extensive fine wine retail sales through all states and capital cities. Cellar-door sales 10 a.m. to 4.15 p.m. Monday to Saturday. Mailing list available; enquiries to Taltarni Vineyards, Moonambel, Vic. 3478.

Prices:
$7.25 to $11 recommended retail; usually not subject to marked discounting.

Overall Quality:
Very good, frequently exceptional.

Vintage Rating 1982–85:
'84, '82, '85, '83.

Outstanding Prior Vintages:
'79.

Tasting Notes:

1985 BLANC DES PYRENEES CHABLIS STYLE [17] *Colour:* light to medium yellow-green. *Bouquet:* rich, full and round peach/apricot aromas; much more a white burgundy than a chablis. *Palate:* most attractive clean, rich and soft wine, with marked chardonnay-like peach/apricot flavours. Drink '86–'87.

1984 FUME BLANC [18.4] *Colour:* pale green-yellow. *Bouquet:* intense grassy/gooseberry aroma with the faintest nuance of oak in the background, a beautifully made wine. *Palate:* similar intense, biting sauvignon blanc character with oak barely perceptible. Finishes crisp and dry. An outstanding example of its style. Drink '85–'86.

1982 RESERVE DES PYRENEES [16.6] *Colour:* medium to full red-purple. *Bouquet:* firm, but rather closed, with just a touch of crisp berry aroma. *Palate:* spicy/pepper background to fruit flavours on fore-palate, then fairly pronounced tannin on the mid-to-back palate. An early drinking style for men only, because the tannin will outlast the fruit. Drink '86–'88.

1982 CABERNET SAUVIGNON [18.2] *Colour:* deep red-purple. *Bouquet:* strong rich and complex, with smoky oak characters intermingling with a hint of blackcurrant. *Palate:* a very clean, generous wine with lovely mid-palate fruit with dark berry flavours; lingering but modulated tannin and excellent balance. An outstanding cellaring special. Drink '88–'98.

1982 FRENCH SYRAH [18.6] *Colour:* deep purple-red. *Bouquet:* voluminous, ripe velvety/berry aromas, perfectly complemented by oak. *Palate:* excellent fruit depth with velvety berry flavours on fore-palate, followed by distinct impact of varietal spice. Tannin is soft and in balance. Drink '86–'92.

WARRENMANG

pp. 251–2

Location:
Mountain Creek Road, Moonambel, 3478;
2 km east of town.
(054) 67 2233.

Winemaker:
Russell Branton.

1985 Production:
Approximately 2000 cases (some additional wine sold in bulk).

Principal Wines:
Chardonnay, Shiraz and Cabernet Sauvignon.

Distribution:
Principally mailing-list and cellar-door sales; wholesale distribution to fine wine retailers through W. J. Seabrook & Son, Victoria and Fesq & Company, New South Wales. Cellar-door sales 9 a.m. to 4.30 p.m. Monday to Friday, 10 a.m. to 5 p.m. Saturday. Mailing-list enquiries to Warrenmang Vineyard, Moonambel, Victoria, 3478.

Prices:
$8 to $11 cellar door.

Overall Quality:
Very good.

Vintage Rating 1982–85:
White: '85, '84 (first vintage).
Red: '82, '84, '85(?), '83.

Outstanding Prior Vintages:
'79, '80.

Tasting Notes:

1983 SHIRAZ [17.4] *Colour:* dense, inky purple. *Bouquet:* deep, concentrated and intense, and in the early part of 1985 still to open up fully. *Palate:* a very big wine, showing clear effects of the drought; ripe, sweet fruit on the fore-palate, then a slight dip in flavour before massive, drying tannin on the finish. Drink '88–'94.

1982 SHIRAZ [15.8] *Colour:* dense purple-red. *Bouquet:* complex, powdery bouquet but with a distinct trace of meaty mercaptan aromas. *Palate:* a big, complex wine with strong fruit and soft but persistent tannin; nonetheless, the wine is marred by a touch of mercaptan-derived hardness. Drink '86–'88.

1983 CABERNET SAUVIGNON [16.8] *Colour:* dense purple, almost opaque. *Bouquet:* rich and dense, with a touch of mint and extraordinary concentration. *Palate:* a huge, concentrated wine with powerful tannin on the finish. Needs years to become approachable. Drink '89–'95.

1982 CABERNET SAUVIGNON [17.6] *Colour:* full purple-red. *Bouquet:* smooth and full, with clean but marked regional mint. *Palate:* follows on logically from the bouquet; full fruit, with marked minty flavours and then firm but not excessive tannin on the finish. Drink '86–'90.

Southern and Central Victoria

1985 Vintage

With the vineyards covered in this chapter spreading across much of southern and central Victoria, generalisations are inevitable. By and large the pattern followed that of the other Victorian regions, with a wet spring followed by a cool, dry summer.

In very broad terms, the year was not so different from 1984, with grapes ripening late in cool conditions. The major difference is that acid levels are generally lower, and fruit flavours a little fuller and softer. For some winegrowers the vintage ended up being significantly better than 1984 (and certainly than 1983); for others the quality was not so exceptional. Embarking on another necessary generalisation, the overall quality was good.

The Changes

No new wineries have obtained commercial licences during the year, but a number of vineyards have had wine made for them which will, in the years to come, provide the foundation for commercial sales operations. There is virtually no part of Victoria—and in particular the southern and central regions—which is not suitable for viticulture, and there is no question that the number of wineries will grow as the years go by.

CHERRITTA WINES

p. 255

Location:
Port Road, Branxholme, 3302;
off Hamilton–Portland Road at Wallacedale North sign.
(055) 78 6251.

Winemaker:
John Sobey.

Principal Wines:
Rhine Riesling, Chardonnay, Shiraz and Cabernet Sauvignon, with Moselle style Rhine Riesling the principal wine, but all wines made in very limited quantities.

Distribution:
By mailing list; cellar-door sales by appointment only. Retail distribution Victorian Wine Centre.

Overall Quality:
Poor to adequate.

Tasting Notes:
1982 CABERNET SHIRAZ [15] *Colour:* medium red, slightly dull. *Bouquet:* leathery mercaptan aromas largely obscure light fruit. *Palate:* light to medium weight, with some spicy varietal shiraz flavours, and good crisp acid. A pity about the mercaptan. Drink '85–'87.

CRAWFORD RIVER

p. 255

Location:
Crawford via Condah, 3303;
turn off Henty Highway.
(055) 78 2267.

Winemaker:
John Thompson.

1985 Production:
320 cases.

Principal Wines:
Rhine Riesling, Beerenauslese Rhine Riesling and Cabernet Sauvignon.

Distribution:
Principally mailing list; enquiries to PO Box 3, Condah, 3303. Cellar-door sales by appointment only. Limited retail distribution through Armadale Cellars and Victorian Wine Centre.

Prices:
$6.50 to $8 per bottle and $8.50 per half bottle of Beerenauslese mailing list.

Overall Quality:
Good.

Vintage Rating 1982–85:
'85, '84, '82, '83.

Tasting Notes:
1985 RHINE RIESLING [17] *Colour:* full yellow-green. *Bouquet:* rich and full with obvious botrytis/lime/tropical fruit characters. *Palate:* a very rich, full wine with flavours almost bordering on apricot, yet not phenolic. A very good, albeit early developing, style. Drink '86–'88.

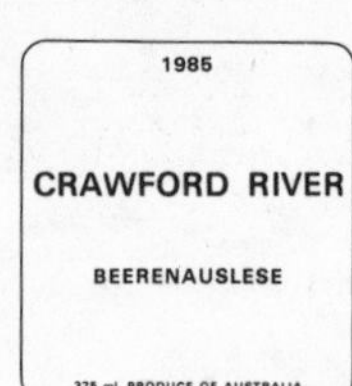

1985 BEERENAUSLESE [18] *Colour:* excellent green-yellow, bright and clear. *Bouquet:* intense lime aromas, with some fermentation characters lingering, but very well-made and volatility kept under tight control. *Palate:* very intense, very luscious lime/pineapple flavours, with excellent acid on the finish; a most impressive wine from a very small winery. Drink '89–'93.

DELATITE

pp. 255–6

Location:
Pollards Road, Mansfield, 3722;
approximately 10 km south-east of town.
(057) 75 2922.

Winemaker:
Rosalind Ritchie.

1985 Production:
5900 cases.

Principal Wines:
A limited range of fine varietal table wines comprising Rhine Riesling, Gewurtztraminer, Sylvaner/Traminer, Late-Picked Rhine Riesling, New Shiraz, Pinot Noir, Cabernet Sauvignon Merlot, Cabernet Sauvignon Shiraz.

Distribution:
Equally divided between cellar-door sales, mail order and fine wine retail distribution. Cellar-door sales 10 a.m. to 6 p.m. 7 days; mailing list to PO Box 246, Mansfield, 3772. Wholesale distribution through Tucker & Co., Sydney; Flinders Wine Company, Melbourne; N. Hollingsworth, Queensland and D. Crossman, South Australia.

Prices:
$8.38 to $11.25 recommended retail. Cellar-door sales $72 to $123 per case.

Overall Quality:
Consistently very good.

Vintage Rating 1982–85:
White: '85, '82, '83, '84.
Cabernet styles: '82, '84, '83, '85.
Pinot Noir: '85, '84, '82, '83.

Tasting Notes:
1984 PINOT NOIR [16.8] *Colour:* vibrant and brilliant light to medium red-purple. *Bouquet:* very clean and fresh, with strong regional minty overtones to light strawberry fruit. *Palate:* light, crisp and fresh, with those same regional mint characters again manifesting themselves; sparkling fresh and clean, but in the final analysis, not distinctively varietal. Drink '85–'86.

1984 NEW SHIRAZ [16.8] *Colour:* vibrant fuchsia-purple. *Bouquet:* clean, fresh and minty, with fruit to the fore and oak not apparent. *Palate:* very fresh, crisp and stylish wine with those vineyard/regional mint characters again to the fore. A stylish light red. Drink '86.

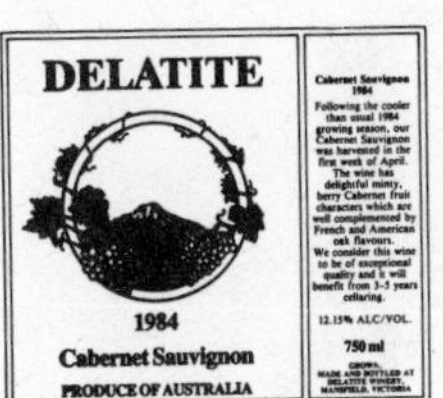

1984 CABERNET SAUVIGNON MERLOT [17.8] *Colour:* vibrant light to medium purple-red. *Bouquet:* intense peppermint aroma underlain with a touch of herbaceous cabernet. *Palate:* an ultra-clean wine with lovely flavours, but lacking a little mid-palate weight and mouth feel; very soft tannin on the finish. Drink '86–'89.

FLOWERDALE

p. 256

Location:
Yea Road, Flowerdale, 3717;
2 km north of Flowerdale Hotel on the main Flowerdale–Yea Road.
(057) 80 1432.

Winemaker:
Peter Geary.

1985 Production:
350 cases.

Principal Wines:

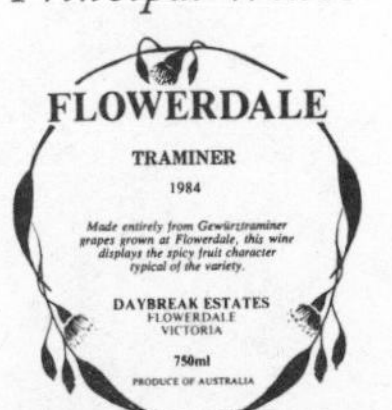

Chenin Blanc, Chardonnay, Traminer and Pinot Noir.

Distribution:
Exclusively cellar-door sales and mailing list; cellar-door sales noon to 5 p.m. Friday and Sunday and 10 a.m. to 5 p.m. Saturday. Mailing-list enquiries to RMB 6513, Yea Road, Flowerdale, 3717.

Prices:
$5 to $9 cellar door.

Overall Quality:
Adequate.

Vintage Rating 1983–85:
'85, '84, '83.

Tasting Notes:
1985 TRAMINER [15] *Colour:* very pale green-yellow. *Bouquet:* neutral to the point where varietal character is not discernible and the fruit is somewhat washed out. *Palate:* better than the bouquet would suggest; clean, and while very light, has been well-made, with good, crisp acid. Drink '86.

1985 PINOT NOIR [15.6] *Colour:* brilliant purple-red of medium depth. *Bouquet:* clean, fresh and crisp, showing relatively little varietal character but well-made. *Palate:* fresh and lifted, to the point of being a little sharp, but very clean. Firm acid on the finish, and the wine may well develop in bottle. Drink '86–'88.

MURRINDINDI VINEYARDS

p. 256

Location:
RMB 6070, Cummins Lane, Murrindindi, 3717.

Winemaker:
Hugh Cuthbertson.

1985 Production:
Approximately 300 cases.

Principal Wines:
Chardonnay and Cabernet Blend (Cabernet Sauvignon, Merlot and Cabernet Franc).

Distribution:
Mail order and through limited retail outlets, principally Talavera Wine Merchants. Vineyard open by appointment only. Mailing-list enquiries as above.

SEPPELT DRUMBORG

p. 257

Location:
Drumborg via Heywood, 3304 (vineyard only).

Winemaker:
Ian McKenzie (chief) heading a large team.

1985 Production:
208 tonnes.

Principal Wines:
Rhine Riesling, Late Harvest Rhine Riesling, Gewurztraminer and Cabernet Sauvignon are principal varietal releases from a very large vineyard planted to a considerable number of varieties. Balance of production is used for blending and in providing base material for Seppelt's sparkling wines.

Distribution:
National retail at all levels.

Prices:
Particularly in the case of main brand sparkling wines, recommended retail prices bear little resemblance to reality. Prices range from $5.50 to over $10.

Overall Quality:
Very good.

Vintage Rating 1982–85:
'84, '82, '85 (no '83).

Outstanding Prior Vintages:
'80 (red), '81 (white).

Tasting Notes:

1981 RHINE RIESLING [17.2] *Colour:* **bright green-yellow of medium depth.** *Bouquet:* **clean; a very firm, fairly austere style, neither aromatic nor particularly fruity.** *Palate:* **excellent, firm and tightly constructed wine; clean-cut, slightly grassy Rhine Riesling flavours; good length and finishes crisp and bone dry. Drink '85–'89.**

1981 TRAMINER [17.6] *Colour:* **medium yellow-green.** *Bouquet:* **very good, clean and spicy varietal aroma, very much in the mould of the wines of Alsace.** *Palate:* **exceptional intensity and style, with surprising weight and some alcohol-derived sweetness. A worthy successor to the great '78 Traminer. Drink '85–'88.**

1980 CABERNET SAUVIGNON [18.2] *Colour:* **very good purple-red of medium depth.** *Bouquet:* **fine cedar/gently sweet, haunting berry aromas of considerable complexity; obvious cool climate characters, yet not green or thin.** *Palate:* **excellent fruit structure and length; an exceptionally stylish wine with beautifully balanced oak against crisp varietal berry fruit flavours. Drink '86–'90.**

1977 RHINE RIESLING [16.8] *Colour:* **glowing yellow-green.** *Bouquet:* **a firm wine which has aged well, although some cheesy/toasty secondary aromas have developed; the underlying fruit is very similar to that of the '81 vintage.** *Palate:* **back palate fleshed out by quite pronounced residual sugar; this jars somewhat after a firm fore-palate. An interesting old wine, still living, but a bit disjointed. Drink '85–'87.**

WANTIRNA ESTATE

pp. 257–9

Location:
Bushy Park Lane, Wantirna South, 3152;
25 km due east of Melbourne.
(03) 221 2367.

Winemaker:
Reg Egan.

1985 Production:
750 cases (less than normal).

Principal Wines:
Clare Rhine Riesling, Chardonnay, Pinot Noir, Cabernet Merlot.

Distribution:
Principally mailing list; enquiries to PO Box 231, Glen Waverley, 3150. No cellar-door sales. Limited fine wine retail distribution through Victorian Wine Centre, Crittendens, Richmond Hill Cellars, Moorfield Vintners and Armadale Cellars.

Prices:
$11.75 recommended retail; less on mailing list.

Overall Quality:
Very good.

Vintage Rating 1982–85:
'84, '82, '85(?), '83.

Outstanding Prior Vintages:
'77, '78.

Tasting Notes:

1983 CHARDONNAY [16.2] *Colour:* medium yellow with a touch of straw. *Bouquet:* shows considerable development with ripe, butterscotch aromas. *Palate:* quite firm, despite the ripeness of the fruit evident in the bouquet; a trace of solids fermentation character has reduced the aromaticity and freshness of the fruit, but this may well build with bottle age. Drink '87–'90.

1981 PINOT NOIR [17.6] *Colour:* medium red-purple, holding both hue and depth. *Bouquet:* surprisingly rich and full, with very complex Burgundian leafy/gravelly aromas. *Palate:* a developed and still surprisingly rich wine, with complex cedar/cigar/leather flavours, strongly reminiscent of developed Burgundies from riper years. A quite striking wine. Drink '85–'89.

1981 CABERNET SAUVIGNON MERLOT [17.8] *Colour:* very good red-purple of medium to full depth; heavy crusting evident on the bottle. *Bouquet:* firm, gentle, herbaceous cabernet fruit, intermingled with well-handled French oak. *Palate:* in the style of the vineyard, shows considerable complexity with most attractive cigar/cedar oak and a long, clean, fruity finish with relatively low tannin. With the heavy crust, should be decanted. Drink '86–'90.

Yarra Valley

1985 Vintage

A late and wet spring caused some problems during flowering, but generally the vineyards showed the benefit of good winter and spring rains, and almost all had totally recovered from the devastation of the 1983 drought. Isolated hail in November caused a few problems, but the major cause of a substantially reduced yield was the exceedingly dry conditions which prevailed from December through to April.

Unirrigated vineyards, in particular, showed considerable stress, and in the very cool conditions it seemed unlikely that the grapes would ripen satisfactorily and fill out. In the end, they did ripen, but acid loss and pH increase was dramatic. Those who picked early were rewarded; those who picked later had their problems compounded by three weeks of rain in the latter part of April.

Overall, the white wines are rated as good to excellent, with red wines variable in the extreme. One or two excellent pinot noirs were made, and—by those whose grapes were picked early—some full-flavoured, deep-coloured cabernet sauvignon. Nonetheless, it will be a year to taste before buying.

The Changes

The major change on the face of the Yarra is the still-to-be-completed Tarrawarra Winery, due to open in time for the 1986 vintage. It will be the largest and most lavish winery in the region, although obviously it will be some time before its wines come onto the market.

How many new wineries will open is debatable. Certainly there is a very large number of vineyards coming into production, some quite large. The imponderables are the effect of changes in the tax laws, which may well discourage some would-be vignerons; and, on the other side, there is the likely buying power of Moet et Chandon. On balance, however, there is no reason to suppose that the Yarra Valley will not continue to be regarded as the most desirable source of premium-quality Victorian table wine.

BIANCHET

p. 262

Location:
Lot 3, Victoria Road, Lilydale, 3140;
4 km north of town.
(03) 739 1779.

Winemaker:
Lou Bianchet.

1985 Production:
1300 cases.

Principal Wines:
Muscadelle, Chardonnay, Gewurztraminer, Pinot Noir, Shiraz and Cabernet Sauvignon.

Distribution:
Exclusively cellar-door sales 10 a.m. to 6 p.m. 7 days.

Prices:
$3.50 to $8.50 cellar door.

Overall Quality:
White wines adequate; red wines good.

Vintage Rating 1982–85:
'82, '85, '84, '83.

Tasting Notes:

1983 CHARDONNAY [15] *Colour:* strong yellow. *Bouquet:* a big, solid and full wine but not exhibiting any varietal aroma. *Palate:* rather heavy, thick and oily; a wine bred to stay rather than to thrill. Drink '86–'89.

1983 PINOT NOIR [16.6] *Colour:* light to medium red-purple. *Bouquet:* clean, fairly light fruit but with distinct strawberry aromas. *Palate:* firm and crisp, if not astringent, but clean and without any fault. Only real criticism is lack of final varietal definition. Drink '86–'88.

1983 CABERNET SAUVIGNON [16] *Colour:* light to medium cherry-red. *Bouquet:* some berry varietal aromas subdued by old oak character. *Palate:* clean, minty fruit flavours of full fore- and mid-palate lead into a rather astringent, bitter finish. Drink '87–'90.

1982 SHIRAZ [16.4] *Colour:* red-purple of medium depth. *Bouquet:* medium to full in depth with a curious, detergent-like aroma. *Palate:* very much better; a touch of varietal crushed pepper/spice on the mid-palate, and the firm finish which is seemingly typical of the vineyard. It will be long-lived wine. Drink '86–'91.

CHATEAU YARRINYA

pp. 263–4

Location:
Pinnacle Lane, Dixon's Creek, 3775;
6 km north of Yarra Glen.
(059) 65 2271.

Winemakers:
Graeme Miller, Leigh Clarnette.

1985 Production:
Not published.

Principal Wines:
Riesling, Kabinett, Gewurztraminer, Traminer Riesling, Beaujolase (sic), Pinot Noir, Shiraz, Cabernet Sauvignon and Vintage Port.

Distribution:
Principally cellar-door sales and mailing list; cellar-door sales 9 a.m. to 6 p.m. Monday to Saturday, noon to 6 p.m. Sunday. Mailing-list enquiries to Chateau Yarrinya, Pinnacle Lane, Dixon's Creek. Limited fine wine retail distribution Melbourne and Sydney.

Overall Quality:
Good to very good.

Prices:
$7.20 to $13.50 cellar door.

Vintage Rating 1982–85:
White: '84, '85, '82, '83.
Red: '82, '84, '85, '83.

Outstanding Prior Vintages:
'76.

Tasting Notes:

1984 GEWURTZTRAMINER [16.6] *Colour:* **medium full yellow-green.** *Bouquet:* **full, very floral and slightly cosmetic/oily varietal aroma.** *Palate:* **rich, soft and full with masses of flavoursome fruit. Drink '86–'87.**

1984 PINOT NOIR [16.6] *Colour:* **light to medium red, developing quickly.** *Bouquet:* **smooth and clean, with a touch of sweet vanillan (probably American) oak.** *Palate:* **good structure and crisp acid finish, but rather simple fruit flavours without distinctive varietal expression. Drink '86–'88.**

1983 SHIRAZ [17.6] *Colour:* **medium red-purple.** *Bouquet:* **full, sweet berry fruit aromas well-integrated with vanillan oak.** *Palate:* **lively and fresh, with sweet cherry/berry fruit flavours; good acid and length. Drink '86–'91.**

1983 CABERNET SAUVIGNON [17] *Colour:* **medium purple-red.** *Bouquet:* **clean; fruit gently ripe with some cherry aromas, but rather one-dimensional.** *Palate:* **good, clean fruit in cherry/blackcurrant spectrum; quite good length, but very low tannin and will develop quickly. Drink '86–'89.**

1982 CABERNET SAUVIGNON [18] *Colour:* **medium purple-red.** *Bouquet:* **smooth and elegant with outstanding fruit/oak balance and integration.** *Palate:* **a firm, yet surprisingly fleshy wine, showing the same balance on the palate as the bouquet; complexing tannins aid the finish, and oak is well-handled throughout. Drink '86–'93.**

DIAMOND VALLEY VINEYARDS

pp. 264–5

Location:
Kinglake Road, St Andrews, 3761.
(03) 710 1484.

Winemaker:
David Lance.

1985 Production:
Not stated; 1984 production 1500 cases.

Principal Wines:

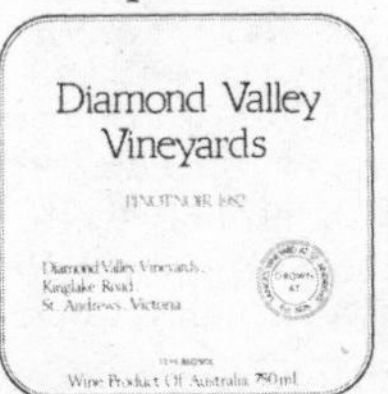

Rhine Riesling, Pinot Noir, Cabernets (a blend of cabernet sauvignon, merlot, cabernet franc and malbec).

Distribution:
Principally by mailing list and and through restaurant and fine wine retail sales in Melbourne. Limited retail distribution in Sydney. Mailing-list enquiries to PO Box 313, Lilydale, 3140.

Prices:
$7.35 to $9.85 recommended retail.

Overall Quality:
Good to very good; Pinot Noir can be exceptional.

Vintage Rating 1982–85:
White: '85, '83, '84, '82.
Red: '85, '84, '83, '82.

Outstanding Prior Vintages:
'81.

Tasting Notes:

1984 RHINE RIESLING [16.8] *Colour:* bright yellow-green. *Bouquet:* highly aromatic and fragrant, outside the usual aroma spectrum for rhine riesling; a touch of spice, and a few other indefinable characters as well. *Palate:* very distinctive fruit flavour, almost pastille-like, and again with some indefinable characters which just don't seem right, and could conceivably have derived from botrytis. Drink '86–'89.

1983 CABERNET [17] *Colour:* light to medium red, with a trace of purple. *Bouquet:* complex, bottle-developed secondary aromas with cedar/tobacco and a touch of mercaptan intermingling; fruit diminished as a result. *Palate:* shows none of the problems of the bouquet with elegant, flavoury cherry/berry flavours. Negligible tannin, and though well-balanced, very light. Drink '86–'89.

1981 PINOT NOIR [18] *Colour:* light to medium red-purple. *Bouquet:* complex leather/sappy aromas, very Burgundian; of light to medium weight. *Palate:* similar very complex leafy/light strawberry flavours; at its peak mid-'85, but good acid will hold the wine. Drink '85–'87.

FERGUSSON'S

pp. 265–6

Location:
Wills Road, Yarra Glen, 3775;
4 km north of Yarra Glen.
(059) 65 2237.

Winemaker:
Andrew Forsell.

1985 Production:
7000 cases approximately.

Principal Wines:
Chenin Blanc, Rhine Riesling, Chardonnay, Shiraz and Cabernet Sauvignon.

Distribution:
Cellar-door sales, mailing list and retail distribution through Redfern Cellars, Sydney and Victorian Wine Consultants, Melbourne. Cellar-door sales 10 a.m. to 5 p.m. Monday to Saturday, noon to 6 p.m. Sunday. Mailing-list enquiries as above.

Prices:
$10.50 to $14.

Overall Quality:
Good.

Vintage Rating 1982–85:
White: '84, '85, '83, '82.
Red: '84, '83, '85, '82.

Outstanding Prior Vintages:
'79, '80.

Tasting Notes:

1983 SHIRAZ [16.8] *Colour:* vibrant purple-red of light to medium depth. *Bouquet:* clean; soft sweet vanillin oak, but fruit a little one-dimensional. *Palate:* very similar to bouquet; sweet oak with light, cherry-flavoured fruit which does not exhibit particularly strong varietal character; a well-made wine which lacks complexity. Drink '87–'90.

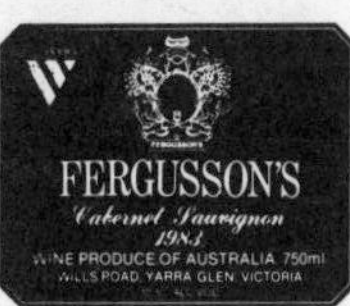

1983 CABERNET SAUVIGNON [17.4] *Colour:* vibrant purple-red. *Bouquet:* very clean; aromatic and fragrant cassis berry/fruit with subtle but fine French oak influence. *Palate:* lovely flavour, but a light hole in the middle which may fill out with a little more bottle development; soft tannin finish. Will probably come on fairly quickly. Drink '86–'90.

KELLYBROOK

p. 266

Location:
Fulford Road, Wonga Park, 3115;
approximately 12 km north-west of Lilydale.
(03) 722 1304.

Winemaker:
Darren Kelly.

1985 Production:
3000 cases.

Principal Wines:
Kellybrook produces both table wines and various forms of cider, the latter produced using classic fermentation and maturation techniques and employing specially grown cider apples. Table wines include Chardonnay Pinot Noir Brut Méthode Champenoise, Rhine Riesling, Late Picked Rhine Riesling, Shiraz Cabernet, Shiraz, Cabernet Sauvignon and Vintage Port. Ciders include Vintage Champagne Cider Brut, Farmhouse Cider, Honeygold, Old Gold (Vintage), Liqueur Cider and Apple Brandy (Calvados).

Distribution:
Almost exclusively cellar-door sales and mailing list; limited restaurant distribution. Cellar-door sales 9 a.m. to 6 p.m. Monday to Saturday and Sunday noon to 6 p.m. Mailing-list enquiries as above.

Prices:
$6 to $9.50 cellar door; Calvados $17.50.

Overall Quality:
Ciders exceptional; table wines good to very good.

Vintage Rating 1982–85:
'82, '84, '83, '85.

Outstanding Prior Vintages:
1975 (Cider).

Tasting Notes:

1983 CHAMPAGNE CIDER [17.4] *Colour:* **glowing, full golden-yellow.** *Bouquet:* **aromatic nutmeg/clove characters, refreshing and very different.** *Palate:* **apple flavour evident but not heavy; the wine has a real delicacy and lightness, with again a touch of clove/spice flavour on the mid-palate, and then finishing bone dry. Drink '85–'87.**

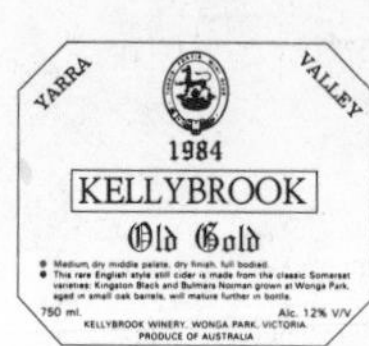

1984 OLD GOLD [17.6] *Colour:* **as the name promises, golden.** *Bouquet:* **highly aromatic, spicy/cinnamon/rich apple characters; sweet, spicy apple flavours on the mid-palate leading to a bone-dry spicy finish. A still wine (made from apples) of great individuality and character. Drink '86–'88.**

1984 SHIRAZ [18] *Colour:* **light, vibrant red-purple.** *Bouquet:* **ultra-varietal aromatic spice/pepper characters; very clean.** *Palate:* **a beautifully crisp and sparkling fresh wine with crushed black pepper spice flavours; of light to medium weight; the type of wine to restore shiraz to popularity. Drink '87–'91.**

1984 CABERNET SAUVIGNON [17.2] *Colour:* **vibrant purple-red.** *Bouquet:* **a little closed, with a slight suggestion of some leathery mercaptan.** *Palate:* **infinitely better than the bouquet promises, with lively fruit counterpoised against charred oak; good weight and structure, with a long life in front of it. Drink '88–'93.**

LILLYDALE VINEYARDS

pp. 266–7

Location:
Davross Court, Seville, 3139.
(03) 277 0262.

Winemakers:
Alex White and Martin Grinbergs.

1985 Production:
Not stated.

1984 Production:
2700 cases.

Principal Wines:
White table wines only; Gewurtztraminer, Rhine Riesling and Chardonnay.

Distribution:
Principally by mailing list and through Melbourne restaurants and fine wine retailers; limited Sydney distribution. Tastings by appointment only. Mailing list PO Box 313, Lilydale, 3140.

Prices:
$8 to $12 retail.

Overall Quality:
Very good; Chardonnay exceptional.

Vintage Rating 1982–85:
'84, '83, '85, '82.

Tasting Notes:
1984 CHARDONNAY [18.8] *Colour:* bright yellow-green. *Bouquet:* intense but fine and delicate grapefruit aromas. *Palate:* a supremely elegant wine, with near-perfect acid/fruit balance, and a long, clean finish. Drink '87–'91.

1983 CHARDONNAY [18.2] *Colour:* bright yellow-green. *Bouquet:* beautifully protected, extremely complex yet very clean fruit aromas in the tropical peach spectrum, although there is also a hint of grapefruit present. *Palate:* medium to full weight; beautifully rich and rounded mid-palate with peach/apricot flavours; long, soft finish. Drink '86–'88.

1984 RHINE RIESLING [16.8] *Colour:* light, bright yellow-green. *Bouquet:* crisp and firm, but still to open up and develop aromatics. *Palate:* firm and crisp, with good acid and undoubted development potential, but will never be particularly generous. Drink '86–'89.

MOUNT MARY

pp. 267–9

Location:
Coldstream West Road, Lilydale, 3140;
3 km west of Coldstream.
(03) 739 1761.

Winemaker:
Dr John Middleton.

1985 Production:
Not for publication; estimated approximately 1500 cases.

Principal Wines:
Chardonnay, Pinot Noir and Cabernets (the latter a blend of cabernet sauvignon, cabernet franc, merlot and malbec). Gewurtztraminer now discontinued.

Distribution:
Exclusively mailing list; very small quantities find their way on to the retail trade and into restaurants. No cellar-door sales.

Prices:
1984/85 releases $12.50 per bottle.

Overall Quality:
Whites good; reds (particularly Cabernets) often exceptional.

Vintage Rating 1982–85:
Dr Middleton is unable to decide.

Outstanding Prior Vintages:
Every year except '77.

Tasting Notes:
1983 CHARDONNAY [16.2] *Colour:* distinct pinking/fawn tints. *Bouquet:* clean and austere, with some green apple aromas. *Palate:* extremely austere and reserved, with light fruit; excellent acid contributes to a long, although as yet notably ungenerous, finish. Made in a very particular style, at odds with most other Australian chardonnay makers. Drink '87–'90.

1983 PINOT NOIR [17.4] *Colour:* bright red-purple of medium depth. *Bouquet:* strong and firm, but as yet closed and still to build fragrance. *Palate:* a firm wine with good structure, demanding time for the latent varietal character to manifest itself. It will never be particularly rich but will always be elegant. Drink '87–'92.

1982 CABERNETS [19] *Colour:* excellent purple-red, brilliantly clear. *Bouquet:* classic cabernet varietal aroma; gently astringent, with exceptional oak/fruit balance and integration; strongly reminiscent of the great wines of Bordeaux. *Palate:* equally classic flavour and structure; they really don't come much better than this; marvellously lingering finish, with fine, soft tannin. Drink '87–'97.

OAKRIDGE ESTATE

p. 269

Location:
Aitken Road, Seville, 3139;
off Wandin Creek Road, 3 km from Seville.
(059) 64 3379.

Winemaker:
Jim Zitslaff.

1985 Production:
Approximately 450 cases.

Principal Wines:

Red wines only produced; Cabernet Shiraz and Cabernet Sauvignon.

Distribution:
Exclusively by mailing list to Oakridge Estate, PO Box 13, Seville, 3139.

Prices:
$8 to $9 cellar door.

Overall Quality:
Very good.

Vintage Rating 1982–85:
'84, '82, '83 ('85 not yet rated).

Tasting Notes:
1983 CABERNET SHIRAZ [17.8] *Colour:* excellent red-purple. *Bouquet:* first impression of some dusty cabernet aroma followed by mint; clean, well-made and overall medium to full in weight. *Palate:* the dusty aromas of the bouquet come again on the fore-palate; then fresh minty/berry flavours follow, with good acid on the finish. Drink '87–'91.

1982 CABERNET SHIRAZ [17.8] *Colour:* outstanding purple-red, deep and vibrant. *Bouquet:* a much stronger, gravelly, robust wine with a suspicion of mercaptan. *Palate:* very firm, with just a trace of leathery astringency, but with abundant fruit on the mid-palate and soft tannin on the finish. Oak is fairly aggressive throughout the wine, which demands cellaring. Drink '88–'94.

PRIGORJE

pp. 269–70

Location:
Maddens Lane, Gruyere via Coldstream, 3770;
12 km north-east of Lilydale.
(059) 64 9279.

Winemaker:
Ivan Vlasic-Sostoric.

1985 Production:
Approximately 1000 cases.

Principal Wines:

Chardonnay and Burgundy (a blend of shiraz and pinot noir). All wines are offered cellar door with considerable bottle age.

Distribution:
Almost exclusively cellar-door sales and mailing list; very limited Melbourne retail distribution. Cellar-door sales 9 a.m. to 6 p.m. Monday to Saturday, noon to 6 p.m. Sunday. Mailing list as above.

Prices:
$8.50 to $9.50 cellar door.

Overall Quality:
Poor, due principally to problems with unsatisfactory oak.

Vintage Rating 1982–85:
'84, '82, '83 ('85 not yet rated).

Outstanding Prior Vintages:
'76.

Tasting Notes:
1980 BURGUNDY [12.8] *Colour:* full red. *Bouquet:* peculiar meaty aromas reminiscent of some Coonawarra red wines; non-vinous. *Palate:* peculiar meaty/gamy flavours suggesting bacterial spoilage.

1979 BURGUNDY [10.6] *Colour:* medium red. *Bouquet:* aggressive pencil shavings aromas. *Palate:* similar shavings/varnishy oak together with marked volatility.

ST HUBERTS

pp. 271–2

Location:
Cnr St Huberts Road and Maroondah Highway, Coldstream, 3770;
6 km north-east of Coldstream.
(03) 739 1421.

Winemakers:
Messrs White, Lance and Grindbergs (contract).

1985 Production:
The equivalent of 12,500 cases.

Principal Wines:
Rhine Riesling, Chardonnay, Beerenauslese Rhine Riesling, Shiraz, Pinot Noir and Cabernet Sauvignon.

Distribution:
National retail distribution through Elders-IXL Wines and Spirits; also substantial cellar-door and mailing-list sales. Cellar-door sales 10 a.m. to 6 p.m. Saturday and noon to 6 p.m. Sunday. Weekdays by appointment. Mailing-list enquiries as above.

Prices:
$10 to $19 recommended retail.

Overall Quality:
Variable and at times idiosyncratic; can be very good, can also be less than good.

Vintage Rating 1982–85:
White: '84, '82, '85(?), '83.
Red: '84, '85, '83, '82.

Outstanding Prior Vintages:
'77, '80, '81.

Tasting Notes:

1984 CLASSIC DRY WHITE [15] *Colour:* light to medium yellow-green. *Bouquet:* unusual, slightly grassy aroma, quite fresh and of medium weight. *Palate:* unusual medicinal oak flavours, not really terribly pleasant; some grassy, fruit characters again present. Drink '86.

1984 CHARDONNAY [16.8] *Colour:* full yellow, almost orange. *Bouquet:* incredibly rich and sweet, almost raisined, with some apricot characters. *Palate:* commensurately rich apricot flavours; a light dip in the flavour in the mid-to-back palate; an odd wine, but highly flavoured. Presumably botrytis has played a role in shaping the wine. Drink '86–'88.

1984 BEERENAUSLESE [18.6] *Colour:* medium to full yellow-green. *Bouquet:* fragrant and aromatic tropical lime aromas, rich and harmonious. *Palate:* an exceedingly rich wine with lime/tropical fruit flavours on the mid-palate and excellent lingering acid on the finish; a wine which manages to be both fine and elegant, yet luscious, at the same time. Variety not stated, but no doubt rhine riesling. Drink '86–'91.

1984 RHINE RIESLING BOTRYTIS CINEREA [16.6] *Colour:* medium full yellow-green. *Bouquet:* firm passionfruit/frangipani/flower aromas. *Palate:* firm; not at all luscious, and a rather hard, phenolic finish; admittedly plenty of flavour throughout. Drink '86–'89.

1982 SHIRAZ [15] *Colour:* red-purple of medium depth. *Bouquet:* peculiar heavy sweaty/meaty/coffee aromas; non-vinous. *Palate:* a very distinctive wine with those peculiar sweaty/meaty flavours again dominant. A distinctive wine which I must admit to thoroughly disliking. Drink '86–'87.

1982 CABERNET SAUVIGNON [16.8] *Colour:* very good red-purple of medium to full depth. *Bouquet:* a complex wine, in vineyard style, with good fruit and a touch of that peculiar sweaty/meaty aroma, although nowhere near as marked as in the shiraz. *Palate:* exceedingly complex sweet berry/plum/tobacco/spice/meat potpourri; the overall result is quite pleasant, and the wine has good weight and structure. Drink '86–'89.

SEVILLE ESTATE

pp. 270–1

Location:
Linwood Road, Seville, 3139.
(059) 64 4556.

Winemaker:
Dr Peter McMahon.

1985 Production:
Estimated normal production of around 1300 cases.

Principal Wines:

Chardonnay, Riesling Beerenauslese, Shiraz, Pinot Noir and Cabernet Sauvignon. Occasional Rhine Riesling Trockenbeerenauslese also made.

Distribution:
Exclusively by mailing list; limited fine wine retail distribution in capital cities. No cellar-door sales. Mailing-list enquiries to Linwood Road, Seville, 3139.

Prices:
$11 to $12.

Vintage Rating 1982–85:
Rating not provided.

Overall Quality:
A little variable, but usually very good. Beerenauslese and Trockenbeerenauslese Rhine Riesling exceptional.

Outstanding Prior Vintages:
'77.

Tasting Notes:

1984 RHINE RIESLING BEERENAUSLESE [18.8] *Colour:* medium to full gold. *Bouquet:* intensely rich, luscious, raisined fruit. *Palate:* an intensely flavoured yet elegant wine with excellent fore- and mid-palate acid left which adds to the overall exceptional concentration of flavour. Drink '86–'92.

1982 PINOT NOIR [17.8] *Colour:* light to medium red, starting to show some tawny hints. *Bouquet:* clean, fragrant and with marked varietal pinot aromas; not heavy but with good vinosity. *Palate:* fine and elegant wine with high-quality, gently sappy pinot flavour. Light-bodied, but with good intensity, and a long finish. Drink '86–'90.

1982 CABERNET SAUVIGNON [17.4] *Colour:* strong, deep vibrant purple-red. *Bouquet:* full, robust and racy cabernet sauvignon with fairly aggressive oak, yet fully integrated. *Palate:* fine, firmly structured fruit still to come to terms with obvious and rather aggressive oak. Simply needs time. Drink '89–'94.

WARRAMATE

p. 273

Location:
4 Maddens Lane, Gruyere via Coldstream, 3770; 20 km north-east of Lilydale.
(059) 64 9219.

Winemaker:
Jack Church.

1985 Production:
Approximately 700 cases.

Principal Wines:
Rhine Riesling, Shiraz and Shiraz Cabernet, Cabernet Sauvignon.

Distribution:
Principally cellar-door sales and mailing list; limited fine wine retail distribution. Cellar-door sales 9 a.m. to 6 p.m. Monday to Saturday, noon to 6 p.m. Sunday. Weekdays by appointment. Mailing list as above.

Prices:
$5.50 to $9.90.

Overall Quality:
Rhine Riesling adequate; reds consistently very good.

Vintage Rating 1982–85:
'85, '82, '84, '83.

Outstanding Prior Vintages:
'77, '80.

Tasting Notes:

1982 CABERNET SAUVIGNON [18] *Colour:* medium to full purple-red. *Bouquet:* soft, rich and highly aromatic plum/spice characters, more commonly encountered in warmer years. *Palate:* very smooth, full, sweet plum/cherry fruit flavours; a round, almost chewy wine in which oak and tannin play second fiddle to the chunky fruit. Drink '86–'92.

1981 SHIRAZ CABERNET [17.4] *Colour:* light to medium red-purple. *Bouquet:* clean but textured, with full fruit and relatively light oak. *Palate:* full, sweet cassis/red berry flavours, very smooth and with low tannin. Drink '85–'89.

YARRA BURN

pp. 273–4

Location:
Settlement Road, Yarra Junction, 3797;
2 km south-east of Wesburn.
(059) 67 1428.

Winemaker:
David Fyffe.

1985 Production:
Approximately 2000 cases.

Principal Wines:
Méthode Champenoise Pinot Noir, and Cabernet Sauvignon.

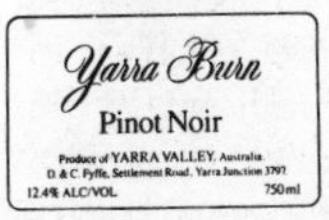

Distribution:
Substantial cellar-door and mailing-list sales; New South Wales wholesale distribution through Haviland Wine Company; Queensland, D. Sutherland; other States direct. Cellar-door sales 10 a.m. to 5 p.m. Monday to Saturday, noon to 5 p.m. Sunday. Mailing list as above.

Prices:
Approximately $10 retail.

Overall Quality:
Usually exceptional.

Vintage Rating 1982–85:
White: '83, '85, '84, '82.
Red: '83, '85, '82, '84.

Tasting Notes:
1984 CHARDONNAY [17] *Colour:* excellent yellow-green of medium depth. *Bouquet:* voluminous spicy oak, not fully integrated, with an overtone of cloves. *Palate:* spicy oak dominant; in mid-1985 the fruit still needing time to come up, which it will most certainly do. Drink '87–'91.

1983 CHARDONNAY [18.4] *Colour:* full yellow. *Bouquet:* extremely rich, clean and full, with round, ripe, peachy fruit. *Palate:* a very big, unctuous and richly textured wine, stylish and arresting. Drink '85–'87.

1984 PINOT NOIR [18.8] *Colour:* light to medium red, tinged with purple. *Bouquet:* fragrant strawberry fruit aromas intermingle with sweet, spicy oak. *Palate:* shows classic pinot flavour and structure, light in body but intense in flavour. Fully deserves its two trophies and gold medals. Drink '86–'90.

1984 CABERNET SAUVIGNON [18.6] *Colour:* clear but strong purple-red. *Bouquet:* fine, elegant and aromatic; bell-clear varietal aroma and perfectly balanced oak. *Palate:* classic cabernet with a touch of herbaceous character underlying sweet dark berry flavours. Low tannin. Drink '88–'93.

YARRA YERING

pp. 274–5

Location:
Briarty Road, Gruyere via Coldstream, 3770; off Maddens Lane, 20 km north-east of Lilydale. (059) 64 9267.

Winemaker:
Dr Bailey Carrodus.

1985 Production:
Approximately 2000 cases.

Principal Wines:
Semillon, Chardonnay, Pinot Noir, No. 1 Dry Red (a blend of cabernet sauvignon, malbec and merlot) and No. 2 Dry Red (85% shiraz plus various other Rhone varieties). Three vintages of No. 1 Dry Red and No. 2 Dry Red usually on offer from the vineyard at any one time. As at mid-1985, '81, '82 and '83 vintages were all available.

Distribution:
Principally cellar-door sales and mailing list; retail distribution through Nicks Wine Merchants, Richmond Hill Cellars and Victorian Wine Centre, Melbourne and The Oak Barrel, Sydney. Cellar-door sales 10 a.m. to 5 p.m. Monday to Saturday, noon to 5 p.m. Sunday. Mailing list as above.

Prices:
$8.50 to $15 cellar door.

Overall Quality:
Whites good, reds exceptional particularly Pinot Noir, and also No. 1 Dry Red.

Vintage Rating:
'82, '85, '84, '83.

Outstanding Prior Vintages:
'80.

Tasting Notes:

1984 CHARDONNAY [15.8] *Colour:* **full yellow with some straw.** *Bouquet:* **strong malty aromas; a solid wine showing evidence of some solids fermentation characters.** *Palate:* **showing far more than the bouquet promises; fruit of medium weight with some grapefruit/citric flavours; good acid and a long, firm finish. Undoubtedly needs time. Drink '88–'91.**

1983 DRY RED NO 1 [18] *Colour:* **very good, full purple-red.** *Bouquet:* **solid and deep; complex fruit with a touch of charred oak aromas.** *Palate:* **most attractive sweet fruit in the dark berry/blackcurrant spectrum; soft tannin on the finish; overall a rich and generous wine. Drink '87–'93.**

1983 DRY RED NO 2 [18.6] *Colour:* **excellent purple-red with a touch of fuchsia.** *Bouquet:* **very complex; softly ripe fruit married with charred/smoky oak aromas.** *Palate:* **excellent soft, dusty/furry structure in the best tradition of the Rhone Valley; vibrant, sweet, dark cherry flavours on the mid-palate, and a long soft finish. Drink '87–'93.**

1982 DRY RED NO 1 [18.2] *Colour:* **medium to full purple-red, strong and promising a long life.** *Bouquet:* **rich, gently sweet, ripe fruit with vanillan oak aromas.** *Palate:* **very full, generous wine with perfectly ripe cassis/blackcurrant fruit; soft tannin rounds off the finish. A perfectly made wine. Drink '86–'93.**

YERINGBERG

pp. 275–6

Location:
Maroondah Highway, Coldstream, 3770;
18 km north-east of Lilydale.
(03) 739 1453.

Winemaker:
Guill De Pury.

1985 Production:
550 cases.

Principal Wines:

Marsanne, Chardonnay, Pinot Noir and Cabernet Sauvignon (the last with small quantities of merlot and malbec in the blend).

Distribution:
Almost exclusively mailing list; small quantities available in Victorian Wine Centre, Nicks of Doncaster, Duke & Moorfield and Sutherland Cellars, Melbourne, and The Oak Barrel, Sydney. Mailing list as above.

Prices:
$9 to $10.50 cellar door.

Overall Quality:
Very good and frequently exceptional.

Vintage Rating:
White: '84, '83, '85, '82.
Red: '84, '83, '85, '82.

Outstanding Prior Vintages:
'80.

Tasting Notes:

1984 CHARDONNAY [16.8] *Colour:* pale straw-yellow. *Bouquet:* clean, with some malty/straw solids ferment characters. *Palate:* crisp, and rather austere, with fruit development held back by solids; will greatly benefit from time in bottle. Drink '87–'91.

1983 PINOT NOIR [18.4] *Colour:* excellent deep red-purple. *Bouquet:* outstanding richness to fruit aroma in the style of a ripe Pommard; plum is the dominant aroma. *Palate:* very full and deep strawberry/plum fruit flavours; a remarkably generous, classic Australian Pinot Noir. Not quite as spectacularly rich as the Yarra Yering Pinot of the same year, but rich by any other standards. Drink '86–'92.

1983 CABERNET [16.6] *Colour:* bright medium to full red-purple. *Bouquet:* ripe berry aromas marred by distinct trace of straw oxidation. *Palate:* almost identical to the bouquet; big, ripe fruit flavours, then a cross-cut of straw. Looked infinitely better as a young wine out of cask, and something of a disappointment. Drink '87–'90.

1983 MARSANNE [17] *Colour:* bright yellow-green. *Bouquet:* clean; slight chalky/solids characters merging into typical honeysuckle fruit. *Palate:* far more life and elegance than earlier vintages of the variety; flavours of green peach and a touch of honeysuckle. Should develop quite well in bottle. Drink '86–'88.

South Australia

Adelaide Hills

1985 Vintage

A very wet winter was followed by a cool spring, resulting in a later than normal bud-burst. Notwithstanding the late start, fruit-set was good and the vines showed unusual early-season vigour.

A cool but dry summer made the use of supplementary irrigation essential, and the relatively few unirrigated vineyards showed considerable stress. Overall, yields were average, with bird damage unusually low. Some rain in the second half of March helped the berries to fill out and ripen, but vintage was still between 10 days and two weeks behind normal.

Base wines for champagne styles were of excellent quality, and on a par with the very good 1984 vintage. Red wines throughout the region have excellent colour and flavour, helped by the warm nights experienced late in the season due to a continuous cloud cover.

For many vignerons, it was the best year since 1980; for others 1984 was more successful. None is unhappy, however.

The Changes

The Adelaide Hills region is one of unparallelled activity, with innumerable vineyards coming into production. Many winemakers have established their homes in the widespread district even before their vineyards are producing, taking fruit in the meantime from other districts. Once the home vineyards all come into bearing, and once the identity of the region is more clearly established in the market place, the Adelaide Hills will become a major force in the cool-climate stakes in Australia.

ASHBOURNE

pp. 283–4

Location:
(Vineyard only) Stafford Ridge, Lenswood, 5240. (08) 272 2105.

Winemaker:
Geoffrey Weaver.

1985 Production:
1200 cases.

Principal Wines:
Rhine Riesling and Cabernet Sauvignon which have historically come from a diversity of sources (from grapes purchased in) but which will come in the future from the new vineyard at Lenswood.

Distribution:
By mailing list only and through selected restaurants and one or two fine wine retailers. Mailing-list enquiries to 2 Gilpin Lane, Mitcham, SA, 5062.

Prices:
$8.30 recommended retail.

Overall Quality:
Very good.

Vintage Rating 1982–85:
White: '85, '83, '82 (no '84 made).

Outstanding Prior Vintages:
'80 (Coonawarra Cabernet).

Tasting Notes:

1983 COONAWARRA RHINE RIESLING [17.8] *Colour:* medium yellow-green, showing some bottle development. *Bouquet:* very rich, very complex lime/tropical fruit aromas, full and satisfying. *Palate:* rich and generous germanic lime fruit flavours; although the wine has a great deal of flavour, there are no phenolics to mar the finish. Drink '85–'88.

1980 COONAWARRA CABERNET SAUVIGNON [19] *Colour:* dark yet brilliant purple-red. *Bouquet:* a very big, but tightly constructed aroma, smooth and clean, with perfectly modulated cabernet varietal aroma. *Palate:* outstanding richness of sweet cherry/berry flavours; perfectly judged ripeness; a quite outstanding and beautifully balanced wine. Drink '85–'92.

CLARENDON ESTATE

p. 284

Location:
Wine made by Andrew Garrett; vineyards in the Adelaide Hills in the course of establishment.

Winemaker:
Andrew Garrett.

1985 Production:
5000 cases.

Principal Wines:
A range of high-class varietal wines, principally from Adelaide Hills and McLaren Vale fruit, including Rhine Riesling, Fumé Blanc, Chardonnay, Beerenauslese, Hermitage and Cabernet Sauvignon.

Distribution:
Fine wine retail through wholesale agents in all states; The Wine Co., Melbourne; Chris Hayes Fine Wines, Sydney; David Kruse, Brisbane; Chateau Barnard, Perth; and the Wine Merchant, Adelaide. No cellar-door sales. Mailing list available; write to PO Box 81, Burnside, 5066 ((08) 79 5951).

Prices:
$7.55 to $9.88 recommended retail.

Overall Quality:
Very good.

Vintage Rating 1982–85:
White: '85, '84, '83, '82.
Red: '84, '85, '83, '82.

Tasting Notes:

1984 CHARDONNAY [18.2] *Colour:* full yellow. *Bouquet:* very rich, ripe, buttery/butterscotch, bottle-developed aromas. *Palate:* very full, ripe and buttery style, reminiscent of Rosemount wines or even Californian; has good fruit, and enormous, mouth-filling flavour. Gold medal winner Canberra National Show 1984. Drink '85–'87.

1984 FUME BLANC [17.8] *Colour:* bright medium yellow-green. *Bouquet:* strong, lemony oak tends to dominate, but there is identifiable sauvignon blanc aroma underneath; overall very complex. *Palate:* better balanced, though the oak is still very much to the fore, showing spicy limousin flavours; rich mouth-feel and good fruit. Drink '86–'88.

1981 HERMITAGE [17] *Colour:* very good purple-red of medium depth. *Bouquet:* clean and full, with sweet vanillan oak balanced against ripe but not jammy fruit. *Palate:* very clean; fully ripe, sweet cherry/berry flavours; as with the bouquet, full flavoured but not jammy. Drink '85–'89.

CRANEFORD

p. 285

Location:
(Cellar-door sales only) Williamstown Road, Springton, 5235.
(085) 68 2220.

Winemaker:
Colin Forbes.

1985 Production:
Approximately 700 cases.

Principal Wines:
Rhine Riesling.

Distribution:
Mailing list only and through selected retailers serviced direct from Craneford.

Overall Quality:
Very good.

HENSCHKE

pp. 285–6

Location:
Keyneton, 5353.
(085) 64 8223.

Winemaker:
Stephen Henschke.

1985 Production:
Approximately 40,000 cases.

Principal Wines:
Ugni Blanc, White Burgundy, Semillon, Rhine Riesling, Rhine Riesling Auslese, Dry White Frontignac, Sauvignon Blanc, Malbec, Mount Edelstone, Hill of Grace, and Cyril Henschke Cabernet Sauvignon.

Distribution:
Substantial fine wine retail distribution in all states, with wholesale agents in each state. Also cellar-door sales 9 a.m. to 4.30 p.m. Monday to Friday, 9 a.m. to noon Saturday. Mailing list to C. A. Henschke & Co., Post Office, Keyneton, 5353.

Prices:
$5.60 to $10.50 cellar door.

Overall Quality:
Still a little variable; has improved greatly over last few years; most wines very good, a few exceptional.

Vintage Rating 1982–85:
White: '84, '82, '85, '83.
Reds: '82, '84, '85, '83.

Outstanding Prior Vintages:
'78, '80.

Tasting Notes:

1984 SEMILLON WOOD-MATURED [18.6] *Colour:* medium yellow-green. *Bouquet:* very rich, complex buttery fruit and spicy/toasty charred oak; stylish and exciting. *Palate:* glorious spicy oak perfectly married with rich, buttery fruit; good acid balance; fresh but deep flavour. A brilliant success just as the chardonnay from the same year was extremely disappointing. Drink '86–'89.

1984 GEWURTZTRAMINER [17.4] *Colour:* medium to full yellow-green. *Bouquet:* extremely rich, soft and full lime/lychee aromas. *Palate:* very full, round and soft lime/lychee/spice flavours, with just a touch of hardness on the finish which seems an almost inevitable companion to full-flavoured gewurztraminer. Drink '85–'87.

1984 RHINE RIESLING AUSLESE [18.2] *Colour:* light to medium yellow-green. *Bouquet:* rich and luscious tropical fruit/pineapply aromas of considerable depth. *Palate:* a round, mouth-filling wine without any hardness and abundant tropical fruit salad fruit flavours; very good acid balance on the finish. Drink '86–'90.

1982 HILL OF GRACE [17.4] *Colour:* bright red-purple. *Bouquet:* spotlessly clean and smooth; fruit moderately but not aggressively ripe. *Palate:* a strikingly textured wine with furry/velvety mouth-feel and soft tannin on the mid- and back-palate; a ripe style, but very well handled. Drink '86–'90.

1982 MOUNT EDELSTONE [18] *Colour:* strong red-purple of medium to full depth. *Bouquet:* distinct new French oak influence adds complexity to the firm, clean fruit. *Palate:* tracks logically on from the bouquet, with the oak handling a further dimension; rich, deep fruit on the mid-palate, with very good balance and a long, lingering finish. Drink '86–'93.

1982 CYRIL HENSCHKE CABERNET SAUVIGNON [17] *Colour:* medium to full red-purple. *Bouquet:* distinctly ripe berry fruit aromas with oak only just evident. *Palate:* a very flavoursome, ripe style with some plum/mulberry flavours; soft and chewy; a wine in a particular style. Drink '85–'89.

HOLMES

pp. 286–7

Location:
Main Street, Springton, 5235;
in centre of town.
(058) 68 2203.

Winemaker:
Leon Holmes.

1985 Production:
Estimated 2000 cases.

Principal Wines:
Rhine Riesling, May Wine, Rosé, Shiraz, Cabernet Sauvignon (with merlot in the blend), Vintage Port and a range of specially packaged fortified wines.

Distribution:
Exclusively cellar-door sales and mailing list. Mailing list provides innovative futures purchase scheme, with payment made shortly after vintage at a saving of approximately half of the ultimate cellar-door per-bottle price. Almost 50% of the wine is sold this way. Highly readable and individualistic mailing bulletins twice a year. Cellar-door sales and restaurant 10 a.m. to 5 p.m. 7 days; mailing-list enquiries to Holmes Winery, PO Box 59, Mt Pleasant, 5235.

Prices:
$4.50 to $6.50 cellar door (1985 'futures' sold at $38.50 per dozen case).

Overall Quality:
Mostly good.

Vintage Rating 1982–85:
'84, '85, '82, '83.

Tasting Notes:
1984 SHIRAZ [17.2] *Colour:* bright purple-red, of medium depth. *Bouquet:* sweet berry/cherry fruit with well-integrated oak; a very aromatic and clean, well-made wine. *Palate:* attractive, cool berry flavours in the cherry/plum spectrum, with good mid-palate fruit and excellent oak handling throughout. Drink '87–'91.

1984 CABERNET SAUVIGNON [16] *Colour:* red-purple of light to medium depth. *Bouquet:* sweet, almost essency, cassis/cherry/strawberry aromas, striking and unusual. *Palate:* carries the attractive fruit flavours of the bouquet a little too far into essency/stewed fruit flavours; too much of an otherwise good thing. Drink '87–'89.

MOUNTADAM

pp. 287–8

Location:
High Eden Ridge Road, High Eden Ridge;
5 km west of Eden Valley township, 5235.
(085) 64 1101.

Winemaker:
Adam Wynn.

1985 Production:
6500 cases.

Principal Wines:
Rhine Riesling, Chardonnay, Pinot Noir and Cabernet Sauvignon.

Distribution:
Fine wine retail distribution through wholesalers in all states. Mail orders to Mountadam Vineyard, High Eden Ridge, Eden Valley, 5235. Tastings and winery tours by appointment; no cellar-door sales.

Prices:
$9.50 to $14 retail.

Overall Quality:
Very good.

Vintage Rating 1982–85:
White: '85, '84, '83, '82.
Red: '85, '84, '83, '82.

Outstanding Prior Vintages:
'81.

Tasting Notes:

1983 CHARDONNAY [18] *Colour:* golden yellow. *Bouquet:* full, rich and developed honey/butter aromas. *Palate:* very rich and smooth, with similar honey/buttery flavours to those evident in the bouquet, together with some grapefruit/melon fruit flavours. A rich and totally enjoyable wine. Drink '85–'88.

1983 PINOT NOIR [16.6] *Colour:* red, but showing first signs of developing tawny hues. *Bouquet:* quite firm, with pinot fruit aroma in a sappy, almost sour, style; oak quite well-balanced. *Palate:* a firm wine, with good structure and mouth-feel, although the oak is a little pedestrian in its flavour. An infinitely better wine than the tired and brown '82; will be long-lived for a pinot. Drink '85–'89.

ORLANDO STEINGARTEN

pp. 288–9

Location:
(Vineyard only) Eastern Barossa Ranges, due east of Rowland Flat, north of Trial Hill Road (off Sturt Highway).

Winemaker:
Robin Day (chief winemaker).

1985 Production:
None made.

Principal Wines:

Only one wine produced: Orlando Steingarten Riesling, normally as an Auslese.

Distribution:
Very restricted output. Selectively available through leading fine wine stockists in capital cities.

Price:
$10.99.

Overall Quality:
Exceptional.

Vintage Rating 1981–84:
'84, '82, '83, '81.

Outstanding Prior Vintages:
'76, '72, '70, '68.

Tasting Notes:
1981 STEINGARTEN RHINE RIESLING [17.6] *Colour:* **full yellow.** *Bouquet:* **magnificently complex, classically developed riesling aroma with soft, lime/honey/toast aromas.** *Palate:* **departs from the more recent trend of spatlese Steingartens; a full, dry style with exceptional fore-palate fruit, which despite the relatively low residual sugar, is quite luscious. At its peak now. Drink '86–'88.**

PETALUMA

pp. 289–90

Location:
Spring Gully Road, Piccadilly, 5151.
(08) 339 4403.

Winemaker:
Brian Croser.

1985 Production:
2500 cases Méthode Champenoise.

Principal Wines:

Rhine Riesling (from Clare Valley vineyard), Botrytis Affected Rhine Riesling (from Coonawarra, using grapes under long-term contract arrangements), Chardonnay (presently Coonawarra but in future utilising estate-grown Adelaide Hills grapes), Petaluma Coonawarra (in fact a red wine with the varietal composition disclosed only on the back label; usually cabernet sauvignon, sometimes with a small percentage of shiraz) and in the future, Adelaide Hills Méthode Champenoise major project with stocks at present maturing. Initial releases of 900 cases likely September 1986; label name not yet determined but will describe the wine as "MC Reserve". Wines other than MC Reserve discussed in separate entries pp. 191 and 212.

Distribution:
National fine wine retail distribution through wholesale agents in each state. Cellar-door sales 10 a.m. to 5 p.m. 7 days at historic Old Mill Building in Adelaide Hills. No mailing-list sales.

Overall Quality:
Exceptional.

Tasting Notes:
1984 MC RESERVE **Early trial disgorgement samples tasted mid-1985 indicate an extremely clean, fine and beautifully balanced wine, which will be made in a distinctively Australian style (as opposed to that of Champagne), but which will have the elegance—and the intensity of flavour—one looks to in Champagne.**

WYNNS HIGH EDEN ESTATE

Location:
(Vineyard only) High Eden Ridge Road, High Eden Ridge, 4 km west of Eden Valley township, 5235.

Winemaker:
Pam Dunsford (chief winemaker).

1985 Production:
Not for publication, but not on scale of most Wynn wines.

Principal Wines:
One wine only made: High Eden Rhine Riesling.

Distribution:
National retail at all levels.

Prices:
Recommended retail irrelevant; real price as little as $3.16 September 1985.

Overall Quality:
Good, and occasionally very good.

Vintage Rating 1982–85:
'85, '84, '82, '83.

Tasting Notes:

1983 HIGH EDEN RHINE RIESLING [16.8] *Colour:* medium to full yellow-green. *Bouquet:* rich, full, soft and generous wine with a touch of district lime and also a hint of pineapple. *Palate:* a soft, mouth-filling wine, with good mid-palate weight and a soft, acid finish. Very advanced for its relative youth. Drink '85–'86.

WYNNS
High Eden Estate
RHINE RIESLING
1984
WINE PRODUCT OF AUSTRALIA 750 ml

1984 HIGH EDEN RHINE RIESLING [17.4] *Colour:* medium yellow-green. *Bouquet:* firm; in a very different style, initially reserved but blossomed in the glass, with fine, lime fruit aromas. *Palate:* firm and clean, with obvious cellaring potential; the wine has good acid, and is relatively undeveloped at this stage. Drink '86–'89.

YALUMBA: HEGGIES AND PEWSEY VALE

pp. 290–3

Location:
Flaxman Valley Road, Eastern Barossa Ranges, due east of Rowland Flat.

Winemakers:
Peter Wall (chief), Alan Hoey and "the Yalumba team".

1985 Production:
Heggies: 10,000 cases. Pewsey Vale: approximately 20,000 cases.

Principal Wines:
Heggies Vineyard: Rhine Riesling and Botrytis Affected Late Harvest Rhine Riesling; Pewsey Vale: Rhine Riesling and Cabernet Sauvignon. Other varietal releases probable in the future.

Distribution:
National through S. Smith & Son Pty Ltd offices in each state.

Prices:
$7.30 to $9.40 (Heggies) and $6.49 to $8.27 (Pewsey Vale) retail.

Overall Quality:
Very good; Rieslings, both dry and botrytised, often exceptional.

Vintage Rating 1982–85:
'84, '82, '85, '83.

Tasting Notes:

1984 HEGGIES RHINE RIESLING [18.4] *Colour:* medium green-yellow. *Bouquet:* very fine yet intense fruit, with outstanding riesling aroma, clean and harmonious. *Palate:* follows on logically from the bouquet; fine lime/toast riesling flavours with excellent structure and feel on the mid-palate, with a clean finish. Drink '85–'88.

1983 HEGGIES BOTRYTIS AFFECTED LATE HARVEST RHINE RIESLING [18.2] *Colour:* deep yellow, with tints of orange. *Bouquet:* intense pineapple/lime aromas with a trace of volatility, which is very much a part of the style. *Palate:* great depth and intensity to the fore- and mid-palate fruit, with that trace of volatility lifting the finish and preventing the wine from cloying. A flavoury and stylish wine of great character. Drink '85–'90.

1984 PEWSEY VALE RHINE RIESLING [16] *Colour:* bright light to medium yellow-green. *Bouquet:* highly protected fruit, but some smelly "armpit" fermentation characters distracting and which really should have settled down by now. *Palate:* lovely, grassy fruit flavours, almost into sauvignon blanc; much better than the bouquet suggests, but a wine which really has not come on in the bottle as one might have expected. Drink '86–'87.

1983 PEWSEY VALE CABERNET SAUVIGNON [16.8] *Colour:* bright purple-red of medium depth. *Bouquet:* utterly unmistakable, lemony oak so much part of the Yalumba style; fragrant and elegant berry cabernet characters well-balanced against the lemony oak. *Palate:* the fine underlying fruit is largely dominated by the lemony oak, and I would quite simply prefer to see more fruit or—better still—less oak. The wine has good structural balance, but not in terms of flavour. Drink '86–'90.

Adelaide Metropolitan Area/ Adelaide Plains

1985 Vintage

A favourable winter and spring prompted vigorous vine growth and good fruit-set. However, the dry and generally warm summer resulted in very rapid ripening and, therefore, in many vineyards, flavour and acid loss.

One of the earliest vintages on record saw all varieties harvested before the end of February in some vineyards, and overall flavours are lighter and softer than normal. Yields were average, and so in general terms was the quality of the vintage. Its principal virtue was that none of the grapes were diseased, and, at the very least, sound wines were made.

The Changes

The major change during the year was the rebirth of the Angle Vale Co-operative under the umbrella of the Berri-Renmano Group. Barossa Valley Wine Estates, as the winery is now known, will be a significant help to the beleaguered growers in the district. The Gordon Sunter label has likewise appeared on the market, and is a new entry in this book.

Within the Adelaide metropolitan region, Normans Winery has finally bowed to urban pressure and, more particularly, taken advantage of its acquisition of the Coolawin Winery in the Southern Vales, to which its manufacturing operations have been transferred.

Perhaps the best news, however, is the rebirth of the Penfolds Magill Vineyard, with the Penfolds Premium Estate Red being made entirely from the remaining 10 or so hectares of vines at Magill. At the time of writing these words, the wine was still to be released but, as Max Schubert had so much to do with its creation, its quality is certain to be very high.

ANGLESEY

pp. 296–8

Location:
Heaslip Road, Angle Vale, 5117;
0.7 km south of Angle Vale, and 10 km south of Gawler.
(085) 24 3157.

Winemaker:
Christopher Hackett; technical adviser, Max Schubert.

1985 Production:
1300 cases.

Principal Wines:

Anglesey hopes to establish QVS White and QVS Red as its flagships. QVS White is blended from semillon, rhine riesling, sauvignon blanc, chardonnay and colombard; QVS Red from cabernet, shiraz and malbec (and as from 1986) merlot. Other wines released are Chablis, Rosé and Cabernet Sauvignon.

Distribution:
National retail through wholesalers in each state. Cellar-door sales 10 a.m. to 5 p.m. Monday to Friday; weekends by appointment. Mailing-list enquiries to PO Box 1, Angle Vale, SA 5117.

Prices:
$6.30 to $6.50 recommended retail.

Overall Quality:
Adequate, but with strong probability of significant improvement.

Vintage Rating 1982–85:
White: '85, '84, '83, '82.
Red: '85, '84, '83, '82.

Outstanding Prior Vintages:
1980.

Tasting Notes:
1983 QVS WHITE [15.4] *Colour:* bright straw-yellow. *Bouquet:* neutral; slightly chalky; lacks fruit richness and certainly any discernible varietal character. *Palate:* neutral fruit flavours; rather heavy, in a somewhat stolid, white burgundy mould, lacking real sparkle or lift, but free from any fault. Drink '86–'87.

1983 QVS RED [16.8] *Colour:* medium red-purple. *Bouquet:* soft butter-vanillan American oak married with soft, sweet fruit. *Palate:* soft, ripe cherry/berry flavours backed with sweet vanillan oak; soft tannin finish. Drink '86–'90.

BAROSSA VALLEY ESTATES

Location:
Heaslip Road, Angle Vale, 5117;
8 km south-east of Gawler.
(085) 24 3100.

Winemaker:
Colin Glaetzer.

1985 Production:
Approximately 2000 tonnes of grapes crushed (equivalent to 150,000 cases).

Principal Wines:
Future releases will include Rhine Riesling, Chardonnay, Sauvignon Blanc, Shiraz and Cabernet Sauvignon; only wine released to date (and the only wine produced in 1984) is Barossa Valley Estates Rhine Riesling.

Distribution:
National retail through Taylor Ferguson. Cellar-door sales 9 a.m. to 5 p.m. Monday to Friday; 11 a.m. to 5 p.m. Saturday and 1 p.m. to 5 p.m. Sunday.

Prices:
Under $5.

Overall Quality:
Too early in the rebirth of the operation to assess.

Tasting Notes:

1984 BAROSSA VALLEY ESTATES RHINE RIESLING [15] *Colour:* medium yellow-green. *Bouquet:* soft, somewhat broad fruit with some secondary bottle-developed aromas already present. *Palate:* a big, full, broad wine, tending to flabbiness, although with plenty of flavour. Drink '85–'86.

GORDON SUNTER

Location:
Winery still to be established; wines made at various South Australian wineries to date, but a permanent (home) winery will be established.

Winemaker:
Stuart Blackwell.

1985 Production:
2900 cases.

Principal Wines:

Chablis, Rhine Riesling and Cabernet Sauvignon.

Distribution:
Presently principally mail order and through isolated retailers serviced direct from administration office. All enquiries to PO Box 658, Gawler, 5118. When cellar door established, cellar-door sales will be 9 a.m. to 5 p.m. Friday to Sunday inclusive.

Prices:
$4 to $8 recommended retail.

Overall Quality:
Good.

Vintage Rating 1982–85:
White: '84, '85, '82, '83.
Red: '85, '84, '82, '83.

Tasting Notes:
1984 CABERNET SAUVIGNON [17] *Colour:* dense purple-red. *Bouquet:* deep and smooth, with dark chocolate and berry aromas intermingling with well-handled oak. *Palate:* a very big, rich wine of great depth, with dark chocolate fruit flavours on the mid-palate and some astringent tannin to provide balance on the finish. Drink '88–'92.

NORMAN'S

pp. 298–9

Location:
183–187 Holbrooks Road, Underdale, 5032; administration only.
(08) 43 7011.
Grants Gully Road, Clarendon, 5157; winery.
(08) 383 6138.

Winemakers:
Jim Irvine (executive winemaker); Brian Light (winemaker manager).

1985 Production:
Approximately 45,000 cases.

Principal Wines:

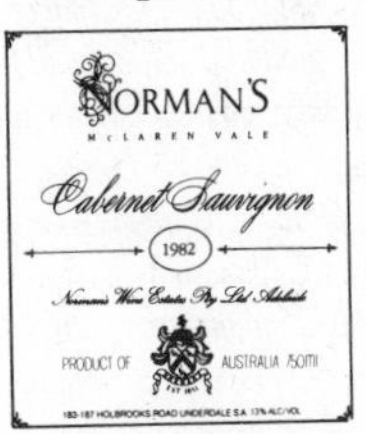

A substantial range of table, fortified and sparkling wines produced predominantly from grapes grown in the company's own vineyards at Evanston Estates in the Adelaide Plains and at Clarendon in the Adelaide Hills. Grapes are also purchased occasionally from growers at Coonawarra, the Barossa Valley, Southern Vales and the Hunter Valley. The regional source of the wine is clearly stated on the label. Winemaking is now all carried out at Chai Clarendon (formerly Coolawin).

Distribution:
National retail distribution through Elders-IXL Wines & Spirits Pty Ltd. Cellar-door sales and mailing list.

Prices:
$6.60 to $8.80 recommended retail other than Coonawarra Cabernet Sauvignon ($13.35).

Overall Quality:
Consistently very good.

Vintage Rating 1982–85:
'82, '85, '84, '83.

Tasting Notes:

NORMANS CONQUEST BRUT [17.6] *Colour:* full yellow. *Bouquet:* strong, complex, buttery fruit with a touch of toasty yeast autolysis. *Palate:* big, ripe buttery/flavoury wine with hints of chardonnay, and good balance. One of the best non-vintage methode champenoise wines available in Australia throughout 1985. Drink '86.

1984 EVANSTON ESTATE–BAROSSA CHARDONNAY [17.2] *Colour:* medium yellow, with a touch of straw. *Bouquet:* clean, of medium weight, with well-integrated lemony oak and fruit. *Palate:* very good oak handling a feature of the wine; the fruit is not strongly varietal nor particularly rich, but the wine nonetheless has good length on the palate. Drink '86–'88.

1984 BAROSSA VALLEY SAUVIGNON BLANC FUME [18] *Colour:* brilliant light to medium green-yellow. *Bouquet:* attractive lemony oak intermingling with some soft gooseberry varietal fruit; very well-made. *Palate:* outstanding oak/fruit balance, with round and soft fruit, yet unmistakably sauvignon. The type of sauvignon blanc Californians would approve of. Drink '86–'88.

1984 ADELAIDE PLAINS PINOT NOIR [18] *Colour:* very good red-purple, with far better than average depth. *Bouquet:* clean, smooth and with gently sweet American oak an important part; not particularly varietal. *Palate:* a sweet, mouth-filling wine with distinct strawberry pinot flavours; excellent balance and style; immaculate winemaking. Drink '86–'89.

1983 McLAREN VALE CABERNET SAUVIGNON [16.8] *Colour:* bright and strong medium to full purple-red. *Bouquet:* clean, with gently sweet berry fruit perfectly balanced against oak. *Palate:* a big wine, with some sweet, slightly squashy flavours; a rich and flavoursome mouthful, but lacks the final finesse and elegance of the best Norman wines. Drink '86–'90.

1981 COONAWARRA CABERNET SAUVIGNON [17.4] *Colour:* medium red, with the first signs of tawny starting to appear. *Bouquet:* a firm and solid wine with a touch of cigar-box oak. *Palate:* good depth and complexity of structure; a soft wine which will probably develop quickly and may ultimately become too soft. An excellent food wine now. Good but not in the class of the quite brilliant 1980 which preceded it. Drink '86–'88.

PRIMO ESTATE

pp. 299–300

Location:
Old Port Wakefield Road, Virginia, 5120;
20 km north of Virginia township.
(08) 380 9442.

Winemaker:
Joe Grilli.

1985 Production:
Approximately 5000 dozen.

Principal Wines:
Rhine Riesling, Sauvignon Blanc, French Colombard, Chardonnay, Auslese, Beerenauslese, Hermitage, Cabernet Sauvignon, and Double Pruned Cabernet Sauvignon.

Distribution:
Significant national fine wine distribution through wholesale distributors in each state. Also cellar-door sales and mailing list. Cellar-door sales 9 a.m. to 5.30 p.m. Monday to Saturday and 10 a.m. to 5 p.m. Sunday. Mailing-list enquiries to PO Box 77, Virginia, SA, 5120.

Prices:
$6.45 to $8.25 recommended retail.

Overall Quality:
Very good.

Vintage Rating 1982–85:
White: '85, '82, '84, '83.
Red: '85, '84, '83, '82.

Tasting Notes:

1985 SAUVIGNON BLANC FUME STYLE [17.2] *Colour:* bright pale green-yellow. *Bouquet:* very fresh, crisp and clean, but not particularly varietal. *Palate:* a very well-balanced and made wine with fresh fruit showing light but perceptible gooseberry/grapefruit flavours; oak no more than a subtle hint. Drink '86–'88.

1984 CHARDONNAY [17.8] *Colour:* bright, glowing green-yellow. *Bouquet:* uncannily like a French burgundy; complex and austere but intense fruit, together with a touch of burgundian sulphide. *Palate:* very fine and elegant; a remarkable achievement for the district, and completely belies its 13.2 degrees of alcohol. On all the indications, should develop very well in bottle. Drink '86–'89.

1984 BOTRYTIS RIESLING AUSLESE [17.6] *Colour:* medium yellow, with a few traces of green. *Bouquet:* complex, and, like the Chardonnay, showing some French sauternes characters with traces of aggressive kerosene and even a touch of compound sulphide. *Palate:* duplicates the bouquet, and can best be described as a French rhine riesling sauternes. Overall of medium lusciousness, and, with that touch of racy astringency, needs time to settle down. Drink '87–'91.

1984 BEERENAUSLESE [16.8] *Colour:* straw-green. *Bouquet:* marked volatile lift, yet again French in style, with strong complex sauternes-like aromas. *Palate:* the high level of volatility is a little distracting, even within the confines of the style; nonetheless, has intense fruit and very good acid. It will be interesting to watch the development of the wine. Drink '87–'92.

1983 CABERNET SAUVIGNON [16.6] *Colour:* dense red-purple. *Bouquet:* rich and full fruit with some tobacco/cigar box/leather complexities, partially derived from a trace of mercaptan. *Palate:* a big, ripe wine with abundant flavour and soft lingering tannin on the finish; again a degree of astringency deriving from the mercaptan. Drink '86–'90.

1983 DOUBLE PRUNED CABERNET SAUVIGNON [17.6] *Colour:* red-purple of medium depth, much lighter than the conventional wine of the same year. *Bouquet:* some vanilla-bean oak aromas intermingling with herbaceous cabernet fruit. *Palate:* a much finer wine than its sister, though still with abundant fruit; good acidity, fine tannin and well-handled oak all add to the class of the wine. (Harvested 12 May, 1983, two months later than normal.) Drink '87–'91.

TOLLEY'S PEDARE

p. 300

Location:
30 Barracks Road, Hope Valley, 5090;
15 km from Adelaide GPO.
(08) 264 2255.

Winemakers:
Christopher Tolley (chief) and Andrew Garrett.

1985 Production:
The equivalent of over 260,000 cases, though only a portion of this sold under the Tolley Pedare label.

Principal Wines:
Rhine Riesling, Gewurtztraminer, Chablis, Wood-aged Semillon, Spatlese White Frontignac, Fumé Blanc, Pinot Noir, Shiraz Cabernet and Cabernet Sauvignon; also limited range of fortified wines and sparkling wine.

Distribution:
National retail through wholesalers in each state. Significant fine wine retail distribution through wholesale agents in all states. Also cellar-door sales at Barossa Valley Winery 10 a.m. to 5 p.m. Monday to Saturday and at Hope Valley 7.30 a.m. to 5 p.m. Monday to Friday and 9 a.m. to 5 p.m. Saturday. Mailing-list enquiries to PO Box 1, Angle Vale, SA, 5117.

Prices:
No recommended retail price set; theoretical price in $4.70 to $7.80 range, usually closer to the bottom end.

Overall Quality:
Reliably good; sometimes very good.

Vintage Rating 1982–85:
White: '82, '85, '84, '83.
Red: '82, '85, '84, '83.

Outstanding Prior Vintages:
1981.

Tasting Notes:

1985 CHABLIS [17] *Colour:* bright yellow-green. *Bouquet:* very good fruit weight which has been carefully protected and preserved; a trace of toasty fermentation character still lingers, but will without question diminish as the wine ages. *Palate:* excellent acidity and freshness gives credence to the use of the word chablis; the wine achieves this without the green, thin fruit characters which are sometimes resorted to. Drink '86–'87.

1984 FUME BLANC [18] *Colour:* brilliant, bright green-yellow. *Bouquet:* aromatic, clean and fragrant; clearly defined sauvignon blanc in the softer style. *Palate:* outstanding winemaking has produced a wine with lovely citric oak/fruit balance and a quite long, although relatively soft, finish. Drink '86.

1983 PINOT NOIR [17.6] *Colour:* outstanding purple-red of medium to full depth. *Bouquet:* soft and clean, sweet oak; considerable weight and style with a touch of strawberry lift. *Palate:* considerable, indeed surprising weight; a fairly firm, astringent finish. A pinot noir built to last. Drink '86–'89.

WOODLEY WINES

pp. 301–3

Location:
Blyth Street, Glen Osmond, 5064;
administration only; winery at Dorrien, Barossa Valley.
(08) 79 9261.

Winemaker:
B. R. Norman.

1985 Production:
Not available for publication but estimated approximately 4500 tonnes at Dorrien and under contract, producing approximately 350,000 cases.

Principal Wines:
Queen Adelaide Riesling, Queen Adelaide Rhine Riesling Spatlese, Queen Adelaide White Burgundy, Queen Adelaide Chablis, Est., Queen Adelaide Claret, St Adele Burgundy, Queen Adelaide Vintage Champagne, Queen Adelaide Vintage Brut Champagne, Lord Melbourne Port, Old Woodley Port, Lord Melbourne Port principal brands, with Queen Adelaide Riesling one of the largest brand sellers in Australia. Also very limited releases of small parcels of high quality Cabernet Sauvignon from Coonawarra and the southern vales from the 1977 to 1980 vintages (called Reference Series). Woodley's was purchased by Seppelt's in July 1985.

Distribution:
National retail distribution at all levels.

Prices:
Recommended retail prices meaningless; subject to periodic savage discounting, particularly in Queen Adelaide range; theoretical price of Queen Adelaide $5.40.

Overall Quality:
Reference Series Cabernet Sauvignons very good; other wines barely adequate; quality will undoubtedly improve following the Seppelt takeover.

Vintage Rating 1982–85:
White: '85, '84, '83, '82.
Red: '85, '84, '82, '83.

Outstanding Prior Vintages:
1980 (Reference Series Cabernet Sauvignon).

Tasting Notes:

WOODLEY EST. [15.8] *Colour:* bright yellow-green. *Bouquet:* strong muscat gordo blanco aroma, rich and fruity. *Palate:* full-flavoured, rich muscat; very good within its terms of reference (a non-vintage, light, sweet wine). Drink now.

1984 QUEEN ADELAIDE RHINE RIESLING [12] *Colour:* medium yellow, straw-tinged. *Bouquet:* unpleasant aroma, lacking fruit and finesse. *Palate:* a very coarse, hard wine without any redeeming features. It is extraordinary that such a wine is so widely accepted in the market-place.

1981 ST ADELE BURGUNDY [14] *Colour:* medium red. *Bouquet:* aged, soft and slightly leathery. *Palate:* a fairly ordinary, old-style commercial wine in which a touch of mercaptan adds the final insult of some bitterness. Drink '86.

1980 REFERENCE SERIES McLAREN VALE CABERNET SAUVIGNON [18.4] *Colour:* very good purple-red. *Bouquet:* strong, concentrated, classic, rich cabernet aroma beautifully blended with oak. *Palate:* fine but generous; perfectly ripe fruit with some cedar/mint flavours; soft tannin and good acid on the finish of a truly outstanding wine. Drink '85–'90.

Barossa Valley

1985 Vintage

An ideal winter and spring, with well-above-average rainfall and mild temperatures, resulted in a spectacular start to the vintage. In the early part luxuriant growth caused extensive outbreaks of powdery mildew, but these disappeared with the onset of hot, dry weather in January, which continued unabated for the next two and a half months.

Unirrigated vineyards suffered badly from stress, and were saved only by late rains in March. With the prolonged hot, dry spell expectations were for a much-reduced harvest.

In fact, yields were well above average, catching all of the wineries by surprise. What is more, during vintage, most vignerons thought quality would be average at best and would not approach the quality of 1984. However, as the wines were cleaned up at the end of fermentation, surprise followed surprise. The whites in particular have marvellously full and soft flavour and, even if the acids are lower than those of 1984, the early flavour development is far better. Rhine riesling, chardonnay, semillon and sauvignon blanc all did well, with some superb rhine rieslings in various styles ranging from delicate to full bodied.

Red wines are likewise full of promise, and only the fortified wines are disappointing.

The Changes

The Barossa Valley soldiers on. There are indications that some of its more progressive inhabitants recognise that other regions, in particular the Southern Vales and the Clare Valley, have upstaged it in attracting tourists. One disenchanted vigneron commented: "When we have a meeting to consider how we can attract tourists back, all the committee argues about is whether or not we should open on Sunday." In an increasingly competitive marketplace, that is simply not good enough.

Rovalley Wines is in liquidation.

BASEDOWS

pp. 309–10

Location:
161–165 Murray Street, Tanunda, 5352; on northern outskirts of township. (085) 63 2060.

Winemaker:
Douglas Lehmann.

1985 Production:
Approximately 30,000 cases.

Principal Wines:
A limited range of table and fortified wines, with some very old reserves of base-fortified wine to draw on. Table wines include Eden Valley Rhine Riesling, White Burgundy, Spatlese White Frontignac, Hermitage, Cabernet Sauvignon and Show Release Cabernet Shiraz. Old Show Tawny Port and Old Liqueur Frontignac are the most distinguished fortified wines.

Distribution:
Substantial cellar-door sales; limited mailing-list sales; wholesale distribution through Classic Wine Marketers, South Australia; Taylor Ferguson, Victoria and Queensland; Chateau Barnard, Western Australia and Carol Anne Classic Wines, New South Wales. Cellar-door sales 10 a.m. to 5 p.m. 7 days. Mailing-list enquiries to PO Box 32, Tanunda SA, 5353.

Prices:
$6.60 to $8.50 recommended retail.

Overall Quality:
Reliably good.

Vintage Rating 1982–85:
White: '82, '83, '84, '85.
Red: '82, '85, '84, '83.

Outstanding Prior Vintages:
'76 (red and white), '80 (red).

Tasting Notes:

1985 WHITE BURGUNDY (WOOD-AGED) SEMILLON [16.8] *Colour:* bright green-yellow. *Bouquet:* clean, with lemony/grassy aromas and oak still to integrate fully. *Palate:* a very lively wine, with crisp acid and good fruit flavour to the fore. Drink '86–'88.

1984 CHARDONNAY [17.4] *Colour:* bright yellow of medium depth. *Bouquet:* a trace of volatile lift apparent; good fruit/oak balance, with some buttery oak married to grapefruit varietal aroma. *Palate:* a well-balanced, lively wine, with light to medium peach/butter flavours; overall well-restrained and not cloying or heavy. Early developing. Drink '85–'87.

1982 BAROSSA HERMITAGE [16.8] *Colour:* clear red-purple of medium depth, holding its hue well. *Bouquet:* a distinctively regional hermitage, with softly sweet fruit and American oak merging imperceptibly into each other. *Palate:* like most of the Basedow wines, very fresh and elegant, with clear fruit flavours; a nice touch of sweet oak, and low tannin. Now close to its peak. Drink '85–'87.

1982 CABERNET SAUVIGNON MERLOT CABERNET FRANC [18] *Colour:* excellent full purple-red. *Bouquet:* marked varietal herbaceous aromas; very clean, with good oak integration and ample weight. *Palate:* balance, both in terms of fruit-ripeness and structure, is the outstanding feature of a very good wine; firm berry/leafy flavours counterpoised against a touch of cedar oak. Drink '86–'91.

BERNKASTEL

p. 310

Location:
Langmeil Road, Tanunda.

Principal Wines:
A limited range of traditional Barossa Valley styles, centred on Rhine Riesling, White Burgundy and Cabernet Sauvignon.

Distribution:
Almost exclusively cellar-door sales.

Overall Quality:
Not rated.

BLASS BILYARA

pp. 310–14

Location:
Sturt Highway, Nuriootpa, 5355;
4 km north of township.
(085) 62 1955.

Winemakers:
John Glaetzer and David Wardlaw.

1985 Production:
A crush of over 5500 tonnes; cases produced not stated.

Principal Wines:

A range of high-quality, bottled table wines which draw on diverse areas and varieties and which are the ultimate expression of the blender's art. They comprise Classic Dry White, Rhine Riesling Traminer, Yellow Label Rhine Riesling, Spatlese Rhine Riesling, Green Label Frontignan Traminer, Yellow Label Hermitage, Grey Label Cabernet Sauvignon, Black Label Cabernet Sauvignon Shiraz, Brut Champagne and 15-year-old Tawny Port.

Distribution:
National retail to virtually all fine wine retailers through wholesale agents in each state. Cellar-door sales 9.15 a.m. to 4.15 p.m. Monday to Friday, 10.15 a.m. to 4.15 p.m. Saturday, noon to 4.15 p.m. Sunday. Mailing list also available, PO Box 396, Nuriootpa SA, 5355.

Prices:
A bastion in the face of the rising tide of discounting; $7.50 to $16 recommended retail is very close to the real price range.

Overall Quality:
Without reservation or qualification, exceptional.

Vintage Rating 1982–85:
White: '82, '85, '84, '83.
Red: '82, '85, '84, '83.

Outstanding Prior Vintages:
'80.

Tasting Notes:

1985 GREEN LABEL FRONTIGNAN TRAMINER [16.8] *Colour:* light to medium yellow. *Bouquet:* clean and soft; surprisingly subdued gentle aromatics. *Palate:* rich flavour; marked residual sugar balanced by good acid; an unashamedly commercial wine but has character and distinctiveness. Drink '86.

1984 GREY LABEL SPATLESE RHINE RIESLING [17.4] *Colour:* bright, light to medium yellow-green. *Bouquet:* full and clean; most attractive lime/tropical fruit aromas. *Palate:* has considerable intensity, with very good acid and residual sugar well under control. Clearly defined riesling fruit flavours; a wine for the terrace or with food. Drink '86–'87.

1981 GREY LABEL CABERNET SAUVIGNON [18.2] *Colour:* medium red, still with a tinge of purple. *Bouquet:* fine and fragrant, gently astringent cabernet married to cedar/lemon oak. *Palate:* much softer and sweeter than the bouquet would suggest, with dark chocolate/caramel flavours to the mid-palate. Not hard to see how it has won two trophies and seven gold medals. Drink '86–'87.

1980 YELLOW LABEL HERMITAGE [18] *Colour:* full red, tinged with purple. *Bouquet:* rich and full, almost dense; sweet, ripe fruit perfectly balanced with vanillin oak. *Palate:* round, soft and ripe yet not jammy; as always a soft and lingering finish, with barely perceptible tannin. Mouth-filling and complete. Drink '85–'87.

1980 SHAREHOLDERS' RESERVE CABERNET SHIRAZ [18.4] *Colour:* medium to full red. *Bouquet:* of medium weight, but very complex, with smoothly integrated lemony/vanillan oak and softly ripe fruit. *Palate:* complex, sweet berry and sweet American oak flavours intermingle, with just a hint of mint on the mid-palate and soft tannin on the finish. A rich, stylistic but, above all else, easy drinking wine. Drink '86–'88.

1980 BLACK LABEL CABERNET SAUVIGNON SHIRAZ [18.8] *Colour:* medium to full red-purple, brilliant and clear. *Bouquet:* a perfectly integrated and balanced wine, with velvety smooth fruit interwoven with oak; despite the abundant aroma, the bouquet is gently complex and beautifully balanced. *Palate:* a totally seductive wine, with sweet fruit, harmonious oak and soft tannin. A wine which fills the mouth with flavour yet does not cloy. Drink '86–'90.

CHATEAU YALDARA

p. 317

Location:
Gomersal Road, Lyndoch, 5351;
4 km north-west of township.
(085) 24 4200.

Winemaker:
Robert Thumm.

1985 Production:
Not stated.

Principal Wines:
A wide and at times somewhat unconventional range of white sparkling and fortified wines are made. Residual sugar has always featured large, extending even to some of the red table wines, resulting in the only Vintage Spatlese Claret available in Australia. Yaldara has nonetheless kept pace with changes in the vineyard, with current releases including a White Burgundy Colombard, Chardonnay, Traminer, Riesling Spatlese, Chablis, Spatlese Frontignac and Lyndoch Valley Riesling; the red wines include Claret, Cabernet Shiraz, Cabernet Sauvignon, Beaujolais, Lambrusco and Vintage Claret Spatlese.

Distribution:
Very substantial cellar-door sales through strikingly ornate and beautifully maintained winery and hospitality complex; Sydney retail distribution through own branch sales office. Cellar-door sales 8 a.m. to 5 p.m. Monday to Saturday. Chateau tours hourly during the week.

Prices:
$3.50 to $5.25 recommended retail.

Overall Quality:
Adequate to very good, depending on one's taste.

CHATTERTONS

p. 317

Location:
Barritt Road, Lyndoch, 5351;
4 km north of township.
(085) 24 4082.

Winemaker:
Roland Chatterton.

1985 Production:
Not known, but limited.

Principal Wines:
Traditional table wines and some unusual fortified wines.

Distribution:
Exclusively the cellar door; cellar-door sales 9 a.m. to 5 p.m. Monday to Saturday. Mailing-list enquiries to PO Box 82, Lyndoch, 5351.

ELDERTON

pp. 317–18

Location:
3 Tanunda Road, Nuriootpa, 5355;
200 metres south of Nuriootpa Post Office.
(085) 62 1058.

Winemakers:
Peter Lehmann, James Irvine (contract winemakers).

1985 Production:
20,000 cases.

Principal Wines:
Rhine Riesling, Hermitage and Cabernet Sauvignon.

Distribution:
Wholesale agents in the course of appointment for eastern states; Western Australia through Lionel Samson. Pending appointment, retail sales supplied direct ex winery. Cellar-door sales 10 a.m. to 5 p.m. Monday to Saturday; 1 p.m. to 5 p.m. Sunday. Mailing list PO Box 394, Nuriootpa, SA, 5355.

Prices:
$6.50 to $8.45 recommended retail.

Overall Quality:
Very good.

Vintage Rating 1982–85:
White: '85, '84.
Red: '82, '85(?), '84, '83.

Outstanding Prior Vintages:
1982 first production.

Tasting Notes:

1984 RHINE RIESLING [16.8] *Colour:* medium to full yellow-green. *Bouquet:* full rich and round rhine riesling with a touch of lime/pineapple; traditional Barossa Valley style. *Palate:* very generous, full and round; traditional Barossa-floor riesling; a touch of hardness on the finish detracts slightly. Drink '85–'86.

1983 HERMITAGE [17] *Colour:* excellent, medium red-purple. *Bouquet:* fresh and lively, with strong, minty fruit aromas. *Palate:* a replica of the bouquet; fresh, lively, sweet, minty fruit; most attractive, although no hint of any varietal spice. Drink '86–'90.

1982 HERMITAGE [17.4] *Colour:* medium to full red, still with a touch of purple. *Bouquet:* solid, smooth wine with an attractive background of cedary oak. *Palate:* excellently balanced fruit and oak; a trace of minty fruit on the mid-palate followed by a long, smooth modulated finish. Drink '85–'89.

1983 CABERNET SAUVIGNON [15.4] *Colour:* strong purple-red, brilliantly clear. *Bouquet:* robust and fairly astringent varietal aroma. *Palate:* a big, rather sweet and obvious style; not jammy, but lacks finesse and elegance. Drink '86–'89.

HIGH WYCOMBE WINES

p. 318

Location:
Bethany;
3 km east of Tanunda, 5352.
(085) 63 2776.

Winemaker:
Colin Davis.

1985 Production:
Not known, but very limited.

Principal Wines:
Limited range of traditional Barossa styles.

Distribution:
Exclusively cellar door 9 a.m. to 5 p.m. 7 days.

HOFFMANS

p. 318

Location:
Para Road, North Para via Tanunda, 5352.
(085) 63 2083.

Winemakers:
Various, but chiefly Peter Lehmann (contract).

1985 Production:
Approximately 1000 tonnes crushed.

Principal Wines:
Table and fortified wines are produced. The table wines are released in two series; premium quality under the Sternagel Estate label (the name of one of the Hoffman vineyards), and the remainder simply under the Hoffmans label, identified by variety and (occasionally) additionally by district. Principal wines include Chablis, Spatlese White Frontignan, Eden Valley Rhine Riesling, Late Harvest Chenin Blanc and Barossa Valley Shiraz under standard label; under Sternagel Estate label, Gewurztraminer, Auslese Rhine Riesling and Cabernet Sauvignon. Fortified wines are headed by Old Tawny Port, with an average age of 15 years.

Distribution:
Retail distribution handled direct from winery. Cellar-door sales and regular mailing list available. Cellar-door sales 9 a.m. to 5 p.m. Monday to Saturday. Mailing-list enquiries to PO Box 37, Tanunda, SA, 5352.

Prices:
$5.75 to $8.95 table wines recommended retail; Old Tawny Port $18.50.

Overall Quality:
Sternagel Estate wines very good; others good; Old Tawny Port exceptional.

Vintage Rating 1982–85:
'82, '85, '84, '83.

Outstanding Prior Vintages:
'80.

Tasting Notes:

1985 CHENIN BLANC [15.8] *Colour:* bright green-yellow. *Bouquet:* quite full; soft, slightly cheesy fruit characters; careful winemaking evident. *Palate:* rather firmer than the bouquet suggests, with clean, crisp acid and some green/grassy fruit flavours. Could well have been labelled chablis. Drink '86.

1984 EDEN VALLEY RHINE RIESLING [16.8] *Colour:* medium to full yellow-green. *Bouquet:* pungent; slightly soapy overlay to firm, lime/tropical regional riesling fruit aromas. *Palate:* very well-made; very rich, lime/tropical fruit flavours, with balancing acid and considerable depth. Has developed fairly quickly. Drink '85–'87.

1984 STERNAGEL AUSLESE RHINE RIESLING [17.4] *Colour:* full yellow. *Bouquet:* an extremely luscious and rich bouquet with botrytis very evident, and marked lime/straw aromas. *Palate:* an exceptionally intense wine, with explosive acid on the mid- to back-palate. A style which others may find too intense, but not me. Drink '86–'90.

1983 STERNAGEL CABERNET SAUVIGNON [16.8] *Colour:* very good, full purple-red, bright and clear. *Bouquet:* clean; a touch of minty fruit, with light but well-handled oak. *Palate:* fresh and crisp minty/berry flavours in a surprisingly light and delicate palate; a wine one would expect from a cool climate. Best enjoyed for its freshness and fruit flavour. Drink '85–'87.

OLD TAWNY PORT [18.4] *Colour:* full, rich, deep tawny, showing obvious age. *Bouquet:* a powerful Australian tawny, with great depth and lusciousness; hints of caramel intermingle with good rancio. *Palate:* a very high-quality wine, with a rich and luscious mid-palate followed by superb cleansing acid on the finish. Drink now.

KAISER STUHL

pp. 318–21

Location:
Sturt Highway, Nuriootpa, 5355.
(085) 62 1633.

Winemakers:
Warren Ward (chief), John Duval and numerous others.

1985 Production:
Not stated; doubtless substantially in excess of 30,000 tonnes.

Principal Wines:
Table wines headed by the Ribbon Range, comprising Green Ribbon Rhine Riesling, Gold Ribbon Spatlese Riesling, Purple Ribbon Auslese Riesling, Red Ribbon Shiraz and intermittent Special Red Ribbon Cabernet Sauvignon releases. Then follow Chablis Colombard, Black Forest Moselle and Kaiser Stuhl Rose. Next come Bin 33 Claret, Bin 44 Riesling and Bin 55 Moselle. Summer Wine is one of the largest-selling sparkling wines (non-bottle fermented) in Australia; Special Reserve Brut Méthode Champenoise also sold. A full range of casks and flagons also marketed, together with 2-litre vintage red wine flagons and the usual range of ports and sherries.

Distribution:
National through retail outlets at all levels. Cellar-door sales Monday to Friday 8.30 a.m. to 5.30 p.m.; Saturdays 10 a.m. to 5 p.m.

Prices:
Realistically, no recommended retail price set by Kaiser Stuhl. Wines subject to periodic heavy discounting; actual prices range from $2.95 to $13 (the latter for premium red releases with theoretical price of $15.80).

Overall Quality:
Standard releases adequate to good. Ribbon releases very good and occasionally exceptional (for example 1978 Green Ribbon Rhine Riesling and 1980 and 1981 Red Ribbon Shiraz and Cabernet Sauvignons).

Vintage Rating 1982–85:
White: '85, '82, '84, '83.
Red: '82, '85, '83, '84.

Outstanding Prior Vintages:
'71, '76 and '80.

Tasting Notes:

1984 *CHABLIS* [16.2] *Colour:* medium to full yellow-green. *Bouquet:* rich and full, with a light touch of smoky/lemony oak; in truth more a white burgundy than chablis style, but nonetheless attractive. *Palate:* a quite rich and distinctly oaky fore-palate, followed by a crisp finish with some green fruit flavours which bring the wine back into chablis style. Very creditable commercial wine. Drink '85–'86.

1984 *GREEN RIBBON RHINE RIESLING* [17] *Colour:* excellent green-yellow. *Bouquet:* considerable fruit depth, with marked lime fruit aroma and some toasty development already apparent. *Palate:* full and soft mid-palate fruit, again showing a touch of the lime juice characters evident in the bouquet; residual sugar well-controlled; firm finish and obvious cellaring potential. Drink '86–'89.

1981 *RED RIBBON SHIRAZ* [18.2] *Colour:* strong purple-red. *Bouquet:* rich, warm, American oak balanced against equally rich and opulent fruit. *Palate:* a very oaky wine, but the fruit has the backbone and depth to support the degree of oak imparted; soft tannin finish. Drink '85–'92.

KARLSBURG

p. 321

Location:
Gomersal Road, Lyndoch, 5351;
4 km north-west of town.
(085) 24 4025.

Winemaker:
Charles Cimicky.

1985 Production:
Not stated.

Principal Wines:

A range of interesting varietal white and red table wines produced from diverse varieties established on Karlsburg's own vineyards in the second half of the 1970s. The wines include Chardonnay, Colombard, Traminer, Rhine Riesling, Shiraz, Cabernet Sauvignon, Ruby Cabernet, Carignane and Pinot Noir.

Distribution:
Chiefly cellar-door sales and mailing list; cellar-door sales through imposing castellated winery 9 a.m. to 5 p.m. Monday to Friday, 10 a.m. to 5 p.m. Saturday and noon to 5 p.m. Sunday. Limited eastern states retail distribution. Mailing-list enquiries to PO Box 69, Lyndoch.

Prices:
$4.95 to $7.90 cellar door.

Overall Quality:
Good.

Tasting Notes:

1984 COLOMBARD [15.4] *Colour:* very pale green-yellow. *Bouquet:* mid-1985, some bottling SO_2 still evident and holding back fruit. *Palate:* a touch of spritz evident; fair mid-palate fruit, and excellent crisp acid (not the oily acid which sometimes marks colombard) on the finish. Drink '85–'86.

1983 PINOT NOIR [17] *Colour:* very good purple-red. *Bouquet:* clean; softly sweet fruit, neatly balanced against light oak. *Palate:* some warm, strawberry flavours on the mid-palate, together with toasty, charred oak, which appears to be limousin. A very well-made wine with ample fruit flavour. Drink '85–'87.

1982 CABERNET SAUVIGNON BIN 117 [16.4] *Colour:* purple-red of medium to full depth and good brilliance. *Bouquet:* clean; gently astringent varietal cabernet with a touch of freshly turned earth. *Palate:* some varietal grassy,' green fruit flavours, but not excessively so; soft but persistent tannin on finish. Well-made, well-balanced wine. Drink '85–'88.

KRONDORF

pp. 321–2

Location:
Krondorf Road, Tanunda, 5352;
7 km south-east of town.
(085) 63 2145.

Winemakers:
Grant Burge and Ian Wilson.

1985 Production:
Approximately 2500 tonnes (or 1,600,000 litres); 75% white, 25% red.

Principal Wines:

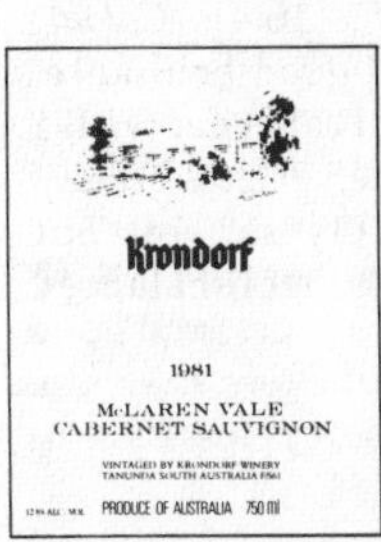

Varietal table wine specialists; highest-quality table wines released under Burge and Wilson label, comprising Rhine Riesling, Chardonnay, Late Harvest Wood Matured Semillon, Cabernet Sauvignon and Cabernet Sauvignon Cabernet Franc; "standard" Krondorf releases, identified both by variety and region, including Fumé Blanc, Chardonnay, Rhine Riesling, Spatlese Frontignac, Hermitage and Cabernet Sauvignon. Also high-quality aged Tawny Port and Méthode Champenoise Brut.

Distribution:
National widespread retail, particularly in fine wine retailers; self-distribution at wholesale level in South Australia, Victoria and New South Wales; distributed by Carlton United Breweries in Queensland. Substantial cellar-door sales 10 a.m. to 5 p.m. 7 days a week. Mailing list also available; enquiries to Box 242, Tanunda, 5352.

Prices:
Have been partially successful in limiting discounting by offering wines at a realistic price in the first place: $6.70 to $9.30 recommended retail is usually not much in excess of the real price.

Overall Quality:
Consistently very good.

Vintage Rating 1982–85:
White: '85, '84, '82, '83.
Red: '85, '83, '84, '83.

Outstanding Prior Vintages:
'79, '80.

Tasting Notes:

1984 BURGE AND WILSON CHARDONNAY [17.6] *Colour:* bright green-yellow. *Bouquet:* smoky/lemony oak tends to dominate fruit, but nonetheless not unattractive. *Palate:* a well-constructed and balanced wine with real pretensions to elegance; varietal fruit is surprisingly restrained and undeveloped mid-1985. Drink '86–'88.

1984 CHARDONNAY [17] *Colour:* pale, bright green-yellow. *Bouquet:* clean and light, with some lemony aromatics. *Palate:* a fresh, well-balanced wine with nice mouth-feel and some lemony/grapefruit mid-palate flavours; oak well-handled. Drink '85–'87.

1984 BURGE AND WILSON EDEN VALLEY RHINE RIESLING [17.8] *Colour:* excellent green-yellow, bright and glistening. *Bouquet:* highly aromatic, with typical Eden Valley lime/pineapple fruit aroma. *Palate:* fulfils the promise of the bouquet; archetypal district character, with weighty fruit with strong lime-juice flavour. Drink '85–'90.

1983 CABERNET SAUVIGNON CABERNET FRANC [18.2] *Colour:* medium red, showing some development. *Bouquet:* fragrant and fresh, with fine fruit/oak integration. *Palate:* light, fresh and crisp but with very good total flavour. Oak in evidence, but not over-done. Best while it retains its freshness and fruitiness. Drink '86–'87.

1982 BURGE AND WILSON BAROSSA VALLEY CABERNET SAUVIGNON [17.8] *Colour:* medium red, still with some purples. *Bouquet:* strongly accented herbaceous cabernet aroma, most unusual for the Barossa Valley. *Palate:* consistent with bouquet; strong, leafy/herbaceous fruit, but with more than adequate mid-palate weight which prevents the wine being thin or astringent. A most elegant, if highly unusual, Barossa cabernet. Drink '85–'91.

LEO BURING

pp. 314–16

Location:
Sturt Highway, Tanunda, 5352;
2 km north-east of township.
(085) 63 2184.

Winemaker:
John Vickery (chief).

1985 Production:
Not stated, but clearly very substantial.

Principal Wines:

A very substantial range of table wines, which fall into a number of groupings. Highest quality wines released under White Label Reserve Bin series, embodying a complicated system of bin numbers which change each year. Foremost among these are Eden Valley and Watervale Rhine Rieslings (with age, some of the greatest in the country). Padthaway and Barossa Valley Rhine Rieslings also released, with Barossa Valley Auslese Rhine Riesling particularly noteworthy. Red wine releases under Reserve Bin Label are in no way comparable to the quality of the white wine releases. Then follow the Leo Buring Varietal Collection of white and red table wines; Chenin Blanc, Fumé Blanc, Chardonnay and Traminer, with a series of Rhine Rieslings additionally identified by district—variously the Eden Valley, Barossa-Eden Valley, and Watervale, with corresponding red wines comprising Barossa Valley Cabernet Sauvignon, Eden Valley Shiraz and Pinot Noir. Next come the Black Label range, Bin 21 Moselle, Bin 33 Rhine Riesling, Bin 48 Chablis, Bin 86 White Burgundy, Bin 7 Cabernet Sauvignon and Bin 13 Burgundy. At the bottom end of the bottled range are the Extra Special generic releases, and finally casks and flagons.

Distribution:
National retail distribution at all levels.

Prices:
Cover the full spectrum of price from $2.26 to $35 recommended retail; discounting is less severe and less frequent at the top end of the range.

Overall Quality:
Standard releases to good, with white wines consistently better than red; Reserve Bin Rhine Rieslings, particularly with age, exceptional.

Vintage Rating 1982–85:
'85, '84, '82, '83.

Outstanding Prior Vintages:
'71, '73, '75.

Tasting Notes:

1985 BAROSSA VALLEY RHINE RIESLING (VARIETAL COLLECTION) [17] *Colour:* **light to medium green-yellow.** *Bouquet:* **round and quite soft, with good fruit-weight; gentle, tropical lime aromas.** *Palate:* **round and soft, with most attractive, gentle lime fruit; smooth, well-balanced and with a soft and relatively full finish. Drink '86–'88.**

1985 CHARDONNAY (VARIETAL COLLECTION) [17] *Colour:* **light to medium yellow-green.** *Bouquet:* **already showing some pleasing complexity; nicely balanced light oak, with toasty/buttery aromas, although the fruit is not especially aromatic.** *Palate:* **good fruit-weight, with some distinctive grapefruit/citric fruit flavours, and good acid. A wine which undoubtedly will blossom over the next 12 months and promises to be the best release yet in this line. Drink '86–'88.**

1985 FUME BLANC (VARIETAL COLLECTION) [16.6] *Colour:* **bright, light green-yellow.** *Bouquet:* **gradually opened up in the glass, with light but distinctive sauvignon blanc aroma, with some slightly cheesy oak.** *Palate:* **good weight and distinctive ripe gooseberry flavours; a round, soft fume style, with no aggression. Drink '87–'89.**

1984 EDEN VALLEY RHINE RIESLING (VARIETAL COLLECTION) [16] *Colour:* **light to medium yellow.** *Bouquet:* **clean; of medium to full weight, with a clearly identifiable touch of the Eden Valley lime juice aroma, together with some emerging toasty characters.** *Palate:* **good middle-of-the-road style; well-balanced, the only fault being a lack of fruit intensity. Drink '85–'87.**

1984 BAROSSA VALLEY RHINE RIESLING (VARIETAL COLLECTION) [16.4] *Colour:* **light to medium yellow-green.** *Bouquet:* **clean; some depth to the fruit but not particularly aromatic.** *Palate:* **much fuller and softer than the bouquet suggests, with good mid-palate fruit fleshed out by a trace of residual sugar. Attractive early drinking style. Drink '85–'86.**

1984 WATERVALE RHINE RIESLING (VARIETAL COLLECTION) [16] *Colour:* **light to medium yellow-green.** *Bouquet:* **light to medium fruit, with typical Clare Valley toasty characters, but lacking richness.** *Palate:* **a light and fairly elegant wine; well-made, and could repay cellaring. Drink '86–'88.**

ORLANDO

pp. 322–8

Location:
Sturt Highway, Rowland Flat, 5350;
immediately north of township.
(085) 63 8545.

Winemaker:
Robin Day (chief) heads a substantial team.

1985 Production:
Not for publication, but very substantial.

Principal Wines:
One of Australia's most important makers of high-quality table wines. At the top end of the premium wines come individual vineyard bin lines with a non-recurring bin number, identified chiefly by variety and region. Orlando takes grapes from all over South Australia, the principal regions being the Barossa, Eden and Clare Valleys, Coonawarra, Keppoch, Southern Vales and the Riverland. The Eden Valley is the most important source of high quality rhine riesling and traminer; Riverland of chardonnay; and Coonawarra/Keppoch of cabernet sauvignon. After the individual vineyard and show wines come St Helga Rhine Riesling and St Hugo Cabernet Sauvignon; then follow the RF series of Chardonnay, Semillon, Fumé Blanc, Pinot Noir and Cabernet Sauvignon. Jacobs Creek Claret is by far the largest-selling bottled red wine in Australia, outselling its nearest competitor (Seaview Cabernet Sauvignon) by three-to-one. Jacobs Creek Rhine Riesling has been more recently introduced, and is also a very large-volume seller, but has a long way to go before approaching the 150,000 cases of Jacobs Creek Claret sold each year. Orlando is also the dominant force in the cask market, well clear of Leasingham in second position. The Coolabah range of casks is consistently of better quality than those of any other company. Orlando have also embarked on a Classic Maturation Release program of show stocks, producing aged white wines of exceptional quality.

Distribution:
National retail at all levels.

Prices:
A wide price range, with Thompsons Liquor Guide price usually bearing little or no relationship to the real price. (There are no recommended retail prices set by Orlando.)

Overall Quality:
Within the respective terms of reference of the various classes, consistently good if not exceptional. St Helga and St Hugo certainly fall in the exceptional category for their price range, as does RF Chardonnay and RF Semillon.

Vintage Rating 1982–85:
White: '85, '84, '83, '82.
Red: '82, '85, '84, '83.

Outstanding Prior Vintages:
'80.

Tasting Notes:

1985 JACOBS CREEK RHINE RIESLING [17] *Colour:* **excellent bright green-yellow.** *Bouquet:* **of remarkable weight and fruit depth, with quite complex lime/toast aromas.** *Palate:* **of exceptional depth and character for such a large-volume commercial wine; true rhine riesling style and structure, and even offers cellaring potential. The wine is balanced and complete; one simply cannot ask for more at the price. Drink '86–'88.**

1985 ST HELGA RHINE RIESLING [17.8] *Colour:* **medium full yellow-green.** *Bouquet:* **a very rich and full soft wine, with deep lime/toast aromas.** *Palate:* **rich, mouth-filling flavours, with unmistakable regional lime characters; round, soft and generous with a long, soft finish. Drink '86–'90.**

1985 RF CHARDONNAY [18] *Colour:* **full yellow-green.** *Bouquet:* **rich, complex, buttery fruit and oak; much bigger and richer than the '84 at the same stage.** *Palate:* **extremely complex, charred/toasty oak, suggestive of some barrel fermentation, although this is presumably impossible in such a large-volume wine. Astonishing flavour and quality. Drink '86–'88.**

1983 ST HUGO CABERNET SAUVIGNON [17] *Colour:* **red-purple of medium depth.** *Bouquet:* **light, plum fruit aromas; a clean wine, with the oak held well in restraint, given the much diminished fruit depth compared with prior releases of this wine.** *Palate:* **smooth and sweet plum flavours; a touch of sweet oak; a well-integrated and balanced wine, but with far less depth of flavour than any of the three preceding vintages. Drink '86–'88.**

1982 RF CABERNET SAUVIGNON [17.2] *Colour:* **medium to full red-purple.** *Bouquet:* **a very big, clean wine, with generous fruit and oak flavours, and the Coonawarra contribution quite marked.** *Palate:* **a generous, soft wine, with quite chewy fruit; very good balance; another absolutely outstanding commercial release, with weight and character far beyond that which one would normally expect from such a widely available wine. Drink '86–'89.**

PENFOLDS

pp. 328–34

Location:
Sturt Highway, Nuriootpa, 5355;
2 km south of township.
(08) 332 6099.

Winemakers:
Don Ditter (group chief winemaker), Warren Ward (Nuriootpa chief winemaker), John Duval and many others.

1985 Production:
Not for publication, but, with Kaiser Stuhl, among the largest in Australia.

Principal Wines:
Specialist red-winemakers of the highest reputation and quality; in descending order of price are Australia's greatest red wine, Grange Hermitage, then St Henri Claret, followed by Bin 707 Cabernet Sauvignon; there is then a price gap to Bin 389 Cabernet Shiraz, Bin 28 Kalimna Shiraz and Bin 128 Coonawarra Claret; a notch under this come Bin 333 Burgundy and (intermittently) Bin 2 Shiraz Mataro. Over the years some quite magnificent show release wines have appeared under non-repeating bin numbers. For many, 1962 Bin 60A is the greatest red produced in Australia in the last 30 years; others of note are Bin 58 of 1961, Bins 61, 62, 63 and 64 of 1963; and Bin 7 of 1967. Penfolds recently released its first Chardonnay (from 1982), and the principal white wine is Bin 202 Traminer Riesling. Koonunga Hill Dry Red has, since 1976, established itself as one of the best value-for-money red wines in the lower half of the market, while Dalwood Hermitage and Penfolds Claret are the two cheapest bottled wines, the latter of similar quality to that which appears in the 2-litre flagons and 4-litre casks.

Distribution:
National through retailers at all levels.

Prices:
As one would expect, an enormous range from a recommended retail of a little over $2 to more than $30 for Grange. Heavy discounting makes a mockery of many of the recommended retail prices, although not so much that of Grange.

Overall Quality:
Grange and Bin 707 exceptional; other reds usually very good, with some variability in the latter part of the 1970s.

Vintage Rating 1982–85:
'82, '84, '83, '85.

Outstanding Prior Vintages:
'71, '73, '76, '80.

Tasting Notes:

1983 KOONUNGA HILL [16.8] *Colour:* medium red-purple. *Bouquet:* very well-balanced, with sweet, berry fruit set against attractive, vanillan American oak. *Palate:* a surprisingly elegant wine, far lighter in style than preceding vintages, with firm berry-cabernet flavours, although the typical Koonunga tannin (from the pressings component) is very much in evidence on the mid- and back-palate. Drink '86–'91.

1982 CHARDONNAY [16.8] *Colour:* full yellow, still with a few touches of green. *Bouquet:* soft and full, with good fruit/oak balance; some complexity to white burgundy characters but varietal aroma now diminished. *Palate:* full, soft and ripe; well-balanced mid-palate fruit, but drying out slightly on the finish and varietal character on the wane. Drink '85–'86.

1982 KALIMNA SHIRAZ BIN 28 [17] *Colour:* very good purple-red of medium depth. *Bouquet:* clean and smooth, with well-balanced fruit and oak, and a touch of bottle-developed tobacco aroma. *Palate:* a quite complex and elegant wine, with some cigar box flavours, good mid-palate fruit and gentle tannin on the finish. Continues the recent return to form of the Penfolds reds. Drink '86–'92.

1981 ST HENRI [15.8] *Colour:* medium to full red-purple. *Bouquet:* a very deep, strong and complex aroma with a hint of sulphide/mercaptan. *Palate:* old-fashioned and robust, with those typical, slightly abrasive, green stalky characters which are part and parcel of the St Henri style, and which I personally do not much like. Drink '86–'90.

1978 GRANGE HERMITAGE [18.4] *Colour:* deep, strong red with no sign of amber yet developing. *Bouquet:* immensely rich and deep fruit, matched by sweet American oak. *Palate:* a massive wine, lifted (and helped) by a touch of the volatility which is deliberately buried into the wine; some astringency on the back-palate still to soften, but a very worthy member of a proud line. Drink '89–'98.

PETER LEHMANN

pp. 334–5

Location:
Off Para Road, Tanunda, 5352;
1.5 km north-west of Tanunda.
(085) 63 2500.

Winemaker:
Peter Lehmann.

1985 Production:
7,750,000 litres.

Principal Wines:
Much of the very large production is made either under contract or for on-sale in bulk to other wine companies. An ever-increasing portion is bottled under the Peter Lehmann and Masterson labels for retail distribution; wines are released under varietal labels, sometimes additionally identified by district, and include Rhine Riesling, Dry Semillon, Chenin Blanc, Late Harvest Traminer, Semillon Sauternes, Pinot Noir, Shiraz and Cabernet Sauvignon (all under the Peter Lehmann label). Under the Masterson label the wines are Dry Chablis, Classic Moselle, Dry Red and Phar Lap Collectors Tawny Port. Peter Lehmann AD2001 Vintage Port (from 1980) completes the range.

Distribution:
Extensive retail distribution through wholesale agents Australian Liquor Marketers in all states except South Australia and Western Australia, where distribution handled by P. F. Caon & Co. Cellar-door sales 8.30 a.m. to 5 p.m. Monday to Friday (tastings only by appointment). A mailing list also operates, offering the full normal range, together with wines exclusive to the list and to cellar-door sales. For enquiries write to PO Box 315, Tanunda, SA, 5352.

Prices:
$5.75 to $9.35 recommended retail.

Overall Quality:
Reliably very good.

Vintage Rating 1982–85:
White: '82, '85, '84, '83.
Red: '82, '85, '84, '83.

Outstanding Prior Vintages:
'80.

Tasting Notes:

1985 CHENIN BLANC [16.2] *Colour:* light green-yellow. *Bouquet:* strong and full, almost aggressive, fruit aromas with a trace of Loire Valley chalky/cheesy character. *Palate:* a strongly flavoured and structured wine with a touch of lemony/green astringency. Drink '86–'87.

1984 BAROSSA VALLEY RHINE RIESLING [17] *Colour:* medium to full yellow. *Bouquet:* classic, dry, toasty Australian rhine riesling, unmodified either by yeast or botrytis. *Palate:* a wine with backbone, firm and flavoursome, with good acid on the finish. A totally traditional style, and none the worse for that. Drink '85–'88.

1982 SEMILLON SAUTERNES [18.4] *Colour:* deep golden-yellow. *Bouquet:* extremely pungent, complex and weighty, with very marked volatility which one either accepts or rejects. *Palate:* magnificently rich, butter/butterscotch, viscous flavours; the volatile lift prevents the wine from cloying. Getting close to its peak. Drink '85–'88.

1982 CABERNET SAUVIGNON [17] *Colour:* medium red-purple. *Bouquet:* fragrant, secondary bottle-developed aromas, with a touch of cedary oak and light, sweet fruit. *Palate:* a very well-made, highly commercial wine, with most attractive light to medium sweet berry flavours intermingling with vanillan American oak. Is picking up character as it ages. Drink '86–'89.

1981 SHIRAZ [17] *Colour:* medium red. *Bouquet:* very smooth and clean, with sweet American oak integrated with moderately ripe fruit. *Palate:* a very smooth, gently sweet wine, with good fruit flavours, and, like the cabernet sauvignon, starting to show some attractive bottle-developed flavours. Drink '85–'88.

1980 BIN AD 2001 VINTAGE PORT [16.8] *Colour:* full red-purple. *Bouquet:* a solid, big and potent aroma with slightly simple but clean spirit. *Palate:* very full, with deep, sweet berry flavours followed by clean spirit on the finish. A little one-dimensional, but will undoubtedly live, although it will be rather tired by 2001. Drink '86–'90.

THE REDGUM VINEYARD

pp. 335–6

Location:
Hoffnungsthal Road, Lyndoch, 5351; cellar-door sales 1 km north of Lyndoch on Barossa Valley highway.
(085) 244511.

Winemaker:
Trevor Jones.

1985 Production:
23,000 cases.

Principal Wines:
Until 1983 the Redgum Vineyard was known as Karrawirra, and the wines marketed under that label. The wines are now marketed under two labels: Premium Selection Wines under the Kies Family Selection Label, comprising Rhine Riesling, Sauvignon Blanc, Rhine Riesling Auslese and Shiraz Cabernet. The remainder are released under the Redgum Vineyard Label, comprising White Barossa, Semillon Blanc de Blanc, Classic Dry White, Fumé Blanc, Frontignan Spatlese, Chablis, Rhine Riesling, Chardonnay, Spring Cabernet, Cabernet Shiraz, Cabernet Sauvignon, Sparkling Burgundy and Kavel Tawny Port.

Distribution:
Reasonably extensive retail distribution through wholesale agents in all states except New South Wales where distributed direct. Cellar-door sales 9 a.m. to 5 p.m. Monday to Friday and 10 a.m. to 5 p.m. weekends and public holidays. Mailing list available; enquiries to PO Box 4, Lyndoch, 5351.

Prices:
$5.33 to $9.60 recommended retail.

Overall Quality:
Somewhat variable; adequate to very good; current releases disappointing.

Vintage Rating 1982–85:
White: '84, '85, '82, '83.
Red: '85, '84, '82, '83.

Outstanding Prior Vintages:
'76, '80.

Tasting Notes:

1984 CLASSIC DRY WHITE [12] *Colour:* distinct browning. *Bouquet:* rather common and coarse, with heavy, undistinguished fruit. *Palate:* A very ordinary wine which ought not to be in a bottle, and only perhaps in a cask.

KIES SAUVIGNON BLANC FUME STYLE [14.6] *Colour:* medium yellow with a touch of straw. *Bouquet:* dominated by intrusive volatile lift. *Palate:* much better than bouquet promises; marked oak influence, with lemon and spice flavours intermingling; volatility apparent but not unacceptable; a high-flavoured wine. Drink '85–'86.

1984 REDGUM FRONTIGNAN SPATLESE [16.6] *Colour:* medium yellow-green. *Bouquet:* very clean, with crystal-clear varietal grapy aroma. *Palate:* full-flavoured, very clean wine, tingling with fresh grape flavours; good balance, and the residual sugar does not cloy. Drink '86.

KIES LYNDOCH HILLS RHINE RIESLING AUSLESE [17] *Colour:* glowing yellow-green. *Bouquet:* of medium richness, with distinct lime aromas and some toasty development. *Palate:* a very well-made wine; strong rhine riesling mid-palate flavours, followed by crisp acid which gives length and provides a cleansing finish. Drink '85–'88.

1979 KIES LYNDOCH HILLS SHIRAZ CABERNET [15.4] *Colour:* medium to full red. *Bouquet:* old-style wine, with medium ripe fruit with some gravelly/earthy aromas, but smooth overall. *Palate:* ripe, soft and chocolatey fruit, with just a fraction of "sweaty saddle" bottle-developed character. Drink '85–'87.

1981 REDGUM BAROSSA CABERNET SAUVIGNON [15.4] *Colour:* medium red. *Bouquet:* rather astringent, with leathery/pencil shavings aromas. *Palate:* rather better, but fair mid-palate fruit is followed by a rather leathery, astringent finish. Drink '86–'87.

ROCKFORD

p. 336

Location:
Krondorf Road, Tanunda, 5352;
3 km south of Tanunda.
(085) 63 2720.

Winemaker:
Robert O'Callaghan.

1985 Production:
2700 cases.

Principal Wines:

A range of varietal wines made from grapes purchased throughout many of South Australia's wine regions including the Eden Valley, the Adelaide Plains, the Barossa Valley, and the Southern Vales. Wines include Eden Valley Rhine Riesling, Adelaide Plains Sauvignon Blanc, Spatlese White Frontignac, Rhine Riesling Botrytis Cinerea, Alicante Bouchet, Shiraz Cabernet, Cabernet Sauvignon, Muscat of Alexandria, Tawny Port and Shiraz Vintage Port.

Distribution:
Exclusively cellar-door sales and mailing lists; cellar-door sales 11 a.m. to 5.30 p.m. 7 days. Mailing-list enquiries to PO Box 142, Tanunda, SA, 5352.

Prices:
$4.90 to $7.70 cellar door.

Overall Quality:
Good.

Vintage Rating 1982–85:
Not relevant because of varied sources of material.

Tasting Notes:

1985 SAUVIGNON BLANC [17.8] *Colour:* medium to full yellow-green. *Bouquet:* complex smoky/charred oak together with clean, crisp fruit. *Palate:* a fresh, surprisingly delicate wine, yet with considerable intensity, and carrying the oak very well; a true chablis style. Drink '87–'89.

1985 SPATLESE WHITE FRONTIGNAC [17] *Colour:* pale straw-green. *Bouquet:* highly aromatic, with pronounced, sweet, tropical fruit aromas and some of the distinctive grapy frontignac aromas. *Palate:* a very clean, gently sweet wine with pristine frontignac grape flavours, balanced by crisp acid on the finish. Drink '86.

1985 ALICANTE BOUCHET [16.6] *Colour:* bright, light to medium red-purple. *Bouquet:* some sweet berry aromas, but not particularly aromatic. *Palate:* fresh and crisp, with some sweet, red cherry flavours; an attractive, light, fresh red in Beaujolais style. Drink '85–'86.

ROSEWORTHY

pp. 336–7

Location:
Roseworthy Agricultural College, Roseworthy, 5371; 4 km from town and 9 km north-west of Gawler. (085) 24 8057.

Winemaker:
Jeff Anderson.

1985 Production:
1000 cases.

Principal Wines:

A limited range of white and red varietal table wines and fortified wines made from diverse sources. Wines include Eden Valley Chardonnay, Sauvignon Blanc, Eden Valley Rhine Riesling, Colombard, Rkaziteli, Chablis, Late Picked Frontignac, Wood Matured Semillon, Pinot Noir Champagne, Shiraz Cabernet Maceration Carbonique, Adelaide Hills Shiraz, Vintage Port, Tawny Port, Fino Sherry, Liqueur Frontignac and Old Liqueur Brandy.

Distribution:
Limited fine wine retail distribution through wholesale distributors in each state; cellar-door sales 10 a.m. to 4.30 p.m. Monday to Friday. No mailing list.

Prices:
$3.50 to $6.95 cellar door; recommended retail higher. Old Liqueur Brandy $14.50.

Overall Quality:
Very good, with occasional exceptional wines.

Vintage Rating 1982–85:
White: '83, '85, '82, '84.
Red: '84, '82, '85, '83.

Outstanding Prior Vintages:
'79 (reds); '81 (whites).

Tasting Notes:

1984 EDEN VALLEY RHINE RIESLING [18] *Colour:* medium yellow-green. *Bouquet:* very full and rich lime/camphor bottle-developed aromas. *Palate:* a strongly flavoured wine, with rich lime fruit on the mid-palate and a firm, almost hard, finish. Very clear regional character throughout the wine. Drink '85–'88.

1983 EDEN VALLEY CHARDONNAY [18.4] *Colour:* medium to full yellow. *Bouquet:* clear and full varietal aromas in the grapefruit/honey spectrum; excellent overall richness and balance. *Palate:* fine and lively grapefruit/melon flavours, with a long, lingering finish. A wine of considerable finesse and elegance. Drink '85–'87.

1983 ADELAIDE HILLS SHIRAZ [16.8] *Colour:* bright medium red-purple. *Bouquet:* very clean and quite complex, with cherry/berry flavours set against lemony oak. *Palate:* powdery, soft tannin appears early and lasts throughout the palate; some soft, berry flavours on the mid-palate; not quite in the class of the earlier vintages of this wine. Drink '86–'89.

ST HALLETT'S

pp. 337–8

Location:
St Hallett's Road, Tanunda, 5352;
4 km south of township.
(085) 63 2319.

Winemaker:
Larry Keetch.

1985 Production:
500 tonnes (the equivalent of 35,000 cases).

Principal Wines:
A fairly traditional range of white and red table wines and fortified wines including Rhine Riesling, Semillon White Burgundy, Chablis, Fumé Blanc, Sauterne Mount Kitchener Shiraz Cabernet Malbec, Carl Special Shiraz Cabernet Malbec and Shiraz Cabernet. Fortified wines include a range of tawny and vintage ports, many graced with various sporting figures and/or horses.

Distribution:
Wholesale distributors in South Australia, Victoria, New South Wales and Queensland provide retail distribution. Substantial cellar-door sales 8.30 a.m. to 5 p.m. Monday to Friday and 10 a.m. to 5 p.m. weekends. Mailing-list enquiries to PO Box 120, Tanunda, SA, 5352.

Prices:
Table wines $4.10 to $9.50 cellar door; fortified wines $8.60 to $11 cellar door.

Overall Quality:
Good; occasional very good wines.

Vintage Rating 1982–85:
White: '85, '84, '82, '83.
Red: '82, '84, '85, '83.

Outstanding Prior Vintages:
'80.

Tasting Notes:

1985 CHABLIS [16.6] *Colour:* pale yellow-green. *Bouquet:* perfumed, full and rich tropical fruit aromas; clean and well-made. *Palate:* similar to the bouquet; full, soft, rich fruit with abundant flavour, and absolutely nothing whatsoever to do with chablis. Drink '86–'87.

NV MT KITCHENER TOKAY RIESLING [15.4] *Colour:* medium yellow, showing some development. *Bouquet:* rather heavy and full, with obvious bottle age, and just a fraction coarse. *Palate:* abundant pastille, fruit flavour on the mid-palate, but finishes rather heavily. Drink '85.

1982 OLD BLOCK SHIRAZ [18] *Colour:* deep red. *Bouquet:* round and soft, with sweet, warm-fruit aromas and some bottle-developed complexity. *Palate:* smooth, showing most attractive bottle development and quite surprising elegance; a touch of cigar-box oak and quite intense fruit flavours, with a long finish. A real surprise. Drink '85–'89.

1981 FRANGOS TROPHY VINTAGE PORT [17.4] *Colour:* dense red. *Bouquet:* ripe, soft and gently complex, with good spirit and considerable development showing. *Palate:* a very developed wine, more in a Late Bottled Vintage style, and looking as if it may almost end up having more to do with a tawny than a vintage port, with some rich caramel flavours evident. A winner of three gold medals and the Frangos Trophy. Drink '85–'88.

SALTRAM WINERY

pp. 338–9

Location:
Angaston Road, Angaston, 5353;
1 km west of township.
(085) 64 2200.

Winemaker:
Mark Turnbull.

1985 Production:
Not available for publication, but very substantial.

Principal Wines:

A wide range of bottled wines and fortified wines is marketed under a number of label series. The highest quality wines are marketed under the Pinnacle Label, comprising Rhine Riesling, Sauvignon Blanc, Gewurztraminer, Auslese Rhine Riesling, Sauternes, Eden Valley Shiraz, 1951 Vintage Tawny Port and 1952 Old Liqueur Muscat. Mamre Brook Chardonnay and Mamre Brook Claret are of similar quality and priced equivalently. Then follows a range of varietal whites and reds including Chablis, Chardonnay, White Burgundy, Rhine Riesling Spatlese, Traminer Riesling, Fumé Blanc, Sauvignon Blanc, Semillon Hermitage, Cabernet Sauvignon, Selected Vintage Claret, Metala Claret and Hazelwood Claret. The fortified wines also include Mr Pickwick Port, of similar age and complexity to the Pinnacle Series.

Distribution:
National retail through Seagram Wines and Spirits. Cellar-door sales 9 a.m. to 5 p.m. Monday to Friday and noon to 5 p.m. weekends. Mailing list/mail orders available; enquiries to PO Box 321, Angaston, SA, 5353.

Prices:
Vary widely according to quality and style, from a recommended retail of around $5 to over $30; discounting is perennial, and at times halves recommended retail prices.

Overall Quality:
Varies greatly according to the standing of the wine in the Saltram hierarchy. Pinnacle Series usually very good and occasionally exceptional; Mamre Brook Chardonnay very good; others vary from adequate to good.

Vintage Rating 1982–85:
'84, '85, '82, '83.

Outstanding Prior Vintages:
'80.

Tasting Notes:

1982 PINNACLE GEWURTZTRAMINER [18] *Colour:* glowing yellow-green. *Bouquet:* full rich and luscious varietal aroma, fruity rather than spicy. *Palate:* an opulently rich and soft wine, with an almost chewy texture and none of the tannic hardness which often appears in traminer. If varietal character is not particularly marked, many would say the wine is all the better for that. Drink '85–'86.

1982 PINNACLE COONAWARRA AUSLESE RHINE RIESLING [17.2] *Colour:* medium yellow. *Bouquet:* very complex, with some aged kerosene character starting to evelop, but still surprisingly firm. *Palate:* much more ife and fruit than the bouquet suggests; rich, lime, botrytis fruit flavours on the mid-palate, and a long, clean, gently luscious finish. Drink '85–'87.

1982 SALTRAM CABERNET SAUVIGNON [15.2] *Colour:* strong red-purple. *Bouquet:* rather closed and slightly dull, lacking fruit; a suspicion of subliminal mercaptan. *Palate:* smooth, of fair weight, but again rather dull, and again the suspicion that a trace of mercaptan may be holding the wine back. Drink '86–'88.

1951 PINNACLE SHOW TAWNY PORT [18.4] *Colour:* pale to medium mahogany, bright and clear. *Bouquet:* exceptionally complex; aged, fine and lingering fruit and spirit aromas; quite magnificent. *Palate:* exceedingly complex and full; some wood-aged volatile lift; a nice touch of acid on the finish lengthens the flavour. Richly deserves its 14 gold and 14 silver medals. Drink now or forever.

1951 PINNACLE AMONTILLADO SHERRY [18] *Colour:* deep straw-brown. *Bouquet:* full, softly complex rancio; smooth and relatively soft spirit. *Palate:* lovely, nutty flavour; marvellously rich, yet not sweet; very fine old Amontillado. Drink now.

1952 PINNACLE OLD LIQUEUR MUSCAT [18.2] *Colour:* brilliant orange-mahogany. *Bouquet:* very soft and light, almost fresh, with harmonious fruit/spirit balance. *Palate:* similarly smooth and harmonious, but much lighter and softer than the muscats of north-eastern Victoria. Very good within its own particular terms of reference. Drink now.

SEPPELT

pp. 339–45

Location:
Seppeltsfield via Tanunda, 5352;
7 km north-east of Tanunda.
(085) 62 8028.

Winemakers:
James Godfrey and Nigel Dolan.

1985 Production:
600 tonnes Barossa Valley; 1100 tonnes Qualco.

Principal Wines:
Seppeltsfield Winery produces Seppelt's famed tawny ports; Para, Old Tawny and Mount Rufus. Each year a 100-year-old vintage Para Port is released in tiny quantities, selling for over $1500 per bottle. Bin DP90 Tawny Port is legendary for its quality and scarcity, while Seppelt's equally distinguished range of sherries (Flor Fino Bins DP44 and DP117, Amontillado Bins DP96 and DP116 and Oloroso Bin DP20) are also matured at Seppeltsfield. Chateau Tanunda ferments the base wines for sherries, and ferments and matures all of the South Australian-based red wine drawn from the Barossa Valley, Eden Valley, Southern Vales, Langhorne Creek, River Murray and Keppoch areas. Seppelt has an exceedingly complex labelling system, with a large number of quality grades and series of wines, complicated by a penchant for constantly changing the design of the labels. The most consistently available wines in the mid-market come out under the Reserve Bin range of Rhine Riesling, Spatlese Rhine Riesling, Chardonnay, Pinot Noir, Hermitage and Cabernet Sauvignon (together with a few others which come and go). An up-to-date summary of table wines is a near impossibility.

Prices:
Basically fall for table wine in the $5 to $7 recommended retail range; discounting significantly reduces these, but not to the extent of some of the major wine companies.

Overall Quality:
Consistently good, if not very good. Seppelt simply does not release poor wines. Fortified wines consistently exceptional.

Vintage Rating 1982–85:
White: '84, '82, '85, '83.
Red: '82, '84, '85, '83.

Tasting Notes:

1984 FUME BLANC [16.2] *Colour:* glowing yellow-green. *Bouquet:* very strong oak aroma, slightly rough, and as yet to integrate satisfactorily. *Palate:* some gently grassy fruit, well-hidden by as yet aggressive oak, but the wine will benefit from bottle age. Drink '86–'88.

1984 CHARDONNAY [18] *Colour:* bright yellow-green. *Bouquet:* perfectly balanced and integrated fruit and oak, so smooth that the wine almost appears bland. *Palate:* a complete change of pace; an immensely rich and viscous, mouth-filling wine, with an alcohol-derived illusion of mid-palate sweetness; some grapefruit flavour; excellent acid on a long, clean finish. Drink '85–'88.

1983 CHARDONNAY/SAUVIGNON BLANC [17.8] *Colour:* outstanding deep, glowing green-yellow. *Bouquet:* deep and full fruit, with chardonnay dominant but just a hint of underlying grassiness. *Palate:* similarly impressive depth of fruit flavour; a very well-balanced wine, with a fresh, lively finish; oak perfectly handled throughout. Drink '85–'88.

DP117 SHOW FINO FLOR SHERRY [18.8] *Colour:* yellow-bronze. *Bouquet:* fine; very clean rancio certainly, a background hint of nuttiness, and spirit smooth and unassertive throughout. *Palate:* gently nutty fore-palate flavours, then a firm and authoritatively cleansing finish. Best served slightly chilled. A multi-trophy and gold medal winner both in Australia and overseas.

DP90 TAWNY PORT [19.2] *Colour:* light tawny-gold. *Bouquet:* immensely complex, showing effects of prolonged wood ageing; a touch of spicy fruit and marked rancio lift. *Palate:* exceptionally complex both in terms of flavour and structure, particularly on the mid-palate, which is almost impossible to describe, so complex is it; in the manner of all great tawny ports, finishes crisp and almost dry, with good acid.

TOLLANA

pp. 345–7

Location:
Tanunda Road, off Sturt Highway, Nuriootpa, 5355; 1 km south of township.
(085) 62 1433.

Winemaker:
Pat Tocaciu.

1985 Production:
Not for publication, but estimated at over 10,000 tonnes.

Principal Wines:

A recent reappraisal of wines (and labels) has led to Tollana diversifying grape sources and no longer relying solely on its excellent Woodbury Vineyard in the High Eden Hills. Woodbury continues to supply Eden Valley Rhine Riesling and Cabernet Sauvignon, but Tollana Chardonnay comes from McLaren Vale and Tollana Merlot from unnamed sources. Full range also includes Chablis, Riesling Beerenauslese, White Frontignan Bin TW5 19, Chenin Blanc, Cabernet Sauvignon Bin TR 222, Shiraz Cabernet Bin TR 16 and Shiraz Cabernet. Some excellent non-vintage champagne and excellent non-vintage Brut Champagne (Méthode Champenoise) wines have also been released in recent years.

Distribution:
National through United Distillers Pty Ltd into retail shops at all levels. Curiously, no attempts whatsoever are made on the public relations front, and the wines are far less well known than they deserve to be.

Prices:
Theoretical retail subject to severe and totally unmerited discounting with trophy-winning '82 Rhine Riesling selling for $2.99 mid-1985.

Overall Quality:
Very good.

Vintage Rating 1982–85:
White: '82, '85, '84, '83.
Red: '82, '84, '85, '83.

Outstanding Prior Vintages:
'76 (white and red); '79 (white).

Tasting Notes:

1984 CHABLIS [15.6] *Colour:* pale green-yellow. *Bouquet:* soft; tropical fruit salad spread on toast; an altogether peculiar definition of chablis. *Palate:* of medium weight, with a slight flavour dip on the mid- to back-palate; quite well balanced and not heavy. Drink '85–'86.

1984 McLAREN VALE CHARDONNAY [17.6] *Colour:* medium to full yellow-green. *Bouquet:* very rich fruit aroma with strong spicy/dusty oak. *Palate:* a very full-flavoured chardonnay in the peachy/creamy mould which has developed with almost frightening rapidity. Drink '85–'86.

1983 EDEN VALLEY RHINE RIESLING [16.8] *Colour:* medium yellow. *Bouquet:* developed and rich to the point of almost being heavy; strongly accented regional lime aromas. *Palate:* an immensely flavoured but very soft wine, singularly advanced and at odds with the usual track record of these wines as able to benefit from prolonged cellaring. No doubt a function of the drought year. Drink '85–'86.

1983 MERLOT [16.6] *Colour:* medium red-purple. *Bouquet:* fairly soft and ripe fruit, graced by leather/cedar aromas, partly from oak. *Palate:* of medium weight; again some cedar/leather flavours apparent; a very interesting although not immediately recognisable varietal character; soft tannin finish. Drink '86–'87.

1983 BEERENAUSLESE [18] *Colour:* full green-yellow. *Bouquet:* deep and concentrated, with straw/malt/honey aromas and almost none of the volatile lift one expects in this style. *Palate:* a marvellously concentrated wine, with a long, lingering palate with lime flavours; excellent acid balance adds zest and life, and promises extended cellaring potential. Varieties not stated. Drink '86–'92.

1982 EDEN VALLEY RHINE RIESLING [18.4] *Colour:* medium to full yellow-green. *Bouquet:* very full, developed toasty/lime aromas in archetypal Eden Valley style. *Palate:* richly flavoured, perfectly balanced wine, with soft but intense lime-fruit; now at its peak. (Trophy Winner Melbourne Show 1985.) Drink '85–'87.

VERITAS

p. 347

Location:
94 Langmeil Road, Tanunda, 5352;
3 km north of township.
(085) 63 2330.

Winemaker:
Rolf Binder.

1985 Production:
Approximately 10,000 cases.

Principal Wines:
A kaleidoscopic range of wines, table, fortified and flavoured, many with a strong Hungarian influence. Labels include White Burgundy, Crouchen Colombard, Leankyia, Rhine Riesling, Tramino, Chri-ro Late Picked Rhine Riesling, Carignan Shiraz, Shiraz Cabernet Sauvignon, Bikaver Bull's Blood, and a range of Ports, Vermouths, Sherries and even Oompah Pah Port.

Distribution:
Exclusively cellar-door sales and mailing list. Cellar-door sales 9 a.m. to 5 p.m. Monday to Friday and 11 a.m. to 5 p.m. weekends and public holidays. Mailing-list enquiries to PO Box 126, Tanunda, SA, 5352.

Prices:
$3 to $7 cellar door.

Overall Quality:
Good.

Vintage Rating 1982–85:
White: '84, '85, '82, '83.
Red: '82, '84, '85, '83.

Outstanding Prior Vintages:
'80.

Tasting Notes:

1985 RHINE RIESLING [16.4] *Colour:* pale straw-green. *Bouquet:* very clean, well-made, fruity wine with no after-effects of fermentation. *Palate:* of light to medium weight; very clean, fresh and flavoursome; residual sugar well-handled in a wine of good overall balance. Drink '86–'87.

1985 TRAMINO [16.2] *Colour:* pale, with a faint, straw tinge. *Bouquet:* clean and gentle, with fairly neutral fruit. *Palate:* a very pleasant, well-balanced wine, with some interesting lychee fruit flavours; once again residual sugar very well handled; a well-made wine from an unusual blend of verdelho, traminer and rhine riesling. Drink '86–'87.

1984 CHRI-RO ESTATE LATE PICKED RHINE RIESLING [17] *Colour:* medium to full yellow. *Bouquet:* rich and clean, with developed butterscotch lime aromas of considerable depth. *Palate:* rich, flavoursome and smooth; very well-made, with no phenolic hardness, although it has developed very quickly. Drink '85–'86.

1982 BIKAVER BULL'S BLOOD BIN 17 [15.6] *Colour:* red-purple of medium depth. *Bouquet:* soft, gently powdery sweet fruit and a suspicion of lactic character. *Palate:* peculiarly powdery texture which comes from prolonged old oak storage; sweet berry flavours underneath; again in a European mould. Drink '85–'87.

1978 SPECIAL TAWNY PORT [16.6] *Colour:* tawny brown. *Bouquet:* rich, raisined liqueur style, seemingly with a contribution from muscadelle or some other white grape. *Palate:* a rich, complex wine, half-way between a tokay and a vintage port; seems to have been left in the cask a fraction too long, but crammed full of flavour. Drink now.

WARD'S GATEWAY CELLARS

p. 347

Location:
Lyndoch, 5351; between Sandy Creek and Lyndoch. (085) 24 4138.

Winemaker:
Ray Ward.

1985 Production:
Estimated approximately 3700 cases.

Principal Wines:
Limited range of traditional Barossa Valley table and fortified wine styles.

Distribution:
Exclusively cellar-door sales (and mail order). Cellar-door sales 9 a.m. to 5.30 p.m. Monday to Sunday.

Overall Quality:
Adequate, and occasionally good.

WILSFORD

p. 348

Location:
Gomersal Road, Lyndoch, 5351;
on outskirts of township.
(085) 24 4019.

Winemaker:
Noel Burge.

1985 Production:
Not stated, but relatively substantial for a family winery.

Principal Wines:
A full range of white and red table wines, fortified wines (a specialty of the winery), flavoured wines and sparkling wines are produced.

Distribution:
Exclusively cellar-door sales and by mail order. Cellar-door sales 8 a.m. to 5 p.m. 7 days. Mail-order enquiries to PO Lyndoch, SA, 5351.

Prices:
Very low.

Overall Quality:
Adequate.

YALUMBA

pp. 348–54

Location:
Eden Valley Road, Angaston, 5353;
3 km south of township.
(085) 64 2423.

Winemakers:
Described by Yalumba as "the Yalumba Team", headed by Peter Wall.

1985 Production:
Approximately 20,000 tons.

Principal Wines:
The wines of S. Smith & Son Pty Ltd are henceforth to be marketed under four distinct labels. The first is the traditional Yalumba label, covering a range of wines and styles made from grapes not necessarily estate-grown. Premium wines include Signature Reserve Dry Red, Brut de Brut Vintage Champagne and Galway Pipe Tawny Port; others include Directors Special Tawny Port, non-vintage Angas Brut Champagne, Carte d'Or Rhine Riesling and Galway Shiraz Cabernet. Next are the Hill-Smith Estate wines made from estate-grown grapes on vineyards owned by members of the family and including Shiraz, Riesling, Wood Matured Semillon and Cabernet Sauvignon; the wines are aimed particularly at the export market. The remaining two labels are Pewsey Vale (principally Rhine Riesling, Botrytis Affected Rhine Riesling and Cabernet Sauvignon), and Heggies Vineyard, destined to produce Rhine Riesling (both dry and botrytis-affected), Chardonnay, Pinot Noir, Cabernet Sauvignon and Sauvignon Blanc.

Distribution:
National retail at all levels, principally through own offices in each of the eastern states.

Prices:
$5.50 to $10.50; some discounting evident, intermittently at distressing levels.

Overall Quality:
Consistently very good; some wines (particularly Heggies) exceptional.

Vintage Rating 1982–85:
White: '84, '82, '85, '83.
Red: '85, '84, '83, '82.

Outstanding Prior Vintages:
White: '65, '76.
Red: '76.

Tasting Notes:

1985 CABERNET SAUVIGNON LDR [18] *Colour:* crystal bright light to medium red-purple. *Bouquet:* very fresh, beautifully modulated cabernet varietal aroma, neither green nor sharp, yet fairy-light. *Palate:* vibrantly fresh, cherry-flavoured wine; by far the best of the light reds from 1985 across Australia; all fruit, and no tannin. Drink '85–'86.

1984 CARTE D'OR RHINE RIESLING [17.4] *Colour:* brilliant yellow-green of medium depth. *Bouquet:* very clean, with strongly accented varietal rhine riesling aroma and just a touch of toastiness. *Palate:* smooth and clean fruit of medium weight on the mid-palate, with a varietal flavour lift on the finish. A very high-quality commercial wine in which the residual sugar has been judged to perfection. Drink '85–'87.

1983 HILL SMITH ESTATE WOOD MATURED SEMILLON [17] *Colour:* full yellow-green, with no brown or straw tints from oak. *Bouquet:* a very rich aroma with marked oak influence; the oak has nonetheless been very well-handled and is in harmony with the fruit. *Palate:* once again lemony oak plays a major role in the flavour, but there is adquate fruit to provide structure and balance. Drink '85–'88.

1983 HILL SMITH ESTATE AUTUMN HARVEST BOTRYTIS AFFECTED SEMILLON [18.4] *Colour:* full yellow-gold. *Bouquet:* very rich and complex; attractive touch of volatile lift in best sauternes style; traces of honey and butter. *Palate:* magnificently rich and intense; extremely luscious; first-class Australian sweet white wine. Drink '85–'92.

1978 SIGNATURE SERIES COLIN HAYES BLEND [17.4] *Colour:* strong red of medium to full depth. *Bouquet:* a very clean, solid wine with abundant fruit to match the oak. *Palate:* a ripe style with considerable complexity, and the same excellent fruit/oak balance evident in the bouquet; gentle tannin rounds off the finish. Drink '85–'89.

Clare Valley

1985 Vintage

The Clare Valley conformed closely to the rest of South Australia, abundant winter and spring rainfall ensuring perfect flowering and the setting of a heavy crop. A cool and abnormally dry summer (December–February rainfall was less than half that of normal) substantially delayed ripening, and in the end led to wines with far lower than normal alcohol.

Not surprisingly, unirrigated vineyards suffered significantly from stress, and yields were significantly reduced. Despite this, the overall yield for the region was well above average, and came as a great surprise to the district's vignerons. The vintage was the latest on record, extending until the third week of May.

Despite the ripening problems and low alcohol, the wines have abundant flavour. It was a particularly successful year for white wines, with rhine riesling—naturally enough—at the fore. A majority of the vignerons of the region rate it as their best vintage in the past four years; however, others still think 1984 will produce greater wines in the long term.

Certainly the wines look as if they will develop fairly quickly, the whites offering much to enjoy in the latter part of 1986 and 1987. The red wines, too, are of very high quality, cabernet sauvignon and shiraz making richly complex wines of good colour and depth.

The Changes

In the Polish Hill River Valley, Paulett's Winery was operational for the 1985 vintage, as was the new winery of Wilson's Polish Hill.

The other major development in the year was Stanley's decision to sell a large part of its older and less productive vineyards. A notably unsuccessful auction was held, but a number of the vineyards subsequently changed hands by private treaty, one of the choicest parcels going to Mitchells.

Robert Crabtree of Watervale Cellars has sold the marvellous old building on the low side of the road, and moved to an equally lovely house on top of the hill on the opposite side, immediately above the town of Watervale.

1985 also witnessed the first, and tremendously successful, wine and food weekend in the Clare Valley. This is to become a regular feature of the district, adding very substantially to the already very great tourist appeal. With its natural beauty, and rich heritage of stone buildings, the Clare Valley can fairly claim to be South Australia's most attractive region for winelovers to visit.

ENTERPRISE WINES

pp. 365–7

Location:
2 Pioneer Avenue, Clare, 5453;
at northern end of town.
(088) 42 2096.

Winemaker:
Tim Knappstein.

1985 Production:
11,000 cases Enterprise label; 7000 cases sold as clean skin; 54,000 litres sold in bulk.

Principal Wines:

Rhine Riesling, Fumé Blanc, Gewurztraminer, Cabernet Sauvignon, Cabernet Shiraz, Beerenauslese Rhine Riesling.

Distribution:
Available through most fine wine retailers in capital cities and in many of the better restaurants. Major eastern states distributor I. H. Baker. Significant cellar-door sales; open 9 a.m. to 5 p.m. Monday to Saturday.

Prices:
$6.95 to $8 cellar door.

Overall Quality:
Rhine Riesling and Cabernet Sauvignon exceptional; others very good.

Vintage Rating 1982–85:
White: '82, '85, '84, '83.
Red: '84, '85, '82 (all '83 sold in bulk).

Outstanding Prior Vintages:
White: '77, '80.
Red: '79, '80, '82.

Tasting Notes:

1984 RHINE RIESLING [17.2] *Colour:* bright green-yellow. *Bouquet:* classically refined, almost steely, with a clear refusal to rely upon aromatic yeasts to add richness. *Palate:* a fine, crisp and elegant wine, still rather closed up and, like the bouquet, needing further bottle age. Will be a lovely wine. Drink '87–'91.

1984 GEWURZTRAMINER [16.8] *Colour:* light yellow-green. *Bouquet:* quite full, with spicy, almost tannic, firmness coming from the traminer which is very evident. *Palate:* a strongly accented wine with pronounced traminer influence throughout and good weight to the middle palate; well-handled touch of residual sugar fleshes out the flavour. Drink '86–'88.

1984 FUME BLANC [16.6] *Colour:* pale green-yellow. *Bouquet:* very undeveloped; clean and fresh with oak held in restraint and gently grassy fruit aromas. *Palate:* light to medium bodied with grassy/tangy fruit and some smoky oak. Like the rhine riesling, still undeveloped mid-'85 and needing time. Drink '87–'89.

1984 CABERNET SAUVIGNON [19.2] *Colour:* excellent medium to full purple-red. *Bouquet:* fragrant, with sweet, berry aromas backed by sophisticated oak handling, with lovely balance and complexity; rich but not over-ripe. *Palate:* a wine which miraculously combines exceptional intensity of flavour with great elegance; a marvellous amalgam of berry and oak flavours, with great length and balance. (The wine contains 10% of merlot and 10% cabernet franc.) Drink '88–'96.

1984 CABERNET SHIRAZ [17.6] *Colour:* bright medium purple-red. *Bouquet:* complex, with some charred oak and considerable richness, yet overall, smooth. *Palate:* some sweet cherry flavours to fruit of medium to full weight; soft tannin and a long finish. Drink '87–'91.

FAREHAM ESTATE

p. 367

Location:
Main North Road, Leasingham, 5452;
3 km north of town.
(088) 49 2098.

Winemaker:
Peter Rumball.

1985 Production:
64,000 cases.

Principal Wines:
A select range of table wines including Blanc de Blancs, Gewurztraminer, Fumé Blanc, Rhine Riesling and Cabernet Sauvignon.

Distribution:
Principally cellar-door sales and mailing list. Cellar-door sales 9 a.m. to 5 p.m. Monday to Saturday. Mailing-list enquiries to PO Box 5, Watervale, 5452. Limited retail and restaurant distribution through Montgomery Smith Adelaide, and Classic Winebrokers, Melbourne.

Prices:
$5.25 to $7.90 cellar door.

Overall Quality:
Has been variable, but improving. Some good to very good.

Vintage Rating 1982–85:
White: '84, '85, '82, '83.
Red: '84, '85, '83 (no '82).

Outstanding Prior Vintages:
'77, '78.

Tasting Notes:

1985 SAUVIGNON BLANC A very clean wine, with some sweet fruit aromas but no varietal aggression; very good palate weight and richness, with considerable depth of soft sauvignon fruit. Appears to have excellent potential. Tasted from cask.

1984 WOOD MATURED SEMILLON [15.4] *Colour:* bright green-yellow. *Bouquet:* distinct lift of volatility, commercially acceptable but technically on or over the border line. *Palate:* again that volatile lift appears but the wine is rich, with nice back-palate feel and flavour and no doubt commercially acceptable. Drink '86.

1984 SAUVIGNON BLANC [17.6] *Colour:* excellent, light to medium green-yellow. *Bouquet:* full, with good fruit/oak integration; some grassy notes but overall rich and tempered. *Palate:* a most attractive wine, with slightly spicy oak, suggestive of limousin, in pleasant counterpoise to fruit; a soft, fruity (though not sweet) style in which the varietal composition is barely relevant. Drink '86–'88.

1983 CABERNET SAUVIGNON [17.8] *Colour:* medium full red-purple. *Bouquet:* rich, minty, sweet, berry fruit aromas bordering on jamminess. *Palate:* intense, sweet fragrant cassis/mint berry flavours. A voluptuous wine, and a great success in a hot and difficult vintage, albeit reflecting that vintage. Drink '87–'90.

HERITAGE WINES

p. 368

(Formerly Robertsons)

Location:
Wendouree Road, Clare, 5453;
5 km south of town.
(088) 42 3212.

Winemaker:
Stephen Hof.

1985 Production:
1700 cases.

Principal Wines:

Will ultimately be Clare Valley-based; in short term Barossa Valley wines made by or for Stephen Hof. Wines will include Clare Rhine Riesling, Wood Matured Semillon, Shiraz and Cabernet Shiraz.

Distribution:
Cellar door, mailing list and some retail/restaurant sales. Cellar-door sales 10 a.m. to 5 p.m. 7 days (advisable to telephone first on weekdays). Mailing-list enquiries PO Box 183, Clare.

Prices:
$4.80 to $6.25.

Overall Quality:
Good, on evidence of Barossa wines.

Tasting Notes:

1984 CLARE RHINE RIESLING [16.8] *Colour:* medium to full yellow-green. *Bouquet:* very rich and full, with soft lime aromas. *Palate:* a very big, full and broad wine with strong lime characters more reminiscent of the Eden Valley. Quite marked residual sugar (11 grams per litre) fills out palate further. Drink '85–'87.

JEFFREY GROSSET

pp. 367–8

Location:
King Street, Auburn, 5451;
0.5 km east of town.
(088) 49 2175.

Winemaker:
Jeffrey Grosset.

1985 Production:
3000 cases.

Principal Wines:

White and red table wines including Eyre Creek Rhine Riesling, Polish Hill Rhine Riesling, Watervale Rhine Riesling, Late Harvest Rhine Riesling, Chardonnay, and Cabernet Sauvignon Cabernet Franc.

Distribution:
Wines sold principally through cellar-door sales and mailing list. Cellar-door sales 10 a.m. to 5 p.m. Wednesday to Sunday while wine available. Telephone to check on availability. Mailing-list enquiries as above. Limited retail and restaurant distribution.

Prices:
$9.50 to $12 cellar door.

Overall Quality:
Very good and frequently exceptional.

Vintage Rating 1982–85:
White: '85, '82, '84, '83.
Red: '85, '84, '82, '83.

Outstanding Prior Vintages:
Not applicable; first vintage 1981.

Tasting Notes:

1984 POLISH HILL RHINE RIESLING [18] *Colour:* bright, light green-yellow. *Bouquet:* clean, highly aromatic fruit with a touch of tropical richness; very stylish. *Palate:* a slightly lighter and more elegant wine than the Watervale Rhine Riesling of the same year, but still having very considerable weight and, in particular, mid-palate richness. Drink '85–'88.

1984 WATERVALE RHINE RIESLING [18.2] *Colour:* bright green-yellow. *Bouquet:* lower aromatics than the Polish Hill, but still with a great depth to the fruit aroma. *Palate:* some tropical/lime fruit flavours running through a deep and long palate. A marvellously rich, yet not heavy, wine which had already gained considerable bottle developed complexity by mid 1985. Drink '85–'87.

1984 CABERNET SAUVIGNON/CABERNET FRANC [18.2] *Colour:* vibrant fuchsia. *Bouquet:* fragrant dancing fruit aromas, spotlessly clean and with wild cherry characters. *Palate:* a typically stylish Grosset red, with minty mid-palate flavours followed by a taste of cloves on the finish. Tasted ex barrel, showed outstanding potential. (As did the 1985 Rhine Riesling.)

1983 CABERNET SAUVIGNON/CABERNET FRANC [17.8] *Colour:* vibrant purple of medium depth. *Bouquet:* soft, berry aromas allied with sweet, vanillan oak. *Palate:* oak fairly evident throughout the wine; some plum/berry mid-palate fruit, and then soft but persistent tannin. A more obvious wine than Grosset would normally wish to make. Drink '86–'88.

JIM BARRY'S WINES

pp. 364–5

Location:
Main North Road, Clare, 5453;
(088) 42 2261.

Winemakers:
Jim, Mark and Peter Barry.

1985 Production:
3600 cases.

Principal Wines:
Limited range of white and red varietal table wines including Lodge Hill Vineyard Rhine Riesling, Watervale Rhine Riesling, Chardonnay, Sauvignon Blanc, Clare Valley Cabernet Sauvignon, and Merlot.

Distribution:
Substantial cellar-door sales 9 a.m. to 5 p.m. Monday to Friday; 10 a.m. to 4 p.m. Saturday and public holidays; 11 a.m. to 2.30 p.m. Sunday. Significant retail and restaurant distribution South Australia; limited distribution eastern states.

Prices:
$8 to $9 per bottle recommended retail.

Overall Quality:
Consistently good.

Vintage Rating 1982–85:
'84, '83, '85, '82.

Outstanding Prior Vintages:
'75, '78, '80.

Tasting Notes:

1985 SAUVIGNON BLANC **Softly rich bouquet, with a touch of varietal sauvignon aroma, followed by a much more generous palate, with strongly accented sauvignon flavours and considerable depth. Showed great promise (tasted from tank).**

1984 WATERVALE RHINE RIESLING [16.4] *Colour:* **light to medium yellow-green.** *Bouquet:* **full, clean; a little broad, but has richness.** *Palate:* **a big, soft wine dominated by slight sweetness on the mid-palate flavour and a fairly soft finish. With 10 grams per litre of sugar, an unashamedly commercial wine, but well put together. Drink '85–'86.**

1984 LODGE HILL RHINE RIESLING [17] *Colour:* **light to medium yellow-green.** *Bouquet:* **quite pronounced aromas, with a touch of tropical fruit and of medium weight.** *Palate:* **some lime flavours immediately apparent in a wine with abundant fruit flavour, good balance, and nice mouth-feel. Significantly less sweet than Watervale Rhine Riesling. Drink '85–'88.**

1984 CHARDONNAY [14.8] *Colour:* **medium yellow-green.** *Bouquet:* **light fruit, with a touch of oak but lacking complexity and depth.** *Palate:* **obvious oak is really the only taste in the wine, which lacks varietal character and is too light, although has been well enough made. Perhaps fruit will develop in bottle. Drink '87.**

1983 CABERNET SAUVIGNON, CABERNET FRANC, MERLOT, MALBEC [17] *Colour:* **light to medium red-purple, bright and clear.** *Bouquet:* **clean with aromatic sweet fruit and a nice touch of vanillan oak.** *Palate:* **very light but fresh, attractive summer red style in good balance; low tannin on the finish. To be enjoyed as a fruit wine rather than a complex wine. Drink '85–'87.**

1981 CABERNET SAUVIGNON [16.4] *Colour:* **light to medium red.** *Bouquet:* **clean fresh and fairly light with gently sweet fruit aromas.** *Palate:* **well balanced but lacking mid palate flesh; again the low tannin structure typical of the vineyard. Drink '85–'87.**

JUD'S HILL

pp. 369–70

Location:
Farrell Flat Road, 2 km east of Clare, 5343; (vineyard only).

Winemaker:
Brian Barry (consultant Brian Croser).

1985 Production:
5000 cases.

Principal Wines:
Only four wines so far offered; Rhine Riesling, Cabernet Sauvignon, Merlot Cabernet and Cabernet Malbec (a Clare Valley-Keppoch blend).

Distribution:
No cellar-door sales or mailing list. Total production distributed through P. F. Caon, Adelaide and Melbourne; Mark Fesq, Sydney; Chateau Barnard, Perth; and The Oak Barrel, Canberra.

Prices:
$9 approximate retail.

Overall Quality:
Consistently very good.

Vintage Rating 1982–85:
White: '84, '85, '82, '83.
Red: '85, '84, '83, '82.

Outstanding Prior Vintages:
Not applicable; 1982 first vintage.

Tasting Notes:

1984 CLARE RHINE RIESLING [18.4] *Colour:* bright green-yellow. *Bouquet:* full, fine and deep fruit with excellent varietal aroma and outstanding potential. *Palate:* abundant flavour, style and intensity; a very long, clean finish with good acid. Drink '86–'92.

1983 CLARE CABERNET SAUVIGNON [17.6] *Colour:* bright medium red-purple. *Bouquet:* clean, with quite marked varietal astringency and French oak in the background. *Palate:* very clean fruit flavours in the dark berry spectrum, counter-balanced by a touch of astringency; low tannin profile. Drink '87–'91.

1983 CLARE/KEPPOCH CABERNET MALBEC [17] *Colour:* medium to full red, distinctly darker than the straight cabernet. *Bouquet:* a much softer and riper style, with distinctive malbec influence. *Palate:* ripe, round and soft sweet fruit, with some vanillan oak flavours; soft tannin, certainly in a burgundy rather than claret style. Drink '86–'88.

LINDEMANS AND LEO BURING

pp. 370–2

Location:
Main North Road, Clare (vineyard only).

Winemaker:
John Vickery (chief winemaker, Leo Buring Tanunda).

Principal Wines:

Leo Buring Rhine Riesling releases headed by White Label Reserve Bin wines, followed by Varietal Collection releases. Lindemans under Watervale 4-figure bin number releases. Also intermittent releases under 4-figure bin number of Shiraz Cabernet.

Distribution:
Widespread national retail distribution.

Prices:
An extremely wide range of prices between current and old classic vintage releases. Prices for current releases subject to heavy discounting; curiously, those for the old releases (up to $35 per bottle) not so liable to discounting.

Overall Quality:
Leo Buring White Label Reserve Bins often exceptional with age; other releases good.

Vintage Rating 1982–85:
White: '85, '84, '82.
Red: '84, '85, '82 (no '83 vintage).

Outstanding Prior Vintages:
White: '68, '70, '72.
Red: '68, '71.

Tasting Notes:

1985 LEO BURING RESERVE BIN RHINE RIESLING [16.4] *Colour:* light to medium green-yellow. *Bouquet:* typical, firm riesling with real backbone, very much in Clare Valley style. *Palate:* a firm, austere wine, sinewy and lean, and virtually guaranteeing a very long cellaring future, during which time it will transform itself. A welcome return to form, although modest points at this juncture no indication of the potential of the wine. Drink '88–'93.

1984 LEO BURING WATERVALE RHINE RIESLING (VARIETAL COLLECTION) [16] *Colour:* light to medium yellow-green. *Bouquet:* clean; light to medium fruit with a touch of toasty character and low overall aroma. *Palate:* a wine with pretensions to elegance, but the light body and lack of fruit richness tells against it in the end; the fault lies more in the fruit than the winemaking. Drink '86–'88.

1982 LINDEMANS WATERVALE RHINE RIESLING BIN 6495 [15.8] *Colour:* medium yellow-green. *Bouquet:* clean, with fairly light but discernible riesling fruit aroma. *Palate:* clean, light to medium fruit but lacking richness; reasonable acid gives some promise for further cellaring. Drink '85–'88.

1981 LINDEMANS WATERVALE SHIRAZ CABERNET BIN 6215 [16.8] *Colour:* medium to full red-purple. *Bouquet:* clean and fresh with ripe/spicy fruit and a touch of stalky, cabernet-derived astringency. *Palate:* a wine with some life and lift, aided by a touch of new oak, and also a little zest from the cabernet component. Flavoursome but not jammy. Drink '86–'90.

MARTINDALE

Location:
Main North Road, Leasingham via Watervale, 5452;
(tasting and sales only; wines made at Jim Barry Wines).
(088) 422 261.

Winemaker:
Mark Barry.

1985 Production:
1000 cases.

Principal Wines:
Rhine Riesling, Late Harvest Frontignac Traminer, Carbonic Maceration Shiraz and Tawny Port.

Distribution:
Exclusively cellar door and mailing list. Cellar-door sales weekends, school holidays and public holidays 10 a.m. to 4 p.m. Mailing-list enquiries to Box 399B, Clare, SA, 5343.

Prices:
$6 to $6.50 cellar door.

Overall Quality:
Quite good.

Tasting Notes:

1984 MARTINDALE RHINE RIESLING [16] *Colour:* pale yellow-green. *Bouquet:* full and solid wine, similar in style to Jim Barry Watervale Rhine Riesling. *Palate:* a rich, solid wine with a little residual sugar apparent; commercially oriented and again very much in the Jim Barry Watervale style. Drink '86–'88.

1984 LATE HARVEST FRONTIGNAC TRAMINER [16] *Colour:* pale straw-yellow. *Bouquet:* clean, clearly defined, pungent varietal fruit, yet not oily. *Palate:* fresh and full of lively flavour with just a touch of spice and not excessively sweet. Most attractive commercial style. Drink '86.

MITCHELL

pp. 373–4

Location:
Hughes Park Road (known locally as Skillogalee or Skilly Road), Skillogalee Valley, Sevenhill via Clare, 5453;
3 km south-west of Sevenhill.
(088) 43 4258.

Winemaker:
Andrew Mitchell.

1985 Production:
7500 cases.

Principal Wines:

Only three wines produced every year: Watervale Rhine Riesling, Late Picked Rhine Riesling, and Cabernet Sauvignon; occasional Shiraz release, and one or two special wines offered only to mailing-list customers.

Distribution:
Principally cellar door and mailing list. Cellar-door sales 10 a.m. to 4 p.m. 7 days. Mailing list as above. Limited fine wine retail and restaurant sales.

Prices:
$7.95 to $9.60 recommended retail; less cellar door.

Overall Quality:
Exceptional.

Vintage Rating 1982–85:
White: '82, '85, '84, '83.
Red: '84, '82, '85, '83.

Outstanding Prior Vintages:
'77, '80 (White); '76, '80 (Red).

Tasting Notes:
1984 SEVENHILL RHINE RIESLING [18.8] *Colour:* brilliant green-yellow. *Bouquet:* powerful and deep, with that typical touch of Clare Valley toasty aroma but promising much for the future. *Palate:* a wine of truly exceptional power and intensity, with equally remarkable balance and length. Superb mid-palate fruit; a lingering finish with just a hint of passionfruit, but overall unaffected by any of the vagaries of yeast or botrytis. Classic Australian rhine riesling at its greatest. Drink '86–'93.

1984 CABERNET SAUVIGNON [18.4] *Colour:* bright purple-red of medium depth. *Bouquet:* fragrant cedar oak, with finely defined, gently grassy cabernet aroma; a wine which proclaims its class. *Palate:* very elegant, fine cool climate style; very much a Mitchell wine and not so much a traditional Clare Valley wine. You take your choice. Drink '88–'94.

1984 SHIRAZ [17.8] *Colour:* medium red. *Bouquet:* very aromatic, with a marvellous amalgam of slightly lemony/smoky oak aromas and fragrant fruit. *Palate:* an outstanding success; lively fruit and oak flavours intermingle with lovely mid-palate fruit and soft tannin on the finish. Drink '87–'91.

MOUNT HORROCKS

p. 369

Location:
Mintaro Road, Leasingham, 5452;
300 metres east of Main North Road.
(088) 43 0005.

Winemaker:
Jeffrey Grosset (consultant).

1985 Production:
4500 cases.

Principal Wines:

White and red table wines, identified by variety and occasionally by vineyard or district, including Watervale Rhine Riesling, Eyre Creek Semillon, Chardonnay, Cordon Cut Rhine Riesling and Cabernet Merlot.

Distribution:
Principally through cellar door and by mailing list. Cellar-door sales 10 a.m. to 4 p.m. 7 days. Mailing-list enquiries to PO Box 72, Watervale, 5452. Retail and restaurant distribution through P. F. Caon, Adelaide; Crittendens, Melbourne; and Carol Anne Classic Wines, Sydney.

Prices:
$9.40 to $11 recommended retail.

Overall Quality:
Very good.

Vintage Rating 1982–85:
'85, '82, '84, '83.

Outstanding Prior Vintages:
Not applicable; first vintage 1982.

Tasting Notes:

1984 WATERVALE RHINE RIESLING [16.8] *Colour:* medium yellow-green. *Bouquet:* a tightly constructed, firm wine; deep, almost dense. *Palate:* follows on logically from bouquet, with deep flavour and a suggestion of some solids fermentation characters although, given the winemaker, such a technique highly unlikely. Perceptible residual sugar adds further weight. Drink '86–'88.

1984 CORDON CUT RHINE RIESLING [17.4] *Colour:* glowing yellow-green. *Bouquet:* strong, smooth fruit, but lacking the aromatic lift of botrytised rieslings. *Palate:* extremely full, with very sweet lime/peach fruit flavours; cloys a little on the finish and just lacks that extra touch of acid. May well be long-lived, however. Drink '86–'91.

1983 CABERNET SHIRAZ MERLOT [17.2] *Colour:* light to medium red-purple, bright and clear. *Bouquet:* fine, elegant, modulated berry aromas. *Palate:* sweet, berry fruit on the fore- and mid-palate with tastes of plum; a background of oak evident throughout the wine and soft tannin on the finish add complexity to the structure. Drink '85–'88.

PAULETTS

p. 374

Location:
Polish Hill Road, Polish Hill River;
4 km east of Sevenhill, 5453.
(088) 43 4328.

Winemaker:
Neil Paulett.

1985 Production:
2000 cases.

Principal Wines:

Main releases Rhine Riesling and Shiraz; tiny quantities of other varietals briefly available cellar door.

Distribution:
Exclusively cellar-door sales and mailing list; cellar-door sales 9 a.m. to 5 p.m. 7 days.

Prices:
$6.60 cellar door.

Overall Quality:
Good to very good, with potential for even better things.

Vintage Rating 1983–85:
'85, '84, '83.

Outstanding Prior Vintages:
Not applicable; first vintage 1983.

Tasting Notes:
1984 SHIRAZ [18.2] *Colour:* **medium full purple-red.** *Bouquet:* **marvellous varietal spice leaps out the glass, a veritable tour de force.** *Palate:* **an elegant wine with spicy crushed pepper/spice dominating the mid-palate, complexed by a touch of smoky oak. Very good overall balance; a lovely fresh red. Drink '87–'90.**

PETALUMA

p. 375

Location:
Off Farrell Flat Road, Clare 5453;
4 km east of township (vineyard only).
(08) 339 4403.

Winemaker:
Brian Croser.

1985 Production:
10,000 cases.

Principal Wines:

Only one Petaluma wine produced: Rhine Riesling. Other varieties grown, but wine sold to other makers.

Distribution:
National fine wine retail distribution through wholesale agents in each state. No cellar-door sales. No mailing list.

Prices:
$10.90 recommended retail.

Overall Quality:
Exceptional.

Vintage Rating 1982–85:
'85, '84, '82, '83.

Outstanding Prior Vintages:
'80.

Tasting Notes:
1984 RHINE RIESLING [18.6] *Colour:* **brilliant glistening light green-yellow.** *Bouquet:* **fine, classic riesling aroma; very tightly knit; touch of Clare toast, and no yeast influence whatsoever.** *Palate:* **intense, fine fruit with outstanding mid-palate flesh and weight; no tropical fruit overlay and a near-perfect example of classic dry Australian riesling. Drink '86–'92.**

QUELLTALER ESTATE

pp. 375–8

Location:
Main North Road, Watervale, 5452;
1 km north-east of town.
(088) 43 0003.

Winemaker:
Michel Dietrich.

1985 Production:
90,000 cases.

Principal Wines:
Released under three quality grades: the first is Quelltaler Estate (Rhine Riesling, Cachet Blanc, Traminer Riesling, Wood-aged Semillon); then Clare Valley range (Rhine Riesling, Chablis and Cabernet Sauvignon); and finally generic releases (principally Grande Reserve Hock). Granfiesta Sherry is also an important, high quality, release.

Distribution:
National through Remy & Associates. Cellar-door sales 8 a.m. to 5 p.m. Monday to Friday, 11 a.m. to 4 p.m. weekends and public holidays.

Prices:
$9.60 to $10.20 recommended retail.

Overall Quality:
Very good, particularly recent vintages.

Vintage Rating 1982–85:
'85, '84, '82, '83.

Outstanding Prior Vintages:
'78, '80.

Tasting Notes:

1984 QUELLTALER ESTATE RHINE RIESLING [18]
Colour: medium full yellow-green. *Bouquet:* very rich, very full, complex lime/vanillan fruit. *Palate:* a very full-flavoured but well-balanced wine, with an intriguing touch of spice on the finish; rich and deep. Drink '86–'92.

1984 QUELLTALER ESTATE CACHET BLANC [17.6]
Colour: bright, light to medium green-yellow. *Bouquet:* very smooth and clean, with well-integrated oak. *Palate:* very firm but markedly crisp fruit; one of the very few Australian white wines to actually have some true chablis flavour and structure. Ironically, not labelled as such. Good acid balance a feature of the wine. Drink '86–'89.

1984 WOOD-AGED SEMILLON [18.2]
Colour: medium yellow, with a touch of oak-derived straw. *Bouquet:* shows much less overt reliance on oak than many of the prior vintages of this excellent wine; some honey/nut fruit flavours adding weight and texture. *Palate:* very smooth, with deep semillon fruit and beautifully handled, gently spicy oak adding richness; a touch of buttery semillon varietal flavour already building. Drink '86–'92.

1984 QUELLTALER ESTATE SAUVIGNON BLANC [16.6] *Colour:* bright yellow-green of medium depth. *Bouquet:* yet to really open up and develop aroma; a touch of astringent gooseberry varietal character, but basically subdued. *Palate:* a very firm wine, with a slight trace of bitterness, and just a suggestion of sulphide. Light oak. Drink '86–'89.

1984 QUELLTALER ESTATE NOBLE RHINE RIESLING [17.8] *Colour:* glowing yellow-green. *Bouquet:* firm and deep, with racy/robust riesling character, with a trace of kerosene. *Palate:* very rich, very flavoursome with viscous mouth-feel, yet avoiding heaviness. A striking wine. Drink '86–'91.

1984 QUELLTALER ESTATE NOBLE SEMILLON [17.6]
Colour: full yellow, bordering on orange. *Bouquet:* complex botrytised semillon aromas; some butterscotch characters, but lifted by a trace of pleasant volatility. *Palate:* very sweet and luscious sauterne style, with deep butterscotch flavours. Simply lacks final intensity to lift it into the highest class. Drink '86–'93.

SEVENHILL

pp. 378–80

Location:
College Road, Sevenhill via Clare, 5453;
1 km north-east of town.
(088) 43 4222.

Winemaker:
Brother John May.

1985 Production:
21,500 cases.

Principal Wines:

A substantial range of wines offered, ranging from varietal releases through to generics. Wines include Rhine Riesling, Traminer Frontignac, Tokay, Moselle, Clare Riesling, Shiraz, Cabernet Sauvignon, Merlot, Cabernet Franc, together with a limited range of fortified wines. Substantial output of sacramental wines in addition.

Distribution:
Principally cellar door and mailing list. Cellar-door sales 9 a.m. to 4 p.m. Monday to Friday; Saturday 9 a.m. to noon. Limited capital city distribution through fine wine retailers. Mailing list as above.

Prices:
$5 to $8 cellar door.

Overall Quality:
Some very good, others adequate to good.

Vintage Rating 1982–85:
'82, '84, '85, '83.

Outstanding Prior Vintages:
'72, '75, '77, '80.

Tasting Notes:

1985 TRAMINER FRONTIGNAC Strong varietal aroma and flavour with the spice of each variety intermingling; very fruity commercial style with abundant flavour. (Tasted from tank.)

1984 CABERNET SAUVIGNON [14.4] *Colour:* very light red-purple. *Bouquet:* light, slightly baggy and lacking fruit depth. *Palate:* similarly lacking fruit richness, with the problems compounded by a rather odd and unsatisfactory oak character. A major disappointment and out of line with the normally very reliable red wines of Sevenhill.

1984 MERLOT CABERNET FRANC CABERNET SAUVIGNON [16] *Colour:* vibrant light red. *Bouquet:* clean but light, with an attractive, sweet, red berry aroma. *Palate:* light-bodied, with crisp fruit; mid-palate flavours suggestive of raspberries; low tannin. Drink '86–'88.

SKILLOGALEE

pp. 380–1

Location:
Off Hughes Park Road, Skillogalee Valley,
Sevenhill via Clare, 5453;
3 km south-west of Sevenhill.

Winemaker:
Andrew Mitchell (contract).

1985 Production:
6500 cases.

Principal Wines:
Rhine Riesling Bin 2, Late Harvest Rhine Riesling, Cabernet Sauvignon, Shiraz, Vintage Port.

Distribution:
Principally cellar door and mailing list. Cellar-door sales 10 a.m. to 5 p.m. 7 days. Mailing list, PO Box 9, Sevenhill via Clare, 5453. Retail sales Melbourne, Richmond Hill Cellars; Sydney, Bankstown Cellars.

Prices:
$5.50.

Overall Quality:
Very good.

Vintage Rating 1982–85:
'84, '85, '82, '83.

Outstanding Prior Vintages:
'78, '80.

Tasting Notes:

1984 RHINE RIESLING BIN 2 [17.6] *Colour:* light to medium green-yellow, quite brilliant. *Bouquet:* firm and deep, with a touch of district toast, and fruit aroma still to fully develop as at mid-1985. *Palate:* very generous flavour, round and full, with a marked touch of residual sugar adding depth. The wine is beautifully balanced against that residual sugar, however, and is an excellent wine in the softer style. Drink '85–'89.

1984 LATE HARVEST RHINE RIESLING [16.8] *Colour:* light to medium yellow-green. *Bouquet:* firm, clean and deep; classic late harvest rhine riesling, yet not particularly aromatic. *Palate:* round flavours verging on butterscotch, but not so much luscious or sweet as simply fruity. An older style spatlese which will repay cellaring. Drink '86–'90.

STANLEY LEASINGHAM

pp. 381–8

Location:
7 Dominic Street, Clare, 5453;
on southern outskirts of town.
(088) 42 2555.

Winemakers:
Chris Proud (chief winemaker), Tim Adams.

1985 Production:
165,000 cases premium wines, further 450,000 cases equivalent in cask and bulk wine.

Principal Wines:

Wide range, headed by Winemakers Selection Series, presently comprising Bin 7 Rhine Riesling, Bin 49 Cabernet Sauvignon, Bin 56 Cabernet Malbec,Chardonnay, Traminer, Sauternes and Beerenauslese Rhine Riesling. Then follow Bin 3 White Burgundy, Bin 4 Traminer Riesling, Bin 5 Rhine Riesling, Bin 6 Rhine Riesling Moselle, Bin 9 Spatlese Rhine Riesling, Bin 14 Chablis, Bin 61 Shiraz and Bin 68 Cabernet Shiraz. Bottled wine range finishes with Spring Gully Rhine Riesling and Hutt Creek Claret. Also extensive cask sales.

Distribution:
National distribution through most liquor stores, chains and hotels. Cellar-door sales 8 a.m. to 5 p.m. Monday to Friday, Saturday 9 a.m. to 4 p.m.

Prices:
$4.30 to $7.80 recommended retail;
Trockenbeerenauslese $13.

Overall Quality:
Very good; occasional exceptional wines.

Vintage Rating 1982–85:
'85, '84, '82, '83.

Outstanding Prior Vintages:
'71, '72, '73, '75, '77 & '80.

Tasting Notes:

1984 GEWURTZTRAMINER WINEMAKERS SELECTION [17] *Colour:* bright yellow-green. *Bouquet:* rich and firm, not especially spicy, but with ample fruit. *Palate:* an elegant wine, with traminer varietal character evident but not overstated. Gentle, spicy fruit, with just a hint of residual sugar. Drink '85–'87.

1984 FUME BLANC [16.8] *Colour:* light to medium yellow-green. *Bouquet:* very attractive light spicy/nutmeg oak aromas, with fruit yet to fully develop. *Palate:* once again the fruit is very light, and the wine relies principally on most attractive, spicy oak. May well develop additional character. Drink '86–'88.

1984 CHARDONNAY [16.6] *Colour:* medium yellow, with a touch of oak-derived straw. *Bouquet:* light fruit, with barely perceptible varietal character and some smoky oak aromas. *Palate:* provides rather more than the bouquet promises, with distinct grassy/grapefruit mid-palate flavours with a touch of lemony/smoky oak; an elegant, "cool" wine which could possibly develop well in bottle. Drink '86–'87.

1984 RHINE RIESLING BIN 7 [17] *Colour:* quite full yellow, with a touch of straw. *Bouquet:* full and smooth, already showing surprising depth and development for the year; some soft lime/vanillan aromas. *Palate:* full, round and soft butterscotch/lime flavours; very attractive, although remarkably advanced. Drink '86–'87.

1983 CABERNET SHIRAZ BIN 68 [16.4] *Colour:* medium red-purple. *Bouquet:* sweet, vanillan American oak together with fairly ripe fruit; clean and overall of medium weight. *Palate:* some life and lift to the point of sharpness; pleasant, clean, cherry fruit flavours; light oak and low tannin. (Due for release 1986.) Drink '86–'89.

1982 CABERNET MALBEC BIN 56 [16.6] *Colour:* light to medium red-purple. *Bouquet:* very clean; delicate and elegant fruit/oak balance and aromas. *Palate:* as the bouquet promises, quite light and elegant, but very well-balanced, with all of the components present, although in moderation. Drink '86–'88.

TAYLORS

pp. 388–9

Location:
Mintaro Road, Auburn, 5451;
3 km north-east of town.
(088) 49 2008.

Winemaker:
Andrew Tolley.

1985 Production:
Approximately 180,000 cases.

Principal Wines:
Chardonnay, Rhine Riesling, White Burgundy, Hermitage, Pinot Noir and Cabernet Sauvignon.

Distribution:
National retail sales through most liquor stores, chains and hotels. Cellar-door sales 10 a.m. to 5 p.m. Monday to Saturday and public holidays, Sunday 10 a.m. to 4 p.m.

Prices:
$6.50 to $7.70 recommended retail.

Overall Quality:
Good.

Vintage Rating 1982–85:
'84, '85, '82, '83.

Outstanding Prior Vintages:
'76, '78, '79.

Tasting Notes:

1984 RHINE RIESLING [16] *Colour:* medium yellow-green. *Bouquet:* a big, fairly broad wine, with a touch of caramel and marked yeast volatility. *Palate:* very generously flavoured; in mainstream of Clare style, although again marred by a degree of volatility which some will accept and others not. Drink '86–'88.

1983 PINOT NOIR [16.2] *Colour:* very good, deep red-purple. *Bouquet:* quite full and sweet fruit, with marked vanillan oak, although relatively little varietal character. *Palate:* solid fruit flavours, but really an indeterminate, medium-bodied red, with only a fleeting glimpse of pinot varietal flavour. Drink '85–'88.

1982 CABERNET SAUVIGNON [16.8] *Colour:* medium red, with obvious development showing. *Bouquet:* of light to medium weight, and quite complex leafy/cedar/cigar box aromas. *Palate:* a quite lively and elegant wine, but the fruit appears to be fading very quickly, particularly given the early promise of the wine tasted previously from cask. Drink '85–'86.

WATERVALE CELLARS

pp. 389–90

Location:
North Terrace, Watervale, 5452;
off Main North Road in township.
(088) 43 0069.

Winemaker:
Robert Crabtree.

1985 Production:
2400 cases.

Principal Wines:
Rhine Riesling, Semillon, Semillon Chardonnay, Shiraz Cabernet and Cabernet Sauvignon.

Distribution:
Principally cellar door and mailing list. Cellar-door sales 9 a.m. to 5 p.m. most days.

Prices:
$6.50 to $7 per bottle cellar door.

Overall Quality:
Good, and improving all the time.

Vintage Rating 1982–85:
'82, '84, '85, '83.

Outstanding Prior Vintages:
'84, '85.

Tasting Notes:

1984 RHINE RIESLING [15.6] *Colour:* **bright yellow-green.** *Bouquet:* **very slight solids character, not particularly aromatic and needing time to settle down and develop.** *Palate:* **much better than the bouquet suggests, with full flavour, and the mid-palate fleshed out by a touch of residual sugar. Drink '86–'87.**

1984 SEMILLON CHARDONNAY [16.8] *Colour:* **medium yellow-straw.** *Bouquet:* **clean, with well-balanced fruit and oak, though no clear varietal characters emerge.** *Palate:* **good overall flavour and balance; while the chardonnay influence is not particularly noticeable overall, good mouth-filling flavour and structure; quite stylish. Drink '86–'89.**

1984 SHIRAZ CABERNET [17.8] *Colour:* **very good purple-red.** *Bouquet:* **clean, fresh, berry fruit of medium to full intensity, backed by a touch of oak.** *Palate:* **shows all hallmarks of skilful winemaking; very well-protected, fresh fruit, with lovely weight and style; should develop superbly. Drink '88–'93.**

1982 SHIRAZ [16.8] *Colour:* **light to medium red-purple.** *Bouquet:* **very clean, gentle, sweet fruit and vanillan American oak aromas intermingle.** *Palate:* **quite a fresh wine, with gently sweet, cherry flavours on the mid-palate, leading on to very soft but persistent tannin on the finish, and again that touch of vanillan oak. Drink '86–'89.**

1982 CABERNET SHIRAZ [17] *Colour:* **medium red-purple.** *Bouquet:* **clean, slightly firmer than the shiraz, but again the sweet, berry aromas make their appearance.** *Palate:* **fuller and slightly firmer than the Shiraz, although overall in similar style. Excellent fruit/oak integration. Drink '86–'89.**

WENDOUREE

pp. 390–2

Location:
Wendouree Road, Clare, 5453;
2 km south of township.
(088) 42 2896.

Winemaker:
Tony Brady.

1985 Production:
3600 cases.

Principal Wines:

Virtually exclusively red wines, with the occasional fortified wine, including fortified Rhine Riesling and fortified Muscat of Alexandria; 1984 saw first dry Rhine Riesling. Red wines include Cabernet Sauvignon, Cabernet Malbec, Cabernet Malbec Shiraz, Shiraz, Shiraz Mataro and Malbec Shiraz.

Distribution:
Principally cellar door and mailing list. Cellar-door sales 10 a.m. to 4.30 p.m. Monday to Saturday. Closed Sundays and between Christmas and New Year. Mailing-list enquiries to PO Box 27, Clare, 5453. Very limited wholesale distribution to Liquor Wholesalers, Adelaide; W. J. Seabrook, Melbourne; Jules Geurassimoff, Brisbane and The Oak Barrel, Sydney.

Prices:
$8 to $9 cellar door.

Overall Quality:
Exceptional.

Vintage Rating 1982–85:
'83, '84, '85, '82.

Outstanding Prior Vintages:
'75, '78, '80.

Tasting Notes:

1984 CABERNET SAUVIGNON [17.4] *Colour:* deep, full purple-red. *Bouquet:* strong, almost aggressive fruit/oak; dense, old-style vin de garde. *Palate:* enormous strength and depth, yet component parts are in balance; all the wine needs is a great deal of patience. Drink '90–'98.

1984 CABERNET MALBEC [17.8] *Colour:* medium full purple-red. *Bouquet:* strong, powerful yet still discrete fruit, with outstanding development potential. *Palate:* rather more open than the bouquet; some sweet fruit flavours from the malbec lift the mid-palate; a lovely, stylish, flavoury wine destined to become superbly complex with age. Drink '89–'95.

1983 CABERNET MALBEC [18.4] *Colour:* deep purple-red. *Bouquet:* very complex, very full fruit, with marked new oak influence adding further to overall weight and complexity. *Palate:* voluptuous, rich, sweet berry flavours on the mid-palate, with excellent balancing acid on the finish, together with substantial but not aggressive tannin. The oak influence evident in the bouquet also makes its mark. Drink '89–'95.

1983 SHIRAZ [18] *Colour:* dense purple, almost impenetrable. *Bouquet:* an enormously powerful wine, high in alcohol, with overtones of cinnamon and clove. *Palate:* great depth, yet surprisingly smooth; tannin quite soft; sweet vanillan/American oak flavours complement the fruit to perfection. Drink '88–'94.

1982 MALBEC CABERNET [17.8] *Colour:* medium to full purple-red. *Bouquet:* smooth and clean with, somewhat surprisingly, the cabernet dominant (it comprises 20% of the blend). *Palate:* by the standards of Wendouree, a light, elegant wine, with medium-weight fruit on the mid-palate and again the cabernet sauvignon is the dominant part of the blend. The American oak used tastes as if it is French, once again probably due to the contribution of the cabernet. Drink '87–'92.

WILSON'S POLISH HILL RIVER VINEYARDS

pp. 392–3

Location:
Near corner Polish Hill Road and Stone Cutting Road, Polish Hill;
5 km east of Sevenhill via Clare, 5453.
(088) 258 9797.

Winemaker:
John Wilson.

1985 Production:
2600 cases.

Principal Wines:

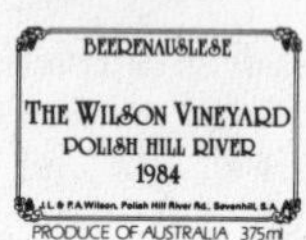

Rhine Riesling, Gewurztraminer, Rhine Riesling Beerenauslese, Pinot Noir, Shiraz Cabernet and Cabernet Sauvignon Malbec.

Distribution:
Principally cellar door and mailing list. Cellar-door sales 10 a.m. to 4 p.m. weekends and public holidays. Limited wholesale distribution through Tollgate Wine Merchants, Adelaide. Mailing list as above.

Prices:
$5 to $6.50 cellar door.

Overall Quality:
Variable; adequate to very good.

Vintage Rating 1982–85:
Red wines: '85, '84, '82, '83.

Tasting Notes:

1984 RHINE RIESLING BEERENAUSLESE [16.8] *Colour:* yellow-green. *Bouquet:* rich, limy aroma, with obvious botrytis influence, and then a peculiar hint of fresh mushroom. *Palate:* very rich, good balancing acid, highly concentrated but again flawed by a peppery/mushroom taste on the back palate, conceivably due to some mould contamination during the botrytis process. Drink '87–'90.

1984 PINOT NOIR [16.8] *Colour:* vibrant fuchsia/purple. *Bouquet:* clean, but rather closed as at mid-1985; should develop in bottle. *Palate:* fresh, light to medium weight with a nice touch of strawberry flavour on the mid-palate and crisp acid on the finish. Overall, a well-structured pinot. Drink '85–'86.

1984 SHIRAZ CABERNET [16.2] *Colour:* medium purple-red. *Bouquet:* pronounced, meaty, carbonic maceration aromas; considerable overall richness. *Palate:* a witches' brew of meaty/stewed fruit aromas which seem so prevalent in Australian carbonic maceration wines. Attractive for all that. Drink '86–'87.

1984 CABERNET SAUVIGNON MALBEC [17.2] *Colour:* dense purple. *Bouquet:* very big, rich and complex wine, with fairly ripe fruit and just a touch of meaty aroma. *Palate:* arresting, voluptuous ripe berry flavours, together with a fraction of volatile lift. Drink '86–'88.

Coonawarra

1985 Vintage

1985 will in all probability be seen as a twin vintage with 1984; both were far cooler than in normal years, with vintage taking place substantially later than normal. Only 1982 is likely to provide any serious competition to the wines of 1984 and 1985, unless, of course, one goes back to 1980. There is no clear-cut preponderance of opinion favouring either 1984 or 1985, but it is clear that both years have produced wines which will live long in the memory of winelovers.

The weather pattern was a familiar one. A wet winter and late spring delayed bud-burst, but a very large crop developed in the wake of a perfect flowering and fruit-set. Dry and cool conditions then prevailed until the third week of March, when a week of hot weather helped lagging maturities.

Botrytis, which caused such havoc in 1983 and which caused some problems in 1984, was kept under far better control than previously, and vine health and fruit quality overall was very good. White wines all show full flavour and good varietal character, but it is the red wines which, in the long term, will be regarded as outstanding. Shiraz, cabernet sauvignon and merlot have produced some magnificent wines, while the pinot noirs will probably be the best so far to come from the region.

The Changes

The major event during the year was the award of the 1985 Jimmy Watson Trophy to Hollick's Neilson Estate Wines (or, as it is now known, Hollick's Wines). In the past few years a large number of small wineries have opened for business in Coonawarra, and many of them are producing superb wines. Hollick's is obviously the front-runner, but James Haselgrove, Ladbroke Grove, Koppamurra and Zema Estate are all exciting newcomers.

There has never been any serious doubt about the quality of Coonawarra. The practices of some of the larger wine companies have been criticised by informed observers, and the battle between the smaller and the larger companies will be of critical importance in determining the future direction of wine quality and style.

BOWEN ESTATE

pp. 401–2

Location:
Main Penola–Naracoorte Road, Penola, 5277;
4 km north of township.
(087) 37 2229.

Winemaker:
Doug Bowen.

1985 Production:
3750 cases.

Principal Wines:
Rhine Riesling, Chardonnay, Shiraz and Cabernet Sauvignon.

Distribution:
Substantial cellar-door and mailing-list sales; cellar-door sales 8 a.m. to 5 p.m. Monday to Saturday. Mailing-list enquiries to PO Box 4B, Coonawarra, 5263. Fine wine distribution through Talavera Wine Company, Melbourne; Tucker and Co., Sydney; and Classic Wine Merchants, Adelaide.

Prices:
$7.20 to $9.20 recommended retail.

Overall Quality:
Exceptional.

Vintage Rating 1982–85:
White: '84, '82, '85, '83.
Red: '84, '85, '82, '83.

Oustanding Prior Vintages:
'79.

Tasting Notes:

1984 RHINE RIESLING [16.6] *Colour:* yellow-green of medium depth. *Bouquet:* rich, lime/botrytis aromas, full of character. *Palate:* pungent and very rich, strongly influenced by botrytis and somewhat exaggerated in style; a slightly phenolic finish. Drink '85–'88.

1982 CABERNET SAUVIGNON [17.8] *Colour:* red-purple of medium depth, showing some signs of development. *Bouquet:* fine, clean, gently-herbaceous fruit, with bell-clear cabernet characteristics. *Palate:* very firm, varietal cabernet sauvignon in typical Bowen style; ample weight, though not by any means heavy; fine and subtle oak handling. Drink '86–'92.

1981 SHIRAZ [18.2] *Colour:* medium red-purple. *Bouquet:* very clean, of light to medium weight, with lively and refreshing pepper/spice aromas. *Palate:* of light to medium weight, but vibrant fruit flavours, with the same pepper/spice characters evident in the bouquet. Outstanding varietal character. Drink '85–'90.

BRANDS LAIRA

pp. 402–3

Location:
Penola–Naracoorte Highway, Coonawarra, 5263; 11 km north of Penola.
(087) 36 3260.

Winemakers:
Bill and Jim Brand.

1985 Production:
6300 cases.

Principal Wines:
Red wine specialists; Shiraz and Cabernet Sauvignon. Lesser quantities of Cabernet Malbec, Malbec and tiny production of Pinot Noir. Intermittent special release of Original Vineyard Shiraz, and an occasional Rhine Riesling.

Distribution:
Fine wine retail distribution through wholesale agents in South Australia, Victoria, New South Wales and Queensland; Tasmania through Aberfeldy Cellars. Cellar-door sales 8 a.m. to 5 p.m. Monday to Saturday and holidays and Sundays of long weekends. Mailing-list enquiries to PO Box 18, Coonawarra, 5263.

Prices:
$6 to $12 cellar door.

Overall Quality:
After some uncertainty and variability, has returned to rightful status of very good.

Vintage Rating 1982–85:
'84, '85, '82, '83.

Outstanding Prior Vintages:
'81, '76, '74, '68.

Tasting Notes:

1984 RHINE RIESLING [16.8] *Colour:* medium straw-yellow. *Bouquet:* pungent lime/botrytis aromas, very much in the regional style of '84 rhine riesling. *Palate:* a big wine, with considerable residual sugar taking it almost into a spatlese class; soft and full; no phenolic hardness. Drink '86–'89.

1983 SHIRAZ [17.4] *Colour:* medium red-purple. *Bouquet:* clean, well-balanced and with just a trace of mint, and not jammy. *Palate:* very clean; of light to medium weight, with good fruit/oak balance and smooth, sweet berry flavours on the mid-palate. A great wine for a very difficult vintage. A winner of several gold medals. Drink '85–'90.

1983 CABERNET SAUVIGNON [17.6] *Colour:* red-purple of medium depth. *Bouquet:* light to medium weight; clean, sweet, fruit aromas, with a touch of cherry. *Palate:* smooth, round and ripe cherry/plum fruit flavours; little evident oak influence and fairly low tannin. Another great success for the year. Drink '86–'90.

1982 ORIGINAL VINEYARD SHIRAZ [17.6] *Colour:* medium red. *Bouquet:* clean; of light to medium weight, with smooth, non-spicy fruit and some lemony French oak. *Palate:* a perfectly clean wine, with fairly light but crisp fruit and a similar light, lemony oak influence to that apparent in the bouquet. A long and lingering soft finish. Drink '85–'89.

1982 CABERNET SAUVIGNON [17.8] *Colour:* medium red-purple. *Bouquet:* firm; a touch of charred/smoky oak aroma, with fine cabernet varietal fruit underneath. *Palate:* firm fruit structure; considerable intensity and style, with good acidity in a lingering, clean finish. Drink '87–'92.

1981 CABERNET MALBEC [17.2] *Colour:* medium red-purple. *Bouquet:* sweet berry/plum contribution from malbec very obvious; of medium weight and developing well, with some secondary complex aromas emerging. *Palate:* of medium to full weight, with berry malbec flavours again to the fore; a clean, crisp, low tannin finish. Drink '85–'89.

CHATEAU REYNELLA

pp. 403–4

Location:
No vineyards owned; fruit purchased from vineyards owned by Coonawarra Machinery Company.

Winemaker:
Geoff Merrill (consultant).

1985 Production:
Total Chateau Reynella production 500,000 litres.

Principal Wines:
Rhine Riesling and Cabernet Sauvignon.

Distribution:
National retail through Thomas Hardy offices in all states.

Prices:
$7 to $7.70 recommended retail.

Overall Quality:
Very good.

Vintage Rating 1982–85:
White: '84, '82, '85, '83.
Red: '84, '82, '85, '83.

Outstanding Prior Vintages:
'80.

Tasting Notes:

1981 COONAWARRA CABERNET SAUVIGNON [17.2] *Colour:* bright red of medium depth. *Bouquet:* clean; some gently astringent, cabernet varietal aroma intermingling with sweet oak. *Palate:* a much riper and sweeter style than most of the earlier wines under this label; soft plum/berry flavours; extremely smooth. Drink '85–'89.

HOLLICK'S WINES

pp. 404–5

Location:
Racecourse Road, Coonawarra, 5263;
first winery north of Penola, 2 km from town.
(087) 37 2318.

Winemaker:
Ian Hollick.

1985 Production:
5500 cases.

Principal Wines:
Rhine Riesling, Chardonnay and Cabernet Sauvignon.

Distribution:
Cellar-door sales, mailing list and fine wine retail distribution through wholesale agents in each state. Cellar-door sales 9 a.m. to 5 p.m. 7 days. Mailing-list enquiries to Box 9B, Coonawarra, 5263.

Prices:
$6.95 to $8.50 recommended retail.

Overall Quality:
Very good; some exceptional wines.

Vintage Rating 1982–85:
White: '84, '85, '83 (first white vintage).
Red: '84, '82, '85, '83.

Tasting Notes:

1985 RHINE RIESLING [18] *Colour:* bright green-yellow. *Bouquet:* full, clean and rich riesling fruit, with some lime overtones. *Palate:* most attractive, soft and almost delicate fruit, devoid of any phenolic hardness yet with ample flavour. Early drinking style. Drink '86–'87.

1984 RHINE RIESLING [18.4] *Colour:* bright, glowing yellow-green. *Bouquet:* very clean, medium to full in weight, with strong aromatic fruit. *Palate:* outstanding classic rhine riesling; perfect balance, weight and structure; considerable intensity of mid-palate flavour and a long, clean, soft finish. Altogether excellent. Drink '85–'88.

1984 CHARDONNAY [16.8] *Colour:* some oak-derived, brown-pink tints. *Bouquet:* lemony/spicy oak tends to dominate fruit but will settle down. *Palate:* better balanced, although oak still tends to dominate; lively fruit and crisp acid will come to the fore with a little more bottle age. Drink '86–'88.

1984 CABERNET SAUVIGNON [18.6] *Colour:* medium full purple-red. *Bouquet:* full, gently sweet, berry aromas; perfectly modulated fruit and impeccable oak balance. *Palate:* smooth and silky, sweet, berry flavours with complementary sweet/vanillan oak to add complexity. Low tannin; not a heavyweight wine, and will be easy to drink early in its true lifespan. (Jimmy Watson Trophy winner Melbourne 1985.) Drink '87–'93.

1983 CABERNET SAUVIGNON [18] *Colour:* bright light to medium purple-red. *Bouquet:* raspberry/blackberry aromas intermingled with fresh oak. *Palate:* most attractive, fresh blackcurrant/raspberry flavours; a great success for a difficult vintage. Drink '86–'91.

HUNGERFORD HILL

p. 404

Location:
Main Penola–Naracoorte Road, 1 km north of Penola (vineyard only—still in course of establishment).

Winemaker:
Ralph Fowler.

1985 Production:
Approximately 20,000 cases.

Principal Wines:

Top varietal releases under 'Collection Series' label led by Coonawarra Rhine Riesling and Coonawarra Cabernet Sauvignon. Shiraz and Pinot Noir also released. Also outstanding Chardonnay Pinot Noir Méthode Champenoise.

Distribution:
Significant fine wine retail distribution through wholesale agents in each state.

Prices:
$9.50 to $14.50 recommended retail, the latter price for Chardonnay and Pinot Noir Champagne. Normally subject to only limited discounting.

Overall Quality:
Very good; several exceptional wines (particularly 1983 Rhine Riesling).

Vintage Rating 1982–85:
White: '82, '83, '85, '84.
Red: '82, '85, '84, '83.

Outstanding Prior Vintages:
1978.

Tasting Notes:

1984 COONAWARRA COLLECTION RHINE RIESLING [17.6] *Colour:* medium yellow-green. *Bouquet:* firm, pungent and authoritative riesling in classic mould, without any botrytis-induced aromas. *Palate:* considerable richness, with lime/pineapple mid-palate flavours; very good depth and balance, aided by a remarkably firm finish. Drink '86–'90.

1981 LATE PICKED RHINE RIESLING (BOTRYTIS AFFECTED) [16.8] *Colour:* deep yellow. *Bouquet:* quite aged, with caramel toffee characters emerging. *Palate:* rich and soft, with unusual toffee flavours; fully ready. Drink '85–'86.

1981 COONAWARRA COLLECTION SHIRAZ [17] *Colour:* medium full tawny-red. *Bouquet:* ageing with considerable grace; sweet, minty fruit, integrated with a touch of tobacco, elegant and complex. *Palate:* a fragrant wine of light to medium weight, still with considerable life but seemingly lacking the fruit depth for real longevity. Drink '86–'88.

1982 COONAWARRA COLLECTION CABERNET SAUVIGNON [17.4] *Colour:* red-purple of medium depth. *Bouquet:* pleasant leafy aromas in a bouquet of quite marked elegance. *Palate:* very smooth and clean berry flavours; despite the low tannin profile has a relatively long finish and feels good in the mouth. Drink '86–'90.

1982 CHARDONNAY PINOT NOIR METHODE CHAMPENOISE [18] *Colour:* bright full yellow. *Bouquet:* marked yeast influence in a cheesy, slightly toasty aroma of far greater complexity than one usually encounters in Australian sparkling wines. *Palate:* even better than the bouquet; lovely, creamy, yeasty, complex fruit with soft, mouth-filling mid-palate flavours, and a clean finish. At its peak. Drink '85–'87.

JAMES HASELGROVE

pp. 405–6

Location:
Main Penola–Naracoorte Road, Coonawarra, 5263; 3 km north of Penola.
(087) 37 2734.

Winemaker:
James Haselgrove (white wines made under contract).

1985 Production:
Approximately 7000 cases.

Principal Wines:

Rhine Riesling, Traminer Rhine Riesling, Later Harvest Riesling, Auslese Riesling, Beerenauslese Riesling, Cabernet Nouveau and Cabernet Sauvignon.

Distribution:
Substantial cellar-door sales in both Coonawarra and McLaren Vale; also mailing list. Cellar-door sales 9 a.m. to 5 p.m. 7 days. Mailing-list enquiries to PO Box 14, Coonawarra, 5263. Significant fine wine retail distribution through wholesale agents in each state.

Prices:
$7.10 to $15.95 cellar door.

Overall Quality:
Very good; some late harvest whites exceptional.

Vintage Rating 1982–85:
White: '85, '84, '82, '83.
Red: '85, '83, '84, '82.

Tasting Notes:

1984 RHINE RIESLING [17] *Colour:* medium yellow-green. *Bouquet:* full and toasty, but lacks clear fruit aroma. *Palate:* a much bigger and richer wine than the bouquet suggests; full mid-palate flavour and weight; however, lacks lift and finesse. Could conceivably cellar well. Drink '85–'88.

1984 TRAMINER RIESLING [18] *Colour:* bright green-yellow. *Bouquet:* very distinctive, spicy, Alsace-like traminer with excellent firm backbone. *Palate:* very Alsatian in its flavour and structure; crisp fore- and mid-palate fruit, with an intense, yet not hard, lingering finish. Drink '85–'91.

1984 AUSLESE RHINE RIESLING [17.4] *Colour:* medium full yellow. *Bouquet:* clean; a faint aroma of rich pineapple, but overall somewhat closed. *Palate:* infinitely better than the bouquet; powerful, rich and intense, with excellent penetrating acid to give lift and balance. (Substantially better than the Beerenauslese of same year.) Drink '86–'92.

1983 CABERNET NOUVEAU [13.6] *Colour:* light to medium red-purple. *Bouquet:* light, rather skinny characters, not attractive. *Palate:* skinny/bitter flavours, incongruously with suggestions of oxidation. Not a success. Drink now.

1982 COONAWARRA CABERNET SAUVIGNON [18.8] *Colour:* medium to full red. *Bouquet:* clean, full and firm; excellent cabernet varietal aroma; good oak handling a feature of a stylish wine. *Palate:* excellent balance and weight; the fruit is ripe but not over-ripe; sweet berry flavours on the mid-palate are followed by gently astringent tannins on the finish. Difficult to think how the wine could be improved. Drink '86–'94.

KATNOOK ESTATE

pp. 406–7

Location:
Off main Penola–Naracoorte Road, Coonawarra, 5263;
4 km north of Penola.
(087) 37 2391.

Winemaker:
Wayne Stehbens.

1985 Production:
Approximately 750,000 litres of wine and grape juice produced each vintage, all but 15,000 cases of which is sold as juice or as finished wine to other wine companies across Australia, including many household names. Katnook (or Coonawarra Machinery Company, its sister organisation and vineyard owner) is the important independent source of high-grade Coonawarra wine.

Principal Wines:

Wines released under the Katnook Estate label comprise Rhine Riesling, Sauvignon Blanc, Chardonnay and Cabernet Sauvignon. A second label, Riddoch Estate, is also used for a similar range of lower-priced wines.

Distribution:
Principal distribution through fine wine retailers in all capital cities. Wholesale agents in each state. Cellar-door sales 9 a.m. to 4.30 p.m. Monday to Friday, 10 a.m. to 4.30 p.m. Saturday and public holidays. No mailing list.

Prices:
$9.60 to $16 recommended retail.

Overall Quality:
Very good; sometimes exceptional.

Vintage Rating 1982–85:
White: '83, '82, '85, '84.
Red: '83, '82, '85, '84.

Outstanding Prior Vintages:
'80.

Tasting Notes:

1985 SAUVIGNON BLANC [18] *Colour:* pale green-yellow. *Bouquet:* brilliantly articulated sauvignon blanc varietal character, with rich, gooseberry aromas, avoiding the rather smelly sulphidic characters which sometimes mar the variety; of medium-full weight. *Palate:* equally clear varietal character; ample mid-palate fruit and a lingering finish. Overall has excellent mouth-feel. Drink '86–'88.

1985 RHINE RIESLING [18.8] *Colour:* bright, light green-yellow. *Bouquet:* very clean and fragrant; very clear varietal definition without the intervention of botrytis; ample depth and style. *Palate:* has excellent structure, with tight, clear riesling flavours, and good crisp acid on the finish. An outstanding wine. Drink '86–'90.

1984 CHARDONNAY [18.2] *Colour:* full yellow-green. *Bouquet:* extremely full, dried fig/peach aromas, ripe and viscous; excellent oak integration. *Palate:* a very rich and ripe wine, almost voluptuous in texture, with strong peach/grapefruit flavours, and kept under control by very good acid on the finish. Drink '87–'90.

1984 PINOT NOIR [17] *Colour:* medium full red-purple. *Bouquet:* extremely ripe, jammy/strawberry aromas, intense and indeed overstated. *Palate:* of immense weight; strong, strawberry fruit flavours; way outside the normal understanding of pinot noir in Australia. Most interesting for the uncontrolled fruit flavour. Drink '87–'90.

1982 CABERNET SAUVIGNON [17.2] *Colour:* strong red-purple. *Bouquet:* firm, with some ripe blackcurrant aromas intermingling with a touch of graves-like, gravelly earth character. *Palate:* fairly high alcohol, and a touch of charred/smoky oak adds to the slightly thick texture; a trace of bitterness on the finish is also evident. May simply need time to come together. Drink '87–'93.

KIDMAN

Location:
Main Penola–Naracoorte Road, Coonawarra, 5263; 14 km north of Penola.

Winemakers:
Ken Ward (red wines) and contract winemakers (white wines).

1985 Production:
2100 cases Rhine Riesling, 1900 cases red.

Principal Wines:
Terra Rossa wines is another major independent grape grower, although on a substantially smaller scale than Coonawarra Machinery Company. Only two wines made; Rhine Riesling and a red wine, now labelled as Cabernet Sauvignon or, in best Australian tradition, Great Red Wine of Coonawarra. Wines with considerable age still available; 1976 and 1981 vintage reds on offer in 1985.

Distribution:
Sold exclusively through Dan Murphy's Cellar, Melbourne and through cellar door. Cellar-door sales 9 a.m. to 5 p.m. Monday to Saturday.

Prices:
$3.45 to $3.99 retail.

Overall Quality:
Variable, very usually representing good value because of very low prices.

Vintage Rating 1982–85:
White: '84, '85, '83, '82.
Red: '82, '85, '84, '83.

Outstanding Prior Vintages:
'76, '80 and '81 (red only).

Tasting Notes:

1983 RHINE RIESLING [17.8] *Colour:* some straw. *Bouquet:* rich tropical/pineapple aromas to full, but obviously botrytis-affected, fruit. *Palate:* very full, soft and rich mid-palate, again with pineapple flavours. The finish is a fraction hard. Drink '85–'87.

1982 RHINE RIESLING [17.6] *Colour:* brilliant, deep green-yellow. *Bouquet:* firm, slightly smoky/toasty classic riesling aroma, showing no signs of botrytis whatsoever. *Palate:* firm, rich and concentrated; will develop but still needs time. Drink '86–'90.

1981 CABERNET SAUVIGNON [15.4] *Colour:* red-purple of medium depth. *Bouquet:* firm; some traces of old oak character; slightly smelly, rubber raincoat aroma, no doubt mercaptan-derived. *Palate:* a big, firm wine, with a touch of astringency, once again probably due to mercaptan. Drink '86–'89.

1980 GREAT RED WINE OF COONAWARRA [16.8] *Colour:* medium to full red. *Bouquet:* sweet, vanillan, American oak, but again there is a distracting suggestion of a trace of mercaptan, which slightly spoils an otherwise attractive aroma. *Palate:* sweet, berry fruit on the mid-palate; soft tannin and good acid on the finish provide balance and length. Drink '85–'90.

KOPPAMURRA

p. 408

Location:
Off main Penola–Naracoorte Road, half-way between Penola and Naracoorte; just south of Struan.
(087) 64 7483.

Winemaker:
Wines fermented under contract and returned to stone winery on estate for ageing and blending by owners Susan Andrews and John Greenshields.

1985 Production:
11,000 litres (the equivalent of 1200 cases).

Principal Wines:
Cabernet Sauvignon, and Cabernet Sauvignon Merlot Cabernet Franc (blend).

Distribution:
Principally cellar-door sales and mailing list. Cellar-door sales 7 days a week, but phone appointment preferred. Mailing-list enquiries to Box 886, Naracoorte, 5271. Limited retail distribution in Sydney and Melbourne direct from vineyard.

Prices:
Approximately $7.50 recommended retail.

Vintage Rating 1982–85:
'85, '84, '82, '83.

Overall Quality:
Very good.

Tasting Notes:

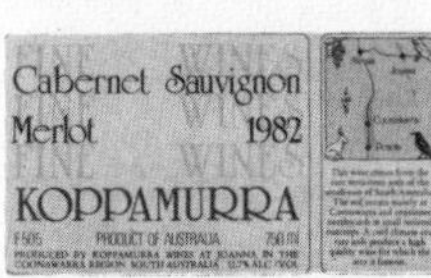

1982 CABERNET MERLOT [17] *Colour:* excellent purple-red. *Bouquet:* firm, deeply structured fruit; an elusive hint of what may be mercaptan lurking deep in the background. *Palate:* sweet, berry fruit flavours on the mid-palate with a touch of mint; beautifully structured and balanced. Would be outstanding were it not for that slight worry about the bouquet. Drink '85–'90.

1980 CABERNET SAUVIGNON [17.8] *Colour:* medium purple-red. *Bouquet:* full, rich and round with excellent ripe berry aromas. *Palate:* strikingly clean and fruity; rich, ripe berry flavours on the mid-palate tempered by just a touch of varietal astringency. Drink '85–'91.

LADBROKE GROVE

p. 408

Location:
Millicent Road, Penola, 5277;
1.5 km south of township.
(087) 37 2997.

Winemaker:
Made under contract at various wineries and matured on estate winery.

1985 Production:
1200 cases.

Principal Wines:
Rhine Riesling, Late Picked Rhine Riesling, Hermitage and Cabernet Sauvignon.

Distribution:
Principally cellar-door sales and mail list. Cellar-door sales 9.30 a.m. to 4.30 p.m. most days. Mailing-list enquiries as above.

Prices:
$7.50 cellar door.

Overall Quality:
Very good.

Vintage Rating 1982–85:
'85, '84, '82, '83.

Tasting Notes:

1984 RHINE RIESLING [17.8] *Colour:* bright green-yellow. *Bouquet:* extremely fragrant and aromatic; lifted lime/pineapple aromas, clean and, within the context of the style, most attractive. *Palate:* stylish, striking and full-flavoured fore- and mid-palate; slight hardness on the finish detracts a little, but nonetheless a most impressive wine. Drink '85–'89.

1984 LATE PICKED RHINE RIESLING [17.4] *Colour:* medium yellow. *Bouquet:* disappointing, rather dull and coarse. *Palate:* there is no resemblance to the bouquet whatsoever; fine wine of great intensity and elegance with a long, clean, lingering finish. A Jekyll and Hyde wine. Drink '86–'90.

1982 HERMITAGE [16.8] *Colour:* purple-red of medium to full depth. *Bouquet:* typical new-generation stewed fruit/plum/leafy aromas of undoubted complexity but, in the final analysis, not a desirable wine character. *Palate:* lively, full of flavour and complex, but exhibiting the same curious melange of flavours apparent in the bouquet. If you like the style, so be it; I don't. Drink '85–'89.

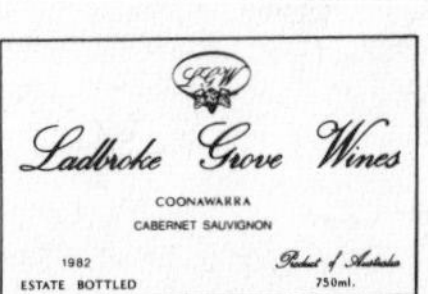

1982 CABERNET SAUVIGNON [18.4] *Colour:* slightly opaque red, showing distinct signs of development. *Bouquet:* complex, with rich and ripe (but not jammy) fruit, intermingling with charred oak. *Palate:* most attractive, softly ripe fruit with plum flavours, backed by a touch of tobacco; an excellent wine with none of the odd new Coonawarra flavours. Drink '86–'93.

LECONFIELD

pp. 408–9

Location:
Main Penola–Naracoorte Road, Coonawarra, 5263; 3 km north of Penola.
(087) 37 2326.

Winemaker:
Dr Richard Hamilton.

1985 Production:
Approximately 6000 cases.

Principal Wines:
Rhine Riesling, Shiraz and Cabernet Sauvignon.

Distribution:
Significant cellar-door sales at Coonawarra and at McLaren Vale; also mailing list. Cellar-door sales 9 a.m. to 5 p.m. Monday to Friday, 11 a.m. to 4 p.m. weekends and public holidays. Mailing-list enquiries to Box 162, Penola, 5277. Fine wine retail distribution in Adelaide, Melbourne, Sydney and Canberra.

Prices:
$5.50 to $10.50 cellar door.

Overall Quality:
White wines have recently improved considerably; red wines very good and Cabernet Sauvignon sometimes exceptional.

Vintage Rating 1982–85:
White: '83, '84, '85, '82.
Red: '82, '84, '85, '83.

Outstanding Prior Vintages:
'78, '80.

Tasting Notes:

1983 RHINE RIESLING BOTRYTIS AFFECTED (DRY STYLE) [16.6] *Colour:* deep yellow with some straw tinges. *Bouquet:* full round and sweet lime aromatics; clean, with no solids fermentation characters; a radical departure in style from earlier Leconfield rieslings. *Palate:* despite the label, not fully dry; residual sugar fleshes out the mid-palate, a legitimate, if not essential, part of the balance of the wine given the massive botrytis influence. Drink '85–'86.

1983 LATE HARVEST RHINE RIESLING BOTRYTIS AFFECTED [16.8] *Colour:* deep yellow. *Bouquet:* rich lime aromas, with strong botrytis influence, yet not heavy or aggressive. *Palate:* very similar to the dry-style wine of the same year, slightly bigger in body and impact; well-made, and full of flavour. Drink '85–'88.

1982 CABERNET SAUVIGNON [18.6] *Colour:* medium to full red-purple. *Bouquet:* fine, herbaceous cabernet in a classic Bordeaux mould, with ample ripeness and weight. *Palate:* a fine, classic wine of good weight and length; beautifully balanced and again reminiscent of a fine red wine of Bordeaux. Richly deserving its 4 gold medals to date. Drink '87–'96.

1981 CABERNET SAUVIGNON [16.2] *Colour:* red-purple of medium depth. *Bouquet:* robust; some leafy, cabernet varietal aroma and a whisper of mercaptan. *Palate:* of medium to full weight, with clearly marked, leafy-varietal cabernet flavours, and a rather leathery finish. Drink '85–'90.

1980 CABERNET SAUVIGNON There were a number of bottlings of this wine; some were absolutely magnificent; one tasted mid-1985 can only be described as a major disappointment.

LINDEMANS

pp. 409–13

Location:
Main Penola–Naracoorte Road, Coonawarra, 5263; 9 km north of Penola.

Winemaker:
Greg Clayfield.

1985 Production:
Not for publication, but estimated approximately 5000 tonnes.

Principal Wines:
An outstanding range of varietal table wines released under two main brands, which Lindemans prefer to keep separate as they are technically owned by and sold by different subsidiaries. Rouge Homme labels comprise Rhine Riesling, Chardonnay, Auslese Rhine Riesling, Pinot Noir, Malbec, Claret and Cabernet Sauvignon. Lindemans Wines labels include Nursery Vineyard Rhine Riesling, St Cedds Vineyard Traminer, Limestone Ridge Shiraz Cabernet and St George Vineyard Cabernet Sauvignon. In addition, Coonawarra provides substantial quantities of wine which go to make up a part of Lindemans blended cellar styles; in particular Auburn Burgundy and Nyrang Hermitage.

Distribution:
National retail at all levels.

Prices:
In the upper half of the market; recommended retail has little relevance to real price, with discounts at fluctuating, but at times considerable, levels. Recommended retail prices theoretically fall in $8.50 to $13.10 range.

Overall Quality:
Very good, with many wines (St George Cabernet Sauvignon a prime example, also Limestone Ridge) exceptional.

Vintage Rating 1982–85:
White: '83, '85, '82, '84.
Red: '82, '85, '84, '83.

Outstanding Prior Vintages:
'76, '78, '80.

Tasting Notes:

1985 NURSERY VINEYARD RHINE RIESLING [17.4] *Colour:* light to medium yellow-green, straw-tinged. *Bouquet:* clean, firm fruit without any obvious botrytis influence. *Palate:* a firm, crisp style, with good fruit weight and depth which builds on the mid-palate and carries through to a long, fruity and relatively soft finish. Much the best rhine riesling from the Nursery Vineyard for many years. Drink '86–'89.

1984 ROUGE HOMME AUSLESE RHINE RIESLING [17] *Colour:* brilliant yellow-green of medium depth. *Bouquet:* very aromatic, with obvious botrytis influence; strong tropical fruit characters which are most attractive. *Palate:* spicy, tropical fruit flavours with riesling character almost totally obscured by influence of botrytis; acid in good balance and not assertive. A voluptuous mouthful. Drink '86–'89.

1983 ROUGE HOMME PINOT NOIR [16.8] *Colour:* red-purple of medium depth, good for the variety. *Bouquet:* a robust style of pinot, with strong lemony oak. *Palate:* carries on logically from the bouquet; fairly racy/robust pinot with some strawberry fruit together with lively, zesty oak; overall of considerable weight and substance. Drink '85–'88.

1982 LINDEMANS LIMESTONE RIDGE SHIRAZ CABERNET [18] *Colour:* medium to full red, still tinged with purple. *Bouquet:* exceptionally complex with a multitude of aromas, basically in the cigar box through to faintly meaty spectrum; a totally distinctive style. *Palate:* most attractive, sweet cherry/berry flavours on the mid-palate, followed by tastes of spice and mint; very soft tannin rounds off the finish. A quite lovely drinking red, albeit in that idiosyncratic, modern-day Coonawarra style. Drink '86–'92.

1982 LINDEMANS ST GEORGE CABERNET SAUVIGNON [18.6] *Colour:* very good medium to full red-purple. *Bouquet:* outstanding, clean, and clear strong fruit without any of the odd aromas and complexities of the Limestone Ridge; a nice touch of cedar oak. *Palate:* one of the best for some time from the stable; lovely balance, and ample depth and length; classic cabernet sauvignon of perfect ripeness and style. A consistent silver medal winner; in my view it should have been a consistent gold medal winner. Drink '87–'95.

MILDARA

pp. 413–15

Location:
Main Penola–Naracoorte Road, Coonawarra, 5263; 9 km north of Penola.
(087) 36 3339.

Winemakers:
Jack Schultz, Tony Murphy and others.

1985 Production:
1500 tonnes.

Principal Wines:

A range of white and red table wines and Coonawarra's only vintage port. Labels comprise Rhine Riesling, Sauvignon Blanc, Chardonnay, Hermitage, Cabernet Shiraz (a label likely to be discontinued), Cabernet Shiraz Malbec, Cabernet Merlot, Cabernet Sauvignon and Vintage Port. J.W. Classic Cabernet Shiraz is a blend of Coonawarra Cabernet Sauvignon and Eden Valley Shiraz, and is an outstanding wine. The famed Yellow Label Bin Series is now also predominantly Coonawarra/Eden Valley sourced.

Distribution:
National retail through all types of outlets.

Prices:
Modest enough to start with, discounting at times reduces the recommended retail to absurdly low levels. Recommended retail ranges between $5.20 and $8.60, but the real prices are inevitably substantially lower.

Overall Quality:
Whites good, reds since 1979 consistently very good, bordering on exceptional.

Vintage Rating 1982–85:
White: '85, '82, '84, '83.
Red: '85, '82, '84, '83.

Outstanding Prior Vintages:
'79, '80.

Tasting Notes:

1984 CHARDONNAY [16.8] *Colour:* pale yellow-green. *Bouquet:* light and clean, some lemony/citrus oak aromas; fresh but rather light. *Palate:* again lightness and elegance, rather than fruit flavour, are the key words; some grapefruit flavours add varietal distinction. Drink '85–'87.

1984 SAUVIGNON BLANC [17.8] *Colour:* bright yellow-green. *Bouquet:* a wine carefully protected during fermentation, with some fermentation characters lingering well into 1985; nonetheless clearly marked grassy varietal character of good depth. *Palate:* a fresh and lively wine on the fore-palate, with very good mid- to back-palate weight and feel. The best sauvignon blanc to come from Mildara so far, even better than the very good '81. Drink '85–'88.

1984 RHINE RIESLING [16] *Colour:* light, bright green-yellow. *Bouquet:* fresh and fragrant with some pineapple/lime aromas. *Palate:* clean; gentle fruit on the mid-palate and a rather hard finish. A commercial wine. Drink '85–'87.

1982 HERMITAGE [17.4] *Colour:* bright red of medium depth. *Bouquet:* most attractive, clean, cherry aromas, sweet and full, but not heavy. *Palate:* a virtual carbon copy of the bouquet; bell-clear cherry/berry fruit flavours to a very well-balanced and modulated wine. Drink '86–'88.

1982 CABERNET MERLOT [18.2] *Colour:* red-purple of medium depth. *Bouquet:* beautifully ripe fruit married with well-handled oak; rich and pleasing. *Palate:* a round, mouth-filling amalgam of berries; typical, ultra-soft Coonawarra tannin on the finish; a balanced, stylish and harmonious wine. Drink '86–'92.

1982 J.W. CLASSIC CABERNET SHIRAZ [17.8] *Colour:* excellent purple-red of medium depth. *Bouquet:* clean and fragrant, with sweet, berry aromas intermingling with cedar oak. *Palate:* an elegant wine with life and lift; attractive sweet berry/plum flavours on the mid-palate, and a soft, low tannin finish. Close to its best now. Drink '85–'88.

PENFOLDS

pp. 416–17

Location:
Main Penola–Naracoorte Road, Coonawarra, 5263;
12 km north of Penola (vineyard only).

Winemakers:
Warren Ward (chief winemaker), John Duval and others.

1985 Production:
Estimated at between 850 and 1000 tonnes; most production used for blending.

Principal Wines:
Only 100 per cent Coonawarra wine on regular release is Bin 128 Claret. Bin 231 Rhine Riesling now discontinued.

Distribution:
National retail at all levels.

Prices:
Recommended retail of Bin 128 in excess of $6 is meaningless; wine usually discounted to $4 and occasionally even less.

Overall Quality:
Good.

Vintage Rating 1982–85:
White: '84, '85, '82, '83.
Red: '82, '84, '85, '83.

Outstanding Prior Vintages:
(Red only) '63, '66, '68, '76, '80.

Tasting Notes:

1981 BIN 128 COONAWARRA SHIRAZ [17] *Colour:* **medium red, but with distinct amber tints and very advanced.** *Bouquet:* **quite aromatic, with some developed tobacco characters, almost Hunter-like, but very stylish for all that.** *Palate:* **rather fresher than the bouquet suggests, a surprisingly elegant and relatively light-bodied wine given the vintage; no varietal spice, but good length to flavour. Drink '86–'90.**

PENOWARRA

p. 417

Location:
Main Penola–Naracoorte Road, Penola, 5277;
3 km north of township.
(087) 37 2458.

Winemaker:
Wine made under contract for Raymond Messenger.

1985 Production:
Not stated but very small.

Principal Wines:
Rhine Riesling, Shiraz and Cabernet Sauvignon.

Distribution:
Substantial cellar-door sales and mailing lists; cellar-door sales 8 a.m. to 5 p.m. Monday to Saturday. Mailing-list enquiries to PO Box 4B, Coonawarra, 5263.

Overall Quality:
Variable, but one or two attractive red wines have been made. Whites adequate.

PETALUMA

pp. 417–18

Location:
Main Penola–Naracoorte Road, Coonawarra, 5263; 13 km north of Penola (vineyard only).

Winemaker:
Brian Croser.

1985 Production:
7000 cases Chardonnay, 6000 cases Coonawarra Red, 500 cases Botrytis Rhine Riesling.

Principal Wines:

Botrytis Affected Rhine Riesling, Chardonnay (presently principally made from Coonawarra fruit, but in the future to come from Adelaide Hills material) and cabernet-dominant red simply entitled 'Coonawarra'.

Distribution:
Through fine wine retailers in all capital cities; no cellar-door sales nor mailing list.

Prices:
$15 to $18.50 recommended retail.

Overall Quality:
Exceptional.

Vintage Rating 1982–85:
Chardonnay: '85, '84, '82, '83.
Botrytis Riesling: '85, '84, '82, (no '83).
Coonawarra Red: '85, '84, '82, '83.

Outstanding Prior Vintages:
'80.

Tasting Notes:
1984 BOTRYTIS RHINE RIESLING [19] *Colour:* glistening, bright green-yellow of medium depth. *Bouquet:* immensely rich and pungent lime aromas, Germanic in style. *Palate:* explosive flavours; intense lusciqusness balanced by very good acid; strong lime/pineapple fruit. Drink '87–'96.

1983 CHARDONNAY [18.2] *Colour:* glowing green-yellow. *Bouquet:* very complex and deep fruit, with an almost bacon-like aroma to the oak. *Palate:* an extremely complex wine, showing the same considerable weight of the bouquet; bone dry and in the austere mould, but perfectly balanced. Drink '86–'90.

1981 COONAWARRA [17.6] *Colour:* medium to full red-purple. *Bouquet:* in mid-1985 going through a development phase, and looking far less attractive than it did as a younger wine, with some leathery/mulberry aromas. *Palate:* gentle mulberry/cherry fruit on the mid-palate; light oak and soft tannin; a fruit wine first and foremost with the palate somewhat at odds with the bouquet. Drink 86–'91.

REDMAN

pp. 418–19

Location:
Main Penola–Naracoorte Road, Coonawarra, 5263; 15 km north of Penola.
(087) 36 3331.

Winemaker:
Bruce Redman.

1985 Production:
200,000 litres (or 22,000 cases).

Principal Wines:
Only two wines made: Claret and Cabernet Sauvignon.

Distribution:
National through Rhine Castle Wines to retailers at all levels. Cellar-door sales 9 a.m. to 5 p.m. Monday to Saturday. No mailing list.

Prices:
Subject to periodic savage discounting; recommended retail $7.20 to $10.10.

Overall Quality:
Extremely disappointing in recent years and no better than adequate.

Vintage Rating 1982–85:
'84, '85, '82, '83.

Outstanding Prior Vintages:
'66, '68, '71.

Tasting Notes:

1983 CLARET [15.4] *Colour:* light to medium red, already developing quickly. *Bouquet:* light, softly scented cherry aromas, with some lactic spoilage present. *Palate:* gently ripe cherry flavours; faintest hint of wood/varietal spice on the back-palate; again a little lactic character intrudes. Drink '86–'89.

1983 CABERNET SAUVIGNON [15.2] *Colour:* light to medium red, very developed. *Bouquet:* soft, gently leathery/earthy aromas deriving from mercaptan. *Palate:* light, leathery fruit; very soft, low tannin and very advanced. A fairly ordinary commercial wine. Drink '86–'88.

ROSEMOUNT ESTATE

p. 420

Location:
Main Penola–Naracoorte Road, Penola, 5270;
on northern outskirts of town (vineyard only).

Winemaker:
Phillip Shaw.

1985 Production:
Not stated; all grapes presently purchased from Coonawarra Machinery Company in any event.

Principal Wines:
Rhine Riesling, Shiraz and Cabernet Sauvignon.

Distribution:
National retail through fine wine merchants; extensive restaurant representation. No cellar-door sales nor mailing list.

Prices:
$7.60 to $9.40 recommended retail.

Overall Quality:
Consistently very good.

Vintage Rating 1982–85:
'82, '85, '84, '83.

Tasting Notes:

1985 RHINE RIESLING [17.8] *Colour:* **bright yellow-green.** *Bouquet:* **highly romatic, with pungent, almost essency, lime fruit aromas.** *Palate:* **classic Coonawarra rhine riesling; long and clean wine with good mid-palate fruit weight and a touch of toast to give structure. Drink '87–'91.**

1982 CABERNET SAUVIGNON [17.8] *Colour:* **bright red-purple of medium depth.** *Bouquet:* **very strong, charred, lemony French oak, but well-handled despite its precocity.** *Palate:* **not surprisingly, oak is again dominant, though similarly well-handled and attractive; good fruit underneath with pleasantly soft acidity. The oak may be obvious but you can't help liking it. Drink '86–'90.**

SKINNER

p. 420

Location:
Cnr Main Penola–Naracoorte Road and Racehorse Road, Coonawarra, 5263;
adjacent to Coonawarra township (vineyard only).

Winemaker:
Contract-made.

1985 Production:
Not stated.

Principal Wines:
Red wines, all sold in bulk to wine merchants, chiefly in Sydney.

WYNNS

pp. 420–5

Location:
Memorial Drive, Coonawarra, 5263;
2 km west of Coonawarra township.
(087) 36 3266.

Winemaker:
John Wade.

1985 Production:
Approximately 6500 tonnes.

Principal Wines:
Rhine Riesling, Chardonnay, Hermitage, Cabernet Sauvignon and John Riddoch Cabernet Sauvignon. Also produces substantial quantities of base wine for *méthode champenoise* wines; other production blended with other Allied Vintners group wines.

Distribution:
National retail at all levels.

Prices:
At least until the acquisition by Penfolds, the most ubiquitous and most unpredictable discounters in the market place. Published prices bear no relationship to reality.

Overall Quality:
Rhine Riesling adequate; Chardonnay good to very good; Hermitage at times excellent; Cabernet Sauvignon good; John Riddoch Cabernet Sauvignon exceptional.

Vintage Rating 1982–85:
'82, '85, '84, '83.

Outstanding Prior Vintages:
'80, '76, '75, '66, '62 and '55.

Tasting Notes:

1984 RHINE RIESLING [16.4] *Colour:* medium full yellow-green. *Bouquet:* clean, fresh, light, riesling aromas; well-made, but lacking depth. *Palate:* clean and gentle light lime/tropical fruit flavours; quite developed; a very good commercial wine at the price at which it sells in the real world. Drink '86–'88.

1984 CHARDONNAY [17.8] *Colour:* full yellow-green. *Bouquet:* extremely rich, ripe and buttery, with a hint of shredded coconut. *Palate:* a very soft, full and generous wine, with ripe buttery/coconut flavours, which must be drunk now and not cellared. Drink '86.

1983 HERMITAGE [17] *Colour:* excellent purple-red of medium depth, bright and clear. *Bouquet:* full and soft, very ripe, plum spice characters verging on the stewed fruit Coonawarra syndrome. *Palate:* very ripe, plum/spice flavours; plenty of weight and character. Not quite in the class of the outstanding '82, but a very good wine nonetheless. Drink '85–'89.

1980 CABERNET SAUVIGNON [16.8] *Colour:* clear, light to medium red. *Bouquet:* marked leafy/tobacco/herbaceous cool-climate aromas, lacking a little flesh. *Palate:* very similar leafy/tobacco/herbaceous flavours; a total contrast to the rich, ripe, fruit flavours of most of the 1980 Coonawarra reds. Drink '85–'88.

ZEMA ESTATE

p. 425

Location:
Main Penola–Naracoorte Road, Coonawarra, 5265; 0.5 km south of Coonawarra township.
(087) 36 3219.

Winemaker:
Ken Ward (consultant).

1985 Production:
2700 cases (will double in next few years).

Principal Wines:

Rhine Riesling, Late Harvest Rhine Riesling, Shiraz and Vintage Port.

Distribution:
Principally cellar-door sales and mailing list; cellar-door sales 9 a.m. to 5 p.m. 7 days. Mailing-list enquiries to PO Box 12, Coonawarra, 5263. Limited retail distribution through Alexander and Patterson, Melbourne and Brackleys in Perth.

Prices:
$6 to $6.50 cellar door.

Overall Quality:
Very good.

Vintage Rating 1982–85:
'82, '84, '85, '83.

Tasting Notes:

1984 RHINE RIESLING [18] *Colour:* bright green-yellow. *Bouquet:* some lime/pineapple aromas; quite rich; good depth. *Palate:* follows on from the bouquet, in the almost mandatory style of modern Coonawarra rhine rieslings; full-flavoured lime/pineapple; excellent soft finish, stylish and balanced. Drink '86–'89.

1984 LATE HARVEST RHINE RIESLING [17.8] *Colour:* medium to full yellow, with just a trace of green. *Bouquet:* obvious botrytis influence, rich and full; very clean. *Palate:* long flavour with intense, lime juice characters and just a touch of pineapple; good acid balance. Drink '86–'90.

1984 SHIRAZ [18.2] *Colour:* dense purple-red. *Bouquet:* full, perfectly ripe fruit, with a touch of coconut/vanillan American oak. *Palate:* lovely cherry fruit flavours married with round, coconut-like oak. A beautifully made and balanced wine of high quality. Drink '87–'92.

1983 SHIRAZ [17.4] *Colour:* medium to full red. *Bouquet:* a lively wine with lifted fruit and coconut-vanillin oak aromas; quite complex. *Palate:* lively and fresh cherry/berry fruit, just a hint of spice and low tannin. A great success for a difficult vintage. Drink '86–'90.

Langhorne Creek

1985 Vintage

Langhorne Creek is a unique viticultural area, depending as it does on being inundated by winter floods of the Bremer River. This year the flooding was heavier than usual, setting the season off to an excellent start.

The cool, dry conditions which prevailed over South Australia until mid-March were followed by intermittent heavy rains which retarded sugar and flavour levels, and caused considerable difficulties during harvest.

Yields varied substantially from slightly lower than average to excessively abundant. Overall quality was patchy, with some disappointments, but cabernet sauvignon and malbec went against the rule by producing excellent, full-bodied wines.

The Changes

The only change has been that Bremer Wines closed its old winery and concentrated its operations in its second and newer facility.

BLEASDALE

pp. 427–9

Location:
Wellington Road, Langhorne Creek, 5255;
17 km east of Strathalbyn.
(085) 37 3001.

Winemaker:
Michael Potts.

1985 Production:
The equivalent of approximately 45,000 cases. Only portion sold under the Bleasdale label; substantial bulk and clean-skin sales.

Principal Wines:

A substantial range of table, sparkling and fortified wines released under both varietal and generic labels. White wines include Wood Aged Semillon, Rhine Riesling, Verdelho, Frontignac and Colombard; red wines include Cabernet Sauvignon, Shiraz Cabernet, Malbec, Special Vintage Shiraz, Private Bin Hermitage and Shiraz Oeillade. Tiny quantities of very old, high-quality Heysen Madeira also available at winery (1 bottle per customer limit). All wines sold with significant bottle age.

Distribution:
National retail through Elders-IXL Ltd. Cellar-door sales 9 a.m. to 5 p.m. Monday to Saturday. Mailing list to PO Box 1, Langhorne Creek, 5255.

Prices:
$5.50 to $9 recommended retail.

Overall Quality:
Good; occasional wines very good.

Vintage Rating 1982–85:
White: '84, '82, '85, '83.
Red: '84, '82, '85, '83.

Outstanding Prior Vintages:
'78, '80.

Tasting Notes:

1983 *WOOD AGED SEMILLON* [16] *Colour:* bright, full yellow. *Bouquet:* marked lemony oak, not fully integrated and tends to dominate light fruit. *Palate:* oak once again dominant and a little rough; the wine will develop, but would have benefited from more fruit. Drink '86–'88.

1981 *CABERNET SAUVIGNON* [16.8] *Colour:* excellent, deep red-purple. *Bouquet:* clean and firm; sweet American oak, together with clearly defined cabernet aroma. *Palate:* abundant berry fruit, tinged with typical cabernet astringency; just a hint of new oak. A good wine. Drink '86–'90.

1980 *SHIRAZ CABERNET SAUVIGNON* [17.6] *Colour:* incredibly deep red-purple. *Bouquet:* clean, very full and dense, gently ripe fruit aroma. *Palate:* a strongly constructed wine, with big fruit, yet somehow delicate; will live for decades; a fraction more lift would have taken it into the highest class. Drink '86–'94.

BREMER WINES

p. 429

Location:
Wellington Road, Langhorne Creek, 5255;
in the centre of the township.
(085) 37 3196.

Winemaker:
Bill Davidson.

1985 Production:
Approximately 3500 cases.

Principal Wines:
A fairly limited range including Chardonnay (the first such release from Langhorne Creek), Cabernet Shiraz and Cabernet Sauvignon.

Distribution:
Almost exclusively cellar-door sales and mailing list, with some Melbourne retail distribution. Cellar-door sales 9.30 a.m. to 5 p.m. Monday to Saturday and 11.30 a.m. to 5 p.m. Sunday. Mailing-list enquiries to PO Box 136, Langhorne Creek, 5255.

Prices:
$8.50 to $9 recommended retail.

Overall Quality:
Adequate; occasional good wines.

Vintage Rating 1982–85:
White: '84, '82, '85, '83.
Red: '84, '83, '85, '82.

Outstanding Prior Vintages:
'80.

Padthaway/Keppoch

1985 Vintage

Not surprisingly, conditions were virtually identical to those of Coonawarra. Yields were well above average, and wine quality is uniformly high.

The white wines have abundant flavour, excellent varietal character and look like being every bit as good as the excellent '84s. Red wines, too, look full of promise, with pinot noir outstanding.

The Changes

There have been no changes. Padthaway remains the preserve of the big companies, producing ever-increasing percentages of those companies' premium wines.

LINDEMANS PADTHAWAY

pp. 433–4

Location:
Padthaway via Naracoorte, 5271;
(vineyard only).

Winemaker:
Greg Clayfield (Coonawarra).

1985 Production:
Not for publication.

Principal Wines:

Rhine Riesling, Rhine Riesling Spatlese, Rhine Riesling Auslese, Fumé Blanc, Chardonnay and Pinot Noir.

Distribution:
National retail through all types of outlets.

Prices:
$6.80 to $9.50 recommended retail; these, however, bear no relationship to the real prices, which are far less.

Overall Quality:
Very good; sometimes exceptional.

Vintage Rating 1982–85:
'84, '85, '82, '83.

Tasting Notes:

1985 FUME BLANC [17.8] *Colour:* light to medium yellow-green. *Bouquet:* highly aromatic, rich gooseberry, verging on passionfruit. *Palate:* very rich, full fruit, exhibiting excellent varietal character in the ripe style; complex and weighty, with a long finish. Drink '86–'87.

1985 RHINE RIESLING [17.8] *Colour:* light, bright green-yellow. *Bouquet:* full, soft and fragrant, with excellent varietal riesling aroma, and promising to build into an extremely rich wine. *Palate:* clean and fresh, with clearly defined and unmodified fruit flavours, free of botrytis; good acid balance. Destined to develop early. Drink '86.

1985 CHARDONNAY [18.4] *Colour:* brilliant medium to full yellow. *Bouquet:* complex, clean fruit and oak, with a touch of peach; a riper style than the magnificent '84, but still has great balance and fruit/oak integration. *Palate:* most attractive, clean, round, peach fruit flavours, with oak judged to perfection. Drink '86–'88.

1984 CHARDONNAY [18.8] *Colour:* bright green-yellow. *Bouquet:* superb balance a feature of the wine; of medium to full weight, with grapefruit aromas intermingling with oak. *Palate:* exceptionally smooth and balanced; fruit flavours across the grapefruit/peach/melon spectrum; a long, harmonious and perfectly weighted wine. Drink '85–'88.

1984 PINOT NOIR [17.8] *Colour:* very good medium to full purple-red. *Bouquet:* clean; good fruit depth, some slightly meaty/burnt burgundian aromas. *Palate:* excellent flavour; overall quite firm, but a most attractive touch of strawberry on the mid-palate; good length to finish. Deserves the gold medals it has won at national shows. Drink '86–'88.

SEPPELT

pp. 434–5

Location:
Adjacent to Padthaway township, approximately 75 km north of Naracoorte; (vineyard only).

Winemakers:
Ian MacKenzie (chief), plus numerous others.

1985 Production:
Over 2000 tonnes of fruit produced from the vineyard.

Principal Wines:

No regular vineyard releases, but Rhine Riesling, Chardonnay and Cabernet Sauvignon in particular play a major role in many of Seppelt's more important wines.

Distribution:
National retail at all levels.

Prices:
Recommended retail barely relevant; real prices in the $5.50 to $7 range.

Overall Quality:
Very good; occasional exceptional wines.

Vintage Rating 1982–85:
White: '84, '82, '85, '83.
Red: '82, '84, '85, '83.

Tasting Notes:

1984 AUSLESE RHINE RIESLING [19] *Colour:* glowing yellow-green. *Bouquet:* intensely perfumed, with strong botrytis influence and a touch of pineapple fruit. *Palate:* a superbly intense, explosively rich wine, with a long, lingering finish. While sweet, does not cloy, and the finish is fresh and tingling. Drink '86–'92.

1983 LATE HARVEST RHINE RIESLING BEERENAUSLESE [17.2] *Colour:* brilliant, glowing green-yellow. *Bouquet:* of medium to full weight; firm germanic lime, richly aromatic. *Palate:* an excellent, rich wine, with a particularly full mid-palate, simply lacking the ultimate intensity and finesse of the '84 Auslese. Drink '85–'87.

1983 SHOW PINOT NOIR [16.8] *Colour:* light to medium red-purple. *Bouquet:* attractive, sweet vanillan oak, together with some strawberry varietal fruit aromas. *Palate:* full, soft, sweet strawberry fruit, but oak a little heavy and pedestrian. (A blend of 70% Keppoch pinot noir and 30% Barossa, show gold medal winner.) Drink '85–'87.

THOMAS HARDY

pp. 432–3

Location:
Midway between Padthaway and Keppoch, adjacent to main highway;
(vineyard only).

Winemakers:
Various in the Hardy team.

1985 Production:
2,500,000 litres.

Principal Wines:

A wide range of varietal table wines are produced, with the Keppoch vineyards providing by far the greatest part of Hardy's wines. Siegersdorf Rhine Riesling is now totally Keppoch material; various varietals under various labels have been released over the years, with the Hardy Collection range introduced mid-1985 and including Chardonnay, Sauvignon Blanc, Fumé Blanc, Chardonnay, Beerenauslese Rhine Riesling, Pinot Noir, Traminer and Rhine Riesling.

Distribution:
National retail.

Prices:
$4.99 to $7.99 recommended retail, but will no doubt be available for substantially less.

Overall Quality:
Has been variable; Collection Series white wines promise to be exceptional.

Vintage Rating 1982–85:
White: '84, '85, '82, '83.
Red: '85, '84, '82, '83.

Outstanding Prior Vintages:
'80.

Tasting Notes:

1984 SIEGERSDORF RHINE RIESLING [17.2] *Colour:* medium full green-yellow. *Bouquet:* soft and clean; some pineapple/tropical fruit aromas, but little or no botrytis influence. *Palate:* soft and fruity, with good sugar balance and a long, soft, fruity finish. Everyman's rhine riesling. Drink '85–'86.

COLLECTION SERIES CHARDONNAY [18.2] *Colour:* medium full yellow-green. *Bouquet:* complex, and rich with strong charred oak aroma and even a touch of Burgundian sulphide. *Palate:* a very rich, complex wine, evidently high in alcohol, as it gives a distinct impression of sweetness, a sweetness which is almost certainly induced by alcohol rather than by residual sugar. (Some cork problems with this wine have resulted in off bottles.) Drink '86–'88.

1984 COLLECTION SERIES FUME BLANC [18.4] *Colour:* medium to full yellow-green. *Bouquet:* very rich, buttery/honeyed aromas, with strong semillon influence contributing much to weight and character. *Palate:* rich and flavoursome honeyed fruit and oak; very good integration and balance. (With rare honesty, the back label discloses the wine as a blend of sauvignon blanc and semillon.) Drink '85–'87.

1984 COLLECTION SERIES BEERENAUSLESE [18.4] *Colour:* full yellow. *Bouquet:* intense raisined lusciousness and tropical fruit aromas of great depth. *Palate:* exceptionally rich, raisined, overwhelmingly luscious wine of a dimension not often achieved in Australia. May be a little too powerful for some. (115 grams per litre of residual sugar and 11.5 degrees of alcohol indicates exceptionally botrytised material was used.) Drink '86–'92.

1984 PINOT NOIR [14.8] *Colour:* light red with some developed tawny hues. *Bouquet:* soft light and caramelised, with little or no varietal character evident, although a touch of mint. *Palate:* light camphor/mint flavours; an irrelevancy as a pinot noir, and only barely acceptable as a very light red. Drink '86.

Riverland

1985 Vintage

Overall, the vintage was the best for many years. Conditions from bud-burst right through to harvest remained unusually cool and temperate, and the absence of rainfall was of no consequence to the vineyards, all of which are irrigated. Indeed, the absence of any rainfall simply resulted in fruit of exceptionally sound condition, free from any mould or rot.

The only problems in the entire season were two days of very hot, windy weather which resulted in some scorching in places. The weather quickly returned to mild conditions, and a protracted vintage took place.

Overall, flavours are finer and fruit quality more delicate yet more intense than in most years. Chardonnay in particular was outstanding, with great aroma. The reds range from average to outstanding, with excellent colour and unusual finesse.

The Changes

The relatively small number of wineries remained unchanged, but give no indication of the overall importance of the region—Australia's largest. This is the heart of cask-land, and its future viability is unquestioned.

ANGOVE'S

pp. 438–9

Location:
Bookmark Avenue, Renmark, 5341 (head office); 1320 North East Road, Tea Tree Gully, 5091 (principal administration branch).
(085) 85 1311.

Winemakers:
Frank Newman and Bob Hill.

1985 Production:
Not stated; however, overall crush is very large and probably in excess of 10,000 tonnes.

Principal Wines:
A complete range of table and fortified wines are made. The table wines are (in descending order of quality) Angove's Varietal releases (8 white wines and a red); next Bin Reference Claret and Shiraz Malbec; then the reserve series (Tregrehan Claret, Brightlands Burgundy, Bookmark Riesling, Nanya Moselle and Golden Murray Sauterne); then Special Riesling, Moselle and Claret; and finally the flagon and cask range in 2-litre and 5-litre sizes. The fortified wines are headed by the St Agnes range of brandies (Very Old Brandy, Old Brandy and Three Star Brandy) and a full range of sherries plus vintage and tawny port. Finally there are the flavoured fortified wines headed by Marko Vermouth and Stones Ginger Wine.

Distribution:
National retail at all levels through company's own distribution network in South Australia, Victoria and New South Wales; other states through independent wholesale distributors. Cellar-door sales at Renmark and Tea Tree Gully 9 a.m. to 5 p.m. Monday to Friday.

Prices:
Vary significantly according to range of wine. Varietal releases between $5.45 and $6.30 recommended retail, but frequently on special for significantly less.

Overall Quality:
Very good indeed given the real price of the wines.

Vintage Rating 1982–85:
White: '84, '85, '83, '82.
Red: '85, '82, '83, '84.

Tasting Notes:

1984 CHARDONNAY [17.2] *Colour:* pale but bright yellow-green. *Bouquet:* quite pungent and aromatic, with a touch of grapefruit and some toasty fermentation characters persisting. *Palate:* a very lively and distinctly fruity wine, with good mid-palate weight. Both bouquet and palate show excellent winemaking, which has protected every last scintilla of fruit aroma and flavour. This is a Riverland chardonnay, and cannot be great; on the other hand, it is exceedingly impressive for what it is. Drink '85–'86.

1984 COLOMBARD [16.8] *Colour:* pale bright green-yellow. *Bouquet:* pungent tropical fruit aromas with lemony overtones, and again immediately protected. *Palate:* rich fruit flavours, impeccably made and balanced; devoid of the oily acid on the finish which sometimes detracts from this variety. Drink '85.

1984 SAUVIGNON BLANC [16.4] *Colour:* very pale colour, almost white. *Bouquet:* marked varietal aroma with that distinctive "armpit" aroma associated both with ultra-careful winemaking and also with the variety sauvignon. *Palate:* very pleasant fruit flavours, although the residual sugar level is distracting; the wine would be better if made bone dry. Drink '85.

1983 CABERNET SAUVIGNON [18] *Colour:* vibrant purple-red of medium depth. *Bouquet:* clean, lively and extremely fragrant sweet cassis/berry aromas. *Palate:* an exceptionally seductive wine with intense, almost perfumed, cherry flavours with marked fruit sweetness (no residual sugar is present in the wine). Drink '85–'87.

BERRI ESTATES

pp. 439–40

Location:
Sturt Highway, Karoom via Berri, 5343;
3 km south-east of Berri.
(085) 83 2303.

Winemaker:
R. J. Wilkinson.

1985 Production:
Almost 40,000 tonnes.

Principal Wines:

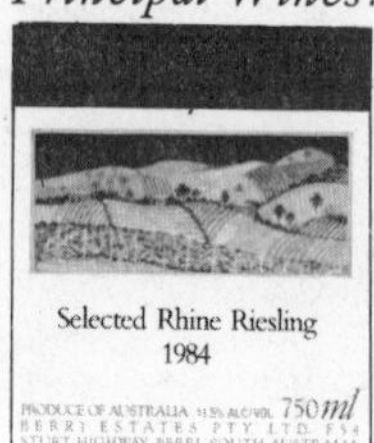

Specialists in 5-litre wine casks and, to a lesser degree, 2-litre flagons. Very substantial sales in bulk to other wineries. Limited range of 750 ml bottles including Spatlese Rhine Riesling, Springvale Chablis, Fruity Gordo Moselle, Chardonnay, Cabernet Shiraz and Cabernet Malbec.

Distribution:
National retail through Taylor Ferguson Limited in all states other than South Australia and Northern Territory, where distributed direct by Berri. Substantial and growing exports to North America, the United Kingdom, Europe and South-East Asia. Fruity Gordo Moselle is said to be the largest volume wine produced in Australia; much is sold to other packagers and re-sellers.

Prices:
The premium range has a theoretical retail price of around $6.70, but in reality, the wines sell for substantially less.

Overall Quality:
At the very least, adequate.

Tasting Notes:

1984 SPATLESE RHINE RIESLING [15.2] *Colour:* medium yellow. *Bouquet:* soft, fairly broad fruit aroma with a hint of caramel and obvious sweetness. *Palate:* similar soft, broad fruit; a reasonable depth of flavour and fair acid. Drink '85–'86.

1983 CHARDONNAY [15.6] *Colour:* bright yellow-green. *Bouquet:* smooth and clean, with a touch of bottle-developed butter/caramel. *Palate:* very light but well-balanced; pleasant feel in the mouth; at its peak late '85. Drink '85–'86.

1980 CABERNET MALBEC SHIRAZ [15.8] *Colour:* medium red, still with a vestige of purple. *Bouquet:* quite fragrant with bottle-developed caramel/tobacco aromas; some oxidation, but not unpleasant. *Palate:* soft, very developed, ripe plum/mulberry fruit flavours, and again a suggestion of some straw oxidation. Drink '85–'86.

FINE OLD TAWNY PORT [18] *Colour:* bright tawny, showing obvious wood-age. *Bouquet:* fine and fragrant, full of character and style; while quite light, has excellent rancio character. *Palate:* a very fine, very elegant tawny, with obvious wood-age; lighter than most Australian tawny ports and verging on Portuguese in style. Understandably a prolific gold medal winner. Drink now.

BONNEYVIEW

p. 440

Location:
Sturt Highway, Barmera, 5345;
due east of Berri.
(085) 88 2279.

Winemaker:
Christopher Sim.

1985 Production:
Approximately 1500 cases.

Principal Wines:
Traminer Riesling, Chardonnay, Frontignan Blanc, Spatlese Trebbiano, Moselle, Riesling, Cabernet Merlot, Cabernet Beaujolais, Nookamka Touriga Port, Shiraz Liqueur Port and Currant Liqueur Port.

Distribution:
Exclusively by cellar-door sales and mail order; cellar-door sales 9 a.m. to 5.30 p.m. 7 days. Mail order as above.

Prices:
$5 cellar door.

Overall Quality:
Adequate to good.

Vintage Rating 1982–85:
'85, '83, '84, '82.

Outstanding Prior Vintages:
'76, '81.

Tasting Notes:
1983 TRAMINER RIESLING [16.8] *Colour:* medium yellow-green. *Bouquet:* clean; quite full tropical lime aromas; has developed very well with surprising richness. *Palate:* abundant lime/pastille/tropical fruit flavours, with very good weight and holding structure and flavour surprisingly. Drink '85–'87.

NV PRIVATE BIN FRONTIGNAN BLANC [15.4] *Colour:* pale, tinged with pink. *Bouquet:* light, soft and clean, gently grapy. *Palate:* a very sweet, rather heavy moselle style; well enough made and no doubt commercially very acceptable. Drink '86.

COUNTY HAMLEY

p. 441

Location:
Cnr Bookmark Avenue and Twenty-Eighth Street, Renmark, 5341;
off Sturt Highway.
(085) 85 1411.

Winemakers:
T. and M. Bodroghy.

1985 Production:
1350 cases.

Principal Wines:
A limited range of table and fortified wines including Vin Fume, Rhine Riesling, Late Harvest Rhine Riesling, Chardonnay, Cabernet Sauvignon Tête de Cuvée, Pinot Noir, Bin 53 Port and Regimental Vintage Port.

Distribution:
Principally cellar-door sales and mailing lists; cellar-door sales 10 a.m. to 5.30 p.m. 7 days. Mailing-list enquiries to PO Box 483, Renmark, 5341.

Overall Quality:
Not rated.

Vintage Rating 1982–85:
White: '82, '85, '83, '84.
Red: '84, '85, '82, '83.

Outstanding Prior Vintages:
'76, '80, '81.

LOXTON MEDIA ESTATE

p. 441

Location:
Bookpurmonong Road, Loxton, 5333;
on north-eastern outskirts of town.
(085) 84 7236.

Winemakers:
K. A. Pfeiffer, A. Harris, P. Taylor and M. Zeppel.

1985 Production:
33,000 tonnes of grapes crushed, almost of all of which sold in bulk as unfermented juice, bulk wine or distilled into brandy, in all cases for on-sale to other wineries.

Principal Wines:
As indicated, virtually all production sold in bulk. Limited sales through cellar door of Loxton Media Estate varietal white and red wines.

Distribution:
Wine sold in bulk both on local and export markets. Substantial sales of grape juice concentrates to south-east Asia and substantial bulk wine exports to Japan. Cellar-door sales of bottled wine 9 a.m. to 5 p.m. Monday to Saturday.

LUBIANA

pp. 441–2

Location:
School Road, Moorook, 5332.
(085) 83 9320.

Winemaker:
Steve Lubiana.

1985 Production:
275,000 litres.

Principal Wines:
A full range of table and fortified wines; premium wines include Chardonnay, special Bin Cabernet Malbec Shiraz, Anniversary Port, 1973 Vintage Port, Old Muscat and Old Liqueur Frontignac; then follow 11 white and 7 red table wines with either varietal or generic labels, and almost 20 fortified wines including vintage ports of 5 vintages from 1974 to 1978.

Distribution:
Principally cellar-door sales and mailing lists; limited wholesale distribution direct ex-winery to selected retailers in capital cities. Cellar-door sales 9 a.m. to 5 p.m. Monday to Friday. Mailing-list enquiries to PO Box 50, Moorook, 5332.

Prices:
$2.50 to $7 per bottle, with most priced at $3.30.

Overall Quality:
Adequate.

Vintage Rating 1982–85:
White: '85, '83, '82, '84.
Red: '82, '83, '84, '85.

Outstanding Prior Vintages:
'74, '76.

Tasting Notes:

NV RHINE RIESLING (INDIVIDUAL VINEYARD) [15.4] *Colour:* bright light to medium green-yellow. *Bouquet:* solid fruit, with a touch of residual SO_2 giving a slight matchbox aroma. *Palate:* soft, clean fruit, with quite good weight, and well-balanced residual sugar. Drink '85–'86.

1981 SPECIAL BIN CABERNET MALBEC SHIRAZ [15.4] *Colour:* medium red. *Bouquet:* some astringent/leathery aromas, derived from mercaptan, with a touch of sweet berry fruit underneath. *Palate:* a pleasant, gently sweet, soft, berry-flavoured wine with low tannin. Drink '85–'87.

SERIES 2 ANNIVERSARY PORT [15.6] *Colour:* medium to full tawny, showing some cask age. *Bouquet:* rich and raisined, with some rancio characters; a very big wine. *Palate:* rich, flavoursome, ripe, tawny port flavours; a slightly biscuity/mousy after-taste mars the wine. Drink now.

RENMANO

p. 443

Location:
Sturt Highway, Renmark, 5341;
on south-western outskirts of town.
(085) 83 2303.

Winemaker:
S. J. Auld.

1985 Production:
Approximately 16,000 tonnes or 11 million litres.

Principal Wines:
Table wines released under Chairmans Selection range comprising Chardonnay Bin 104, Traminer Riesling Bin 204, Fumé Blanc, Rhine Riesling Bin 604, Cabernet Sauvignon Bin 460 and Merlot Bin 540. As with its sister company, Berri, the company specialises in immaculately presented wine casks (and to a lesser degree flagons); very large sales in bulk also made.

Distribution:
National through Taylor Ferguson except for Queensland (Condons), and self-distribution in South Australia and the Northern Territory. Very substantial export sales. Cellar-door sales 9 a.m. to 5.30 p.m. Monday to Saturday and 9 a.m. to noon on Sundays of long weekends. Mailing-list enquiries to PO Box 238, Berri, SA, 5343.

Prices:
Chairmans Selection range has theoretical retail price of around $5.80, but in fact sells for significantly less.

Overall Quality:
Chairmans Selection wines reliably good value for money, occasionally excelling themselves.

Tasting Notes:

1984 CHAIRMANS SELECTION RHINE RIESLING BIN 604 [18.2] *Colour:* medium-yellow green. *Bouquet:* very clean, full and soft with exceptional depth for Riverland fruit. *Palate:* similarly, of unusual depth and richness. Soft but very well balanced; a prolific gold medal winner at National Shows. Drink '85–'86.

1984 CHAIRMANS SELECTION CHARDONNAY BIN 104 [15.2] *Colour:* medium yellow-green. *Bouquet:* pronounced, slightly raw, lemony oak, which seems unlikely to integrate fully; fairly light fruit. *Palate:* light fruit, with raw, lemony oak dominant; little expectation that the wine will ever come fully into balance. Drink '86–'87.

1984 CHAIRMANS SELECTION MERLOT BIN 540 [15.6] *Colour:* red-purple. *Bouquet:* clean; good fruit/oak balance, though the oak itself is a little pedestrian; clean plum/mulberry aromas. *Palate:* similar, soft plum/mulberry flavours on the fore-palate, followed by a light, gently astringent, finish; low tannin. Drink '86–'87.

1981 CHAIRMANS SELECTION CABERNET BIN 460 [15.4] *Colour:* medium red, holding hue well. *Bouquet:* clean; slightly dull, sweet American oak and fruit now fading somewhat. *Palate:* has held fruit flavour and structure better than the bouquet suggests; light fruit, with soft, persistent tannin on the finish, and again a touch of that American oak. Drink '85–'86(?).

Southern Vales

1985 Vintage

Sandwiched between a cool and moist start and a cool, moist and late vintage were three months of drought. Unirrigated vineyards suffered stress, while others were subjected to periodic outbreaks of powdery mildew, particularly during vintage-time rain.

The saving grace was undoubtedly the very cool summer; against all expectations, yields overall were well above average. Equally against all expectations, grape quality in many (but not all) vineyards was very high.

Overall, rhine riesling was disappointing, yet chardonnay and sauvignon blanc were outstanding, and possibly the best so far to come from the district. These latter two varieties show unusually intense varietal character.

The red wines, too, show great fragrance and fruit intensity, even if the colour is slightly lower than normal. Some makers have produced superb cabernet sauvignon, while others are distinctly less happy.

There is no question that those growers with good viticultural practices and with supplementary water at their disposal have reaped the benefits of those techniques, while the less progressive growers had more than their fair share of problems. Weighing these two conflicting extremes, 1985 was a very good year indeed, challenged only by 1984—unless, of course, one goes back to 1980.

The Changes

With more wineries than any other single region in Australia, the Southern Vales remains a hotbed of change. It is perhaps for this reason that, try as I might, I could not elicit reliable up-to-date information on Merrivale, Old Clarendon Wines or Taranga Estate; other longer-established enterprises such as Genders and Saint Francis seemingly preferred to be left alone.

Wineries come and go, owners come and go, and names change. Elysium has finally shut its doors, but the gap will quickly be filled by others. It is a busy region, full of enterprising people, and close to a major market. It deserves its title of "Home of the Small Winery".

CAMBRAI

p. 446

Location:
Hamiltons Road, McLaren Flat, 5171.
(08) 383 2051.

Winemaker:
Graham Stevens.

1985 Production:
Approximately 5000 cases.

Principal Wines:

An unusual offering of varietal table wines including Chablis, Chardonnay, Chardonnay Sylvaner, Rhine Riesling, Gewurtztraminer, Zinfandel, Pinot Hermitage, Cabernet Sauvignon, Shiraz, Cabernet Malbec Merlot, Pinot Cabernet and Vat 52 Show Burgundy.

Distribution:
Principally cellar door and mailing list. Cellar-door sales 10 a.m to 5 p.m. 7 days; mailing-list enquiries to PO Box 206, McLaren Vale, 5171. Limited retail and restaurant distribution in South Australia through Montgomery Smith.

Prices:
$7.15 to $8.25 cellar door.

Overall Quality:
Extremely variable, but has produced some very good wines from time to time.

Vintage Rating 1982–85:
'84, '85, '83, '82.

Outstanding Prior Vintages:
'81.

Tasting Notes:

1984 RHINE RIESLING [16.6] *Colour:* light to medium green-yellow. *Bouquet:* soft, slightly broad, of ample weight; in regional style, with some toasty aromas. *Palate:* a clean, full, round and flavoursome rhine riesling, utterly typical of McLaren Vale. Drink '85–'87.

1983 WOOD AGED CHABLIS [15.6] *Colour:* full yellow, with glints of green. *Bouquet:* slightly stringy/lemony oak; full, with quite good aroma. *Palate:* strong lemony oak is again very evident, although there is also ample fruit; a full wine, but hardly a chablis. Drink '86–'88.

1982 CABERNET SAUVIGNON [16.8] *Colour:* medium red, still with a few hints of purple. *Bouquet:* some leafy, gently astringent, cabernet varietal aroma intermingling with sweet oak; developing bottle complexity. *Palate:* a big, high-flavoured wine, with tastes of gravelly, earthy cabernet; not over-ripe, and finishes firm. Drink '87–'90.

1982 VINTAGE PORT [16.8] *Colour:* dense purple/red. *Bouquet:* exceedingly ripe, rich, sweet and generous old style, with just a trace of straw. *Palate:* very sweet, very ripe caramel/dark chocolate flavours; a heavy, almost liqueur style of vintage port. Drink '87–'93.

CHAPEL HILL

p. 448

(Formerly Chapel Vale Cellars)

Location:
Chapel Hill Road, McLaren Vale, 5171; off Chaffeys Road, due east of McLaren Vale. (08) 383 8429.

Winemaker:
Robert Paul.

1985 Production:
2100 cases.

Principal Wines:

A limited range of traditional McLaren Vale styles including Rhine Riesling, Rhine Riesling Spatlese, Shiraz, Shiraz Cabernet, Cabernet Sauvignon, Vintage Port and Muscat de Fleurieu. Fortified wines offered ex cellars with some bottle age.

Distribution:
Almost exclusively cellar door and mailing list. Cellar-door sales 11 a.m. to 5 p.m. 7 days. Mailing-list enquiries to PO Box 194, McLaren Vale, 5171. Occasional restaurant listing in Adelaide.

Prices:
$6 to $7 cellar door.

Overall Quality:
Variable; some wines very good.

Vintage Rating 1983–85:
White: '85, '84, '83.
Red: '85, '84.

Tasting Notes:

1984 RHINE RIESLING (GOLD CAP) [16.6] *Colour:* bright yellow-green of medium depth. *Bouquet:* clean, solid, slightly toasty deep fruit. *Palate:* soft and gently rich, with abundant flavour, in typical McLaren Vale style. Well-made, but like most rieslings of the district, will develop early. (Second bottling with white cap far inferior.) Drink '85–'87.

1984 RHINE RIESLING AUSLESE [15.2] *Colour:* medium yellow with a touch of straw. *Bouquet:* a big wine, rather heavy but lifted by a touch of lime in the background. *Palate:* rather heavy and phenolic, flavour-some but coarse. Drink '86.

1984 CHAPEL HILL SHIRAZ [17] *Colour:* strong purple-red. *Bouquet:* very full; pronounced, fragrant, sweet fruit, balanced by good vanillan oak. *Palate:* a very big, but beautifully clean wine which belies its high alcohol (over 13%); a nice touch of varietal spice on the mid- and back-palate; extremely well-made. (The Cabernet Sauvignon of the same vintage was destroyed by rubber-raincoat mercaptan.) Drink '89–'94.

MUSCAT DE FLEURIEU [17.8] *Colour:* medium yellow. *Bouquet:* intense, grapy/spicy frontignan aroma with just a hint of spirit. *Palate:* explosively rich grape-spice-muscat flavours; a lightly fortified dessert wine of great flavour and style. Drink now.

CORIOLE

p. 448

Location:
Chaffeys Road, McLaren Vale, 5171;
6 km north of township.
(08) 383 8305

Winemaker:
Mark Lloyd.

1985 Production:
160 tonnes (the equivalent of 11,200 cases).

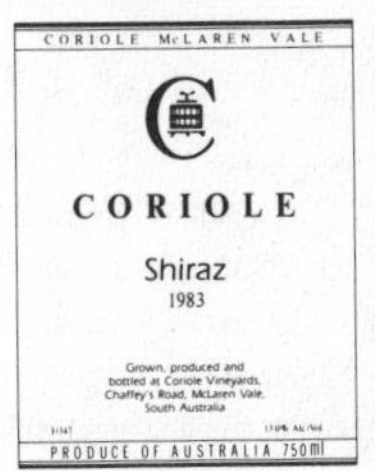

Principal Wines:
Limited range of table wines, with special emphasis on red wines; wines comprise Rhine Riesling, Chenin Blanc, Chardonnay, Shiraz, Special Burgundy and Cabernet Shiraz. Bulk wine for home bottling also sold.

Distribution:
Substantial cellar-door and mailing-list sales; cellar-door sales 9 a.m. to 5 p.m. Monday to Friday, 11 a.m. to 5 p.m. Saturday and Sunday. Mailing-list enquiries to PO Box 9, McLaren Vale, 5171. Fine wine retail distribution through wholesale agents in all states other than South Australia and Victoria (distributed direct).

Prices:
$5 to $7.50 cellar door.

Overall Quality:
Whites good; reds consistently very good.

Vintage Rating 1982–85:
White: '84, '85, '82, '83.
Red: '85, '82, '84, '83.

Outstanding Prior Vintages:
'75, '78.

Tasting Notes:

1984 RHINE RIESLING [16.4] *Colour:* medium green-yellow. *Bouquet:* full fruit, showing obvious signs of careful winemaking; some bottle-developed, toasty characters emerging. *Palate:* a generous, full-flavoured wine, in typical McLaren Vale style; slightly hard back-palate. Drink '85–'87.

1984 CHENIN BLANC [16.6] *Colour:* medium green-yellow. *Bouquet:* rich, distinctive honey/melon fruit aromas, again showing careful winemaking. *Palate:* relies chiefly on residual sugar and balancing acid; does not have the excellent fruit character suggested by the bouquet. Well-made nonetheless. Drink '85–'86.

1982 FRENCH OAK SHIRAZ CABERNET [17.6] *Colour:* dense purple-red. *Bouquet:* complex, clean and rich with tangy/lemony Nevers oak pitted against full fruit. *Palate:* rather thick, and oak very obvious, but masses of fruit flavour and character; will be very long-lived. Drink '86–'93.

1981 SPECIAL BURGUNDY [17.4] *Colour:* medium to full purple-red, holding hue very well. *Bouquet:* clean, a touch of grassiness to the fruit and, despite the label, more a claret style. *Palate:* lively, fresh and crisp wine, yet at the same time exhibiting very considerable fruit-weight and depth. (A blend of 70% shiraz, 15% cabernet sauvignon, 15% grenache.) Drink '85–'89.

D'ARENBERG

pp. 449–50

Location:
Osborn Road, McLaren Vale, 5171;
4 km north of township.
(08) 383 8206.

Winemakers:
F. D'A. Osborn and C. D'A. Osborn.

1985 Production:
480,000 litres (the equivalent of 60,000 cases).

Principal Wines:

Rhine Riesling, Burgundy, Show Shiraz, Cabernet Sauvignon, Gold Medal Burgundy, Shiraz Cabernet, Claret, Cabernet Sauvignon, Tawny Port and Vintage Port. All red table wines offered with considerable bottle age, and a wide range of vintages usually available.

Distribution:
Substantial retail distribution through Taylor Ferguson in all states except South Australia (R. L. Moore Agencies). Cellar-door sales 9 a.m. to 5 p.m. Monday to Friday and 10 a.m. to 5 p.m. Saturdays and public holidays.

Prices:
$5 to $7.80 cellar door.

Overall Quality:
Good, if somewhat traditional.

Vintage Rating 1982–85:
White: '84, '85, '83, '82.
Red: '85, '82, '84, '83.

Outstanding Prior Vintages:
'67, '68, '71, '76.

Tasting Notes:

1984 RHINE RIESLING [16] *Colour:* bright yellow of medium depth. *Bouquet:* soft and toasty, showing considerable bottle development for its age. *Palate:* a clean, soft and ripe wine with flavours verging on caramel/butterscotch; consistently with the bouquet, the wine is very developed. Drink '85–'86.

1982 WHITE MUSCAT OF ALEXANDRIA [16.8] *Colour:* medium yellow tinged with straw. *Bouquet:* fragrant, pungent essence-of-grape aromas, spotlessly clean. *Palate:* similar fragrant flavours, with delicate mid-palate fruit before the light fortifying spirit gives power and authority to the finish. Very well-handled. Drink now.

1981 CABERNET SAUVIGNON [16.8] *Colour:* medium to full red, holding hue well. *Bouquet:* smooth, sweet berry aromas with a gentle trace of astringency and a touch of cedar; overall quite rich. *Palate:* a complex wine, with ripe fruit and soft but persistent tannin picking up on the mid-palate and lasting through to the finish. A very traditional style of red in which oak has made no contribution whatsoever to flavour. Drink '86–'90.

1980 SHIRAZ [17] *Colour:* light to medium red. *Bouquet:* fragrant and light, but with authentic spice/pepper varietal character. *Palate:* a very lively wine, with a delicacy and elegance not often encountered in McLaren Vale; a touch of spice, and crisp acid on the finish. Different but appealing. Drink '85–'88.

1978 SHIRAZ CABERNET [16.4] *Colour:* medium to full red, holding hue well. *Bouquet:* a big, robust wine with a trace of cowshed character, but not overly marked. *Palate:* a big, old style with a slightly hollow back-palate, and some tannin. Drink '85–'87.

SELECTED PORT [17] *Colour:* deep tawny. *Bouquet:* robust and deep, but with some good cask-developed rancio. *Palate:* rich, raisined and flavoury; while very full-flavoured, some of the material is just a fraction young; nonetheless, very good flavour. (The blend does date back to 1964.) Drink now.

DENNIS'S DARINGA CELLARS

p. 450

Location:
Kangarilla Road, McLaren Vale, 5171;
on northern outskirts of township.
(08) 38 3665.

Winemaker:
Peter Dennis.

1985 Production:
3000 cases.

Principal Wines:
Limited range of high-quality varietal table wines; Chardonnay, Sauvignon Blanc, Rhine Riesling, Shiraz Cabernet, Cabernet Sauvignon, Vintage Port, Old Tawny Port and Mead.

Distribution:
Principally cellar-door sales and mailing list. Cellar-door sales 10 a.m. to 5 p.m. 7 days; mailing-list enquiries to PO Box 30, McLaren Vale, 5171. Limited fine wine retail distribution in Sydney, Melbourne and Adelaide.

Prices:
$7.50 to $13.80 recommended retail.

Overall Quality:
Very good; occasional exceptional wines.

Vintage Rating 1982–85:
White: '82, '84, '83, '85.
Red: '84, '82, '83, '85.

Outstanding Prior Vintages:
'78, '79, '80.

Tasting Notes:

1984 SAUVIGNON BLANC [17] *Colour:* excellent bright light to medium green-yellow. *Bouquet:* of medium to full weight; some smoky oak aromas in the wine showing more fume style than distinctive sauvignon blanc character. *Palate:* full and rich, ripe/sweet fruit, in full-blown fume blanc style; richly textured, and very well-made. Drink '85–'87.

1984 CHARDONNAY [17.8] *Colour:* medium to full yellow-green. *Bouquet:* rich and ripe, slightly buttery fruit with complex smoky oak. *Palate:* strong, charred/smoky oak flavours, very burgundian in the style, just a fraction strong now, but will come back with more bottle age as the fruit undoubtedly is there. Drink '86–'89.

1982 CABERNET SAUVIGNON [17.4] *Colour:* red-purple of medium depth. *Bouquet:* firm, clean and robust, with good, dark blackcurrant aromas. *Palate:* strong and ripe, but not overripe, fruit; clean and flavoursome mid-palate with soft tannin on the finish. Drink '86–'90.

1981 CABERNET SAUVIGNON [15.4] *Colour:* dark red, still with a trace of purple. *Bouquet:* fragrant and complex ripe fruit aromas, with just a touch of mercaptan-derived leather. *Palate:* the leathery flavours dominate and rob the wine of its fruitiness. Drink '85–'86.

THE ESTATE

p. 468

Location:
Kangarilla Road, McLaren Vale, 5171;
1 km east of township.
(08) 383 8911.

Winemaker:
Charles Hargrave.

1985 Production:
5000 cases.

Principal Wines:
Limited range of quality table wines including Rhine Riesling, Chardonnay, Sauvignon Blanc, Cabernet Sauvignon and Cabernet Merlot.

Distribution:
Substantial cellar-door and mailing-list sales. Cellar-door sales 11 a.m. to 5 p.m. 7 days; mailing-list enquiries to The Estate, Kangarilla Road, McLaren Vale. Fine wine retail distribution through wholesale agents in Sydney (David Bainbridge) and Melbourne (Van Cooth and Co.).

Prices:
$7.60 to $10.75 recommended retail.

Overall Quality:
Consistently very good.

Vintage Rating 1982–85:
White: '82, '85(?), '84, '83.
Red: '82, '85(?), '83, '84.

Tasting Notes:

1984 CHARDONNAY [18] *Colour:* bright light to medium green-yellow. *Bouquet:* very full, complex, toasty/smoky oak, with some burgundian overtones. *Palate:* very good weight, yet has retained excellent freshness to the gentle peachy fruit flavours; the wine has excellent acid and length, and will age well. Drink '86–'89.

GENDERS

p. 451

Location:
Recreation Road, McLaren Vale, 5171; on north-eastern outskirts of township. (08) 383 8689.

Winemaker:
Keith Genders.

1985 Production:
Not stated.

Principal Wines:
Limited range of traditional McLaren Vale table and fortified wines, many offered with substantial bottle age.

Distribution:
Virtually exclusively cellar door.

Overall Quality:
Not rated.

GEOFF MERRILL

pp. 451–2

Location:
Kangarilla Road, McLaren Flat, 5171; (vineyard only and eventual winery site). (08) 271 2267.

Winemaker:
Geoff Merrill.

1985 Production:
4500 cases.

Principal Wines:
Only two wines made each year, one white, one red. White wine either Semillon or Semillon Sauvignon Blanc and red wine a Cabernet Sauvignon.

Distribution:
Principally through superbly produced mailing list; enquiries to PO Box 386, McLaren Vale, 5171. Limited fine wine retail and restaurant distribution in capital cities.

Prices:
$7.90 (semillon) and $11.50 (cabernet sauvignon) cellar door.

Overall Quality:
Exceptional.

Vintage Rating 1982–85:
White: '84, '82, '85, '83.
Red: '82, '84, '85, '83.

Outstanding Prior Vintages:
'80.

Tasting Notes:

1983 SEMILLON [18.4] *Colour:* medium full yellow-green. *Bouquet:* very rich, very complex, full and buttery fruit and oak. *Palate:* an extremely rich and weighty wine with some spicy/nutmeg oak flavours and very full, ripe fruit; an enormous mouthful. (Gold Medal Winner Melbourne 1985. Due for release mid-'86.) Drink '86–'87.

1982 SEMILLON [17.8] *Colour:* full yellow. *Bouquet:* of medium to full weight, with clean lemony oak and a touch of grassy aroma to the fruit. *Palate:* less weighty but potentially longer-lived than the '83; excellent balance and integration of fruit and oak flavours; some honeyed semillon flavours developing. Drink '85–'88.

1982 CABERNET SAUVIGNON [18.4] *Colour:* medium to full red, with just a tinge of purple. *Bouquet:* fragrant, with complex lemony French oak and excellent clean, crisp fruit. *Palate:* a stylish, lively and fragrant wine, with good flavour intensity and a touch of soft tannin to add to texture. Soft lingering cherry flavours on the mid-palate; a very civilised wine. Drink '86–'91.

HARDY'S

pp. 452–4

Location:
Reynell Road, Reynella, 5161;
on southern outskirts of township. Also at Willunga Road, McLaren Vale, 5171 (Tintara Cellars).
(08) 381 2266.

Winemakers:
Robert Dundon (red wines, brandies and fortified wines), Geoff Weaver (white wines).

1985 Production:
Approximately 15,000 tonnes (the equivalent of more than 1 million cases).

Principal Wines:
Hardy's produces the fullest imaginable range of wines in 750 ml bottles (and the occasional 1.5-litre flagon) but resolutely refuses to participate in the cask market. For all that, the range of wine covers all ends of the market from Edelweiss (a somewhat pale imitation of Ben Ean) through to Australia's greatest vintage ports. McLaren Vale remains the principal source for these great wines, with the bulk of the premium table wines now coming from Padthaway. Hardy's leading brand sellers such as Old Castle Rhine Riesling are of unspecified South Australian origin and no doubt contain fruit from many districts within South Australia.

Distribution:
National retail distribution at all levels through own distribution network.

Prices:
Theoretical retail of $4.20 to $13.80 (for Eileen Hardy Cabernet Sauvignon), but like all major producers, Hardy's is an enthusiastic participant in the discount game.

Overall Quality:
Consistently very good; occasional exceptional wines.

Vintage Rating 1982–85:
White: '85, '82, '84, '83.
Red: '82, '85, '84, '83.

Outstanding Prior Vintages:
'80.

Tasting Notes:

1984 OLD CASTLE RHINE RIESLING [16.2] *Colour:* light to medium yellow-green. *Bouquet:* soft and clean, with clear riesling varietal aroma and quite good weight. *Palate:* a soft, clean, well-made riesling, with adequate fruit flavour and depth, and good balance; residual sugar kept just at threshold perception. A very commercial wine. Drink '85–'86.

1982 COLLECTION CABERNET SAUVIGNON [16.6] *Colour:* medium to full red. *Bouquet:* clean; of light to medium weight, with some leafy/tobacco aromas. *Palate:* rather light, with some bottle developed camphor/leather characteristics, and the fruit showing signs of fading. Drink '85–'86.

1980 VINTAGE PORT [18.4] *Colour:* full red-purple. *Bouquet:* that utterly unmistakable Hardy style; complex brandy spirit; potent, slightly earthy fruit, rich and yet not jammy. *Palate:* a marvellously rich and textured wine, with superb fruit/spirit balance; an opulent mid-palate then a cleansing finish. Drink '87–'96.

1975 VINTAGE PORT [18.8] *Colour:* medium to full purple-red. *Bouquet:* infinitely complex, with full and deep spicy fruit and that Hardy brandy spirit very much to the fore. *Palate:* a marvellously complex, powdery/spicy wine with a touch of aniseed, and fine spirit on the finish. Drink '85–'93.

1973 VINTAGE PORT [17.8] *Colour:* dark red, with just a trace of tawny starting to appear on the rim. *Palate:* full and complex, with attractive gravel/tobacco, secondary, bottle-developed aromas intermingling with that complex brandy spirit. *Palate:* amazingly complex cedar/leather fruit and tobacco flavours, still with great richness on the back-palate. Drink '85–'90.

HUGO WINERY

p. 454

Location:
Elliott Road, McLaren Flat, 5171;
off Kangarilla Road, approximately 2 km from McLaren Flat.

Winemaker:
John Hugo.

1985 Production:
Not stated, but very small.

Principal Wines:
Four wines made: Rhine Riesling, Shiraz, Muscat of Alexandria and Tawny Port. Shiraz offered with substantial age; usually kept in oak for up to 3 years.

Distribution:
Exclusively cellar-door sales and mail order. Cellar-door sales 9 a.m. to 5 p.m. Monday to Saturday.

Prices:
$5 to $6.50 cellar door.

Overall Quality:
Good.

Tasting Notes:

1983 RHINE RIESLING [15.4] *Colour:* full yellow, with some green tinges. *Bouquet:* clean, but rather big and heavy, in more obvious regional style. *Palate:* clean, medium- to full-bodied, with a rather hard finish. A stolid, long-lived wine. Drink '85–'88.

1980 SHIRAZ [16.4] *Colour:* medium full red. *Bouquet:* quite attractive and complex powdery bouquet, typical of prolonged storage in sound old oak. *Palate:* a soft, fairly ripe style with sweet fruit, and again that particular texture and structure which prolonged ageing in large oak vessels imparts. Drink '85–'88. (Both wines tasted late 1984.)

MUSCAT OF ALEXANDRIA [17] *Colour:* orange-gold. *Bouquet:* complex aromas of tea, orange peel and raisins. *Palate:* marvellously rich and ripe, raisiny flavours, deep and persisting in the mouth long after the wine is swallowed. One of the light fortified wines which McLaren Vale does so well. Drink now.

INGOLDBY

p. 454

Location:
Ingoldby Road, McLaren Flat, 5171;
1 km north of township.
(08) 383 0005.

Winemaker:
Bill Clappis.

1985 Production:
80,000 litres (the equivalent of almost 9000 cases).

Principal Wines:

Rhine Riesling, Chablis, Sauvignon Blanc, Cabernet Shiraz and Cabernet Sauvignon; Sauvignon Blanc and Cabernet Sauvignon sold in 500 ml (half-litre) bottles.

Distribution:
Significant cellar-door sales and mailing list. Cellar-door sales 9 a.m. to 5 p.m. Monday to Friday, 11 a.m. to 5 p.m. weekends and public holidays. Mailing-list enquiries as above. Retail distribution in Sydney, Melbourne and Perth to be finalised prior to the end of 1985.

Prices:
Approximately $7 retail for 500 ml bottle.

Overall Quality:
Adequate to good.

Vintage Rating 1982–85:
White: '84, '85, '82, '83.
Red: '84, '85, '82, '83.

Outstanding Prior Vintages:
'75.

Tasting Notes:

1985 SAUVIGNON BLANC [16.6] *Colour:* bright straw-yellow. *Bouquet:* clean; crisp fruit with some light gooseberry varietal character in evidence, and a very faint touch of oak. *Palate:* fresh, light and crisp, with some smoky/armpit fruit characters; oak light, but a little raw. Clean and well enough made. Drink '86–'88.

1983 CABERNET SAUVIGNON [15.4] *Colour:* medium to full red, slightly opaque. *Bouquet:* astringent, traditional McLaren Vale style; good fruit weight but rather leathery. *Palate:* a big robust wine, with plenty of flavour but an astringently bitter, leathery finish. Mercaptan has without doubt marred the wine. Drink '87–'89.

JAMES HASELGROVE

p. 455

Location:
Foggo Road, McLaren Flat, 5171.
(08) 383 8706.

Winemaker:
James Haselgrove (together with contract winemakers).

1985 Production:
45,000 litres, half sold in bulk and half bottled to produce 2500 cases.

Principal Wines:
Both Coonawarra and McLaren Vale wines released. For Coonawarra wines see Coonawarra entry. McLaren Vale wines comprise Rhine Riesling, Chablis, Cabernet Shiraz, Vintage Port and Tawny Port; also a Coonawarra-McLaren Vale Shiraz.

Distribution:
Substantial cellar-door and mailing-list sales. Cellar-door sales 9 a.m. to 5 p.m. 7 days; mailing-list enquiries to PO Box 231, McLaren Vale, 5171. Retail distribution through fine wine retailers in capital cities.

Prices:
$5.70 to $8.70 cellar door.

Overall Quality:
Good.

Vintage Rating 1982–85:
White: '85, '84, '82, '83.
Red: '85, '83, '84 (no '82).

Tasting Notes:

1985 CHABLIS [15.2] *Colour:* bright yellow-green of medium depth. *Bouquet:* perfumed and a fraction oily, showing an apparent blend of ripe rich fruit with some much greener material. *Palate:* a similar blend of green fruit intermingling with riper material; a commercial wine, without any great varietal distinction. Drink '86–'87.

1984 METHODE CHAMPENOISE BRUT [17.6] *Colour:* medium to full yellow, almost verging on buttercup. *Bouquet:* very rich, full, clean fruity wine with buttery fruit aromas suggestive of chardonnay. *Palate:* rich, full peach/apricot fruit flavours suggesting chardonnay, but the wine is in fact a blend of rhine riesling, colombard and traminer. An unusual but very successful sparkling wine. Drink '86–'87.

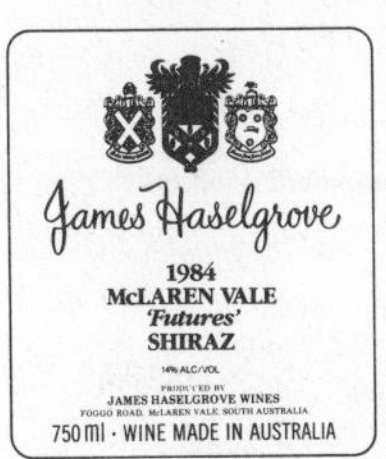

1984 FUTURES SHIRAZ [16.8] *Colour:* medium red-purple. *Bouquet:* very clean, quite elegant wine of medium weight, with very smooth fruit. *Palate:* firm, clean and well-balanced, with firm mid-palate fruit and a gently astringent tannic finish. Drink '87–'90.

1983 CABERNET SHIRAZ [16.6] *Colour:* strong purple-red. *Bouquet:* a solid, clean wine with a trace of flower-like aroma but otherwise rather closed. *Palate:* a well-made, clean wine with some astringent/green characters on the back palate. Drink '86–'88.

KAY BROTHERS AMERY

pp. 455–6

Location:
Kays Road, McLaren Vale, 5171;
5 km north of township.
(08) 383 8211.

Winemaker:
Colin Kay.

1985 Production:
Approximately 140,000 litres (the equivalent of 15,500 cases).

Principal Wines:
A full range of table and fortified wines comprising Rhine Riesling, Traminer, Fumé Blanc, Late Harvest White Frontignan, Sauvignon Blanc (sweet), Late Harvest Rhine Riesling, Shiraz Cabernet, Pinot Noir, Blackwood Estate Shiraz, Cabernet Sauvignon, Vintage Port, Tawny Port, and Liqueur Muscat. Cabernet Shiraz and Cabernet Sauvignon also offered in 10- and 20-litre casks. Most red wines offered with substantial bottle age, up to nine years.

Distribution:
Principally cellar-door and mailing-list sales, with very limited eastern states retail distribution in capital cities. Cellar-door sales 8 a.m. to 5 p.m. Monday to Friday, 10 a.m. to 5 p.m. Saturday and Sundays and public holidays noon to 5 p.m. Mailing-list enquiries to PO Box 19, McLaren Vale, 5171.

Prices:
$3.50 to $9 recommended retail in South Australia.

Overall Quality:
Adequate; style very consistent.

Vintage Rating 1982–85:
White: '85, '84, '83, '82.
Red: '85, '84, '83, '82.

Outstanding Prior Vintages:
White: '71, '72, '79.
Red: '64, '67, '70, '71.

Tasting Notes:

1984 LATE HARVEST WHITE FRONTIGNAN [16.6] *Colour:* pale bright green-yellow. *Bouquet:* strong, highly aromatic and clearly expressed varietal aroma, perfumed and spicy. *Palate:* fresh and strong varietal flavour again evident; pronounced residual sugar in conformity to style. By far the best of the Kay white wines. Drink '85–'87.

1983 PINOT NOIR [15] *Colour:* light to medium red. *Bouquet:* some stalky aromas and a trace of leathery mercaptan. *Palate:* better than bouquet suggests, but fruit is nonetheless diminished and varietal character virtually non-existent; the wine does however have quite good structure. Drink '85–'86.

1981 CABERNET SAUVIGNON [15.8] *Colour:* red-purple of medium depth. *Bouquet:* firm and quite full, but with marked astringent leathery aromas. *Palate:* firm, full, gently ripe cabernet sauvignon with attractive mid-palate weight and soft tannin. Drink '86–'88.

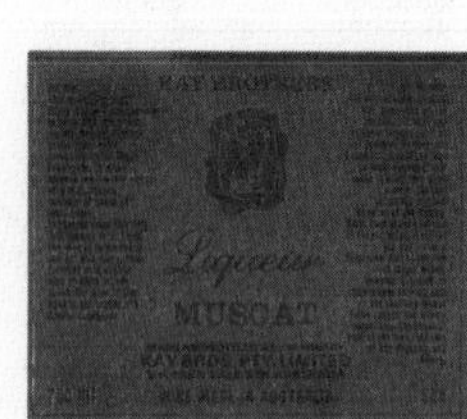

LIQUEUR MUSCAT [17] *Colour:* pale orange-brown. *Bouquet:* grapy aroma, vigorous and vibrant, and with clean, fortifying spirit. *Palate:* most attractive, dried apricot flavours; a lovely younger, lighter style of muscat. Nothing to do with the wines of north-east Victoria, but immensely attractive for all that. Drink now.

MAGLIERI

p. 457

Location:
Douglas Gully Road, McLaren Flat, 5171;
3 km north of township.
(08) 383 0177.

Winemaker:
John Loxton.

1985 Production:
450,000 litres (the equivalent of 50,000 cases).

Principal Wines:
A range of wine styles sold in bottles and flagons including Semillon Trebbiano Pedro, Rhine Riesling, Traminer Riesling, Shiraz, Cabernet Shiraz, Lambrusco Grande Spumante, Demi-sec Spumante, Rossa Spumante, Vintage Port and Flagon Port. All wines offered with some considerable bottle age.

Distribution:
Principally cellar-door sales and mailing list. Cellar-door sales 9 a.m. to 4 p.m. Monday to Saturday and 12.30 p.m. to 4 p.m. Sunday. Mailing-list enquiries as above. Wholesale agents Karana and Co., Adelaide; Gully Wines, Melbourne; and Condon and Co. Pty Ltd, Brisbane.

Prices:
Premium white and red wines $5.50 recommended retail.

Overall Quality:
Quite good; occasional very good wines.

Vintage Rating 1982–85:
White: '85, '83, '82, '84.
Red: '85, '83, '82, '84.

Outstanding Prior Vintages:
'77, '79, '80.

Tasting Notes:

1985 TRAMINER RHINE RIESLING [15.4] *Colour:* a trace of pink evident. *Bouquet:* quite aromatic, with slightly oily contribution from traminer dominant. *Palate:* a light and crisp wine, with marked traminer flavour; well-made apart from the pinking in the colour. A slightly bitter finish needs to soften. Should come on nicely in the bottle. Drink '86–'87.

1984 RHINE RIESLING [16.4] *Colour:* light, bright green-yellow. *Bouquet:* a very full and rich wine with a touch of volatile lift. *Palate:* an extremely rich wine, with quite pronounced residual sugar, bordering on spatlese in style; full of flavour and character. Drink '85–'86.

NV RIESLING [16.8] *Colour:* bright yellow-green. *Bouquet:* complex, with obvious, grassy, semillon varietal flavour, light oak, and very much in a white burgundy style. *Palate:* full and soft round fruit, with a light coating of sweet oak; an excellent food wine (made from semillon) and outstanding at the price. ($35 per case cellar door.) Drink '86.

1983 RHINE RIESLING [17] *Colour:* bright yellow-green of medium depth. *Bouquet:* most attractive, generous soft lime aromas. *Palate:* delightful, bottle-developed flavours; gentle lime fruit on the mid-palate and no obvious reliance on residual sugar. Drink '85–'87.

1981 CABERNET SAUVIGNON [16] *Colour:* red-purple of medium depth, holding hue quite well. *Bouquet:* dusty, powdery aromas suggestive of prolonged old oak storage; soft, green, leafy characters. *Palate:* quite full, but rather one-dimensional and simple ripe fruit flavours. Drink '85–'88.

1979 SHIRAZ [16.8] *Colour:* red-purple of medium depth, holding hue very well. *Bouquet:* very regional, with strong leathery aromas and rich fruit underneath. *Palate:* old traditional McLaren Vale style, robust and strong; ferruginous and slightly leathery, but with very considerable depth to fruit. (Bushing King Red Wine Trophy 1979.) Drink '85–'89.

MARIENBERG

p. 457

Location:
Black Road, Coromandel Valley, Blackwood, 5051; between Clarendon and Blackwood.
(08) 270 2384.

Winemaker:
Ursula Pridham.

1985 Production:
Approximately 10,000 cases.

Principal Wines:
White Burgundy, Chablis, Rhine Riesling, Gewurztraminer, Rosengarten, Auslese, Beerenauslese, Shiraz, Cabernet Shiraz and Cabernet Sauvignon. Red wines all offered with at least 5 years bottle age; white wines with 2 to 3 years bottle age.

Distribution:
Substantial retail distribution through wholesale agents in Victoria, New South Wales, South Australia and Queensland; also some exports. Cellar-door sales 9 a.m. to 5 p.m. Monday to Friday, 10 a.m. to 5 p.m. Saturday and noon to 5 p.m. Sunday. Mailing-list enquiries to Box 220, Blackwood, SA, 5051.

Prices:
$6.65 to $8.25 recommended retail.

Overall Quality:
Wines made in particular style and which have a loyal following. They are not always to my taste but recent tastings have favourably surprised me.

Vintage Rating 1982–85:
White: '84, '85, '83, '82.
Red: '83, '85, '82, '84.

Outstanding Prior Vintages:
'77, '81.

Tasting Notes:

1984 CHABLIS [15.8] *Colour:* bright green-yellow. *Bouquet:* some lifted buttery aromas, more in white burgundy style. *Palate:* full and round, gentle butter flavours; a pleasant wine but not a chablis. Drink '86–'88.

1984 GEWURTZTRAMINER [14] *Colour:* yellow-green, straw tinged. *Bouquet:* chalky/paddy solids fermentation aromas, and very little fruit evident. *Palate:* chalky/solids fermentation characters, with almost no fruit and certainly no varietal character.

1979 LIMITED RELEASE SHIRAZ [17] *Colour:* light to medium red, clear and bright. *Bouquet:* light, clean and smooth, and holding both fruit aroma and structure very well. *Palate:* clean, gently sweet fruit on the mid-palate; soft acid and tannin on the finish. Very well-balanced, and has developed remarkably well in bottle. A most pleasant surprise. Drink '85–'87.

1979 CABERNET SAUVIGNON [16.6] *Colour:* light red-purple. *Bouquet:* clean, but very light; while lacking fruit depth, has not gone over the edge. *Palate:* a light, fully mature wine, with gentle fruit on the mid-palate and a crisp finish. Again, something of a surprise. Drink '85–'87.

MAXWELL

p. 458

Location:
24 Kangarilla Road, McLaren Vale, 5171; on northern outskirts of township.
(08) 383 8200.

Winemaker:
Mark Maxwell.

1985 Production:
Approximately 5000 cases.

Principal Wines:
A limited range of table and fortified wines; also mead specialists. Wines comprise Semillon White Burgundy, Rhine Riesling, Chenin Blanc Rhine Riesling, Cabernet Sauvignon, Cabernet Shiraz, Vintage Port, Sweet Mead, Spiced Mead and Mazer Liqueur Mead.

Distribution:
Principally cellar-door sales and mailing list. Cellar-door sales 10 a.m. to 5 p.m. 7 days; mailing-list enquiries as above. Limited retail distribution services principally direct ex winery.

Prices:
Table wines $6 to $7.65 retail; meads $3.90 retail; liqueur mead $10.40 retail.

Overall Quality:
Very good.

Vintage Rating 1982–85:
White: '82, '85, '84, '83.
Red: '84, '82, '85, '83.

Outstanding Prior Vintages:
'78, '80.

Tasting Notes:

1983 CABERNET SHIRAZ [18] *Colour:* dense purple-red. *Bouquet:* deep and concentrated, gently ripe fruit; quite complex with sweet berry/spice aromas. *Palate:* a beautifully rounded, full and fleshy wine, with most attractive, soft tannin to provide balance to the abundant mid-palate fruit. Again a touch of spice to go with the sweet, berry flavours and vanillan oak. Drink '86–'91.

1982 CABERNET SHIRAZ [16.4] *Colour:* medium full purple-red. *Bouquet:* strong, distinctly herbaceous cabernet aromas of medium to full weight, and in radically different style to the '83. *Palate:* complex, with some leafy/meaty tastes, not in the same style (or, in my view, class) as the '83, notwithstanding the vintage rating given by Maxwells. Drink '85–'87.

SPICED MEAD [N/A] *Colour:* light, pinkish bronze. *Bouquet:* pungent, herbal/spice aromas; almost medicinal, but very attractive. *Palate:* dominated by strong spice/herbal flavours; sweet mid-palate is followed by a pleasantly dry finish. Drink now.

SWEET MEAD [N/A] *Colour:* bronze. *Bouquet:* distinct honey/malt aromas taking one directly back to the base material. *Palate:* obvious honey origins with honey tastes lingering; medium sweet mid-palate, again finishes pleasantly dry. Drink now.

MAZER LIQUEUR MEAD [N/A] *Colour:* bronze-pink of medium depth. *Bouquet:* intense aromatics, with a fine herbal infusion and hints of clove and spice. *Palate:* extremely rich, with strong clove flavours and a lingering finish of remarkable intensity. A unique experience. Drink now.

MIDDLEBROOK

p. 459

Location:
Sand Road, McLaren Vale, 5171;
4 km east of McLaren Vale.
(08) 383 0004.

Winemaker:
Caroline Burston.

1985 Production:
18,000 cases.

Principal Wines:
A carefully chosen range of varietal wines, principally made from locally grown grapes but occasionally incorporating material from elsewhere (principally Padthaway) including Gewurztraminer, Highcrest Chablis, Padthaway Rhine Riesling, McLaren Vale/Kangarilla Rhine Riesling, Chardonnay, Late Harvest Rhine Riesling, Highcrest Shiraz, Padthaway Hermitage, Tawny Port, Old Liqueur Sauvignon Blanc and finally Durus, a marvellous, cumquat-flavoured wine, fortified with old brandy and sweetened with honey.

Distribution:
Fine wine retail distribution in all states through agents and (in New South Wales) own branch. Also cellar-door sales 10 a.m. to 5 p.m. 7 days, together with excellent restaurant noon to 3 p.m. 7 days. Mailing list PO Box 320, McLaren Vale, 5171.

Prices:
$6 to $10 cellar door.

Overall Quality:
Very good.

Vintage Rating 1982–85:
'85, '84, '82, '83.

Tasting Notes:

1985 GEWURTZTRAMINER [16.2] *Colour:* bright, light, medium yellow-green. *Bouquet:* very clean and soft, lacking in varietal definition, however. *Palate:* an extremely well-made, clean, light, fresh and crisp wine in which varietal flavour presumably has been sacrificed deliberately for freshness and crispness. Drink '86.

1984 McLAREN VALE/KANGARILLA RHINE RIESLING [16.8] *Colour:* glistening medium to full yellow. *Bouquet:* a very rich, highly flavoured wine, strong and deep in regional style. *Palate:* rich camphor/lime flavours on the mid-palate of a very big and soft full wine. Early developing. Drink '85–'86.

1984 CHARDONNAY [17.6] *Colour:* medium full yellow-green. *Bouquet:* very full, buttery/peachy fruit; oak not fully integrated but of good complexity. *Palate:* oak a little intrusive on the fore-palate, and comes again on the finish. There is adequate mid-palate fruit, with good varietal flavour, and the wine will come together in the bottle. Drink '86–'89.

1984 HIGHCREST SHIRAZ [17.8] *Colour:* medium to full red-purple. *Bouquet:* rich, full spicy/peppery wine, crammed full of character. *Palate:* marvellous pepper/spice edge; a rich wine, yet has firmness and good acid. Will develop very well, although the finish is fractionally disappointing at this stage. Drink '87–'92.

NOONS

p. 459

Location:
Rifle Range Road, McLaren Vale, 5171;
5 km south-east of township.
(08) 383 8290.

Winemaker:
David Noon.

1985 Production:
1500 cases.

Principal Wines:
Red wine specialists, offering just the occasional white wine. Wines comprise Rhine Riesling, Claret, Unfiltered Claret, Burgundy, Shiraz Cabernet, Shiraz Grenache, Maceration Carbonique, Rose and Vintage Port. Most reds sold with two or three years bottle age.

Distribution:
Exclusively cellar-door sales; 9 a.m. to 5 p.m. every day of the year.

Prices:
$5.50 to $8 cellar door.

Overall Quality:
Consistently very good.

Vintage Rating 1982–85:
'85, '82, '84, '83.

Outstanding Prior Vintages:
'76, '80.

Tasting Notes:

1983 SHIRAZ GRENACHE [17.4] *Colour:* medium to full purple-red. *Bouquet:* clean, quite aromatic, with an unexpected touch of grassy lift. *Palate:* ripe, sweet, minty/berry flavours, yet not thick or jammy; gentle tannin on the finish. Drink '87–'92.

1983 SHIRAZ CABERNET [17.6] *Colour:* dense purple-red. *Bouquet:* spotlessly clean, full and deep yet not jammy or over-ripe. *Palate:* immense, velvety, round and gently chewy structure; a touch of oak to a beautifully clean, rich, yet gentle wine. An extraordinary result given its 14.2 degrees of alcohol. Drink '87–'96.

1982 BURGUNDY [17.2] *Colour:* medium to full red-purple. *Bouquet:* fragrant and clean; very full; with a touch of American oak. *Palate:* an extremely smooth, but firm, wine, drawing power from its astonishing 14.4 degrees of alcohol; a clean, low tannin finish without bitterness or heaviness. Drink '87–'94.

1981 CLARET [17] *Colour:* medium to full red-purple. *Bouquet:* clean and firm, gently astringent and much less aromatic than many of the other Noon wines. *Palate:* a youthful, firm wine with deep flavour and structure, still developing complexity and aroma; again, that cleanliness and smoothness which is the hallmark of all of these wines. Drink '87–'93.

1981 BURGUNDY [17.4] *Colour:* red-purple of medium depth. *Bouquet:* very clean and very soft, with a touch of mint aroma; starting to build secondary, bottle-developed characters. *Palate:* very full and deep, sweet, cassis/berry flavours; miraculously avoids being heavy or jammy, despite its thunderous 14.9 degrees of alcohol. Drink '86–'93.

OLIVERHILL WINES

pp. 460–1

Location:
Seaview Road, McLaren Vale;
4 km north of township.
(08) 383 8922.

Winemaker:
Vincenzo Berlingieri.

1985 Production:
40,000 litres (the equivalent of 4500 cases).

Principal Wines:
Fortified wines specialist offering Tawny Port, Liqueur Muscat, Oloroso Sherry and, in the future, a range of vintage ports.

Distribution:
Exclusively cellar-door sales and mailing list. Cellar-door sales 10 a.m. to 5 p.m. 7 days. Mailing-list enquiries to PO Box 22, McLaren Vale, 5171.

Prices:
$10 to $13.20 cellar door.

Overall Quality:
Not rated.

Vintage Rating 1982–85:
'84, '82, '85, '83.

Outstanding Prior Vintages:
'78.

PIRRAMIMMA VINEYARDS

p. 461

Location:
Johnston Road, McLaren Vale, 5171;
2 km west of township.
(08) 383 8205.

Winemaker:
Geoff Johnston.

1985 Production:
Over 300,000 litres.

Principal Wines:
Chardonnay, Rhine Riesling, Rhine Riesling Spatlese, Palomino, Cabernet Sauvignon, Shiraz, Special Selection Shiraz, Mataro, Maceration Carbonique Shiraz, Vintage Port, Tawny Port and Liqueur Port. Shiraz and Shiraz-Grenache sold in 20-litre packs and in 205-litre drums; 5-year-old tawny port also sold in 205-litre drums.

Distribution:
Limited fine wine retail distribution in Sydney, Melbourne and Adelaide through wholesalers L. Laforgia, Adelaide; Melbourne Wine Advisers, Melbourne and I. D. Hunt Wines, Sydney. Significant cellar-door sales 8.30 a.m. to 5 p.m. Monday to Friday, 10 a.m. to 6 p.m. Saturday and noon to 4 p.m. Sunday. Mailing-list enquiries to PO Box 7, McLaren Vale, 5171.

Prices:
$4 to $7.70 cellar door.

Overall Quality:
Very good.

Vintage Rating 1982–85:
White: '84, '85, '83, '82.
Red: '83, '82, '85, '84.

Outstanding Prior Vintages:
'67, '70, '72, '80.

Tasting Notes:

1984 RHINE RIESLING [16.2] *Colour:* pale bright green-yellow. *Bouquet:* very clean, but surprisingly delicate and fresh; some aromatic fruit. *Palate:* a very light style for the region, with fresh, crisp fruit, but somehow or other lacking depth and intensity. Perhaps this will build with more age. Drink '86–'87.

1983 CHARDONNAY [16.6] *Colour:* full yellow. *Bouquet:* complex bottle-developed aromas with a touch of burgundian sulphide and a suggestion of some barrel fermentation. *Palate:* quite marked bottle development with some grapefruit characters persisting, but suggesting it has already reached its peak. Drink '85–'86(?).

1983 CABERNET SAUVIGNON [18] *Colour:* medium to full red-purple. *Bouquet:* rich and dense, with very good and complex fruit/oak integration and balance; full of weight and character. *Palate:* a ripe and flavoursome textured wine, with lovely sweet berry fruit augmented by a touch of charred oak. A wine of the standard one expects from Pirramimma. Drink '87–'92.

1982 MACERATION CARBONIQUE [16.6] *Colour:* medium red, with a trace of purple remaining. *Bouquet:* marked spice/meat aromatics in ultra-typical carbonic maceration style; has held on surprisingly well. *Palate:* complex flavours; some leafy bitterness starting to develop on the back-palate, but still a most interesting wine. Drink '85–'86.

1978 VINTAGE PORT [17] *Colour:* dark red. *Bouquet:* full, rich and complex sweet berry aromas with good brandy spirit. *Palate:* rich and sweet caramel/berry fruit flavours with considerable complexity and fine brandy spirit; not a heavyweight and now reaching its peak. Drink '85–'88.

REYNELLA

pp. 462–3

Location:
Reynell Road, Reynella, 5161;
on southern outskirts of township.
(08) 381 2266.

Winemaker:
Geoff Merrill (consultant).

1985 Production:
Approximately 500,000 litres (the equivalent of 45,000 cases).

Principal Wines:

Wines made from both Coonawarra and Southern Vales grapes. (See separate entry for Coonawarra.) Southern Vales wines comprise Vintage Reserve Chablis, Chardonnay, Rosé, Vintage Reserve Claret, Cabernet Sauvignon, Cabernet Malbec Merlot, and Vintage Port (one of Australia's two greatest).

Distribution:
National retail distribution through Rhine Castle Wines Pty Ltd.

Prices:
Discounting makes recommended retail largely irrelevant, but recommended retail falls in the $5.20 to $11 range.

Overall Quality:
Consistently very good; vintage port exceptional.

Vintage Rating 1982–85:
'84, '82, '85, '83.

Outstanding Prior Vintages:
'47, '64, '80.

Tasting Notes:

1984 VINTAGE RESERVE CHABLIS [17] *Colour:* straw-yellow, with obvious oak influence. *Bouquet:* full, developed, ripe and rich white burgundy, as far removed from chablis as it is possible to imagine. The oak, dominant when the wine was first released, has come back into balance. *Palate:* a big, soft vanillan/honey/oaky wine, fresh and flavoursome. Drink '86–'87.

1980 CABERNET SAUVIGNON [17.6] *Colour:* medium red. *Bouquet:* clean; pronounced, crisp cabernet varietal aromas, with a touch of grassy/leafy fruit; oak well-balanced. *Palate:* crisp wine, with pronounced varietal cool-climate cabernet flavours, gently astringent, and with light tannin on the finish. The small Coonawarra component of this wine, less than 20%, has a very marked influence on its style and structure. Drink '85–'90.

RICHARD HAMILTON

pp. 463–4

Location:
Willunga Vineyards, Main South Road, Willunga, 5172;
2 km north of township.
(085) 56 2288.

Winemaker:
Dr Richard Hamilton.

1985 Production:
5000 cases.

Principal Wines:
A range of white table wines (no reds made since 1982) in a once-distinctive style, and which have recently become more conventional. Wines include Rhine Riesling, Spatlese Riesling, Chenin Blanc, Chardonnay and Méthode Champenoise Sparkling Wine.

Distribution:
Significant retail distribution through wholesale distributors in New South Wales (Lionel Nell Pty Ltd), Victoria (Emerald Wines Pty Ltd) and through direct distribution in South Australia. Cellar-door sales 9.30 a.m. to 5.30 p.m. Monday to Saturday; mailing-list enquiries to PO Box 421, Willunga, SA, 5172.

Prices:
$5.50 to $8.50 cellar door.

Overall Quality:
Good.

Vintage Rating 1982–85:
'84, '85, '83, '82.

Outstanding Prior Vintages:
'72, '73, '75.

Tasting Notes:

1984 FLEURIEU RHINE RIESLING [16.6] *Colour:* strong yellow-green. *Bouquet:* considerable richness and complexity; almost honeyed roundness, with hints of lime. *Palate:* deep, full-flavoured wine, with very marked residual sugar and somewhat heavy, but no doubt in the style intended. Drink '85–'87.

1984 FUME BLANC [17.2] *Colour:* medium yellow-green. *Bouquet:* softly ripe gooseberry fruit, well-balanced against attractive oak; a quite complex wine of medium to full weight. *Palate:* strong, spicy/nutmeg oak adds flavour to a big, fully ripe sauvignon blanc wine; masses of flavour, and a slightly heavy finish. Drink '86–'89.

1984 CHARDONNAY [16.6] *Colour:* bright straw-yellow. *Bouquet:* elegant fruit, partially obscured by slightly raw/oily oak. *Palate:* a curious wine, with rich flavours, before that slightly oily oak comes again and, lurking in the background, a faint hint of astringent mouldy character, suggesting one or two barrels not sound. Drink '86–'87.

1982 FLEURIEU METHODE CHAMPENOISE [15.4] *Colour:* pale green-yellow. *Bouquet:* very firm green aromas, with a suggestion of some slightly raw oak in the base wine. *Palate:* odd lemony/camphor flavours; a very youthful wine still, but something not quite right with the base wine. Drink '86–'87.

SANTA ROSA

p. 464

Location:
Winery Road, Currency Creek;
due south of Strathalbyn.
(085) 55 4069.

Winemakers:
White wines Brian Croser/Petaluma (contract); red wines Phillip Tonkin, Brian Barry (consultant).

1985 Production:
6300 cases.

Principal Wines:
Limited range of high-quality table wines comprising Semillon, Rhine Riesling, Late Harvest Rhine Riesling, Chardonnay, Sauvignon Blanc, Shiraz, Cabernet Sauvignon and Pinot Noir. Other generic wines available cellar door.

Distribution:
Significant cellar-door and mailing-list sales. Cellar-door sales 10 a.m. to 5 p.m. 7 days; mailing-list enquiries to PO Box 545, Currency Creek, 5214. Limited fine wine retail distribution principally through The Wine Merchant, Adelaide.

Prices:
Premium wines $4.90 to $7 cellar door.

Overall Quality:
Very good; white wines frequently exceptional.

Vintage Rating 1982–85:
White: '84, '85, '83, '82.
Red: '82, '83, '84, '85.

Tasting Notes:

1984 WOOD AGED SEMILLON [17.4] *Colour:* medium yellow-green. *Bouquet:* complex toasty/lemony fruit and oak aromas intermingling; starting to develop richness and will become even fuller and richer given the time it deserves. *Palate:* fine and elegant fruit/oak integration; a wine still at the threshold of its life. Drink '87–'91.

1984 SAUVIGNON BLANC [17.8] *Colour:* bright green-yellow. *Bouquet:* exciting fruit aromas; sweet gooseberry edging into fig aromas; excellent fruit weight. *Palate:* round and rich, almost flowery varietal fruit, in the style to which Californian winemakers aspire. No phenolic hardness. Drink '86–'90.

1984 CHARDONNAY CHABLIS [18] *Colour:* medium yellow-green. *Bouquet:* fine citrus/grapefruit aromas followed by warm smoky oak. *Palate:* lovely fresh flavours and mouth-feel; of medium weight and good acid, with some of those grapefruit characters in the bouquet coming again. It is a relatively light and crisp wine, and the chablis tag fits. Drink '86–'89.

1984 DEER PARK LATE HARVEST RHINE RIESLING [17.4] *Colour:* glowing, deep green-yellow. *Bouquet:* very aromatic, with obvious botrytis influence, though not aggressively so; rich and clean. *Palate:* modulated, but full, lime-juice flavours on the mid-palate; quite intense but only moderately sweet. Very good balance. Gold medal winner Canberra National Show 1984. Drink '86–'90.

1983 CABERNET SAUVIGNON [16.8] *Colour:* bright and brilliant red, tinged with purple. *Bouquet:* smooth, clean and fresh in a fairly light mould. *Palate:* light to medium in weight, with some complex herbaceous/berry flavours; lively and fresh. Early drinking wine. Drink '85–'87.

SCARPANTONI ESTATES

pp. 464–5

Location:
Kangarilla Road, McLaren Flat, 5171; directly opposite Post Office. (08) 383 0186.

Winemaker:
Domenico Scarpantoni.

1985 Production:
Approximately 3500 cases.

Principal Wines:

Block 1 Rhine Riesling, Late Picked Rhine Riesling, White Burgundy, Cabernet Sauvignon, Block 3 Shiraz, Shiraz, Vintage Port, Tawny Port and Liqueur Riesling. Most red wines offered with three or four years bottle age.

Distribution:
Almost entirely cellar door and mailing list. Cellar-door sales 10 a.m. to 5 p.m. seven days. Mailing-list enquiries to PO Box 84, McLaren Vale, 5171.

Prices:
Table wines $4.50 to $5.50 cellar door.

Overall Quality:
Good.

Vintage Rating 1982–85:
'85, '84, '82, '83.

Outstanding Prior Vintages:
'80.

Tasting Notes:

1985 PREMIER [16.8] *Colour:* vibrant royal purple, quite striking. *Bouquet:* very complex meaty/spicy aromas, deep and full; obvious carbonic maceration influence. *Palate:* lively yet curiously velvety structure, with vibrant sweet plum/strawberry fruit flavours. A great success. Drink '85–'86.

1984 BLOCK 1 RHINE RIESLING [16] *Colour:* medium yellow-green. *Bouquet:* big, slightly broad yeasty/toasty aromas, in traditional McLaren Vale style. *Palate:* very full-flavoured, soft and slightly broad, but with abundant fruit. Drink '85–'86.

1981 BLOCK 3 SHIRAZ [16] *Colour:* strong red, with no tawny hints yet developing. *Bouquet:* firm, and with a particular slightly powdery aroma deriving from prolonged storage in large old oak and in tank; clean and fault-free. *Palate:* remarkably fresh, given that it was not bottled until January 1984; good fruit weight and very smooth. All of the flavour comes from fruit and none from oak. Drink '85–'89.

1981 CABERNET SAUVIGNON [15.8] *Colour:* red-purple of medium depth. *Bouquet:* firm and slightly leathery; again a traditional style. *Palate:* quite marked varietal flavour to the point of being rather thin and astringent on the finish. Good mid-palate fruit flavour helps the wine. Drink '85–'87.

SEAVIEW

pp. 465–6

Location:
Reynell Road, Reynella, 5161.
(08) 381 2566.

Winemaker:
Pam Dunsford.

1985 Production:
Not for publication, but very substantial.

Principal Wines:
Seaview is in fact more a brand name than a geographic entity. The grapes for the Seaview brand wines come from a variety of sources, with only a small part coming from the original Seaview vineyards at Chaffey Road, McLaren Vale. The wines comprise Rhine Riesling, Sauvignon Blanc, Semillon, White Burgundy, Vintage Moselle, Spatlese Rhine Riesling, Cabernet Sauvignon (one of the bottled wine brand leaders in Australia), Cabernet Shiraz, Vintage Port and Tawny Port.

Distribution:
National retail through all types of liquor outlets.

Prices:
Recommended retail prices have been absolutely meaningless in the case of Seaview products; most sell between $3.99 and $5.99.

Overall Quality:
Particularly good considering the volume of the wines sold.

Vintage Rating 1982–85:
White: '85, '84, '83, '82.
Red: '84, '85, '82, '83.

Outstanding Prior Vintages:
'75, '77.

Tasting Notes:

1985 RHINE RIESLING [16.8] *Colour:* medium green-yellow. *Bouquet:* clean; soft, gentle fruit of good style and weight. *Palate:* very soft, clean, extremely well-made wine, with clear, unmodified rhine riesling flavours. Given the volume in which it is made, of high quality. Drink '86–'87.

1982 CABERNET SHIRAZ [16.6] *Colour:* bright, light to medium purple-red. *Bouquet:* soft, sweet, cherry aromas with light vanillan oak. *Palate:* very sweet, almost essency cherry/strawberry fruit flavours on the mid-palate, and a soft, clean finish. Another excellent commercial wine. Drink '85–'87.

1982 CABERNET SAUVIGNON [17] *Colour:* medium to full red. *Bouquet:* attractive fruit aromas ranging from sweet berry into dark chocolate. *Palate:* round, sweet plum/berry flavours, suggesting a substantial Coonawarra contribution; low tannin; yet another excellent commercial release given the volume. Drink '86–'88.

THE SETTLEMENT WINE COMPANY

p. 466

Location:
Settlement Road, McLaren Flat,
5 km north-east of McLaren Vale.
(08) 383 0225.

Winemaker:
Dr David Mitchell.

1985 Production:
Approximately 6000 cases.

Principal Wines:
Red wine specialists, with range extending from Carbonic Maceration Red through to Liqueur Port. The ports are sold in an amazing variety of containers and under equally amazing names, including Plasma Port and Koala Port, the latter in a ceramic koala bear with a slouch hat. Also offered is the golf club series, Number 1 Wood, Number 3 Wood and so on. (Get it?)

Distribution:
Principally cellar-door sales and mailing list; cellar-door sales 10 a.m. to 5 p.m. Monday to Friday and noon to 5 p.m. weekends and public holidays. Mailing-list enquiries as above. Limited retail distribution in eastern states, serviced direct from winery.

Prices:
$4.50 to $8.50 cellar door.

Overall Quality:
Good.

Vintage Rating 1982–85:
'84, '82, '85, '83.

Outstanding Prior Vintages:
'76, '78.

Tasting Notes:

1985 CARBONIC MACERATION [17] *Colour:* medium full red-purple. *Bouquet:* firm and rich, with excellent, spicy varietal aroma; clean, and no errant carbonic maceration aromas. *Palate:* rich pepper/spice fruit, with gentle but quite persistent tannin, surprising given the carbonic maceration treatment. A structured but not heavy wine. Drink '86–'89.

1983 CABERNET SAUVIGNON [14.8] *Colour:* dense purple-red. *Bouquet:* enormous gravelly and extractive, dense and astringent *Palate:* a huge wine, heavy and astringent, with some volatility. A blend of 75% Mt Barker cabernet sauvignon (Western Australia) and 25% McLaren Vale material. At one stage it won a gold medal, but something went wrong along the way.

OLDE COTTAGE LIQUEUR PORT [16.6] *Colour:* aged tawny, with no red hues at all. *Bouquet:* obvious rancio, a touch of caramel, smooth and stylish, with considerable weight. *Palate:* a high-flavoured, complex, old tawny port in typical Australian style. Some obviously old material included, and would have scored very highly were it not for a slightly biscuity after-taste. Drink now.

SIMON HACKETT

p. 466

Location:
Aldinga Wine Company Pty Ltd, PO Box 166, Walkerville, 5081; (distribution company only). (08) 223 1685.

Winemaker:
Simon Hackett.

1985 Production:
3200 cases.

Principal Wines:
Initial 1985 release (from '84 and '82 respectively) of only two wines, Semillon and Cabernet Sauvignon. Wines made from McLaren Vale grapes (the cabernet sauvignon has a Coonawarra component) made at various wineries under Simon Hackett's personal direction. Accordingly Simon Hackett is a brand only, with neither vineyard nor winery.

Distribution:
Exclusively through fine wine retailers. Enquiries to PO Box 166, Walkerville, SA, 5081.

Prices:
$8.50 recommended retail.

Overall Quality:
Very good.

Vintage Rating 1982–85:
White: '85, '84.
Red: '83, '82, '84, '85.

Tasting Notes:

1984 SEMILLON [17.8] *Colour:* bright yellow-green, with just a touch of oak-derived straw. *Bouquet:* skilful winemaking evident, with lemony oak and sauvignon blanc (a minor component of the wine). *Palate:* very good fruit/oak balance; some slight buttery/honey semillon flavours already emerging, augmented by the oak. Good crisp acid on the finish rounds off a high quality wine. Drink '86–'90.

1982 CABERNET SAUVIGNON [17.6] *Colour:* excellent purple-red of medium depth, brilliant and clear. *Bouquet:* of medium weight, with some gently astringent cabernet aromas; oak held well in restraint, but evident. *Palate:* most attractive, smooth berry flavours with a nicely judged touch of spicy oak; a well-made and well-balanced wine now close to its peak. Drink '86–'89.

SOUTHERN VALES WINERY

p. 467

Location:
Main Road, McLaren Vale, 5171.
(08) 383 8656.

Winemaker:
Stephen Bennett.

1985 Production:
Not stated, but substantial.

Principal Wines:

SOUTHERN VALES

The wines are distributed under two labels: Tatachilla for the top of the range premium wines, and Southern Vales for the commercial wines. Releases under the Tatachilla label so far include Sauvignon Blanc, Cabernet Sauvignon and Fine Old Tawny Port; those under the Southern Vales label comprise Bin 11 Rhine Riesling, Bin 13 Spatlese Rhine Riesling, Bin 15 White Frontignan Late Picked, Bin 17 Chablis and Bin 27 Cabernet Sauvignon.

Distribution:
Retail, cellar-door and export sales all important. Cellar-door sales 10 a.m. to 5 p.m. Monday to Friday, 10 a.m. to 4 p.m. Saturday and 11 a.m. to 3 p.m. Sunday. Wholesale distributors Ian Loftus and Co., Victoria; Vintage Wine Co., Western Australia; Walter Reed and Co., Queensland. Export sales through George M. Lau (Holdings) Pty Ltd.

Prices:
$6.60 to $9.95 retail.

Overall Quality:
Adequate.

Vintage Rating 1982–85:
'85, '84, '82, '83.

Tasting Notes:

1984 TATACHILLA SAUVIGNON BLANC [15.8] *Colour:* **light to medium yellow-green.** *Bouquet:* **very full and pungent gooseberry aromas; overall impression of ripe fruit.** *Palate:* **varietal flavour is downright aggressive, with a stalky/skinny edge; very flavoursome, however. Drink '85–'87.**

1982 CABERNET SAUVIGNON [16.8] *Colour:* **red-purple of medium depth.** *Bouquet:* **rich, ripe and slightly extractive, indeed thick, fruit aromas.** *Palate:* **far less heavy and aggressive than the bouquet suggests; full, round, gently sweet berry flavours on the mid-palate, and soft tannin on the finish. Drink '86–'90.**

TATACHILLA FINE OLD TAWNY PORT [16.8] *Colour:* **deep, tawny colour, indicative of substantial wood ageing.** *Bouquet:* **rich, almost raisiny; smooth spirit.** *Palate:* **good fruit weight, with sweet plum pudding/caramel flavours, still showing vestiges of the frontignac base wine. Good, wood-developed rancio. Drink now.**

THOMAS FERNHILL ESTATE

p. 468

Location:
Ingoldby Road, McLaren Flat, 5171; on northern outskirts of township. (08) 383 0167.

Winemaker:
Wayne Thomas.

1985 Production:
3500 cases.

Principal Wines:
Rhine Riesling, Chardonnay, Sauvignon Blanc, Shiraz, Cabernet Franc and Cabernet Sauvignon.

Distribution:

Substantial cellar-door sales 10 a.m. to 5 p.m. 7 days; mailing-list enquiries to Ingoldby Road, McLaren Flat, 5171. Limited fine wine retail distribution through wholesalers in New South Wales (Fesq and Co.); Adelaide (Classic Wine Brokers); Victoria (Harvey Long Winebrokers) and Queensland (Barrique Fine Wines).

Prices:
$7.95 to $13.95 retail.

Overall Quality:
Very good.

Vintage Rating 1982–85:
White: '84, '85, '83, '82.
Red: '85, '82, '84, '83.

Outstanding Prior Vintages:
'78.

Tasting Notes:
1985 CHARDONNAY [17.6] *Colour:* **medium yellow-green.** *Bouquet:* **round, soft and full, with rich, buttery fruit and oak; an outstanding white burgundy style.** *Palate:* **round and rich, with very smooth, slightly buttery fruit, and balancing acid to prevent the wine from cloying. Drink '87–'90.**

TORRESAN'S HAPPY VALLEY WINERY

p. 469

Location:
Manning Road, Happy Valley, 5159. (08) 270 2239.

Winemaker:
Stephen Clarke.

1985 Production:
Substantial total crush; approximately 2000 cases premium red wine (shiraz cabernet) and 1000 cases white wine (riesling crouchen).

Principal Wines:
A basic range of bottled and bulk wines produced which sell principally on price.

Overall Quality:
Adequate at best.

WIRRA WIRRA VINEYARDS

pp. 469–70

Location:
McMurtrie Road, McLaren Vale, 5171;
2 km south-east of township.
(08) 38 3414.

Winemakers:
Greg Trott; Oenotec Pty Ltd consultants.

1985 Production:
20,000 cases.

Principal Wines:
A limited range of very high-quality table wines, made from grapes grown both within and outside of the Southern Vales, the majority of the Southern Vales material being estate-grown or grown on associated vineyards. Wines included Hand Picked Rhine Riesling, Late Picked Rhine Riesling, Chardonnay (from various specified sources), Sauvignon Blanc Semillon, Cabernet Shiraz, Cabernet Sauvignon, and Church Block Cabernet Merlot.

Distribution:
Substantial cellar-door sales 9 a.m. to 5 p.m. Monday to Saturday; 11 a.m. to 5 p.m. Sunday. Also significant fine wine retail distribution through Rutherglen Wine Co., Victoria; I. H. Baker, New South Wales and Queensland; Tasmanian Fine Wines, Hobart; The Oak Barrel, ACT; South Australian distribution handled direct.

Prices:
$8 to $11.50 recommended retail.

Overall Quality:
Exceptional.

Vintage Rating 1982–85:
White: '84, '82, '85, '83.
Red: '84, '82, '83, '85.

Outstanding Prior Vintages:
'79.

Tasting Notes:

1984 SAUVIGNON BLANC [18.4] *Colour:* bright green-yellow of light to medium depth. *Bouquet:* intense, pristine grassy/gooseberry varietal aroma, Loire-like in character. *Palate:* exceptionally clear varietal flavour with good mid-palate weight and a lingering finish. An absolute tour-de-force for a warm-climate sauvignon. Drink '86–'88.

1984 HAND PICKED RHINE RIESLING [17.4] *Colour:* brilliant, strong green. *Bouquet:* very clean, with pronounced lime aromas; of medium weight only; and with more finesse and life than most McLaren Vale rieslings. *Palate:* typically generous fore- and mid-palate fruit, but lifted out of the ruck by the excellent acid on the finish. Drink '86–'87.

1984 CHARDONNAY [18] *Colour:* brilliant green-yellow. *Bouquet:* complex smoky oak balanced against intense and fine grapefruit/melon flavours. *Palate:* very complex, with some barrel ferment characters adding complexity to toasty/smoky oak flavours, together with similar grapefruit/melon fruit to that evident in the bouquet. On evidence of earlier Wirra Wirra chardonnays, will certainly stand bottle-age. Drink '86–'89.

1983 CHURCH BLOCK CABERNET MERLOT SHIRAZ [17] *Colour:* medium red-purple. *Bouquet:* of the complexity one expects from Wirra Wirra; caramel/cigar aromas intermingle with obviously ripe shiraz, with secondary bottle aromas already developing. *Palate:* some of those caramel cigar/leather characters of the bouquet again manifest themselves with fairly soft fruit and low tannin; oak held well in restraint. Will not be a long-lived wine. Drink '86–'88.

WOODSTOCK

pp. 470–1

Location:
Douglas Gully Road, McLaren Flat, 5171;
3 km north-east of township.
(08) 383 0156.

Winemaker:
Scott Collett.

1985 Production:
Approximately 300,000 litres; approximately 70% sold in bulk to other wineries.

Principal Wines:
Small range of very high-quality table and fortified wines comprising Rhine Riesling, Sauvignon Semillon, Botrytis Sweet White, Muscat of Alexandria, Cabernet Sauvignon, Tawny Port and Vintage Port. Tawny Ports also sold in 25-litre containers.

Distribution:
Substantial cellar-door sales 9 a.m. to 5 p.m. Monday to Friday and noon to 5 p.m. weekends. High-quality mailing list; enquiries to PO Box 151, McLaren Vale, SA, 5171. National distribution through John Cawsey and Co. except South Australia where distribution through R. L. Moore Agencies.

Prices:
$6 to $10.50 cellar door.

Overall Quality:
Exceptional.

Vintage Rating 1982–85:
White: '85, '84, '83, '82.
Red: '82, '85, '84, '83.

Tasting Notes:

1984 BOTRYTIS SWEET WHITE [18.4] *Colour:* brilliant and glowing yellow-green. *Bouquet:* intense honeyed/lime fruit aromas, very rich and clean. *Palate:* great complexity; pronounced honeyed chenin blanc flavour, with very good acid; just a fraction hard on the finish, which time will rectify. (A blend of 75% chenin blanc and 25% rhine riesling picked at 22 baume.) Drink '88–'94.

1983 CABERNET SAUVIGNON [17] *Colour:* bright red-purple of medium to full depth. *Bouquet:* a big, full and robust fruit aroma with a touch of sweet American oak. *Palate:* generously flavoured, sweet red berry/cassis flavours, just avoiding jamminess. An excellent wine for a difficult year, though not in the class of the magnificent '82. Drink '87–'91.

1982 CABERNET SAUVIGNON [19] *Colour:* full purple-red. *Bouquet:* extraordinarily complex, with aromas of mint, cassis and green leaf, all intermingling. *Palate:* of great flavour intensity and elegance; rich cabernet varietal flavour with some minty overtones. Drink '86–'94.

1984 VINTAGE PORT [18.4] *Colour:* impenetrable purple-red. *Bouquet:* powerful; superbly complex brandy spirit with dense, deep fruit aromas. *Palate:* magnificently rich cassis/blackcurrant mid-palate fruit, then complex spirit. A most striking and unusual vintage port. Drink '87–'96.

Western Australia

Lower Great Southern Area

1985 Vintage

If the eastern states had their great drought in the lead-up to the 1983 vintage, the West had its in the lead-up to 1984's. Vignerons hoping for abundant winter rains for the 1985 vintage were only partially satisfied, although spring was unusually wet and cool, which partly made up for the deficit. Overall, flowering and fruit-set were good, though subsequent bunch development was less than satisfactory in some vineyards. One of the coolest Januaries on record was followed by extremely hot conditions in February and March, relieved only by the afternoon sea breezes which are a feature of the district.

Vintage commenced in mid-March, two to three weeks earlier than normal. In retrospect, this was fortunate timing, for the dry season broke earlier than normal, in mid-April, when vintage was largely but not totally completed.

After the very low yields of 1984, tonnages returned to normal, with fruit quality regarded almost uniformly as exceptional. The white wines are very aromatic and well balanced, with clearly defined varietal character. The reds have abundant flavour and equally good varietal character, and promise to develop into wines of greater than normal elegance and finesse.

The Changes

The Lower Great Southern Area is both exceedingly remote and exceedingly far-flung. It seems to have developed a distinct neurosis about the publicity accorded the Margaret River, and is drawing in on itself. The number of producing wineries (or at least producing labels) is on the decrease. Mount Shadforth, Narrikup, Perillup and Redmond are all effectively withdrawing from commercial sale; Hay River is becoming decidedly shadowy; and several others are more than reticent about supplying information. One such was Watermans, now reincarnated as Chatsfield Wines, which, perversely, seems clearly destined to produce some excellent wine.

The obvious exceptions to the above comments are Plantagenet and Forest Hill and, to a lesser degree, Alkoomi and Goundrey. Shemarin, Rob Bowen's weekend retreat, is a new entry: here the low profile is very deliberate, as Bowen is most anxious he should not be seen to compete in any way with Plantagenet, where he is employed as winemaker.

To all intents and purposes, Alkoomi, Goundrey and Plantagenet are the driving forces in the region. The only other producing winery of significance is Chateau Barker, and it more than any other prefers to keep itself to itself. I do not believe that such attitudes are appropriate in today's marketplace.

ALKOOMI

p. 481

Location:
Wingeballup Road, Frankland, 6396;
11 km west of township.
(098) 55 2229.

Winemaker:
Merv Lange.

1985 Production:
Approximately 12,000 cases.

Principal Wines:
Rhine Riesling, Semillon/Sauvignon Blanc, Cabernet Shiraz, Malbec, Cabernet Malbec Shiraz and Cabernet Sauvignon.

Distribution:
Mailing list, cellar-door sales and through wholesale distributors in Western Australia, Regional Vineyard Distributors; New South Wales, David Bainbridge and Victoria, Sutherland Cellars. Limited exports through Craig Mostyn Limited. Mailing-list enquiries to RMB 234, Frankland, 6396. Cellar-door sales 10 a.m. to 5 p.m. Monday to Saturday and 1 p.m. to 5 p.m. Sunday.

Prices:
$7.50 to $9.50 retail.

Overall Quality:
White wines adequate; red wines good to very good.

Vintage Rating:
'85, '84, '82, '83.

Outstanding Prior Vintages:
'77, '80.

Tasting Notes:
1984 RHINE RIESLING [14.6] *Colour:* light to medium straw-yellow. *Bouquet:* a heavy wine, with distinct malty/cheesy solids characters. *Palate:* as the bouquet promises, rather heavy and phenolic. It will certainly improve with bottle age, but it is difficult to see the wine ever becoming really attractive. Drink '87–'89.

1984 SEMILLON SAUVIGNON BLANC [15] *Colour:* medium yellow-green. *Bouquet:* a wine of greater fruit depth and character, although there are still some rather heavy and slightly cheesy solids characters. *Palate:* of considerable weight and flavour, although varietal character is somewhat obscured by honey/malt solids fermentation flavours. A wine which will develop into a particular style of white burgundy with bottle age. Drink '87–'90.

1983 MALBEC [17] *Colour:* full purple-red, slightly opaque. *Bouquet:* complex, berry/leaf aromas, with just a touch of meaty/spice character. *Palate:* complex, tobacco/plum flavours, with good mid-palate weight and soft tannin; crisp acid also helps the wine. Drink '87–'91.

1983 CABERNET SAUVIGNON [17.8] *Colour:* deep purple-red. *Bouquet:* strong, dense and gravelly/robust wine with absolutely unmistakable cabernet characteristics. *Palate:* deep, powerful and strong with integrated tannin; very good mid-palate ripeness and weight, with firm berry flavours and then a typically authoritative finish. Drink '89–'96.

CHATEAU BARKER

pp. 481–2

Location:
Albany Highway, Mount Barker, 6324;
7 km north of Mount Barker.
(098) 51 1452.

Winemaker:
James Cooper.

1985 Production:
Not for publication.

Principal Wines:
A limited range of table wines released under registered brand names including Quondyp Rhine Riesling, Quondyp Traminer, Tiger's Eye Pinot Noir, Pyramup Cabernet Shiraz Malbec and Pyramup Cabernet Sauvignon.

Distribution:
Chiefly cellar-door sales and mailing list. Limited eastern states retail distribution through Taylor Ferguson. Mailing-list enquiries as above.

Overall Quality:
Not known currently; neither samples nor up-to-date information forthcoming.

CHATSFIELD

Location:
34 Albany Highway, Mount Barker, 6324; at township.
(098) 51 1266.

Winemaker:
Capel Vale (contract).

1985 Production:
Not for publication.

Principal Wines:

Only wines presently available are Rhine Riesling and Traminer.

Distribution:
Principally cellar-door sales and mailing list; cellar-door sales 10 a.m. to 4 p.m. Tuesday to Saturday. Mailing-list enquiries to PO Box 65, Mount Barker, WA, 6324. Limited wholesale distribution in Western Australia through Lionel Sampson, Perth.

Prices:
$8.50.

Overall Quality:
Very good.

Vintage Rating 1982–85:
Not relevant because of change of ownership and winemaking.

FOREST HILL

pp. 482–3

Location:
142 km peg, Muir Highway, Forest Hill via Mount Barker, 6324.
(098) 51 3231.

Winemaker:
Rob Bowen (contract).

1985 Production:
2500 cases.

Principal Wines:
A limited range of white, red and fortified table wines comprising Rhine Riesling, Traminer, Chardonnay, Cabernet Sauvignon and Vintage Port.

Distribution:
Chiefly mailing list and cellar-door sales. Limited retail distribution serviced direct ex vineyard. Mailing-list enquiries to Forest Hill Vineyard, PO Box 49, Mount Barker, WA. Cellar-door sales 10 a.m. to 4 p.m. 7 days and public holidays except Good Friday and Christmas Day.

Prices:
$7.50 to $10.60 cellar door.

Overall Quality:
Exceptional.

Vintage Rating 1982–85:
Not relevant, as contract winemaker (and winery) changed 1984.

Outstanding Prior Vintages:
'75.

Tasting Notes:

1984 *RHINE RIESLING* [18.4] *Colour:* medium yellow-green. *Bouquet:* very clean, strong, firm and robust riesling aroma; quite steely, and with real backbone. *Palate:* superb style, depth and weight; a wine which exhibits exceptional concentration and intensity of flavour, yet avoids heaviness. A classic cellaring style. Drink '86–'91.

1984 *TRAMINER* [16.4] *Colour:* medium to full green-yellow. *Bouquet:* soft, gentle lime/fruit aromatics; of medium to full weight. *Palate:* a big wine, but with a soft mid-palate structure, with lime/spice flavours, and then marred by a slightly hard finish, a characteristic endemic to traminer. Drink '86–'87.

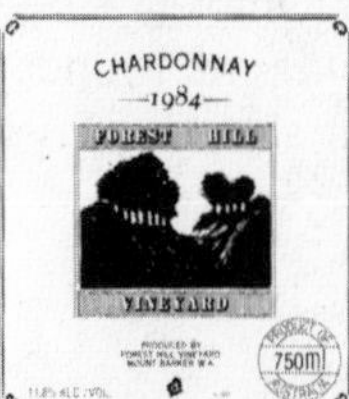

1984 *CHARDONNAY* [18.4] *Colour:* bright green-yellow. *Bouquet:* full and rich, with outstanding varietal character in the grapefruit spectrum; clean and deep. *Palate:* a vibrant, lively and elegant wine, with stylish fruit flavour and excellent structure. Very similar to the Plantagenet Chardonnay of the same year. An each-way proposition for drinking or cellaring. Drink '86–'89.

1984 *RUBY PORT* [16.2] *Colour:* medium to full red-purple. *Bouquet:* clean, but shows some slightly inappropriate green/astringent aromas. *Palate:* very sweet, and again a curious counterposition between sweetness and some green flavours. Despite considerable show success, not a wine that I found especially successful. Drink '86–'88.

GALAFREY

p. 483

Location:
145 Lower Sterling Terrace, Albany, 6330; in township.
(098) 41 6533.

Winemaker:
Ian Tyrer.

1985 Production:
Approximately 1000 cases.

Principal Wines:
Rhine Riesling, Shiraz, Pinot Noir and Cabernet Sauvignon.

Distribution:
Exclusively cellar-door sales and mail order; cellar-door sales 10 a.m. to 5 p.m. most days; preferable to ring for appointment. Mailing-list address as above.

Prices:
$7.50 cellar door.

Overall Quality:
Not rated; wines not available for assessment.

GOUNDREY

pp. 483–4

Location:
11 North Street, Denmark, 6333; in township.
(098) 48 1515.

Winemaker:
Michael Goundrey.

1985 Production:
Approximately 4500 cases.

Principal Wines:

Rhine Riesling, Cabernet Shiraz and Cabernet Sauvignon.

Distribution:
Chiefly mailing list and cellar-door sales; limited retail distribution through wholesale distributor Lionel Sampson (Perth). Cellar-door sales 10 a.m. to 4 p.m. Monday to Saturday. Mailing-list enquiries as above.

Prices:
$8.10 to $8.50 recommended retail; 10 per cent less cellar door.

Overall Quality:
Good to very good.

Vintage Rating 1982–85:
White: '82, '85, '84, '83.
Red: '84, '83, '85, '82.

Outstanding Prior Vintages:
'77, '81.

Tasting Notes:

1985 *RHINE RIESLING* [18] *Colour:* bright green-yellow. *Bouquet:* clean; rich spicy/nutmeg aroma, unusual but attractive and deriving from fruit, not oak. *Palate:* attractive full fruit with some lime flavours; very good palate weight, and the wine finishes with crisp acid. Drink 86–'90.

1983 *CABERNET SAUVIGNON* [17.4] *Colour:* medium to full red-purple. *Bouquet:* a very strong, robust and concentrated wine, needing time to soften and open up. *Palate:* has very firm structure; some sweet, berry/vanillan oak flavours on the mid-palate, followed by gently astringent tannin on the finish. Will be long-lived. Drink '89–'94.

HAY RIVER

p. 484

Location:
Denmark Road, Mount Barker, 6324;
30 km west of Mount Barker (vineyard only).

Winemaker:
Michael Goundrey (contract).

1985 Production:
Not known but limited.

Principal Wines:

Only one grape is grown and only one wine made: Cabernet Sauvignon.

Distribution:
Limited Perth retail distribution. No cellar-door sales nor eastern states distribution.

HOUGHTON FRANKLAND RIVER

pp. 484–5

Location:
(Vineyard only) off Rocky Gully to Frankland Road, north of Muir Highway (vineyard leased by Houghton from owners, Frankland River Wines).

Winemaker:
Peter Dawson.

1985 Production:
Approximately 600 tonnes of grapes crushed (the equivalent of 45,000 cases).

Principal Wines:
Rhine Riesling, Traminer and Cabernet Sauvignon.

Distribution:
National retail through Thomas Hardy distribution network.

Prices:
$6.50 to $6.85 recommended retail.

Overall Quality:
Good to very good.

Vintage Rating 1982–85:
White: '85, '83, '82, '84.
Red: '85, '83, '82, '84.

Outstanding Prior Vintages:
'80.

Tasting Notes:

1983 AUSLESE RHINE RIESLING [16.8] *Colour:* **medium yellow-green.** *Bouquet:* **a little closed, with some bottle-developed camphor aromas.** *Palate:* **a total contrast to the bouquet, lively and with intense, mouth-puckering acid to balance considerable sweetness and fruit weight. Drink '85–'87.**

1982 CABERNET SAUVIGNON [17] *Colour:* **medium to full purple-red.** *Bouquet:* **strongly accented cabernet varietal aroma, but a touch leathery and astringent.** *Palate:* **firm, herbaceous fruit, with a long, crisply acid finish. Much better than the bouquet suggests. Drink '85–'88.**

NARANG

p. 485

Location:
Woodlands, Porongurup,
19 km east of Mount Barker (vineyard only).

Winemaker:
Rob Bowen (contract).

1985 Production:
75 cases.

Principal Wines:
Only Rhine Riesling grown and made.

Distribution:
Exclusively cellar-door sales and through private mailing list.

Overall Quality:
Not rated.

PLANTAGENET

pp. 486–7

Location:
Albany Highway, Mount Barker, 6324; on northern outskirts of township. (098) 51 1150.

Winemaker:
Rob Bowen.

1985 Production:
Approximately 7500 cases.

Principal Wines:
An ever-expanding range of table and fortified wines is made, produced from a variety of grapes estate-grown, purchased from other vineyards in the district, but also coming from the Bindoon region. The source of all of the grapes is clearly stated on the label. Small releases of high-quality table wines, restricted to cellar-door and mailing-list sales, appearing under the Kings Reserve Series; others simply under the Plantagenet label, but indicating both the district and vineyard of source. Wines include Rhine Riesling, Chenin Blanc, Traminer, Chardonnay, Frontignan, Blanc Cabernet, Fleur de Cabernet, Cabernet Sauvignon and Cabernet Hermitage.

Distribution:
Significant retail distribution through wholesale agents in each state; also active mailing list and cellar-door sales. Cellar-door sales 9 a.m. to 5 p.m. Monday to Saturday; mailing-list enquiries to PO Box 155, Mount Barker, WA, 6324. Wholesale distributors are West Coast Wines, Perth; Fesq & Company, Sydney; Rutherglen Wine Company, Melbourne and Montgomery Smith, South Australia.

Prices:
$6 to $10 recommended retail.

Overall Quality:
Exceptional.

Vintage Rating 1982–85:
White: '84, '83, '85, '82.
Red: '83, '84, '85, '82.

Outstanding Prior Vintages:
'81.

Tasting Notes:

1985 FRONTIGNAN (BINDOON) [18] *Colour:* very pale bright green. *Bouquet:* spotlessly clean, intense and perfumed spicy grape aromas. *Palate:* marvellous fresh essence-of-grape, sweet fruit flavours with some residual sugar; a great Australian wine style, and they really don't come any better than this wine. Drink '85–'86.

1985 FLEUR DE CABERNET [17] *Colour:* vibrant light to medium purple-red. *Bouquet:* fresh, light, crystal clear cabernet varietal character, with a touch of sweet berry and a hint of some carbonic maceration character. *Palate:* fresh and crisp, appreciably astringent, with good cabernet varietal character, but adequate fruit weight to carry that astringency. A success. Drink '86.

1984 WYJUP RHINE RIESLING [17.8] *Colour:* light to medium green-yellow. *Bouquet:* very clean and soft, gently fragrant/flowery fruit aromas. *Palate:* a beautifully balanced, fresh and elegantly flowery wine, full of flavour, and with a clean, soft finish. Drink '85–'88.

1984 KINGS RESERVE CHARDONNAY [18.4] *Colour:* glowing bright green-yellow. *Bouquet:* magnificently aromatic grapefruit characters; quite outstanding fruit character, with the oak only incidental. *Palate:* intense and elegant varietal fruit; avoids the heaviness of so many Australian chardonnays, and derives its style and character from the grape rather than from the oak cask in which it was matured. Drink '85–'89.

1983 CABERNET HERMITAGE [17.8] *Colour:* dense, dark purple-red. *Bouquet:* enormously powerful, concentrated and deep wine with a hint of black pepper/spice from the shiraz component. *Palate:* amazing concentration, as if reduced by a form of evaporation; some black pepper characters again apparent; very deep fruit, and fairly soft tannin on the finish both surprising and a relief. A wine like they used to make in north-eastern Victoria. Drink '88–'93.

1983 CABERNET SAUVIGNON [17.2] *Colour:* dense, dark purple. *Bouquet:* potent, deep, concentrated and unfathomable wine, yet to build any semblance of aromatic character. *Palate:* very concentrated but surprisingly smooth; a slight dip in the mid-palate flavour which may fill out; some ripe minty/berry flavours and soft tannin. A striking wine which needs time. Drink '87–'91.

SHEMARIN

p. 487

Location:
18 Muir Street, Mount Barker, 6324.

Winemaker:
Rob Bowen.

1985 Production:
Approximately 300 cases.

Principal Wines:

Shemarin is the label for the very small quantities of wine which Plantagenet winemaker Rob Bowen has made on his own account on and off since 1980. Bowen is adamant that the quantities of wine made will always be very restricted and that the wines will never compete with Plantagenet. 1985 was the first vintage from estate grown grapes; intermittently since 1980 parcels of wine have been made from grapes purchased in from other growers in the region. The estate will concentrate on Sauvignon Blanc. Other releases have included and will in the future include Hermitage, Zinfandel and Cabernet Sauvignon.

Distribution:
Informal mailing list and through the Oak Barrel, Sydney and Nicks of Doncaster, Melbourne. No cellar-door sales.

Prices:
$7 to $9 recommended retail.

Overall Quality:
Very good.

Vintage Rating 1982–85:
Not applicable.

Tasting Notes:

1985 SAUVIGNON BLANC [16.8] _Colour:_ pale bright green-yellow. _Bouquet:_ light fruit, with some slightly sweaty armpit varietal aroma. _Palate:_ clean, light fresh and clean, with very delicate grassy/gooseberry varietal character. Little or no oak apparent. Will always be an elegant rather than full-flavoured wine. Drink '86–'87.

1982 ZINFANDEL [17] _Colour:_ medium red-purple. _Bouquet:_ strong, crushed black pepper aroma dominates all other characters. _Palate:_ lively black pepper flavours on the fore- and mid-palate; a crisply acid, low tannin finish. A most unusual and striking wine. Drink '86.

TINGLE-WOOD WINES

pp. 487–9

Location:
Glenrowan Road, Denmark, 6333;
8 km north-west of town.
(098) 40 9218.

Winemaker:
Bob Wood.

1985 Production:
45 cases.

Principal Wines:
Rhine Riesling and Cabernet Shiraz.

Distribution:
Exclusively cellar-door sales and mailing list; cellar-door sales 9 a.m. to 6 p.m. Monday to Saturday, Sunday by appointment. Mailing-list enquiries to PO Box 160, Denmark, 6333.

Prices:
$6 cellar door.

Overall Quality:
A little variable; adequate to very good.

Vintage Rating 1982–85:
'84, '85, '82, '83.

Tasting Notes:

1983 RHINE RIESLING [17.6] _Colour:_ medium yellow, quite developed. _Bouquet:_ clean, deep and solid, with concentrated lime aromas. _Palate:_ rich and very Germanic in style; strikingly intense and concentrated flavours of most unusual depth. Certainly a wine from a very low yielding vineyard. Drink '85–'89.

1983 CABERNET SAUVIGNON SHIRAZ [16.4] _Colour:_ dense purple-red, brilliantly clear yet almost impenetrable. _Bouquet:_ potent and deep, with a background of black pepper/spice. _Palate:_ a very firm wine in which slightly bitter tannin builds early and throws out the balance on the back-palate; while there is some attractive pepper spice on the mid-palate, it is doubtful if the wine will ever come into balance. Drink '88–'92.

Margaret River

1985 Vintage

Since 1980, Margaret River has had two outstanding vintages: 1982 and 1985. Only with a longer perspective will it be possible to tell which deserves the higher overall rating, but it is already certain that the 1985 wines—particularly the whites, but also the reds—will be sought after eagerly.

Excellent spring rains were followed by a very cool, dry summer, interrupted only by two weeks of extremely hot weather at the end of February. Had that two weeks of hot weather not intervened, it is anyone's guess as to what the quality might have been. Certainly it had some impact, but the high quality of the wines as they settle down in the second half of 1985 is undoubted. All of the white wines show excellent depth of fruit flavour and clearly articulated varietal character. The red wines are very aromatic and fruity, although many tend to be a little lighter-bodied than normal. Given the strength of so many of the Margaret River reds, this may be no bad thing.

The Changes

With the exception of one major vineyard development planned to lead to a winery in 1986 (or possibly 1987) there have been no major changes. Output continues to increase, and the overall reputation of the region continues to grow. Even if David Hohnen failed in the impossible dream of winning three Jimmy Watson Trophies in a row, Leeuwin Estate has stepped into the breach in publicising the virtues of Margaret River from Melbourne to London, chiefly through the instruments of the London Philharmonic Orchestra.

Certification, or appellation, call it what you will, appears to be faltering, just at the time when it is gaining momentum in Victoria. However, the district has probably already established its identity and is in any event virtually guaranteed immunity from malpractice by virtue of its isolation from other regions.

ASHBROOK ESTATE

p. 495

Location:
Harman's South Road, Cowaramup, 6284;
10 km north-east of Margaret River.
(097) 55 6238.

Winemaker:
Tony Devitt.

1985 Production:
3000 cases.

Principal Wines:

A limited range of varietal table wines comprising Semillon, Chardonnay, Verdelho, Sauvignon Blanc and Cabernet Sauvignon.

Distribution:
Principally cellar-door sales and mailing list; cellar-door sales 10 a.m. to 5 p.m. weekends and public holidays. Mailing list to PO Box 263, West Perth, 6005. Telephone (09) 321 6474. Limited intermittent retail distribution through the Oak Barrel, 60 Darling Street, and Summer Hill Cellars, Sydney; Sutherlands, Melbourne; Farmer Bros, Canberra and through Caon & Co., Adelaide and Perth.

Prices:
$7.50 to $8.50 cellar door.

Overall Quality:
Not rated.

Vintage Rating 1982–85:
Tony Devitt is unable to express any preference.

Outstanding Prior Vintages:
'80.

CAPE MENTELLE

p. 495–7

Location:
Off Walcliffe Road, Margaret River, 6285;
3 km west of town.
(097) 27 2439.

Winemaker:
David Hohnen.

1985 Production:
12,000 cases.

Principal Wines:

Now famous as a cabernet sauvignon specialist, but offers an eclectic choice of Rhine Riesling, Semillon (which includes a little sauvignon blanc and chenin blanc), Zinfandel, Hermitage and Cabernet Sauvignon.

Distribution:
Retail, cellar-door and mailing-list sales. Cellar-door sales 9 a.m. to 4.30 p.m. Monday to Saturday. Substantial sales in fine wine retailers with wholesale distributors in each state. For mailing list (and regular handsome bulletins) write to PO Box 110, Margaret River, 6285.

Prices:
$10 to $16.50 cellar door.

Overall Quality:
Very good, Cabernet Sauvignon exceptional.

Vintage Rating 1982–85:
White: '82, '85, '84, '83.
Red: '82, '85(?), '84, '83.

Outstanding Prior Vintages:
'78.

Tasting Notes:

1983 HERMITAGE [18.4] *Colour:* dense purple-red. *Bouquet:* very clean, intense, crushed black pepper aroma; superb style and varietal character. *Palate:* a gloriously clean wine, with intense pepper flavours, yet not heavy; may well achieve delicacy with time as the tannin is uncharacteristically low. Drink '87–'93.

1983 ZINFANDEL [18] *Colour:* medium to full red-purple. *Bouquet:* a complex aroma of smooth berries, merging with a hint of tobacco and caramel, no doubt from the oak. *Palate:* intense, almost essency, cherry/red berry fruit, then soft tannin on the finish. A striking wine. Drink '86–'90.

1983 CABERNET SAUVIGNON [18.6] *Colour:* dense purple-red, almost impenetrable. *Bouquet:* a very big, robust wine with deep and complex firm cabernet fruit, with a touch of herbaceousness balanced by oaky richness. *Palate:* a powerful, intense wine, with very complex fruit flavours; oak present but subservient; fine, complexing tannin on the finish. Drink '89–2000.

CHATEAU XANADU

p. 497

Location:
Railway Terrace, off Wallcliffe Road, Margaret River, 2685;
3 km east of town.
(097) 5 7281.

Winemaker:
John Smith.

1985 Production:
Not for publication.

Principal Wines:
Chardonnay, Semillon, Semillon Spatlese, Sauvignon Blanc, Cabernet Sauvignon, Cabernet Shiraz, Fine Cabernet.

Distribution:
Principally cellar-door sales and mailing list. Significant retail sales in Perth; eastern states limited to Crittenden, Melbourne; Farmer Bros, Canberra and Harris, Sydney. Cellar-door sales 10 a.m. to 4.30 p.m. Monday to Saturday, 11 a.m. to 4.30 p.m. Sunday. Mailing-list enquiries to PO Box 144, Margaret River, 6285.

Prices:
$7 to $8 cellar door.

Overall Quality:
Good to very good.

Vintage Rating 1982–85:
White: '85, '82, '84, '83.
Red: '82, '83, '85, '84.

Tasting Notes:
1985 SEMILLON (WOOD MATURED) [18] *Colour:* medium yellow-green. *Bouquet:* strong, pungent herbaceous/grassy fruit aroma, with little oak evident mid-August 1985. *Palate:* very good palate weight and feel to go with grassy herbaceous character; a New Zealand-style semillon which is far closer to the traditional perception of a sauvignon blanc. By any standards a quite excellent wine. Drink '87–'90.

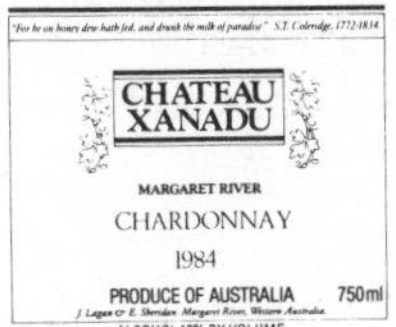

1984 CHARDONNAY [17.2] *Colour:* Medium yellow-green. *Bouquet:* highly aromatic fruit with some tropical fruit aromas. *Palate:* very rich, voluptuous flavours with an illusion of sweetness. Drink '86–'88.

CLAIRAULT

p. 497

Location:
Henry Road, Willyabrup via Cowaramup, 6284;
19 km north-east of Margaret River.
(097) 55 5229 or (097) 55 6225.

Winemaker:
Ian Lewis.

1985 Production:
2000 cases.

Principal Wines:
Semillon Sauvignon Blanc, Rhine Riesling, Dry Rose, Light Bodied Cabernet Sauvignon, Cabernet Sauvignon and Vintage Port.

Distribution:
Principally cellar door and mailing list. Cellar-door sales 10 a.m. to 5 p.m. Monday to Saturday (and Sunday during school holidays). Limited retail sales through Melbourne, Sutherland Cellars; Sydney, Mobbs Hill Cellars and Campsie Bodega; Perth, various retailers. Mailing-list enquiries to CMB Carbunyup River, 6280.

Prices:
$8.50 to $9.50 cellar door.

Overall Quality:
Very good; some exceptional wines.

Vintage Rating 1982–85:
White: Not applicable; first vintage '85.
Red: '82, '85, '84, '83.

Tasting Notes:
1984 DRY ROSE [15.2] *Colour:* medium to full pink, with just a touch of salmon. *Bouquet:* clean, but lacking in fruit aromatics; adequate at best. *Palate:* clean; quite well-made with fair fore- and mid-palate fruit, but lacking crispness on the finish, though bone dry. Drink '85–'86.

1984 CABERNET SAUVIGNON PORT [18] *Colour:* medium purple-red. *Bouquet:* brilliantly clean; scented, almost minty, fruit with clean, brandy spirit aroma. *Palate:* exceptionally smooth, sweet, mid-palate fruit; good brandy spirit and a touch of tannin complexity on the finish. Drink '86–'90.

1982 CABERNET SAUVIGNON [18.4] *Colour:* purple-red of medium depth. *Bouquet:* beautifully clear and clean, full herbaceous cabernet with some capsicum aromas. *Palate:* a wine of great elegance with some berry/cherry flavours on the mid-palate, with cigar/herbaceous flavours coming again on the finish; despite the low tannin, the flavour lingers. Drink '85–'89.

CULLENS' WILLYABRUP

pp. 498–9

Location:
Caves Road, Willyabrup via Cowaramup, 6284;
15 km north-west of Margaret River.
(097) 55 5277.

Winemaker:
Diana Cullen.

1985 Production:
7800 cases.

Principal Wines:

Substantial range of white and red table wines: Chardonnay, Semillon, Sauvignon Blanc, Auslese Rhine Riesling, Sauvignon Blanc Sauternes style, Pinot Noir, Spatlese Cabernet Sauvignon, Cabernet Sauvignon, Cabernet Merlot.

Distribution:
Largely cellar door and mailing list. Cellar-door sales 10 a.m. to 4 p.m. Monday to Saturday. Mailing list PO Box 17, Cowaramup, 6284.

Prices:
$9.50 to $10 cellar door; $11.50 retail.

Overall Quality:
Very good; often exceptional.

Vintage Rating 1982–85:
White: '82, '85, '84, '83.
Red: '82, '85, '83, '84.

Outstanding Prior Vintages:
'75, '77.

Tasting Notes:

1984 CHARDONNAY [17.8] *Colour:* pale straw-yellow. *Bouquet:* very complex; penetrating grapefruit/citric fruit characters, together with some slight "sweaty armpit" barrel ferment characters. *Palate:* very full and rich mid-palate, with strongly accented grapefruit flavours; overall spectacular depth and power; perhaps a little short on elegance, but who cares? Drink '86–'89.

1984 SAUVIGNON BLANC [17.6] *Colour:* pale bright green-straw. *Bouquet:* marzipan oak aromas overlying clear varietal gooseberry fruit; lovely richness and balance. *Palate:* complex fruit/oak barrel ferment characters; rich, lingering and full finish. Drink '86–'90.

1984 SPATLESE CABERNET *Colour:* light vibrant fuchsia, with some spritz. *Bouquet:* interesting peppery/herbaceous aromas, dry and crisp. *Palate:* utterly incongruous marked residual sugar and high acidity clash both with each other and with the bouquet. Some may like the style, but I most certainly do not. Impossible to give any meaningful points to the wine.

1983 CABERNET MERLOT [18] *Colour:* medium purple-red. *Bouquet:* in typical Cullen style, robust, firm and deep with an added impact from the warm vintage. *Palate:* enormous depth and power to fruit; a ripe style but of undeniable quality; persistent soft tannin on the finish. Drink '87–'93.

1983 SAUVIGNON BLANC SAUTERNE STYLE [17] *Colour:* yellow-orange. *Bouquet:* marked volatile lift which is just within the parameters of the style; rich caramel/butter underlay; very complex. *Palate:* rich coffee/caramel/butter fruit flavours; volatile lift again apparent on the finish. A most striking wine. Drink '85–'89.

GHERARDI WINES

p. 499

Location:
Gnarawary Road, Margaret River, 6285;
6 km south-west of town.

Winemaker:
Peter Gherardi.

1985 Production:
Very limited.

Principal Wines:
Chenin Blanc (blend) only wine so far released.

Distribution:
Exclusively cellar door and mailing list.

GILLESPIE VINEYARDS

p. 499

Location:
Davis Road, Witchcliffe, 6286;
10 km south of Margaret River.
(097) 57 6281.

Winemaker:
Alastair Gillespie.

1985 Production:
2000 cases.

Principal Wines:
Two wines only marketed: Semillon Sauvignon Blanc and Cabernet Sauvignon.

Distribution:
Principally cellar door and mailing list. Cellar-door sales 10 a.m. to 4 p.m. Monday to Saturday during summer; during winter Saturday 10 a.m. to 4 p.m. or by appointment. Mailing-list enquiries as above. Very limited retail distribution in Sydney and through Sutherland Cellars, Melbourne. Reasonable Perth retail and restaurant distribution.

Prices:
$6.50 to $10.50.

Overall Quality:
White wines adequate; Cabernet Sauvignon improving each year.

Vintage Rating 1982–85:
White: '85, '84, '82, '83.
Red: '85, '82, '83, '84.

Outstanding Prior Vintages:
Cabernet Sauvignon '79.

Tasting Notes:
1984 SEMILLON SAUVIGNON BLANC [14.8] *Colour:* light to medium yellow, with just a touch of straw. *Bouquet:* very heavy and slightly oily, with marked solids fermentation characters. *Palate:* a very big, rather heavy and phenolic wine, as yet not really approachable; may surprise given enough time. Drink '88–'92.

1983 CABERNET SAUVIGNON [17.2] *Colour:* dark, deep purple-red. *Bouquet:* strong and firm, with attractive cassis/berry fruit aromas. *Palate:* firm, full and robust cabernet fruit, with good oak integration; typical tannin of the vintage; needs many years. Drink '89–'95.

GRALYN CELLARS

pp. 499–500

Location:
Caves Road, Willyabrup via Cowaramup, 6284;
15 km north-west of Margaret River.
(097) 55 6245.

Winemakers:
Graham & Merilyn Hutton.

1985 Production:
Not published; estimated approximately 2500 cases.

Principal Wines:
Vintage Port specialists, also offering Rhine Riesling, Hermitage, Cabernet Sauvignon, Hermitage Port, Cabernet Port and White Port (made from Rhine Riesling).

Distribution:
Exclusively cellar door and mailing list. Cellar-door sales 10.30 a.m. to 4.30 p.m. 7 days. Mailing list c/o PO Cowaramup, 6284.

Overall Quality:
Adequate to good.

HAPP'S

p. 500

Location:
Commonage Road, Yallingup;
5 km south of Dunsborough, 6281.
(097) 55 3300.

Winemaker:
Erland Happ.

1985 Production:
2500 dozen.

Principal Wines:
Chardonnay, Shiraz, Merlot, Cabernet Sauvignon and Vintage Port.

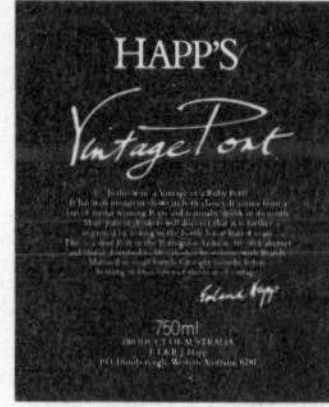

Distribution:
Principally cellar door and mailing list. Cellar-door sales 10 a.m. to 5 p.m. 7 days. Mailing list PO Dunsborough, 6281. Perth wholesale: Vintage Wine Company.

Prices:
$8 cellar door.

Overall Quality:
Consistently very good; some exceptional fragrant light-bodied vintage ports.

Vintage Rating 1982–85:
'84, '85, '83, '82.

Tasting Notes:

1985 VINTAGE PORT [18.4] *Colour:* vibrant purple of medium depth. *Bouquet:* beautifully crisp, clean and elegant; light to medium weight, with a distinctive touch of brandy spirit. *Palate:* lively, dancing, vibrant and spicy fruit made quite dry, but absolutely chock-full of elegant flavour. A bottle is consumed as easily as a glass. Drink '86–'87.

1984 CABERNET SAUVIGNON [17.2] *Colour:* medium to full purple-red. *Bouquet:* full, deep and robust, yet not aggressive, and with considerable richness. *Palate:* much fuller than the Merlot of the same vintage; good mid-palate fruit and marked tannin on the back palate, yet still very very elegant. Drink '87–'92.

1983 SHIRAZ [17.8] *Colour:* very good purple-red. *Bouquet:* a robust wine, quite complex and with just a hint of leathery mercaptan. *Palate:* deep, strong and complex with richly textured berry flavours and excellent structure and balance. Drink '86–'92.

1983 CABERNET SAUVIGNON [17.8] *Colour:* dark purple-red. *Bouquet:* ripe, deep and smooth fruit, with a touch of cedar complexity. *Palate:* mouth-filling, sweet, ripe, berry flavours followed by soft, lingering tannin on the finish to add complexity. Drink '87–'92.

1983 VINTAGE PORT [18.4] *Colour:* medium to full red-purple. *Bouquet:* much fuller than the '85; very clean with excellent fruit/spirit balance and overall of medium weight. *Palate:* crisp, clean mid-palate fruit, but tannin/spice on the back-palate, together with the fine brandy spirit, result in a great wine of very considerable complexity. Drink '86–'89.

LEEUWIN ESTATE

pp. 500–2

Location:
Gnarawary Road, Margaret River, 6285;
5 km south of town.
(097) 57 6253.

Winemaker:
Bob Cartwright.

1985 Production:
Approximately 22,000 cases.

Principal Wines:
Chardonnay, Rhine Riesling Reserve Bin, Rhine Riesling, Pinot Noir and Cabernet Sauvignon. All wines offered with significant bottle age, and immaculate packaging. The labels add a new dimension to Australian wine marketing.

Distribution:
Extensive fine wine retail distribution (wholesale agents I. H. Baker & Co. and Van Cooth & Co.). Cellar-door sales 10 a.m. to 4.30 p.m. 7 days. Mailing list PO Box 7196, Cloisters Square, Perth, 6000.

Prices:
Breathtaking: Chardonnay and Pinot Noir $25 to $35 per bottle.

Overall Quality:
Good to very good; Chardonnay can be exceptional, which at the price it should be.

Vintage Rating 1982–85:
White: '82, '84, '85, '83.
Red: '85, '83, '82, '84.

Outstanding Prior Vintages:
'80.

Tasting Notes:

1983 RHINE RIESLING [16.6] *Colour:* **medium to full yellow.** *Bouquet:* **clean and solid-indeed weighty-riesling fruit, but lacks lift and fragrance.** *Palate:* **very big flavour with ripe fruit, and a slightly thick back-palate. Drink '86–'88.**

1980 CABERNET SAUVIGNON [16.6] *Colour:* **medium to full red-purple, holding its hue very well indeed.** *Bouquet:* **complex bottle age aromas have developed, with a touch of cigar box and gently ripe fruit; overall of medium to full weight.** *Palate:* **cedary/cigar box flavours on the fore-palate; fruit then dips sharply in face of persistent tannin on the back palate and finish. A classic doughnut cabernet. Drink '85–'88.**

1982 CHARDONNAY [18.6] *Colour:* **medium yellow-green.** *Bouquet:* **fine, fragrant grapefruit aromas inter-mingling with nutmeg/spice limousin oak; marvellously full and complex.** *Palate:* **exceedingly fine; a long and intense flavour, yet delicate; some of the same nutmeg characters of the bouquet manifest themselves in a wine of exceptional balance and style. Drink '85–'89.**

1982 PINOT NOIR **(Samples were hard to come by, so here are the winemaker's notes on release of the wine in July 1985).** *Colour:* **light brick-red.** *Bouquet:* **strong, fresh, typical pinot gamy character, enhanced by gentle oak.** *Palate:* **full, rich, pinot flavour, with a lovely blend of French oak; full and round, yet soft with a subtle tannin finish. (Other first-hand accounts are a little less enthusiastic.)**

MOSS WOOD

pp. 502–3

Location:
Metricup Road, Willyabrup, via Cowaramup, 6284; 18 km north-east of Margaret River.
(097) 55 6266.

Winemaker:
Keith Mugford.

1985 Production:
3000 cases.

Principal Wines:
Chardonnay, Semillon, Pinot Noir and Cabernet Sauvignon.

Distribution:
Fine wine retail distribution, cellar door and mailing list. Cellar-door sales 10 a.m. to 4 p.m. (preferably by appointment). Mailing list PO Box 52, Busselton, 6280.

Prices:
$9 to $13 cellar door.

Overall Quality:
Exceptional.

Vintage Rating 1982–85:
White: '85, '84, '83, '82.
Red: '83, '85, '82, '84.

Outstanding Prior Vintages:
'75, '77, '80.

Tasting Notes:

1984 CHARDONNAY [17.4] *Colour:* yellow-green of medium depth. *Bouquet:* rather withdrawn and closed fruit as at August 1985, but with latent power; nice oak. *Palate:* a very smooth, firm wine with good fruit/oak balance and integration; crisp acid and once again the basic structure is there. Drink '87–'89.

1984 SEMILLON [17.8] *Colour:* light to medium yellow-green. *Bouquet:* quite full, and reminiscent of 1980 vintage tasted at the same time; some grassy aromas. *Palate:* rich fruit and weight to mid-palate; a wine of backbone and unmistakable varietal character, with considerable potential. Drink '87–'91.

1984 SEMILLON WOOD MATURED [17.6] *Colour:* medium full yellow-green. *Bouquet:* most attractive, spicy/nutmeg oak, adding another dimension of richness and depth to the aroma. *Palate:* intense spicy cinnamon oak utterly dominant at this stage, with the wine needing time to come back into balance. Should mature very well. Drink '87–'90.

1983 PINOT NOIR [16.8] *Colour:* bright red of light to medium depth. *Bouquet:* crisp fruit with a touch of fresh earth; oak just a fraction dull. *Palate:* a light, clean and fresh wine with some varietal strawberry fruit on the mid-palate, but overall rather one dimensional. Pales into insignificance against the towering magnificence of the '81 Pinot Noir. Drink '87–'90.

1983 CABERNET SAUVIGNON [18.4] *Colour:* strong, dense, red-purple. *Bouquet:* very clean, firm and deep wine, still to develop bottle aromas. *Palate:* excellent fruit modulation with cassis-berry flavours in a riper style, yet avoiding jamminess or heaviness. Soft tannin and oak handling impeccable throughout. Drink '87–'94.

PIERRO

p. 503

Location:
Caves Road, Willyabrup, via Cowaramup, 6284; 17.5 km north-west of Margaret River. (097) 55 6232.

Winemaker:
Michael Peterkin.

1985 Production:
1000 dozen.

Principal Wines:
Chardonnay, Sauvignon Blanc, Pinot Noir and Cabernet Sauvignon.

Distribution:
Cellar-door, mailing-list and limited fine wine retail sales through The Oak Barrel and 60 Darling Street, Sydney and Sutherland Cellars, Melbourne. Cellar-door sales 10 a.m. to 5 p.m. weekends and public holidays. Closed June, July and August. Mailing list PO Box 522, Busselton, 6280.

Prices:
$6 to $12 cellar door.

Overall Quality:
Good to very good; some samples tasted in eastern states not representative.

Vintage Rating 1982–85:
White: '84, '85, '82, '83.
Red: '82, '84, '85, '83.

Outstanding Prior Vintages:
'80.

Tasting Notes:

1984 SAUVIGNON BLANC [16.2] *Colour:* pale straw-yellow with a suggestion of pinking. *Bouquet:* a trace of bottling SO_2 lingers on; of medium weight and just a touch of varietal grass. *Palate:* soft, sweet, lantana-like fruit, almost into lychee; slight hardness on the back-palate. Drink '86–'87.

1984 SPATLESE RIESLING [17.4] *Colour:* medium to full yellow, with a touch of straw. *Bouquet:* clean, fragrant and flowery peach/tropical fruit aromas. *Palate:* a marvellously rich wine with strong peach flavour; most unusual, but very attractive. Drink '85–'87.

1983 PINOT NOIR [17.6] *Colour:* bright light to medium red-purple. *Bouquet:* very clean; excellent fruit/oak balance and with a hint of strawberry fruit aroma. *Palate:* very firm, with far higher-than-usual tannin; may well have the potential to develop into an extremely good wine. Drink '86–'90.

1982 CABERNET SAUVIGNON [17] *Colour:* dense red-purple. *Bouquet:* an immense wine with deep, dark fruit aromas and rich, chewy oak. *Palate:* corresponds to the bouquet, with very strong, sweet oak flavours matched by ripe berry fruit and furry tannin throughout. A huge wine, particularly for the vintage. Drink '88–'96.

REDBROOK

pp. 503–4

Location:
Metricup Road, Willyabrup, 6284 (vineyard only).

Winemaker:
Bill Crappsley.

1985 Production:
6800 cases.

Principal Wines:
A limited range of fine varietal table wines comprising Semillon, Sauvignon Blanc, Chardonnay, Hermitage, Merlot and Cabernet Sauvignon.

Distribution:
Substantial cellar-door sales (through Perth winery—see separate entry) and mailing list; mailing-list address: Evans and Tate, Swan Street, Henley Brook, 6055. Also fine wine retail distribution through wholesale agents Caon & Co., South Australia and John Cawsey & Co. Pty. Limited, eastern states.

Prices:
$8 to $10 recommended retail.

Overall Quality:
Consistently very good; exceptional wines will be made as the vineyard matures.

Vintage Rating 1982–85:
White: '85, '84, '82, '83.
Red: '82, '84, '83, '85(?).

Outstanding Prior Vintages:
'79, '81.

Tasting Notes:

1985 SEMILLON [17.6] *Colour:* pale green-straw. *Bouquet:* intense, pungent, grassy/powdery, unlike almost any other Australian semillon, and reminiscent of New Zealand sauvignon blanc; striking and unusual. *Palate:* extraordinary zesty, grassy, fruit flavours, crisp and tingling. Virtually unrecognisable as semillon early in its life. Drink '86–'90.

1985 SAUVIGNON BLANC [17.8] *Colour:* light but bright green-yellow. *Bouquet:* of light to medium weight, with crystal clear, grassy/gooseberry aromas, not so different from that of the semillon of the same year. *Palate:* fine, crisp, sauvignon blanc; excellent mouth-feel on the back-palate; some softness, and avoids outright aggression. Drink '86–'89.

1984 CHARDONNAY [17.4] *Colour:* medium straw-yellow. *Bouquet:* some malty/honey aromas with a backbone of tight fruit. *Palate:* of medium weight, with attractive, honey/peach fruit flavours, together with integrated and balanced oak. A very stylish wine in a lighter mould. Drink '85–'88.

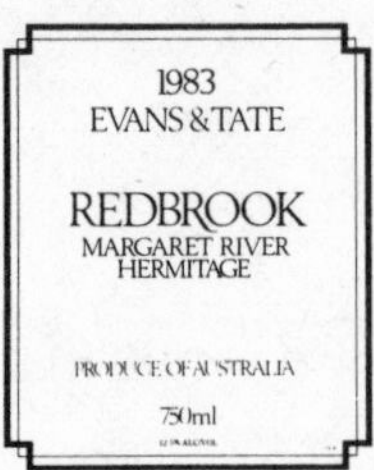

1983 HERMITAGE [17.8] *Colour:* crystal bright red-purple of medium depth. *Bouquet:* clean and very complex, with hints of cigar box, a touch of gravel and sweet, berry fruit; a stylish and classy wine. *Palate:* bell-clear berry flavours; has abundant flavour yet a very delicate feel in the mouth; gentle tannin rounds off the finish. Drink '86–'90.

1983 MERLOT [18.2] *Colour:* medium purple-red. *Bouquet:* a firm, spotlessly clean wine, with immaculate balance and some gentle berry aromas. *Palate:* very good, slightly leafy, varietal flavour, the best so far to be seen in Australia; some incipient, secondary bottle-developed flavours in the cedar/cigar range; soft tannin adds to the structure and finish of the wine. Due for release mid-1986. Drink '87–'91.

1983 CABERNET SAUVIGNON [17.4] *Colour:* bright, clear red-purple. *Bouquet:* very firm cabernet varietal aroma, a touch of gravel and even perhaps the faintest trace of mercaptan. *Palate:* firm, berry/cherry flavours, backed by gentle tannin throughout; a quite lovely wine, which comes alive on the palate after the fractionally uncertain bouquet. Due for release May '86. Drink '87–'92.

REDGATE

p. 504

Location:
Boodjidup Road, Margaret River, 6285;
8 km south-west of town.
(097) 57 6208.

Winemakers:
Bill and Paul Ullinger.

1985 Production:
2600 cases.

Principal Wines:
Semillon, Rhine Riesling, Spatlese Riesling and Cabernet Sauvignon.

Distribution:
Principally cellar-door sales and mailing list; limited Perth restaurant and retail distribution. Melbourne, Sutherland Cellars. Cellar-door sales 10 a.m. to 5 p.m. 7 days. Mailing-list enquiries to PO Box 117, Margaret River, 6285.

Prices:
$6.50 to $10.50 cellar door.

Overall Quality:
White wines good; red wines very good.

Vintage Rating 1982–85:
'85, '84, '83, '82.

Tasting Notes:

1985 RHINE RIESLING [17.2] *Colour:* very light yellow-green. *Bouquet:* soft, clean and fruity, with unmodified riesling aroma in quite different style to the '84. *Palate:* good weight and mid-palate richness, with a correspondingly full, soft finish. Will develop fairly quickly. Drink '86 –'87.

1984 RHINE RIESLING [17] *Colour:* bright straw-green. *Bouquet:* full and clean; very rounded pineapple/tropical fruit aromas. *Palate:* most attractive fruit flavours almost into apricot spectrum; soft but not cloying. Drink '85–'88.

1984 SPATLESE RIESLING [15.8] *Colour:* straw-yellow. *Bouquet:* solid, rather closed and lacking varietal aroma, but clean. *Palate:* firm riesling, only just into spatlese classification; in regional style which tends to provide solidity rather than finesse. Drink '86–'87.

1984 SEMILLON [16.8] *Colour:* straw-yellow. *Bouquet:* solid and a little dull, with a touch of solids fermentation characters leading to a degree of oiliness; despite all this, some grassy fruit. *Palate:* very full-flavoured and of excellent structure; the wine comes alive on the mid- to back-palate with a most attractive, soft, acid, clean finish. Drink '86–'89.

1983 CABERNET SAUVIGNON [18] *Colour:* dark purple-red of very good hue and depth. *Bouquet:* strong and robust, typical of the year; very good depth to sweet fruit, which is neither coarse nor aggressive. *Palate:* round, full, sweet berry/cherry/redcurrant flavours, with gentle but persistent tannin on the finish. Drink '87–'92.

RIBBON VALE ESTATE

p. 504

Location:
Lot 5, Caves Road, Willyabrup via Cowaramup, 6284;
19 km north-east of Margaret River.
(09) 272 3364.

Winemaker:
John James.

1985 Production:
Not stated but very small.

Principal Wines:
Semillon, Semillon Sauvignon Blanc and Cabernet Sauvignon.

Distribution:
Principally mailing list and through direct sales to retailers, principally in Perth; no interstate agents so far appointed. Mailing list 5/15 Regent Street East, Mount Lawley, 6050. (09) 276 4821.

Prices:
$7.45 to $7.95.

Overall Quality:
Good.

Vintage Rating 1982–85:
'84, '85(?), '82, '83.

Tasting Notes:

1984 SEMILLON [16.8] *Colour:* straw-yellow. *Bouquet:* rather closed and somewhat austere, but has potential. *Palate:* much more generous and open than the bouquet would suggest, already developing some honey/nut/butter flavours, with good overall weight and balance. Drink '86–'89.

1984 SEMILLON SAUVIGNON BLANC *Colour:* yellow-green, tinged with straw. *Bouquet:* firm, with marked, grassy, varietal aromas. *Palate:* quite firm and rich, with an added edge deriving from the sauvignon blanc; however, the wine was difficult to assess finally because of a slight corkiness. No second sample could be obtained. Accordingly, not marked.

SANDALFORD MARGARET RIVER ESTATE

p. 505

Location:
Metricup Road, Cowaramup, 6284;
20 km north-west of Margaret River (vineyard).

Winemaker:
Dorham Mann.

1985 Production:
500–600 tonnes of grapes (or 37,000 cases).

Principal Wines:
Semillon (Graves style), Gewurztraminer, Rhine Riesling, Verdelho, Late Harvest Rhine Riesling, Auslese Rhine Riesling and Cabernet Sauvignon.

Distribution:
National retail through Rhine Castle Wines.

Prices:
$7.50 to $10.50 retail.

Overall Quality:
Variable, with some very good wines.

Vintage Rating 1982–85:
White: '85, '82, '84, '83.
Red: '82, '84, '85, '83.

Outstanding Prior Vintages:
'77 (white); '78 (red).

Tasting Notes:

1985 RHINE RIESLING [16.8] *Colour:* light, bright straw-green. *Bouquet:* very clean, floral and fragrant soft fruit, with a hint of lime. *Palate:* soft, floral and fragrant; an easy, round, mouth-filling wine with a soft finish, and again some of the lime flavours apparent in the bouquet. Drink '86–'88.

1985 VERDELHO [17.6] *Colour:* light to medium yellow-green. *Bouquet:* full, with that distinctive honey/banana/passionfruit blend of aromas which is the hallmark of good verdelho. *Palate:* excellent flavour and style; good mid-palate weight and richness; a long, gentle acid finish. Drink '86–'90.

1983 CABERNET SAUVIGNON [15] *Colour:* deep red, with some purple tints. *Bouquet:* a very big, ripe, robust wine, with some harsh astringency. *Palate:* very big, with distinct burnt fruit tastes and a bitter, astringent finish. It is very doubtful whether age will soften the wine. Drink '88–'90.

1983 SHIRAZ [16.2] *Colour:* full red-purple. *Bouquet:* full and firm, with some ripe fruit, but rather closed. *Palate:* much more open and giving; some attractive pepper/spice varietal character; firm tannin and some astringency on the finish. Drink '87–'90.

VASSE FELIX

pp. 505–6

Location:
Harmans South Road, Cowaramup, 6284;
7 km west of town.
(097) 55 5242.

Winemaker:
David Gregg.

1985 Production:
5500 cases.

Principal Wines:
Rhine Riesling, Hermitage and Cabernet Sauvignon.

Distribution:

Cellar door, mailing list and fine wine retailers in most capital cities (Sydney, Oak Barrel; Melbourne, Sutherland Cellars); also limited exports. Cellar-door sales 10 a.m. to 4 p.m. Monday to Saturday. Mailing list as above.

Prices:
$10.80 cellar door.

Overall Quality:
Consistently very good.

Vintage Rating 1982–85:
White: '82, '85, '84, '83.
Red: '82, '85, '83, '84.

Outstanding Prior Vintages:
'76, '79.

Tasting Notes:
1983 CABERNET SAUVIGNON [17.6] *Colour:* clear and bright red-purple of medium depth. *Bouquet:* gentle fruit; soft, cedary complexities; hint of leaf/asparagus. *Palate:* elegant and fine cigar/leafy aromas; quite intense fruit and low tannin; vineyard style triumphing over the vintage. Drink '87–'90.

WILLESPIE WINES

p. 506

Location:
Harmans Mill Road, Willyabrup via Cowaramup, 6284;
24 km north of Margaret River.
(097) 55 6248.

Winemakers:
White wines David Hohnen (contract); red wines Kevin Squance (at Willespie winery).

1985 Production:
600 cases white wines; 320 cases red and vintage port.

Principal Wines:

Rhine Riesling, Semillon, Verdelho and Cabernet Sauvignon and Vintage Port.

Distribution:
Principally cellar-door sales and mailing list. Cellar-door sales 10.30 a.m. to 4.30 p.m. weekends, school and public holidays. Retail sales: Sydney, Oak Barrel, Bondi Junction Liquor Store, 60 Darling Street and Roseville Cellars; Melbourne, Marmacks and Sutherland Cellars.

Prices:
$6.50 to $8.50 cellar door.

Overall Quality:
Reds not tasted; whites surprisingly variable.

Vintage Rating 1982–85:
White: '85, '84, '82, '83.
Red: '85, '84, '83, '82.

Tasting Notes:
1983 RHINE RIESLING [15.8] *Colour:* pale green-yellow. *Bouquet:* neutral, lacking fruit aroma and slightly paddy. *Palate:* a fair wine; clean with good sugar/acid balance and reasonable mid palate fruit. Drink '85–'86.

1983 VERDELHO [12.6] *Colour:* some browning. *Bouquet:* dank, matchbox aroma. *Palate:* curious bitter, stalky wine with little or no fruit flavour and certainly no varietal character.

WOODLANDS

p. 506

Location:
Corner Caves Road and Metricup Road, Willyabrup via Cowaramup, 6284;
19 km north-east of Margaret River.
(09) 294 1869.

Winemaker:
David Watson.

1985 Production:
550 cases.

Principal Wines:

One wine made only, labelled Cabernet Sauvignon but containing small percentages of malbec, with cabernet franc and merlot planned for the future.

Distribution:
By mailing list and through selected Perth and Sydney retailers. Substantial Perth retail distribution; Sydney, Summer Hill Wine Shop and The Oak Barrel. Mailing-list enquiries to 21 Cairnhill Court, Greenmount, WA, 6056.

Prices:
$11 cellar door, $13.50 retail Perth.

Overall Quality:
Sometimes exceptional.

Vintage Rating 1982–85:
'82, '84, '83, '85.

Outstanding Prior Vintages:
'81.

Tasting Notes:
1984 CABERNET SAUVIGNON [15.8] *Colour:* bright light to medium red-purple. *Bouquet:* leafy/cedary aromas with a suspicion of leathery mercaptan, and lacking the richness of earlier vintages. *Palate:* not a success; rather thin and somewhat stringy. A wine which came as a considerable disappointment; it could have been a bad bottle, or for that matter an off-day for the author. However it may be, the wine did not live up to expectations. Drink '87–'89.

WRIGHTS

p. 507

Location:
Harmans South Road, Cowaramup, 6284;
18 km north-west of Margaret River.
(097) 55 5314.

Winemaker:
Henry Wright.

1985 Production:
2350 cases (much lower than usual).

Principal Wines:
Rhine Riesling, Semillon, Chardonnay, Hermitage, Cabernet Sauvignon and Vintage Port.

Distribution:
Principally cellar door and mailing list. Cellar-door sales 10 a.m. to 4.30 p.m. 7 days. Mailing list PO Cowaramup, 6284. Limited fine wine retail merchants in eastern states; substantial Perth retail sales.

Prices:
$8 cellar door.

Overall Quality:
Usually very good; '83s in different style and of lesser quality.

Vintage Rating 1982–85:
'82, '85, '84, '83.

Outstanding Prior Vintages:
'80.

Tasting Notes:
1983 HERMITAGE [16.8] *Colour:* deep purple-red, almost opaque. *Bouquet:* very big, robust, slightly raw wine, with just a suspicion of mercaptan. *Palate:* unequivocally the product of a ripe vintage, with big, mid-palate fruit and strong tannin on the mid- to back-palate. Needs years to come into perspective. Drink '88–'94.

1983 CABERNET SAUVIGNON [15.8] *Colour:* dark purple-red. *Bouquet:* very robust, slightly gravelly/stalky aromas with strong cabernet fruit. *Palate:* rather aggressive at this stage, with vanilla oak pitted against slightly stalky fruit flavours; in my view the least successful wine from Wrights so far made. Drink '87–'89.

South-West Coastal Plain

1985 Vintage

The wettest November on record was followed by two months of cool and dry weather, holding promise of a classic vintage. The heat wave which came to the Margaret River inevitably extended along the south-west coastal plain, leading to extremely rapid ripening in some varieties and causing fruit damage in the younger vines in particular.

To a degree, therefore, the 1985 vintage was a story of what might have been. However, some magnificent white wines were made, none better than by Capel Vale. Varietal fruit flavours are little short of extraordinary, and one is only left to wonder what might have been produced had it not been for that February heat.

The red wines do not quite match the magic of the white wines, but are nonetheless substantially better than the rather mediocre 1983 and 1984 vintages.

The Changes

No new wineries, and no departures, but we have witnessed the extension of some of the remarkable vintage ports of the Margaret River onto the South-West Coastal Plain through the agency of Leschenault.

BRIAR HOLME VINEYARD

pp. 509–10

(Thomas Wines)

Location:
23–24 Crowd Road, Gelorup, 6230.
(097) 21 7228.

Winemaker:
Gill Thomas.

1985 Production:
450 cases.

Principal Wines:
Pinot Noir and Cabernet Sauvignon.

Distribution:
By mailing list and through regional vineyard distributors, Perth. Mailing-list enquiries to PO Box 286, Bunbury, 6230.

Prices:
No wines available for sale mid-1985.

Overall Quality:
Variable, but very good at their best.

Vintage Rating 1982–85:
'84, '83, '85, '82.

CAPEL VALE

p. 510

Location:
Lot 5, Capel North West Road, Sterling Estate, Capel, 6271;
1 km west of town.
(097) 27 2439.

Winemakers:
Dr Peter Pratten and Alan Johnson.

1985 Production:
Approximately 6500 cases.

Principal Wines:
A full range of varietal table wines comprising Rhine Riesling, Gewurtztraminer, Traminer Riesling, Semillon, Sauvignon Blanc, Chardonnay, Shiraz and Cabernet Sauvignon.

Distribution:
Cellar-door sales, mailing list and fine wine retailers through agents in Perth, Vintage Wine Company; Melbourne, Sutherland Cellars; Sydney, Tucker and Company and Brisbane, Barrique. Cellar-door sales 10 a.m. to 4.30 p.m. 7 days. Mailing-list enquiries to Box 692, Bunbury, 6230.

Prices:
$7.70 to $12 cellar door.

Overall Quality:
Exceptional.

Vintage Rating 1982–85:
White: '85, '83, '84, '82.
Red: '85, '84, '83, '82.

Tasting Notes:

1985 SEMILLON SAUVIGNON BLANC [18.4] *Colour:* bright green-yellow of light to medium depth. *Bouquet:* intense and clean fruit aromas, with gooseberry from sauvignon blanc and a backing of richness from the semillon; great weight and strength. *Palate:* vibrantly fresh sauvignon blanc flavour is the dominant feature, with the majority semillon component playing a minor flavour role. A brilliantly successful wine. Drink '86–'90.

1985 CHARDONNAY [18.8] *Colour:* medium yellow-green. *Bouquet:* intense and pungently aromatic grapefruit of exceptional richness and quality. *Palate:* a superb wine in the making, with lively grapefruit balanced by just a degree of oak which will be augmented with further maturation prior to bottling (tasted August 1985). Drink '87–'91.

1984 GEWURTZTRAMINER [17.6] *Colour:* brilliant green-yellow. *Bouquet:* softly aromatic lychee/pastille characters, neither spicy nor oily. *Palate:* a fresh and delicate wine with pronounced traminer flavours but at the same time preserving delicacy. If you like traminer, they don't come a great deal better from Australia. Drink '85–'87.

1985 TRAMINER RIESLING [17.4] *Colour:* brilliant medium green-yellow. *Bouquet:* a trace of fermentation characters lingering, with the rhine riesling dominant and the traminer barely perceptible. *Palate:* excellent weight and balance, with a firm and fruity finish featuring soft but lingering acid; a wine which doesn't do or say much until the finish, and then comes alive. Drink '85–'87.

1984 SHIRAZ [18.2] *Colour:* vibrant purple-red. *Bouquet:* clean, full and deep, but seemingly lacking varietal sparkle or spice. *Palate:* magnificently sweet, rich, cherry fruit flavours intermingling with very complex oak, and a long, soft tannin finish. An outstanding wine, although the bouquet did not lead one to expect this in August 1985. Drink '87–'91.

HARTRIDGE

p. 511

Location:
Lot 36, 35 km peg, Wanneroo Road, Wanneroo, 6065.
(09) 407 5117.

Winemaker:
Perry Sandow.

1985 Production:
Not stated.

Principal Wines:
Chenin Blanc, Pinot Noir and Cabernet Sauvignon.

Distribution:
Almost exclusively cellar-door sales and mailing list. Cellar-door sales 10 a.m. to 6 p.m. Monday to Saturday. Mailing list enquiries to PO Box 37, Wanneroo, 6065.

Overall Quality:
Some very good wines have from time to time appeared under the Hartridge label.

Tasting Notes:
1984 CHENIN BLANC [17] *Colour:* bright light yellow-green. *Bouquet:* fresh, clean, well-made wine with lime aromas, not unlike riesling. *Palate:* clean and crisp; quite marked residual sugar but sufficient fruit to carry the sweetness, and very good total flavour. Drink '85–'86. (Tasted June 1984.)

LESCHENAULT WINES

pp. 511–12

Location:
Minninup Road, off Lakes Road, Gelorup, 6230; 10 km south of Bunbury.
(097) 25 7222.

Winemaker:
Dr Barry Killerby.

1985 Production:
3000 cases.

Principal Wines:
Chardonnay, Traminer, Semillon, Shiraz, Pinot Noir, Cabernet Sauvignon and Vintage Port.

Distribution:
Principally cellar-door sales and mailing list; distributed by Lionel Sampson in Western Australia. Sporadic eastern states distribution. Cellar-door sales 10 a.m. to 5 p.m. Monday to Friday, 10 a.m. to 6 p.m. weekends and holidays. Mailing-list enquiries PO Box 1058, Bunbury, 6230.

Prices:
$7 to $8 cellar door.

Overall Quality:
Table wines variable; Vintage Ports good to very good.

Vintage Rating 1982–85:
'82, '85, '84, '83.

Outstanding Prior Vintages:
'78 (Red), '79 (White).

Tasting Notes:
1984 KEMPSTON VINTAGE PORT [17] *Colour:* deep, youthful purple. *Bouquet:* beautifully clean and fragrant, with very smooth spirit; in that typical Margaret River style, all on its own, and with unique delicacy. *Palate:* sweet, minty/berry fruit on the mid-palate with a slightly peppery finish; a lively, light and crisp vintage port to be drunk in copious quantities. Drink '88–'92.

1983 KEMPSTON VINTAGE PORT [16.4] *Colour:* youthful purple-red. *Bouquet:* fuller and more complex than the '84, but still very clean and smooth, with soft spirit. *Palate:* richer and riper fruit, with some medicinal overtones, but not at all unpleasant; curiously, the more aggressive fruit seems also to lift the profile of the spirit. Should be long-lived. Drink '87–'92.

LUISINI

p. 512

Location:
17 km peg, Wanneroo Road, Wanneroo, 6065;
17 km north of Perth.
(09) 409 9007.

Winemaker:
D. I. Cooper.

1985 Production:
Approximately 70,000 litres.

Principal Wines:
Chablis, Chenin Blanc, Late Picked Chenin Blanc, Shiraz, Shiraz Cabernet and a wide range of fortified wines including Liqueur Verdelho, Ruby Port, Liqueur Port, Tawny Port and Muscat Constantia.

Distribution:
Principally cellar-door sales 8.30 a.m. to 5.30 p.m. 7 days. Mailing orders filled; enquiries as above. Limited retail distribution including Summer Hill Liquor Store, Sydney.

Prices:
$3.50 to $11.80 cellar door.

Overall Quality:
Variable; from poor to good; recent vintages show marked improvement.

Tasting Notes:

1984 CHABLIS [16.4] *Colour:* medium yellow-green. *Bouquet:* lively, fresh, fruit aromas, demonstrating very competent winemaking. *Palate:* crisp, slightly peppery fruit flavours; a trace of phenolic character on the finish, but well-made nonetheless. Drink '85–'87.

1984 CHENIN BLANC [15.8] *Colour:* medium yellow-green. *Bouquet:* again light, fresh and with some honey varietal character building. *Palate:* of light to medium weight; well-constructed and flavoured. Drink '85–'86.

1984 RUBY PORT [15.4] *Colour:* medium purple-red. *Bouquet:* clean with some nice ripe fruit characters. *Palate:* lively, lifted cabernet with clean spirit. Drink '85–'86.
(All wines tasted June 1984.)

PAUL CONTI

pp. 510–11

(Formerly Contiville)

Location:
19 km peg Wanneroo Road, Wanneroo, 6065;
19 km north of Perth.
(09) 409 9160.

Winemaker:
Paul Conti.

1985 Production:
85,000 litres (the equivalent of 9300 cases).

Principal Wines:
Chenin Blanc, Chardonnay, Rhine Riesling, Late Bottled White Frontignac, Spatlese White Frontignac, Marginiup Hermitage and Cabernet Sauvignon. All wines now sourced from estate-grown grapes following discontinuance of the contract making arrangements with Pearse's Forest Hills Vineyard.

Distribution:
Principally cellar-door sales 8.30 a.m. to 5.30 p.m. Monday to Saturday. Extensive Perth retail distribution; limited retail distribution in eastern states through Domaine Wine Shippers, Victoria.

Prices:
Table wines: $6.21 to $6.95 recommended retail; Vintage Port: $8.56.

Overall Quality:
Very good.

Vintage Rating 1982–85:
White: '83, '84, '85, '82.
Red: '82, '83, '84, '85.

Outstanding Prior Vintages:
'72, '74.

Tasting Notes:

1984 WANNEROO CHARDONNAY [17.2] *Colour:* medium yellow. *Bouquet:* clean and very smooth, with considerable weight but diminished fruit aromatics. *Palate:* of medium weight with clearly marked light peachy varietal character; oak well-balanced, and the wine has good structure. No hint of sweetness. Drink '85–'88.

1984 WANNEROO CHENIN BLANC [17] *Colour:* medium yellow with just a touch of straw. *Bouquet:* very full and rich, with soft honey fruit. *Palate:* of medium to full weight, well-balanced with good length and a soft acid finish. Typical Western Australian chenin blanc, with that extra bit of substance. Drink '86–'88.

1984 SPATLESE WHITE FRONTIGNAC [17] *Colour:* full yellow. *Bouquet:* rich and clean with almost essence-like grape aromas, ultra varietal. *Palate:* firmer than the '83; full, firm berry flavours, clean and flavoursome. Drink '85–'88.

1983 LATE BOTTLED WHITE FRONTIGNAC [18] *Colour:* medium yellow-green. *Bouquet:* clean; very full and highly aromatic varietal character. *Palate:* lovely, luscious peachy/lychee flavours, rich and mouth filling; beautifully balanced; an outstanding wine of its style. Drink '85–'87.

1982 MARGINIUP HERMITAGE [17.2] *Colour:* light, bright cherry-red. *Bouquet:* sweet, not overripe, with light cherry aromas. *Palate:* very smooth, sweet, light, cherry fruit with low tannin and crispness. In the mainstream of Marginiup hermitage from Conti. Drink '85–'89.

PEEL ESTATE

pp. 512–13

Location:
Fletcher Road, Baldivis, 6171;
15 km north of Mandurah and 60 km south of Perth, off Main Coastal Highway.
(095) 24 1221.

Winemaker:
Will Nairn.

1985 Production:
5000 cases.

Principal Wines:
Chenin Blanc, Wood Matured Chenin Blanc, Chardonnay, Verdelho, Zinfandel, Shiraz and Cabernet Sauvignon.

Distribution:
Substantial cellar-door and mailing-list sales; cellar-door sales 10 a.m. to 5 p.m. 7 days. Mailing-list enquiries to PO Box 37, Mandurah, 6210. Limited retail distribution through wholesalers in Perth, Chateau Barnard; Melbourne, Van Cooth and Co. and Sydney, Bill Graham.

Prices:
$6.95 to $8.50 recommended retail.

Overall Quality:
Somewhat variable; wines can be very good.

Vintage Rating 1982–85:
White: '84, '85, '83, '82.
Red: '84, '85, '82, '83.

Outstanding Prior Vintages:
'80 (red wines), '81 (white wines).

Tasting Notes:

1984 CHENIN BLANC WOOD MATURED [17.6] *Colour:* light to medium yellow-green. *Bouquet:* clean, smooth and soft fruit with an attractive backing of gentle oak. *Palate:* very good weight with extremely smooth honeyed fruit and oak; crisp acid contributes a lively finish to a full-flavoured and very well-made wine. Drink '86–'89.

1983 CHENIN BLANC WOOD MATURED [17.8] *Colour:* full yellow. *Bouquet:* attractive, honeyed, bottle-developed aromas, rich and full of character, with beautifully integrated oak. *Palate:* a carbon copy of the bouquet, with honeyed/buttery fruit and oak, and soft acid on the finish. A wine full of style and character. Drink '85–'87.

1982 SHIRAZ [16.8] *Colour:* bright red-purple of medium depth. *Bouquet:* highly aromatic, with excellent varietal spice, clean and yet quite complex. *Palate:* light-bodied, but exhibiting attractive cherry flavours, together with a touch of varietal spice; some volatility evident but does not detract from the wine. Drink '85–'87.

1981 SHIRAZ [15.4] *Colour:* light to medium red, with just a trace of purple remaining. *Bouquet:* light fruit, with some slightly leathery overlay which detracts. *Palate:* while quite fresh and crisp and in structure, is once again marred by that touch of leather mercaptan. Drink '85–'86.

Swan Valley

1985 Vintage

Good winter rains were followed by a moist and mild spring, and then in turn an exceptionally cool summer. Vintage in the Swan Valley normally commences at the end of January, and 1985 was no exception. Despite the very substantial crops, the early-picked varieties—with chardonnay leading the way—were of exceptional quality.

The heat then set in, leading to severe stressing of the vines and to substantial crop reductions. The later-picked table wines inevitably suffered, but it was a vintage year of monumental proportions for fortified wines. Grapes for these styles were picked at 27 baume and higher, levels which would make even north-east Victoria green with envy.

Apart from the early-picked varietals and, of course, the fortified wines, quality was average in an abundant harvest.

The Changes

The Swan Valley is slowly but surely contracting. The Perth market is simply not big enough to sustain even the existing population of wineries, and the corner store selling eastern state casks for substantially less than the local product is an irresistible force. Houghton, Evans and Tate and also Sandalford—particularly with its trophy for its 1985 Cabernet Rosé at the 1985 Melbourne Show—remain firm bulwarks. The days of the ethnic winery, with its strength deriving from the once very significant Yugoslav population, must surely be numbered.

BASSENDEAN

pp. 517–18

Location:
147 West Road, Bassendean, 6054;
7 km east of Perth GPO on the Swan River.
(09) 276 1734.

Winemaker:
Laurie Nicoletto.

1985 Production:
Approximately 3500 cases.

Principal Wines:
A red wine specialist who magically creates soft and clean, burgundy-style wines without the aid of any form of oak maturation and very often from fruit of humble variety and origin. Wines include Shiraz, Burgundy, Cabernet Shiraz, Chenin Blanc and Vintage Port. Wine usually available cellar door with up to 5 years bottle age.

Distribution:
Has now largely shrunk to cellar-door sales and mailing list; principal retail distribution in Perth metropolitan area. Cellar-door sales 5.15 p.m. to 6.30 p.m. Monday to Friday, 9 a.m. to 5 p.m. Saturday. Other hours by appointment.

Prices:
$4.90 to $5.80 for reds; $6.90 to $12 for ports.

Overall Quality:
Most adequate.

Tasting Notes:

1980 BASSENDEAN ESTATE BURGUNDY **[15.8]** *Colour:* **light to medium red.** *Bouquet:* **very sweet fruit, with a distinct touch of straw oxidation.** *Palate:* **strong minty flavours, more akin to a central Victorian red. Drink '85–'87.**

1981 BASSENDEAN CABERNET SHIRAZ **[16]** *Colour:* **medium to full red.** *Bouquet:* **very similar sweet, minty fruit, and again just a suspicion of oxidation.** *Palate:* **a complex, spicy wine, with good mid-palate fruit and again a touch of mint. Drink '85–'88.**

COORINJA

p. 518

Location:
Box 99, Toodyay Road, Toodyay, 6566;
50 km north-east of the Swan Valley.
(096) 26 2280.

Winemakers:
Doug and Hector Wood.

1985 Production:
Approximately 5500 cases.

Principal Wines:
A basic range of non-vintage red and fortified table wines are made, which despite their lack of vintage date and unpretentious packaging, often provide surprising value for money. Not truly part of the Swan Valley, and having no viticultural neighbours, Coorinja has remained a backwater, largely unchanged for half a century or more.

Distribution:
Cellar-door sales and mail order; local retail distribution only. Cellar-door sales 8.30 a.m. to 6 p.m. Monday to Saturday.

Prices:
$2.50 to $4.50 cellar door.

Overall Quality:
More than adequate given the price.

ELLENDALE ESTATE WINES

pp. 518–19

Location:
18 Ivanhoe Street, Bassendean, 6054;
in Bassendean township, 0.5 km north of Bassendean railway station.
(09) 279 1007.

Winemaker:
John Barrett-Leonard.

1985 Production:
Approximately 150,000 litres.

Principal Wines:

A wide range of table and fortified wines sold either in bottle or flagon, with special emphasis on young, lightly fortified wines. The 28 wines available cellar-door include Riesling, Shiraz, Cabernet Sauvignon, Sauternes, White Liqueur Muscat, Vintage Port and Cabernet Port.

Distribution:
Exclusively cellar-door sales and mail order. Cellar-door sales 8.30 a.m. to 6 p.m. Monday to Saturday. Mailing-list enquiries as above.

Prices:
All wines, whether in bottle or flagon, are very modestly priced.

Overall Quality:
Adequate.

Tasting Notes:

1984 SAUTERNES [14] *Colour:* pale straw-yellow. *Bouquet:* pungent, aromatic muscat aroma, with some slightly smelly off-characters. *Palate:* a very big and rather coarse, sweet wine, but with the possibility of improvement in bottle. Drink '86–'87.

1984 WHITE LIQUEUR MUSCAT [15.4] *Colour:* very pale yellow. *Bouquet:* strong, pungent muscat aroma with clean spirit. *Palate:* fresh, with very considerable sweetness balanced by cleansing spirit. A fair wine of its somewhat unusual style. Drink now.

1982 CABERNET PORT [14.4] *Colour:* medium to full red-purple. *Bouquet:* clean fruit; light, slightly peppery spirit. *Palate:* similar curious pepper-spice flavours, apparently associated with the spirit, dominate. Drink '85–'86.

EVANS AND TATE

pp. 519–20

Location:
Swan Street, West Swan, 6055;
28 km north-east of Perth.
(09) 296 4666 and (09) 296 4329.

Winemaker:
Bill Crappsley.

1985 Production:
3200 cases.

Principal Wines:
High-quality table wines made from two vineyards; Redbrook in the Margaret River (see separate entry) and Gnangara Estate in the West Swan. The latter produces Gnangara Shiraz (a blend of 80% Shiraz and 20% Cabernet Sauvignon); a wider range of wines come from Redbrook.

Distribution:
National fine wine retail through John Cawsey and Co. except in Western Australia; distributed direct. Cellar-door sales 8 a.m. to 5 p.m. Monday to Saturday. High-quality mailing list; special wines offered to mailing-list subscribers.

Prices:
$7 recommended retail.

Overall Quality:
Exceptional.

Vintage Rating 1982–85:
'82, '84, '83, '85(?).

Outstanding Prior Vintages:
'76, '77, '79, '81.

Tasting Notes:
1983 GNANGARA SHIRAZ [18.2] *Colour:* medium purple-red. *Bouquet:* soft, gentle, cherry/berry aromas with well-integrated oak; very fragrant. *Palate:* rich, gently textured cherry/berry flavours, sweet yet not heavy; soft tannin and light oak. A lovely wine. For release May '86. Drink '86–'91.

1982 GNANGARA SHIRAZ [17.6] *Colour:* brilliant red of medium depth. *Bouquet:* very clean, well balanced, gently complex wine with light, crisp fruit. *Palate:* very smooth wine with long and harmonious fruit/oak flavours; near perfect balance, and only the faintest backstop of tannin. Drink '85–'89.

1982 THREE VINEYARDS CABERNET SAUVIGNON [18.4] *Colour:* light to medium bright red-purple. *Bouquet:* a wine of great style and complexity; clean and firm berry varietal flavour with a touch of cedar/cigar oak. *Palate:* beautifully balanced, complex flavours from sweet berry through to leafy tobacco; now approaching its peak. (A blend of cabernet sauvignon from the Gnangara, Redbrook and Bakers Hill Vineyards.) Drink '86–'89.

GLENALWYN

p. 520

Location:
West Swan Road, West Swan, 6055;
10 km north of Guildford.
(09) 296 4462.

Winemaker:
Len Pasalich.

1985 Production:
Approximately 35,000 litres.

Principal Wines:
Once a fortified wine specialist with output sold principally in flagons, Glenalwyn is increasingly oriented to varietal table wines and fortified wines sold in 750 ml bottles. Wines include Chenin Blanc, Verdelho, Late Picked Verdelho, Cabernet Sauvignon, Liqueur Frontignac and Vintage Port.

Distribution:
Chiefly cellar-door sales; very limited fine wine specialist shops in Perth and Melbourne.

Overall Quality:
Extremely variable; some poor wines but also some good wines.

HENLEY PARK WINES

p. 520

Location:
Swan Street, West Swan, 6055;
near Henley Brook, 22 km north of Perth.

Winemaker:
Mark Yujnovich.

1985 Production:
Approximately 3500 cases.

Principal Wines:
A full range of table and fortified wines are made, and offered both in bottle and flagon, with increasing emphasis on bottle sales. Wines include Chenin Blanc, Rhine Riesling, White Burgundy, Shiraz and Vintage Port.

Distribution:
Exclusively cellar door; tastings and sales 8.30 a.m. to 6 p.m. Monday to Saturday.

Overall Quality:
White wines poor, suffering from mercaptan; fortified wines can be very good, particularly vintage port.

HIGHWAY WINES

p. 520

Location:
Great Northern Highway, Herne Hill, 6056;
17 km north-east of Perth.
(09) 296 4353.

Winemaker:
Anthony Bakranich.

1985 Production:
Approximately 90,000 litres.

Principal Wines:
A wide range of traditional table and fortified wines available, chiefly sold in flagons.

Distribution:
Exclusively cellar-door sales, 8 a.m. to 6 p.m. Monday to Saturday.

Overall Quality:
Adequate at best.

HOUGHTON

pp. 520–2

Location:
Dale Road, Middle Swan, 6056;
15 km north-east of Perth.
(09) 274 5100.

Winemaker:
Peter Dawson.

1985 Production:
Approximately 3500 tonnes (the equivalent of over 260,000 cases).

Principal Wines:
A full range of table wines released under two different labels and from three distinct vineyard areas. The Houghton label includes White Burgundy, Chablis, Late Picked Verdelho, Autumn Harvest Semillon, Chardonnay, Wood Aged Chenin Blanc, Private Bin Rhine Riesling, Auslese Rhine Riesling, Cabernet Rosé (invariably one of Australia's best), Claret and Cabernet Sauvignon, all from the Swan Valley or from an unstated blend. Houghton Frankland River releases presently comprise Rhine Riesling, Cabernet Sauvignon and Shiraz, but are likely to be extended. The Moondah Brook Estate, with fruit from the Gingin Vineyard, offers Verdelho, Chenin Blanc and Cabernet Sauvignon. The fortified wines are all released under the Houghton label, comprising Centenary Port, Show Tawny Port, Vintage Port, Liqueur Tokay and Liqueur Frontignac.

Distribution:
National retail through own distribution network.

Prices:
As with any large company, recommended retail has but limited meaning; recommended retail ranges from around $4.90 to $8 for table wines and $15 for Liqueur Tokay and Frontignac.

Overall Quality:
Consistently very good; some exceptional wines.

Vintage Rating 1982–85:
White: '82, '85, '83, '84.
Red: '83, '85, '82, '84.

Outstanding Prior Vintages:
'80.

Tasting Notes:

1984 MOONDAH BROOK ESTATE CHENIN BLANC [18] *Colour:* **medium yellow.** *Bouquet:* **rich fruit in the honey/tropical fruit spectrum; oak well-restrained though clearly present.** *Palate:* **rich and flavoury, with honey flavours and textures; good depth and length, with balance an outstanding feature. Drink '85–'88.**

1984 MOONDAH BROOK ESTATE VERDELHO [17.8] *Colour:* **medium yellow, with a touch of straw.** *Bouquet:* **voluminous apricot/honey aroma, crammed full of character.** *Palate:* **rich apricot fruit, reminiscent of chenin blanc in the Loire Valley. A wine of great character and fruit flavour. Drink '85–'88.**

1984 HOUGHTON WHITE BURGUNDY [17.6] *Colour:* **medium full straw-yellow.** *Bouquet:* **complex fruit and oak in true white burgundy style, even including a touch of sulphide.** *Palate:* **perfectly made, rich, full-bodied wine; the ultimate commercial white burgundy, beautifully balanced in typical Houghton style. Drink '85–'89.**

1982 HOUGHTON AUTUMN HARVEST SEMILLON [17.8] *Colour:* **glowing yellow.** *Bouquet:* **rich, ripe butterscotch aromas.** *Palate:* **intense and concentrated, with raisined lusciousness and exceptional sugar/acid balance. In a particular style, non-botrytised, but a wine which has matured beautifully and will still live. Drink '85–'88.**

1983 HOUGHTON CABERNET SAUVIGNON [17.6] *Colour:* **bright and clear, fresh red.** *Bouquet:* **clean, gently herbaceous fruit with soft, gently charred oak.** *Palate:* **a very clean, fresh style with elegant, crisp, cherry/berry flavours on the mid-palate; as always, balance is an outstanding feature. (A Frankland River wine.) Drink '86–'89.**

1982 MOONDAH BROOK CABERNET SAUVIGNON [18] *Colour:* **bright red-purple of medium depth.** *Bouquet:* **complex, almost powdery, fruit/oak balance and integration, with real elegance and overtones of Bordeaux.** *Palate:* **fine, elegant and smooth wine, at the peak of perfection, and again pointed so highly because of its superb balance. Drink '85–'88.**

JADRAN WINES

p. 522

Location:
445 Reservoir Road, Orange Grove, 6109;
13 km south-east of Perth (winery not in the Swan Valley.
(09) 459 1110.

Winemaker:
Stephen Radojkovich.

Principal Wines:
Substantial but unstated production of table wine, sparkling wine and fortified wines produced from a variety of sources and sold in containers of all sizes.

Distribution:
Exclusively cellar-door sales 8.30 a.m. to 8.30 p.m. Monday to Saturday.

Overall Quality:
Adequate, particularly given price.

JANE BROOK ESTATE

p. 523

Location:
Toodyay Road, Middle Swan, 6056;
3 km north of Midland
(formerly Vignacourt Wines).
(09) 274 1432.

Winemaker:
David Aitkinson.

1985 Production:
Approximately 3500 cases plus additional bulk sales.

Principal Wines:
A range of table wines from diverse vineyard sources including Wood Aged Chenin Blanc, Mount Barker Rhine Riesling, Mount Barker Semillon Rhine Riesling, Jane Brook Chenin Blanc, Jane Brook Frontignac, Wood Aged Chenin Blanc, Late Harvest Chenin Blanc, Mount Barker Cabernet Sauvignon, and Cabernet Beaujolais; fortified wines include Tawny Port, Vintage Port, Liqueur Muscat and Liqueur Verdelho.

Distribution:
Principally cellar-door sales and mailing list; limited exports through Hicks and Hayes; Perth retail distribution. Cellar-door sales 10 a.m. to 5 p.m. Monday to Saturday, noon to 5 p.m. Sunday.

Prices:
Table wines $5.50 to $7.50 cellar door.

Overall Quality:
Extremely variable, from poor to very good.

Tasting Notes.

1984 MOUNT BARKER SEMILLON RHINE RIESLING [14.8] *Colour:* light, but with some distinct pink hues. *Bouquet:* full fruit, with some soft, spicy, oak aromas. *Palate:* very rich, full flavour with passionfruit on the fore-palate but marred by a hard, coarse finish. Drink '85–'87.

1984 JANE BROOK CHENIN BLANC [13.8] *Colour:* pink-orange. *Bouquet:* stalky, oily, aggressive aroma from excessive German oak extraction. *Palate:* heavy, oily and aggressive oak spoils good fruit. A gold medal winner at the Swan Valley Show, presumably early in its life.

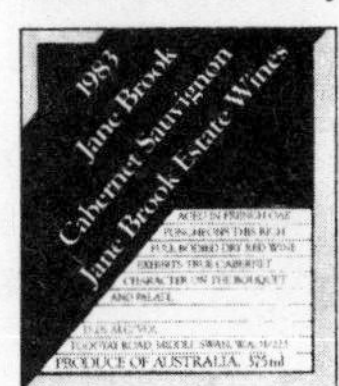

1983 JANE BROOK CABERNET SAUVIGNON [17.2] *Colour:* bright light to medium red-purple. *Bouquet:* clean, with strong minty aromas, fresh and attractive. *Palate:* a clean, well-balanced wine with fresh minty fruit, and just a touch of oak. Drink '85–'88.

LAKEVILLE VINEYARDS

p. 523

Location:
1921 Albany Highway, Maddington, 6109;
16 km south of Perth.
(09) 459 1637.

Winemakers:
Jose and Mate Maras.

1985 Production:
Approximately 3500 litres.

Principal Wines:
Limited range of table and fortified wines, made from estate-grown grapes and sold exclusively to local clientele.

Distribution:
Cellar-door sales 8.30 a.m. to 8 p.m. 7 days.

Overall Quality:
Not rated.

LAMONT WINES

p. 524

Location:
Bisdee Road, Millendon, 6056;
17 km north-east of Perth.
(09) 296 4485.

Winemaker:
Jack Mann.

1985 Production:
Approximately 2800 cases; some bulk sales.

Principal Wines:
Limited range of table and fortified wines including White Burgundy, Cabernet Rosé, Shiraz, Cabernet Sauvignon and Vintage Port.

Distribution:
Almost exclusively cellar-door sales; one retail outlet in each of Melbourne and Hobart; and two retail outlets in Perth. Cellar-door sales 9 a.m. to 5 p.m. Wednesday to Sunday or by appointment.

Overall Quality:
Good.

MOONDAH BROOK ESTATE

p. 524

(See Houghton)

OLIVE FARM

p. 524

Location:
77 Great Eastern Highway, South Guildford, 6055;
3 km north of Perth Airport.
(09) 277 2989.

Winemaker:
Ian Yurisich.

1985 Production:
Approximately 3500 cases and 40,000 litres in flagon.

Principal Wines:
A substantial range of table, sparkling and fortified wines is made; wines include Verdelho, Chenin Blanc Semillon, Late Harvest Chenin Blanc, Chardonnay, Chablis, Hock, Cabernet Shiraz, Cabernet Sauvignon, Oloroso Sherry, Old Madeira, Vintage Port and Tawny Port.

Distribution:
Limited and sporadic retail distribution outside of Perth; principally cellar-door sales and mailing list. Cellar-door sales 10 a.m. to 5.30 p.m. Monday to Friday, 9 a.m. to 3 p.m. Saturdays and public holidays.

Prices:
$5.50 to $12.60.

Overall Quality:
Variable but the majority of the wines are good, particularly fortified wines.

Tasting Notes:

1984 VERDELHO [16.2] *Colour:* medium to full yellow. *Bouquet:* full, quite aromatic with soft gently tropical fruit aromas. *Palate:* full, soft and fleshy, with some honey starting to develop. Drink '85–'88.

OLOROSO SHERRY [16.8] *Colour:* pale yellow-bronze. *Bouquet:* complex, spirity earthy aromas which are most attractive. *Palate:* excellent base material, lusciously sweet, but tending to be a little one-dimensional. With a little wood-age would be outstanding. Drink now.

REVELRY

p. 525

Location:
200 Argyle Street, Herne Hill, 6056;
5 km south of Midland.
(09) 296 4271.

Winemaker:
Stephen Illich.

1985 Production:
Approximately, 28,000 litres.

Principal Wines:
A range of table wines sold chiefly in flagon.

Distribution:
Exclusively cellar door to local clientele; cellar-door sales 2 p.m. to 8 p.m. Monday to Saturday.

Overall Quality:
Not rated.

SANDALFORD

p. 525

Location:
West Swan Road, Caversham, 6055;
5 km north of Guildford.
(09) 274 5922.

Winemaker:
Dorham Mann.

1985 Production:
Approximately 70,000 cases, coming from both Caversham Estate in the Swan Valley and from Margaret River Estate (see separate entry).

Principal Wines:

Unusually for the Swan Valley, only one fortified wine made (Liqueur Sandalera). Caversham Estate wines comprise Chablet, Parmelia Moselle, Parmelia Riesling, Verdelho, White Burgundy, Matilde Rose, Caversham Estate Cabernet and Zinfandel.

Distribution:
National Fine Wine Retail distribution, principally through Taylor Ferguson. Extensive cellar-door sale facilities in historic surroundings 9 a.m. to 5 p.m. Monday to Saturday and noon to 3 p.m. Sunday. Mailing list available; address as above.

Prices:
Lack of real volume in the eastern states limits discounting, but recommended retail prices are still above the real price. Recommended retail ranges from $6.40 to $6.80.

Overall Quality:
Variable, chiefly due to recurrent problems of mercaptan; when this is avoided, wines vary from good to very good, with the best wines coming from Margaret River Estate.

Tasting Notes:

1985 CHENIN VERDELHO [15.6] *Colour:* light to medium yellow, straw-tinged. *Bouquet:* a firm, quite robust wine, with a trace of bottling SO_2; needs time. *Palate:* a fairly plain wine with a slightly hollow mid-palate, partly contributed to by evidently early-picked fruit designed to produce a chablis style. Drink '86–'87.

1985 MATILDE ROSE [17.6] *Colour:* pale crimson-pink. *Bouquet:* very clean and soft, but with little or no varietal aroma to indicate the cabernet sauvignon from which the wine is made. *Palate:* very clean, light, fresh and fault free; to my palate simply needs a little more fruit definition. Trophy Winner Melbourne Show 1985. Drink '86.

1984 WHITE BURGUNDY [15.6] *Colour:* bright yellow-green of medium depth. *Bouquet:* weighty, with some slightly cheesy characters and even some malic/apple hardness. *Palate:* smooth and quite well-balanced; simply lacks any outstanding definition or style; has not been helped much by new oak; may fill out. Drink '86–'87.

TALIJANCICH WINES

pp. 525–6

Location:
121 Hyem Road, Millendon, 6056; just off Great Northern Highway, 1 km north of Herne Hill. (09) 296 4289.

Winemaker:
James Talijancich.

1985 Production:
Approximately 1500 cases plus bulk wine sales.

Principal Wines:
Fortified wine specialists, with spectacular old single vintage Muscat from time to time available. Limited range of basic table wines.

Distribution:
Principally cellar-door sales (75%) with the remainder sold to Perth restaurants. Cellar-door sales 8.30 a.m. to 5.30 p.m. Monday to Saturday and Sundays 10 a.m. to 5.30 p.m. Mailing list available; address as above.

Prices:
$6 to $15 (wines).

Overall Quality:
Table wines adequate; old Muscats very good.

Tasting Notes:
1961 LIQUEUR MUSCAT [17.8] *Colour:* **dark olive with brown-green rim, indicating extreme barrel age.** *Bouquet:* **enormous concentration and richness, but as with any very old single-vintage muscat, lacks the lift provided by a small component of fresh material.** *Palate:* **similarly magnificently rich, but lacking that touch of freshness to lift it into gold medal standard. Drink now.**

TWIN HILLS

p. 526

Location:
Great Northern Highway, Baskerville, 6056; 10 km north of Midland. (09) 296 4272.

Winemakers:
Mark and Eddie Kraljevich.

1985 Production:
Approximately 70,000 litres.

Principal Wines:
A wide range of table and fortified wines, each one of which is offered in bulk, in flagons or in bottles, without differentiation.

Distribution:
Exclusively cellar-door sales 8.30 a.m. to 6 p.m. Monday to Saturday.

Overall Quality:
At the very least, adequate.

VINDARA

p. 526

Location:
Northern Highway, Herne Hill, 6065;
7 km north of Midland.

Winemaker:
Ivan Viskovich.

1985 Production:
Approximately 12,000 litres.

Principal Wines:
Limited range of table wines, usually offered non vintage and by generic descriptions such as Dry White and Burgundy.

Distribution:
Exclusively cellar-door 8 a.m. to 6 p.m. Monday to Saturday.

Overall Quality:
Poor.

WESTFIELD

pp. 526–7

Location:
Cnr Memorial Avenue and Great North Highway, Baskerville, 6056;
10 km north of Midland.
(09) 296 4356.

Winemaker:
John Kosovich.

1985 Production:
Approximately 3000 cases.

Principal Wines:
Chardonnay, Verdelho, Semillon, Riesling, Shiraz, Cabernet Sauvignon and tiny quantities of Méthode Champenoise made from Cabernet Sauvignon.

Distribution:
60% sold through cellar door, 20% through mailing list and 20% to Perth restaurants. Cellar-door sales 8.30 a.m. to 5. p.m. Monday to Saturday. Mailing list address as above.

Prices:
$4.80 to $7.90.

Overall Quality:
White wines adequate to good; red wines and fortified wines good.

Tasting Notes:

1982 CABERNET SAUVIGNON [16.2] *Colour:* medium red. *Bouquet:* clean; light to medium weight with hints of cherry. *Palate:* similar, ripe, cherry flavours; oak very much in the background and a little one-dimensional. Drink '85–'87.

1981 VINTAGE PORT [15.6] *Colour:* dark red. *Bouquet:* clean spirit with sweet, minty aromas. *Palate:* an elegant vintage port, with sweet berry flavours and a cleansing, gently spirity finish. Drink '85–'87.

Canberra District, Queensland and Tasmania

Canberra District

1985 Vintage

As one tracks the 1985 vintage from the far south-west of Western Australia across to the furthest extremes of eastern Australia, one is struck by the similarity of the vintage conditions. This pattern occurred in 1980, and again in 1985. But in truth it is exceedingly rare to find a vintage in which the story is so similar.

The distinguishing feature for New South Wales was the late frosts and, predictably enough, Canberra suffered badly, first in mid-October and then again in the days immediately before Christmas. Coupled with an abnormally dry summer, in which only 25 per cent of the average rainfall fell, the effect on grape yield was inevitably devastating.

In some small recompense, overall quality was exceptional, and for once the birds felt that the remaining crop was not worthy of their attention. The wines are similar to those of 1983, the region's best vintage to that time. The red wines have far greater depth of flavour than usual and share with the white wines clear varietal characteristics and good levels of natural acid.

The district still continues to operate on a doll's-house scale, producing wine by the teaspoonful, sufficient to serve the local Canberra market and a small mailing-list clientele. The cumulative effects of seven years of more or less continuous drought have forced many vignerons who came into the region with high ideals to look elsewhere for their fruit until their own vineyards recover. Cowra and Young have been particularly useful, but there is more than a passing degree of tension between those who restrict themselves to grapes from within the district, and those who are content to look outside. The fact that most of those who go to outside sources make full disclosure on their labels is insufficient to assuage the sensitivities of the purists.

The Changes

The one new winery is Benfield Estate, which made its first wines in 1985. By the standards of the district, it is a very large operation and inevitably relied exclusively on grapes grown in other regions (the Hunter Valley and Mudgee).

Public misconceptions notwithstanding, the Canberra district is not a particularly cool region, and will always be viticulturally marginal because of the extremely dry summers. The grim realisation that irrigation is absolutely essential is slowly coming home to the vignerons, much as it goes against the grain of many. If and when supplementary water becomes commonplace, it may be possible to assess the full potential of the region.

AFFLECK VINEYARD

p. 533

Location:
RMB 244, Gundaroo Road, Bungendore, 2621.

Winemaker:
I. A. Hendry.

1985 Production:
50 cases.

Principal Wines:

Pinot Noir.

Distribution:
Exclusively mailing list; enquires as above.

Prices:
$8.

Overall Quality:
Not rated.

Vintage Rating 1984–85:
'84, '85.

BENFIELD ESTATE

Location:
Fairy Hole Road, Yass, 2582;
off Wargeila Road, 8 km south of Yass.
(062) 26 2427.

Winemaker:
David Fetherston, (Roland Kaval consultant).

1985 Production:
45 tonnes (the equivalent of approximately 3300 cases).

Principal Wines:

All of the 1985 wines (Benfield Estate's first vintage) were made from grapes purchased from other regions, pending the estate vineyards of 18 hectares coming into production. The vineyards are planted to chardonnay, rhine riesling, semillon, traminer, cabernet sauvignon, merlot, cabernet franc and shiraz. Annual crush is planned to be 100 tonnes, and it is proposed to supplement estate-grown grapes with outside sources to compensate for seasonal variations and to provide additional wine styles. The initial vintage produced Semillon Vat 1 (from Upper Hunter Valley fruit, with brief oak storage), Semillon Vat 2 (fruit from same source, with longer oak storage), Dry Rhine Riesling (from Mudgee grapes), Semi-Sweet Rhine Riesling (from Mudgee fruit), Cabernet Sauvignon (Mudgee fruit), Shiraz (Mudgee) and Cabernet Shiraz (Mudgee).

Distribution:
Cellar-door sales, mailing list and progressive retail and restaurant distribution planned for Canberra and Sydney. Cellar-door sales 10 a.m. to 3 p.m. Monday to Friday, 10 a.m. to 5 p.m. weekends. Mailing-list enquiries: PO Box 336, Yass, 2582.

Prices:
$6.60 cellar door.

Overall Quality:
Consistently good; some wines have the potential to be very good.

Tasting Notes:

1975 SEMILLON VAT 1 [17] *Colour:* **full yellow, with a touch of straw.** *Bouquet:* **a well-made wine, with quite rich fruit exhibiting lime/toast aromas; smooth and round, with no solids ferment characters.** *Palate:* **very good fruit depth to well-defined, smooth semillon varietal character. Drink '87–'90.**

1985 SEMILLON VAT 2 [15.6] *Colour:* **medium yellow-green.** *Bouquet:* **a greener style, with some appley aromas and a touch of oak.** *Palate:* **similar green apple/solids flavours; well enough handled within parameters of this heavier style. Drink '88–'91.**

1985 RHINE RIESLING [15.6] *Colour:* **bright green.** *Bouquet:* **clean; some firm, slightly toasty riesling aroma; again well-made.** *Palate:* **a hint of matchbox character but quite good, clear, unmodified rhine riesling flavour on the mid-palate, followed by somewhat hard finish. Drink '86–'89.**

1985 CABERNET SAUVIGNON [17.8] *Colour:* **vibrant, youthful cherry-purple.** *Bouquet:* **fresh and sweet cassis/cherry berry aromas, most attractive.** *Palate:* **fragrantly sweet, cassis berry plus smoky, charred oak flavours; very complex; a very good wine in the making. Drink '89–'94.**

CLONAKILLA

p. 533

Location:
Crisps Lane, off Gundaroo Road, Murrumbateman.
(062) 51 1938 (after hours).

Winemaker:
John Kirk.

1985 Production:
Approximately 2 tonnes (the equivalent of 150 cases).

Principal Wines:
Riesling Sylvaner, Cabernet Sauvignon and Muscat.

Distribution:
Cellar-door sales only 10.30 a.m. to 5 p.m. Sunday.

Prices:
$5.50 to $7.50 cellar door.

Overall Quality:
Good.

Vintage Rating 1984–1985:
'83, '85, '82, '84.

Tasting Notes:

1984 CABERNET SAUVIGNON [16.2] *Colour:* light to medium red-purple. *Bouquet:* fragrant and lifted, with cherry/cassis fruit aromas which came up in glass and displaced some odd, cosmetic/hand lotion aromas which briefly manifested themselves. *Palate:* fragrant cherry/cassis flavours and spicy oak; a distinct mousy/biscuity aftertaste prevented higher marks. Drink '86–'88.

MUSCAT [15.8] *Colour:* pink-orange. *Bouquet:* clean but very light, with some sweet pastille aromas and gentle spirit. *Palate:* fresh and light, with good spirit and adequate fruit; a drinking muscat rather than a sipping muscat. Drink now.

DOONKUNA ESTATE

pp. 533–4

Location:
Barton Highway, Murroo Road, Murrumbateman, 2582;
20 km south-east of Yass.
(062) 27 1636.

Winemaker:
Roland Kaval.

1985 Production:
160 cases (a fraction of normal).

Principal Wines:
Rhine Riesling, Chardonnay, Sauvignon Blanc, Pinot Noir, Shiraz and Cabernet Sauvignon.

Distribution:
Almost exclusively by mail order; mailing-list enquiries as above. Cellar-door sales by appointment only. Isolated restaurant sales.

Prices:
$7.50 to $8 mailing list.

Overall Quality:
Improving; recent wines good to very good.

Vintage Rating 1984–1985:
White: '83, '85, '82, '84.
Red: '83, '85, '84, '82.

Tasting Notes:

1985 SAUVIGNON BLANC SEMILLON [15.6] *Colour:* light to medium green-yellow. *Bouquet:* intense pungent and rich gooseberry aromas, bordering on outright aggression. *Palate:* pronounced gooseberry/grassy varietal flavours, with some added weight and palate-feel from semillon. Drink '87–'89.

1984 PINOT NOIR [17.6] *Colour:* light to medium red-purple. *Bouquet:* fragrant aromas of cherries and strawberries, backed by a subtle hint of cedary/cigar box oak; an exciting bouquet. *Palate:* fine, elegant and fragrant, with lovely, light, strawberry fruit and some touches of cigar box oak. Drink '86–'89.

1983 CABERNET SAUVIGNON [17.4] *Colour:* dense purple-red. *Bouquet:* clean; a very rich, textured wine with good oak integration and a touch of cool climate mint. *Palate:* a very big wine; a lifted blackcurrant/cassis mid-palate and marked tannin on the finish, all rounded off by good oak handling. A complex and potentially long-lived wine. Drink '87–'93.

HELM'S

pp. 534–5

Location:
Butts Road, Murrumbateman, 2582;
20 km south-east of Yass and 35 km north of Canberra, off Yass River Road.
(062) 27 1536.

Winemaker:
Ken Helm.

1985 Production:
Approximately 900 tonnes (reduced by half by December 21 1984 minus 2 degrees celsius frost).

Principal Wines:

Muller Thurgau, Rhine Riesling, Gewurtztraminer, Spatlese, Cabernet Franc, Cabernet Sauvignon Beaujolais Style, Sherry and School Teacher Port. Cabernet Franc purchased from Cowra and blended with 20% estate-grown Cabernet Sauvignon.

Distribution:
Exclusively cellar-door sales and mailing list; cellar-door sales 10 a.m. to 5 p.m. weekends and public holidays, or by appointment. Mailing-list enquiries as above.

Prices:
$5.50 to $8 per bottle cellar door (discount for case prices).

Overall Quality:
Adequate to good.

Vintage Rating 1984–1985:
White: '83, '84, '85, '82.
Red: '83, '84, '82, '85.

Tasting Notes:

1984 RHINE RIESLING [15.6] *Colour:* light to medium yellow-green, tinged with straw. *Bouquet:* some bottle-developed aromas; nuances of lime, but also some slightly chalky characters. *Palate:* good bottle richness and development; building a quite full mid-palate with some lime flavours, and a soft finish. Drink '85–'86.

1984 CABERNET SAUVIGNON BEAUJOLAIS STYLE [15.8] *Colour:* light to medium red-purple. *Bouquet:* soft and clean wine, with more weight and complexity than the label would suggest and good varietal aroma. *Palate:* a light, early-drinking cabernet, with very good mid-palate flavour and a slight mousy/biscuity aftertaste. Nonetheless a success. Drink '85–'86.

1984 CABERNET FRANC [16.4] *Colour:* light to medium red-purple. *Bouquet:* very clean and fresh, gently herbaceous fruit; very well-made. *Palate:* light, clean, crisp and gently herbaceous fruit flavours; pleasant acidity and low tannin on the finish. Drink '85–'87.

1984 CABERNET SAUVIGNON [16.4] *Colour:* light, bright fuchsia-purple. *Bouquet:* clean, fragrant and gently minty fruit, with undertones of grass. *Palate:* clean, minty/cherry fruit; crisp; very well-balanced acid and, again, low tannin finish. Drink '86–'88.

LAKE GEORGE

p. 535

(Formerly Cullarin)

Location:
Federal Highway, Collector, 2581;
50 km north-east of Canberra.

Winemaker:
Dr Edgar Riek.

1985 Production:
475 cases.

Principal Wines:
Semillon, Riesling, Sauvignon Blanc, Chardonnay, Pinot Noir and Cabernet (labelled such and not Cabernet Sauvignon because it has a percentage of Merlot and Cabernet Franc blended in).

Distribution:
Neither cellar-door nor mailing-list sales. Limited distribution to Canberra restaurants and clubs; the remainder consumed by Dr Riek and his large circle of friends and acquaintances

Prices:
$70 a dozen.

Overall Quality:
Variable, due in no small part to Dr Riek's fearless experimentation.

Vintage Rating 1984–1985:
White: '85, '83, '84, '82.
Red: '85, '83, '84, '82.

Tasting Notes:

1983 CHARDONNAY [14.8] *Colour:* traces of pink and brown evident. *Bouquet:* strong skin contact characters, perhaps from solids fermentation; marked lemony oak. *Palate:* lemony oak dominates the flavour and structure, with some light fruit lurking underneath. Drink '85–'87.

1983 PINOT NOIR [15] *Colour:* red-purple of medium depth, bright and clear. *Bouquet:* some pleasant sappy pinot aromas and quite good fruit/oak balance. *Palate:* rather sappy/astringent fruit flavours, augmented by slightly raw oak; a wine which lacks generosity. Drink '85–'87.

1983 CABERNET [16.8] *Colour:* medium red, with a few traces of purple lingering. *Bouquet:* clean; of light to medium weight with gently ripe fruit well-balanced by sweet, vanilla-bean American oak. *Palate:* fresh, quite fragrant and gently sweet red berry flavours; oak well-handled; a smooth wine with a long finish. Drink '85–'89.

LARK HILL

pp. 535–8

Location:
RMB, 281 Gundaroo Road, Bungendore, 2621;
30 km north-east of Canberra.
(062) 38 1393.

Winemakers:
David and Sue Carpenter.

1985 Production:
1000 cases.

Principal Wines:

Spatlese Rhine Riesling, Botrytis Rhine Riesling, Late Harvest Rhine Riesling, Semillon Chardonnay, Carbonic Maceration Shiraz and Cabernet Sauvignon. Most wines are a blend of estate-grown grapes together with grapes from Moppity Park Vineyard at Young. Botrytis Rhine Riesling 100% estate-grown.

Distribution:
Almost entirely cellar-door sales and mailing list; cellar-door sales 10 a.m. to 5 p.m. weekends and public holidays. Mailing-list enquiries as above.

Prices:
$5 to $9 cellar door (less 10% for case purchases).

Overall Quality:
Never less than good, and sometimes very good.

Vintage Rating 1983–1985:
White: '85, '84, '83.
Red: '85, '83, '84.

Tasting Notes:

1985 BOTRYTIS RHINE RIESLING [16.6] *Colour:* medium yellow, with just a touch of green. *Bouquet:* very good varietal fruit aroma, with some lime characters from the botrytis but not masking the essential riesling character. *Palate:* excellent intensity of fruit flavour; not particularly luscious, but well-balanced; with good acid, and will undoubtedly develop in bottle. Drink '87–'89.

1985 SPATLESE RHINE RIESLING [16.8] *Colour:* bright light to medium green-yellow. *Bouquet:* light to medium weight; clean, with a touch of lime; very well-made. *Palate:* lovely fresh flavours, very gently sweet and just into spatlese class; good balance between sugar and acid. Drink '86–'88.

1984 CARBONIC MACERATION SHIRAZ [17.4] *Colour:* excellent red-purple of medium depth. *Bouquet:* solid and rich with that unmistakable touch of plum/spice which is the hallmark of carbonic maceration reds; ample flavour throughout. *Palate:* most attractive, rich plum/spice flavours, almost Pommard-like, of medium to full weight. A great success. Drink '86–'90.

1983 CABERNET SAUVIGNON [16.2] *Colour:* medium red-purple. *Bouquet:* robust with a touch of leathery astringency, possibly due to mercaptan; quite complex. *Palate:* a generously flavoured and robust wine, although again a hint of mercaptan partially smothers some cassis/berry flavours on the mid-palate. Quite firm tannin finish. Drink '86–'90.

MIDDLETONS

p. 538

Location:
Barton Highway, Murrumbateman, 2582;
30 km north of Canberra.
(062) 27 1584.

Winemaker:
Geoffrey B. Middleton.

1985 Production:
Approximately 1100 cases.

Principal Wines:

Chablis, Rhine Riesling, Traminer and Shiraz Cabernet, principally using grapes purchased from other districts including Young and Griffith, but with estate-grown contribution increasing with each vintage.

Prices:
$6 to $8 cellar door.

Overall Quality:
Adequate to good.

Vintage Rating 1982–85:
White: '83, '85, '82, '84.

Tasting Notes:

1983 SHIRAZ CABERNET [16] *Colour:* medium to full purple-red. *Bouquet:* some lifted, minty aromas with considerable fruit depth and just a touch of oxidation. *Palate:* lifted minty/berry fruit with just a trace of volatility; a generously flavoured wine with good balance and considerable fruit. Drink '86–'90.

SHINGLE HOUSE

p. 538

Location:
RMB 209 Gundaroo Road, Bungendore, 2621;
35 km north-east of Canberra.

Winemakers:
Max and Yvonne Blake.

1985 Production:
Nil.

Principal Wines:

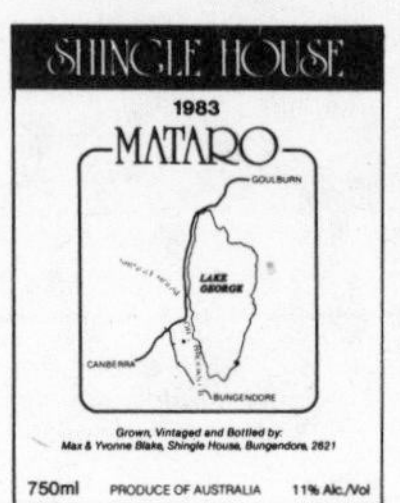

Vineyard planted to mataro, cinsaut, malbec and chardonnay. 1983 Mataro only wine so far produced in sufficient quantity for commercial sale. 1985 vintage destroyed by downy mildew devastation in 1984. Commercial vintage expected in 1986.

WESTERING VINEYARD

p. 538

Location:
Federal Highway, Collector, 2581;
10 km south of town.
(062) 95 8075.

Winemaker:
Captain G. P. Hood.

1985 Production:
177 cases (30% of normal).

Principal Wines:

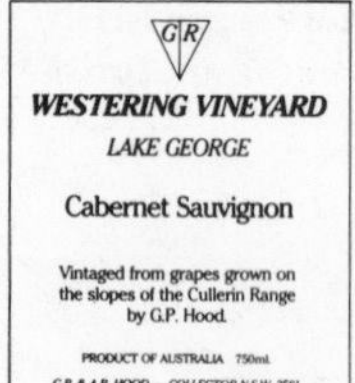

Dry Sherry, Chardonnay, Shiraz and Cabernet Sauvignon.

Distribution:
Exclusively mail order. Enquiries to 97 Jansz Crescent, Griffith, ACT, 2603.

Prices:
$60 to $75 a case.

Overall Quality:
Variable; some wines good.

Vintage Rating 1984–1985:
White: '82, '85, '84, '83.
Red: '82, '83, '85, '84.

Tasting Notes:

1984 CHARDONNAY [14.2] *Colour:* full yellow, tinged with straw. *Bouquet:* heavy, rather austere oak sits on top of whatever fruit may be present. *Palate:* high acid and oak dominant; may well soften with more time, but for the time being the fruit is totally obscured. Drink '88–'89.

1983 SHIRAZ [16.8] *Colour:* medium red-purple. *Bouquet:* smooth and clean fruit of medium weight, with some sweet, berry/vanillan aromas. *Palate:* an elegant, well-balanced wine, with gently astringent tannin on the mid- and back-palate and a touch of cigar box oak. Drink '85–'88.

LAKE GEORGE SHERRY [16.6] *Colour:* golden yellow. *Bouquet:* soft and nutty, with a touch of mellow oak. *Palate:* in dry amontillado style; nice weight and mouth-feel, with some nutty flavours. A most impressive amateur sherry. Drink now.

YASS VALLEY WINES

p. 539

(Formerly Telofa Vineyard)

Location:
Crisps Lane, Murrumbateman, 2582:
30 km north of Canberra.
(062) 27 1592.

Winemaker:
Peter J. Griffiths.

1985 Production:
Negligible, owing to successive attacks of downy mildew and spring frosts.

Principal Wines:

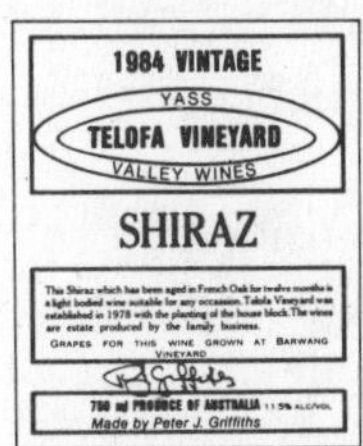

Rhine Riesling, Semillon, Rosé and Shiraz. 1983 Rhine Riesling only estate-grown wine so far released; other wines made from grapes grown at Barwang Vineyard, Young.

Distribution:
Exclusively cellar-door sales and mailing list. Cellar-door sales 10 a.m. to 5 p.m. weekends or by appointment. Mailing-list enquiries to PO Box 18, Murrumbateman, 2582.

Prices:
$4 to $5 cellar door.

Overall Quality:
Variable; so far adequate at best.

Vintage Rating 1984–1985:
'83, '82, '85, '84.

Tasting Notes:

1984 SEMILLON [14.4] *Colour:* full yellow, tinged with straw. *Bouquet:* pungent, dried apricot fruit aromas, very rich but strongly suggestive of some oxidation. *Palate:* similar rich dried apricot flavours, with a very phenolic finish. An unusual wine.

1984 SHIRAZ ROSE [14.8] *Colour:* medium pink-salmon. *Bouquet:* some sweet fruit aromas and a hint of oxidation. *Palate:* of quite distinctive style, reminiscent of the rosés of Tavel; finishes bone dry, but marred by oxidation.

1985 SHIRAZ [15] *Colour:* very developed, light, tawny red. *Bouquet:* light, with some leathery/mercaptan aromas. *Palate:* light, sweet, fruit flavours with just a hint of spice, quite attractive. Drink '86.

Queensland

1985 Vintage

Incredibly, the Australia-wide pattern repeated itself even here. A wet winter led to strong spring growth. The normal summer monsoons did not arrive; instead, cool but dry conditions prevailed throughout much of summer, resulting in rarely encountered vine-stress, particularly on shallower soils.

Vintage began late, at the end of February, and continued for far longer than usual. All of this added up to the best vintage on record, with the grapes ripening in sequence and coming into the wineries in near-perfect condition.

Both white and red wines show good varietal fruit character, as well as considerable depth and ample alcohol. The big four—semillon, chardonnay, shiraz and cabernet sauvignon—were the best performers.

The Changes

The rate of development in the Granite Belt area is unparallelled throughout Australia, with new wineries appearing overnight and others changing hands and names. Kominos and Winewood commenced production in 1985; and Mt Magnus has been reborn.

But perhaps the most significant development in the year was that of Balandean Nouveau. Each of the wineries in the region produced a carbonic maceration red from shiraz, which was then released under a largely identical label (only the winery name, in extremely small type, distinguishes one from the next). The wine was all released at the same time and at the same price. Before accreditation, it was required to pass a masked tasting test.

Southern eyebrows may rise at the gaudy, tropical, pink-purple label, but the fact remains that the move was a brilliantly conceived one to publicise the district, and also to produce a wine style which has considerable relevance for the local market. All in all, one of the most imaginative and constructive marketing efforts of any district anywhere in Australia over the past decade.

BUNGAWARRA

p. 545

Location:
Marshalls Crossing Road, Ballandean, 4382.
(076) 84 1128.

Winemakers:
Phillip Christensen, Kathleen Quealy (assistant).

1985 Production:
Approximately 3000 cases.

Principal Wines:
Chardonnay, Late Harvest Semillon, Balandean Nouveau, Shiraz, Shiraz Cabernet, Light Dry Red, Cabernet Sauvignon, Vintage Port and Liqueur Muscat.

Distribution:
Principally cellar-door sales and mailing list; cellar-door sales 10 a.m. to 4 p.m. 7 days. Mailing-list enquiries to PO Box 10, Ballandean, 4382. Very limited eastern states retail distribution, mainly in Sydney.

Prices:
$5 to $8.50 cellar door.

Overall Quality:
Extremely variable; very good '82s, volatile and poor '83s.

Vintage Rating 1982–85:
White: '85, '84, '82, '83.
Red: '85, '82, '84, '83.

Outstanding Prior Vintages:
'80.

Tasting Notes:
1985 BALANDEAN NOUVEAU [15.6] *Colour:* vibrant purple-red. *Bouquet:* complex, aromatic spice/berry/meat aromas, very much in the style of all the Nouveaus of the region. *Palate:* very fresh, lively, dancing fruit; obvious carbonic maceration flavours; good acid. Drink '85.

1984 L.D.R. LIGHT DRY RED [15.6] *Colour:* bright medium to full purple-red. *Bouquet:* clean, quite firm and with some crisp fruit. *Palate:* clean, with very good cherry flavours, so fruit-sweet there is almost a hint of passionfruit; fresh and attractive. Drink '85–'86.

LIQUEUR MUSCAT [15.6] *Colour:* deep salmon-pink. *Bouquet:* clean, strong grapy muscat aroma and clean spirit. *Palate:* extremely young material, light but of good style, and if one ignores all preconceptions of what one expects from an Australian liqueur muscat, refreshing and flavoursome. Once bottled will never change its spots. Drink now.

ELSINORE WINES

Location:
Back Creek Road, Glen Aplin, 4381;
10 km south of Stanthorpe.
(07) 391 7314.

Winemaker:
Peter Love.

1985 Production:
Not stated but small.

Distribution:
Exclusively cellar-door sales and mail order; cellar-door sales 9 a.m. to 5 p.m. weekends and public holidays. Mailing-list enquiries to PO Box 106, Coorparoo, 4151.

KOMINOS WINES

pp. 545–6

Location:
Off Thorndale Road, Severnlea, 8 km south of Stanthorpe.

Winemakers:
Tony Comino and Stephen Comino.

1985 Production:
Over 1500 cases.

Principal Wines:
Balandean Nouveau, Shiraz and Cabernet Sauvignon.

Distribution:
Principally cellar-door sales and mailing list. Cellar-door sales 9 a.m. to 5 p.m. weekends and weekdays by appointment. Mailing-list enquiries to PO Box 225, Stanthorpe, 4380.

Prices:
No wines to be released until 1986 other than Balandean Nouveau.

Overall Quality:
Initial vintage (1985) very good.

Tasting Notes:

1985 BALANDEAN NOUVEAU [15.6] *Colour:* outstanding, vibrant, crimson-purple. *Bouquet:* strong carbonic maceration aromas, meaty/spicy/biscuity. *Palate:* biscuity flavours on fore-palate diminished after the wine stood in the glass for a while; clean, crisp finish. Drink '85

MOUNT MAGNUS

p. 546

Location:
Donnelly's Castle Road, off New England Highway, 4 km south of Pozieres, 4352.
(076) 85 3213.

Winemaker:
Kevin McCarthy.

1985 Production:
1800 cases.

Principal Wines:
Semillon, Traminer, Balandean Nouveau and Shiraz are top releases. Granite Hills White and Western Hills Moselle also sold.

Distribution:
Exclusively cellar-door and mailing list for the time being. Cellar-door sales 9 a.m. to 5 p.m. 7 days.

Prices:
$5 to $7.50 cellar door.

Overall Quality:
Good.

Vintage Rating 1984–1985:
'85, '84.

Outstanding Prior Vintages:
Not relevant; change of ownership and refurbishment of winery.

Tasting Notes:
1985 BALANDEAN NOUVEAU [16.4] *Colour:* strong, bright purple-red. *Bouquet:* richest and fullest of the '85 Nouveaus; unmistakable spicy/berry fruit aromas. *Palate:* richest and best-balanced wine, with ripe plum flavours on mid-palate and clean, crisp finish. Drink '85.

1984 SHIRAZ [16.6] *Colour:* light to medium purple-red. *Bouquet:* clean, firm, shows good winemaking, although lacks a little new oak sparkle. *Palate:* firm and clean, with an attractive touch of pepper spice. The wine has good depth of flavour and good length, is well-made, but just lacks that bit of lift and life to take it into top class. Drink '86–'89.

OLD CAVES WINERY

p. 546

Location:
New England Highway, Stanthorpe, 4380; on northern outskirts of town.
(076) 81 1494.

Winemaker:
David Zanatta.

1985 Production:
Approximately 40 tonnes (the equivalent of 3000 cases).

Principal Wines:
A wide range of wines, from premium varietals through to generic table wines, thence to Sweet Sherry, Tawny Port, Rummy Port, Blackberry Nip and Coffee Marsala.

Distribution:
Exclusively cellar-door sales and by mailing order; cellar-door sales 9 a.m. to 5 p.m. 7 days. Mailing-list enquiries to PO Box 368, Stanthorpe, 4380.

Prices:
$4 to $6.50.

Overall Quality:
The premium table wines can be very good.

Tasting Notes:

1984 SHIRAZ [16.8] *Colour:* medium red-purple. *Bouquet:* slightly dusty, gentle, old-style shiraz, with a touch of cigar-box oak. *Palate:* clean; well-made, with light to medium-weight sweet fruit, and a very light but clean finish. Champion wine Stanthorpe Show 1985. Drink '85–'87.

1984 CHARDONNAY Gross lactic spoilage evident on both bouquet and palate.

1983 RIESLING [17] *Colour:* full yellow, almost buttercup. *Bouquet:* very full toasty/honey, reminiscent of a rich but old Hunter semillon. *Palate:* very well-made, with most attractive, honey/butter fruit flavours and good acid. A quite lovely wine. Drink '85–'87.

1983 CABERNET SAUVIGNON [16] *Colour:* medium to full purple-red. *Bouquet:* a big wine with leafy/leathery aromas, mercaptan-influenced. *Palate:* a big, rich and full wine with considerable complexity and a trace of volatile lift in the finish. Gold medal Stanthorpe 1985. Drink '85–'88.

ROBINSONS FAMILY

p. 547

Location:
New England Highway, Lyra, 4352;
(south of Ballandean).
(076) 32 8615.

Winemaker:
John Robinson.

1985 Production:
5000 cases.

Principal Wines:

Chardonnay, Rhine Riesling, Late Harvest Traminer, Shiraz, Cabernet Sauvignon, Pinot Noir.

Distribution:
Cellar door, mailing list, own Toowoomba retail outlet and nationally through Rhine Castle Wines. Cellar-door sales 9 a.m. to 5 p.m. 7 days. Mailing list PO Box 613, Toowoomba, 4350.

Prices:
$7 to $8 retail.

Overall Quality:
Good, and steadily improving.

Vintage Rating 1982–85:
'85, '82, '83, '84.

Outstanding Prior Vintages:
'79, '81.

Tasting Notes:

1985 BALANDEAN NOUVEAU [15.4] *Colour:* vibrant light to medium cherry-purple. *Bouquet:* obvious carbonic maceration aromas, with that typical meaty/spice character. *Palate:* excellent flavour on the fore-palate, but a slightly biscuity/mousy finish detracts from the wine. Drink '85–'86.

1985 CHARDONNAY [16.2] *Colour:* medium yellow-green. *Bouquet:* quite full, a touch of lift, and also a suggestion of slightly oily oak. *Palate:* much the richest chardonnay to so far come from the Granite Belt; very rich and giving an impression of sweetness; big, round and soft mouth-filling flavours which do cloy slightly on the finish. Nonetheless, a vast improvement on earlier versions of this variety. Drink '86–'87.

1984 CABERNET SAUVIGNON [17] *Colour:* medium red-purple. *Bouquet:* quite full fruit with complex vanillan/spicy oak which appears to be a blend of American and Portuguese. *Palate:* richly textured, spicy oak (Portuguese?) contributes to a very full-flavoured wine, with good balance and ample fruit to carry that idiosyncratic oak. Drink '87–'91.

1983 CABERNET SAUVIGNON [17.6] *Colour:* strong purple-red. *Bouquet:* clean and complex, with very good fruit/oak integration and balance; quite weighty and stylish. *Palate:* a very well-made wine, with considerable richness to the fruit, well-handled oak, and soft tannin on the finish to add complexity and authority. Drink '87–'91.

ROMAVILLA

pp. 547–8

Location:
Northern Road, Roma, 4455;
on northern outskirts of township.
(074) 22 1822.

Winemaker:
David Wall.

1985 Production:
45,000 litres (the equivalent of 5000 cases).

Principal Wines:
A full range of table wine and fortified wine is produced, with fortified wines a long-standing specialty of the winery but table wines assuming increasing importance.

Distribution:
Exclusively cellar-door sales and mail order; cellar-door sales 8 a.m. to 5 p.m. Monday to Friday and 9 a.m. to noon Saturday. Mailing-list enquiries to PO Box 38, Roma, 4455.

Overall Quality:
Old fortified wines of distinctive style and good quality.

Vintage Rating 1982–85:
'84, '85, '82, '83.

Outstanding Prior Vintages:
'79.

RUMBALARA

p. 548

(Granite Belt Vignerons)

Location:
Fletcher Road, Fletcher, 4381;
15 km south of Stanthorpe.
(076) 84 1206.

Winemaker:
Chris Gray.

1985 Production:
30,000 litres (the equivalent of 3300 cases).

Principal Wines:
Rhine Riesling, Semillon, Chardonnay, Rosé, Shiraz and Muscat. The Girrawheen and Rumbalara labels are now merged into Rumbalara as the sole label of the Granite Belt Vignerons Partnership.

Distribution:
Principally cellar-door sales and mail order; cellar-door sales 9 a.m. to 5 p.m. 7 days. Mailing-list enquiries as above. Limited retail and restaurant distribution in Brisbane.

Prices:
$4.25 to $8.50 cellar door.

Overall Quality:
Good; Semillon frequently very good, if not exceptional.

Vintage Rating 1982–85:
White: '84, '83, '82, '85.
Red: '84, '85, '83, '82.

Outstanding Prior Vintages:
'79.

Tasting Notes:

1984 SEMILLON [17.8] *Colour:* deep, glowing, yellow-green. *Bouquet:* enormously rich, pineapple/tropical fruit aromas, more akin to late-picked chenin blanc; quite extraordinary. *Palate:* intensely rich, perfumed, honeysuckle/tropical/pineapple fruit flavours of utterly particular style. Slightly flawed by a trace of hardness on the back-palate. Drink '85–'87.

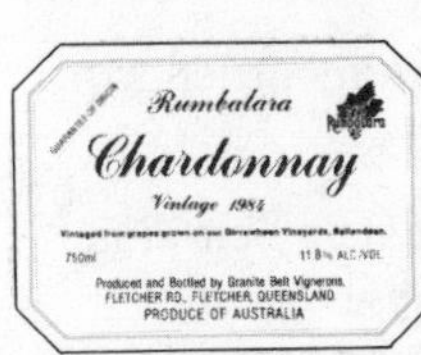

1984 CHARDONNAY [16.8] *Colour:* bright green-yellow. *Bouquet:* very clean; rich and full passionfruit aromas, seductively opulent. *Palate:* similar sweet passionfruit flavours to a wine of light to medium weight and a soft finish. Drink '85–'87.

1983 SEMILLON [15.6] *Colour:* full yellow. *Bouquet:* big aroma, slightly smoky and a faint touch of sulphide, but good fruit. *Palate:* quite a full wine, with plenty of fruit flavour and some typical honey varietal characters. Well-made. Drink '85–'86.

1984 ROSE [15] *Colour:* pale bright pink. *Bouquet:* clean, but rather closed and not particularly fruity. *Palate:* well enough made; a touch of sweetness on the mid-palate and the finish cloys a little. Drink '85–'86.

SUNDOWN VALLEY VINEYARDS

p. 548

(Formerly Angelo's Wines)

Location:
Sundown Road, Ballandean, 4382:
4 km west of town, and 18 km south of Stanthorpe.
(076) 84 1226.

Winemaker:
Rodney Hooper.

1985 Production:
100,000 litres (including 4500 dozen bottled wine).

Principal Wines:
Premium releases include Valley Estate Semillon, Rhine Riesling, Chardonnay, Auslese Sylvaner Hermitage and Cabernet Sauvignon, most released with a Bin number and vineyard identification. Also generic releases of Moselle, Sparkling Moselle, Sparkling Rosé, Spumante, Old Tin Miners Rum Port and so on.

Distribution:
Chiefly cellar door and mailing list. Cellar-door sales 9 a.m. to 5 p.m. 7 days. Mailing list as above.

Prices:
$5.50 to $7.70 cellar door.

Overall Quality:
Good.

Vintage Rating 1982–85:
'85, '83, '84, '82.

Outstanding Prior Vintages:
'74, '78, '79, '81.

Tasting Notes:

1985 CHARDONNAY [16.2] *Colour:* full straw-yellow. *Bouquet:* slightly smelly/cheesy aromas, which improved in the glass and which undoubtedly will not affect the wine once it is bottle-mature. *Palate:* very good fruit weight and acid balance; a well-made wine with considerable potential. Drink '87–'89.

1985 AUSLESE SYLVANER [16.6] *Colour:* light and bright straw-yellow. *Bouquet:* clean; extremely rich jujube/tropical fruit aromas. *Palate:* a most striking and unusual wine; marked tropical fruit with a topping of caramel ice-cream. Unusual, but very well made. Drink '87–'90.

1985 BALANDEAN NOUVEAU [15] *Colour:* light to medium red; just a trace of purple. *Bouquet:* slightly astringent and stalky, with a suspicion of volatile lift. *Palate:* again stalky/astringent flavours evident but redeemed by the crisp acid finish evident in all the Balandean Nouveaus. Drink '85.

1983 SHIRAZ BIN 43 [16.4] *Colour:* excellent purple-red of medium to full depth. *Bouquet:* smooth, with fair weight and complexity, showing some attractive leather/plum aromas. *Palate:* similar flavours manifest themselves in the plum/leather/spice spectrum; of adequate weight and with a soft finish. Drink '86–'88.

1982 CABERNET SAUVIGNON BIN 51 [16.6] *Colour:* very good purple-red. *Bouquet:* some ripe, slightly oxidised fruit aromas with straw/cigar characters. *Palate:* very rich and ripe plum fruit, full of flavour with soft, complexing tannin on the finish. Drink '85–'86.

WINEWOOD

p. 549

Location:
Sundown Road, Ballandean, 4352;
17 km south of Stanthorpe.
(076) 84 1187.

Winemaker:
Ian Davis.

1985 Production:
780 cases (first vintage).

Principal Wines:
Semillon and Balandean Nouveau.

Distribution:
Exclusively cellar-door sales and mailing list at this juncture; cellar-door sales 9 a.m. to 5 p.m. weekends and weekdays by appointment. Mailing-list enquiries to PO Box 84, Ballandean, 4352.

Prices:
$6.50.

Overall Quality:
Not rated.

Tasting Notes:

1985 BALANDEAN NOUVEAU [15.6] *Colour:* excellent bright light to medium red-purple. *Bouquet:* firm and fresh, with less carbonic maceration characters than in other Nouveau wines, but still within the parameters of the style. *Palate:* a fraction astringent and bitter, but still fresh, crisp and lively. Drink '85.

Tasmania

1985 Vintage

Tasmania alone broke free of the pattern across mainland Australia. Adverse dry cold and windy conditions at flower-set led on to a prolonged period of dry, windy weather, with the inevitable result that yields were down by 50 per cent in most vineyards, and in one (the Bream Creek Vineyard of Moorilla) no grapes were picked at all.

An extended Indian summer saved the vintage from total disaster and, while yields were pitifully low, their quality was extremely high. In the north, base wines for champagne look to be excellent, and the pinot noir and chardonnay diverted to table wine use are correspondingly excellent. Rhine riesling in the north is good, but overall the white table wines are no better than average, and it seems almost certain the cabernet sauvignon from both regions will be very green and grassy.

The Changes

Overall, once one looks beyond the big three of Heemskerk, Moorilla and Pipers Brook, Tasmanian wineries are in truth producing wine on a sub-economic scale. If they are to survive in the long term, and if others waiting in the wings are to join them, production levels must substantially increase. It is not possible to run effectively a winery (even as a weekend hobby) with an output of less than 1000 cases a year, and many very well-informed observers of the industry say the real level ought to be a minimum of 10,000 cases.

On the other hand, the joint venture between Louis Roederer and Heemskerk announced during the year will bring considerable benefits to the Pipers Brook area in particular, and most probably to Tasmania as a whole. It is believed that Dominique Portet has purchased land in Tasmania to grow grapes for base wine for *méthode champenoise*, and that a major Swiss viticultural enterprise has likewise commenced a vineyard. Initiatives such as these, with financial strength and technical expertise, will prove of lasting importance for Tasmania.

CHATEAU ELMSLIE

p. 556

Location:
McEwins Road, Legana, 7251;
10 km north of Launceston on the West Tamar Highway.
(003) 30 1225.

Winemaker:
Ralph Power.

1985 Production:
Approximately 500 litres (the equivalent of 55 cases).

Principal Wines:
Chardonnay, Pinot Noir and Cabernet Sauvignon.

Distribution:
Exclusively mailing list and cellar door (by appointment).

Prices:
$8 to $12 cellar door.

Overall Quality:
Very good indeed.

Vintage Rating 1982–85:
White: '85, '84.
Red: '84, '85, '82.

Tasting Notes:

1984 CABERNET SAUVIGNON [18.4] *Colour:* dense, almost impenetrable purple. *Bouquet:* rich, deep and concentrated slightly gravelly fruit; a potent, clean, fruit aroma. *Palate:* enormous flavour and concentration, with pristine varietal fruit and gentle but persistent tannin. An outstanding wine. Drink '89–'96.

1982 CABERNET SAUVIGNON [16.6] *Colour:* light red tinged with purple. *Bouquet:* clean; pronounced green-leaf herbaceous, cool climate aromas. *Palate:* also clean and fault-free; cedary/leafy flavours, but lacking mid-palate flesh. Very well-made for such a small winemaking situation. Drink '86–'88.

FREYCINET

p. 556

Location:
Tasman Highway via Bicheno, 7215.

Winemaker:
1984—Julian Alcorso (contract); 1985 and subsequently—Geoffrey Bull.

1985 Production:
Approximately 50 cases (less than 1984).

Principal Wines:
Chardonnay, Muller Thurgau Sauvignon Blanc, Riesling, Pinot Noir and Cabernet Sauvignon.

Distribution:
White wine available, by cellar-door sales 10 a.m. to 4 p.m. 7 days. Mailing-list enquiries welcome; address as above.

Overall Quality:
Not rated.

GLENGARRY VINEYARD

p. 556

Location:
Luke Road, Glengarry, 7251.
(003) 96 1141.

Winemaker:
Gavin Scott.

1985 Production:
Estimated approximately 200 cases.

Principal Wines:
Pinot Noir and Cabernet Sauvignon.

Distribution:
Principally cellar door and mailing list whilst wine available. Mailing-list enquiries write to PO Box 30, Exeter, 7251.

Overall Quality:
Not rated.

HEEMSKERK

pp. 556–7

Location:
Pipers Brook, 7254;
20 km west of Bridport and 50 km north of Launceston.
(003) 82 7133

Winemaker:
Graham Wiltshire.

1985 Production:
Not available for publication; 1984 crush in excess of 100 tonnes (equivalent to 7500 cases).

Principal Wines:
Chardonnay, Pinot Noir and Cabernet Sauvignon.

Distribution:
Exclusively fine wine retailers; distributed by Fesq and Company in New South Wales, Victoria and Tasmania. No cellar-door sales or mailing lists; winery visits by appointment only.

Prices:
$10 to $12 recommended retail.

Overall Quality:
Very good to exceptional.

Vintage Rating 1984–1985:
White: '82, '84, '83, '85 uncertain.
Red: '85(?), '82, '84, '83.

Tasting Notes:
1985 RHINE RIESLING [16.8] *Colour:* pale bright green-yellow. *Bouquet:* somewhat closed when assessed August 1985, being a tank sample. *Palate:* very lively, but with some slightly aggressive, green/edgy characters to high-flavoured fruit. Could very easily develop into an excellent wine. Drink '87–'90.

1984 CHARDONNAY [17.8] *Colour:* bright yellow-green of medium depth. *Bouquet:* complex, and of substantial weight, with quite luscious fruit intermingling with some charred oak. *Palate:* similar smoky charred oak flavours with fine, crisp fruit; a much more elegant wine than the bouquet would suggest; a long, lingering finish. Drink '87–'91.

1983 CABERNET SAUVIGNON [17] *Colour:* fairly light red, suggesting it will develop quickly. *Bouquet:* intense green capsicum/herbaceous aromas; crystal clear cool climate cabernet sauvignon. *Palate:* fine, astringent ultra-cool climate leafy/capsicum/tobacco flavours. Very well-made, although would have benefited from a touch more depth and richness on the mid-palate. Drink '86–'91.

McEWINS

p. 557

Location:
Loop Road, Glengarry, 7251.
(003) 96 1141.

Winemaker:
Gavin Scott.

1985 Production:
Approximately 5 tonnes (normally 10 tonnes or 500 cases).

Principal Wines:
Pinot Noir and Cabernet Sauvignon.

Distribution:
Exclusively mail order; write to PO Box 30, Exeter, 7251.

Prices:
Not yet determined.

Overall Quality:
On evidence of '84 vintage, very good.

Vintage Rating 1984–1985:
'85, '84.

Tasting Notes:

1984 CABERNET SAUVIGNON [17.6] *Colour:* dense purple-red. *Bouquet:* rich fruit together with excellent French oak; full, complex and most impressive. *Palate:* a big, richly flavoured wine; a very slight dip in the mid-palate before fine-grained oak and fruit tannins manifest themselves on the finish. Drink '88–'93.

MARIONS VINEYARD

p. 557

(Formerly Tamar Valley Vineyards)

Location:
Foreshore Road, Deviot, 7251;
(in best Tasmanian tradition, Deviot, Legana, Glengarry and Exeter all have the same postcode);
25 km north of Launceston.
(003) 94 7434.

Winemaker:
Mark Semmens.

1985 Production:
9600 litres (the equivalent of over 1000 cases).

Principal Wines:
Muller Thurgau, Chardonnay, Pinot Noir and Cabernet Sauvignon.

Distribution:
Cellar-door sales 10 a.m. to 5 p.m. seven days; wines also available retail through Aberfeldy Cellars and Websters Wines.

Prices:
$7 to $8 cellar door.

Overall Quality:
Very good.

Tasting Notes:

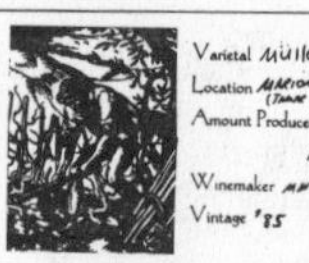

1985 MULLER THURGAU [16.6] *Colour:* pale bright green-yellow. *Bouquet:* very clean and crisp; of light to medium weight; fair fruit but not varietally distinct. *Palate:* an attractive, crisp wine with a hint of nutmeg spice on the back-palate; very well-made for a small winery. Drink '86–'87.

1984 PINOT NOIR [17.8] *Colour:* excellent strong purple-red. *Bouquet:* very complex rich fruit merging with even richer fruit. *Palate:* dominated by extremely complex and seductive oak, but the fruit is there; a striking wine, with some minty/strawberry flavours on the mid-palate and a fine grained, persistent tannin finish. Drink '87–'91.

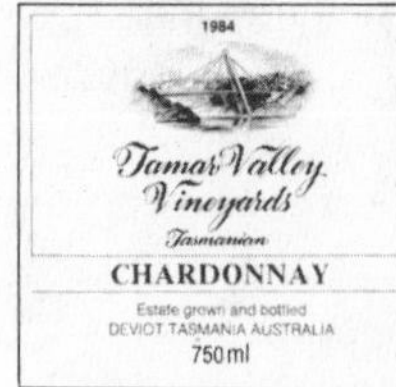

1984 CHARDONNAY [14.8] *Colour:* some pink-brown tints evidencing oxidation. *Bouquet:* slight pastille fruit aromas with light oak, but overall rather closed. *Palate:* similar sweet non-varietal light pastille fruit. Drink '86.

MEADOWBANK

p. 558

Location:
Glenora, Derwent Valley;
75 km north-west of Hobart (vineyard only).

Winemaker:
Hickinbotham Winemakers.

1985 Production:
None made (drought).

Principal Wines:
Rhine Riesling and Cabernet Sauvignon.

Distribution:
All grapes sold to, and wine made and distributed by, Hickinbotham Winemakers of Geelong.

Prices:
$9.95 recommended retail.

Overall Quality:
Very good.

Vintage Rating 1982–85:
White: '83, '82 (no wine made '84 or '85).
Red: '83, '84, '82.

Tasting Notes:

1983 CABERNET SAUVIGNON [17.4] *Colour:* medium red-purple. *Bouquet:* very complex and markedly fragrant leafy/berry aromas, suggestive of carbonic maceration. *Palate:* fragrant, lively berry flavours, with some plum/spice characters, once again suggestive of carbonic maceration. A very clean wine overall, with low tannin. Drink '86–'90.

MOORILLA ESTATE

pp. 558–9

Location:
655 Main Road, Berriedale, 7011;
10 km north of Hobart.
(002) 49 2949.

Winemaker:
Julian Alcorso.

1985 Production:
700 cases.

Principal Wines:
Rhine Riesling, Botrytis Riesling, Chardonnay and Pinot Noir.

Distribution:
Mailing list, selected retailers and restaurants. Principal retailers: Aberfeldy Cellars, Tasmania; The Oak Barrel, Sydney; Sutherland Cellars, Melbourne and Farmer Bros, Canberra. Mailing-list enquiries (well-produced bulletins) as above. No cellar-door sales; winery visits by appointment.

Prices:
$13 to $17 retail.

Overall Quality:
Exceptional.

Vintage Rating 1984–1985:
White: '83, '84, '82, '85.
Red: '85, '84, '82, '83.

Outstanding Prior Vintages:
'75, '77.

Tasting Notes:

1985 BOTRYTIS RHINE RIESLING [17.6] *Colour:* bright green-yellow. *Bouquet:* intense but quite light and crisp aroma, not particularly luscious, and with some fermentation characters lingering. *Palate:* explodes into life; intense elegant lime fruit flavours and the expected outstanding acid on the back-palate. Will be a great late harvest style. Drink '88–'92.

1985 GEWURZTRAMINER [15.8] *Colour:* pale green-yellow. *Bouquet:* very light, very delicate and only barely discernible varietal aroma. *Palate:* very fine and very delicate wine, showing only a trace of varietal character and generally lacking excitement and flavour in August 1985. May develop. Drink '86–'88.

1984 CHARDONNAY [18] *Colour:* pale bright green-yellow. *Bouquet:* fine but complex aromas, with obvious barrel ferment characters, with fruit aroma in the grapefruit spectrum. *Palate:* pungently intense yet fine and delicate grapefruit flavours; a long, lingering finish with good acid. Drink '86–'90.

1984 PINOT NOIR [18.4] *Colour:* bright purple-red, of light to medium depth. *Bouquet:* intense, fine sappy pinot noir aroma with a touch of cigar/oak. *Palate:* magnificently articulated varietal character, with sappy/strawberry flavours intermingling; a clean, long, crisp finish. First-class cool-climate pinot noir. Drink '87–'90.

PIPERS BROOK VINEYARD

pp. 559–60

Location:
Pipers Brook, 7254;
20 km west of Bridport and 50 km south of Launceston.
(003) 82 7197.

Winemaker:
Andrew Pirie.

1985 Production:
Approximately 35,000 litres (the equivalent of 3900 cases).

Principal Wines:
Riesling, Noble Riesling, Traminer, Chardonnay, Pinot Noir and Cabernet Sauvignon.

Distribution:
Principally by mailing list with high quality bulletins; limited Sydney restaurant distribution through I. H. Baker & Co.

Prices:
Approximately $10.50.

Overall Quality:
Exceptional.

Vintage Rating 1984–1985:
White: '82, '85, '84, '83.
Red: '82, '84, '85, '83.

Outstanding Prior Vintages:
'81 Pinot Noir—magnificent.

Tasting Notes:

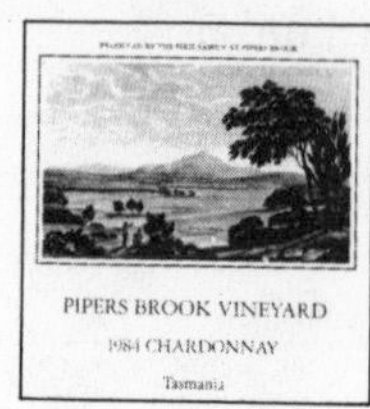

1984 CHARDONNAY [17.8] *Colour:* glowing medium yellow-green. *Bouquet:* very firm and deep wine, with grapefruit citrus aromas; some light, botrytis-like characters; latent richness. *Palate:* extraordinarily complex fruit flavours in the peach/apricot spectrum; lingering soft acid on the finish. A very unusual chardonnay. Drink '85–'89.

1984 PINOT NOIR [17.8] *Colour:* very good purple red of medium depth. *Bouquet:* fine and elegant; a haunting touch of cinnamon/spice behind strawberry fruit; very clean and very well-balanced. *Palate:* a crisp wine with gentle strawberry fruit and very pronounced acid; sensitive oak handling. One of the rare Australian pinot noirs which demands time in the bottle, for the acid really does need to soften and the fruit to come up. If this happens, the wine will be exceptional. Drink '87–'91.

1984 CABERNET BLEND [17.2] *Colour:* medium purple-red. *Bouquet:* clean; of light to medium weight with marked herbaceous/leafy characters, and the merlot influence in the blend quite obvious. *Palate:* strong herbaceous/grassy/crisp flavour and structure; uncompromising, cool-climate wine, possibly showing some young vine characters, and rather tart at this juncture. Drink '88–'90.

1984 CABERNET SAUVIGNON [17.8] *Colour:* medium red-purple, with slightly more reds in the hue. *Bouquet:* a riper style, with slightly sweeter fruit, although still very crisp; oak well-controlled. *Palate:* while unmistakably cool-climate, is fuller and better balanced than the blend, with good mid-palate weight, and crisp acid. The cabernet sauvignon vines are no doubt older than the merlot and cabernet franc which contributed to the blend. Drink '87–'92.

ROTHERLYTHE

p. 560

Location:
Hendersons Lane, Gravelly Beach, Exeter, 7251.
(003) 34 0188.

Winemaker:
Gavin Scott.

1985 Production:
Approximately 30 cases.

Principal Wines:
Pinot Noir and Cabernet Sauvignon.

Distribution:
Exclusively mailing list; enquiries to Dr S. Hyde, 19 Canning Street, Launceston, 7250.

Overall Quality:
Not rated.

STONEY VINEYARD

pp. 560–1

Location:
Campania, 7202;
35 km north-east of Hobart.
(002) 62 4174.

Winemaker:
George Park.

1985 Production:
Approximately 200 cases.

Principal Wines:

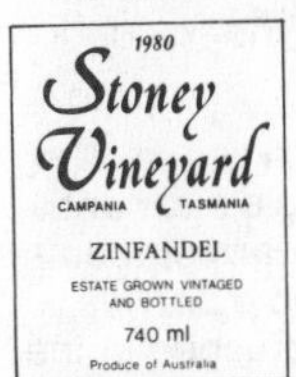

Rhine Riesling, Cabernet Sauvignon and Pinot Noir (Zinfandel and Shiraz recently discontinued).

Distribution:
Exclusively mailing list; enquiries as above. Cellar-door sales by appointment only; no tastings permitted.

Prices:
$8 to $9 cellar door.

Overall Quality:
Exceptional.

Tasting Notes:

1983 RHINE RIESLING [18.2] *Colour:* medium to full yellow. *Bouquet:* very clean; full, soft and richly honeyed; no solids ferment character. *Palate:* very good, deep fruit with fine balancing acid; clean and with far greater richness than one usually encounters in Tasmanian riesling. Drink '85–'87.

1983 CABERNET SAUVIGNON [18.4] *Colour:* intense, dense purple. *Bouquet:* intense, perfumed cassis/berry aromas, yet retaining lightness and elegance. *Palate:* exceptionally rich and deep flavours; soft yet intense sweet berry flavours on the mid-palate. Drink '87–'92.

1982 CABERNET SAUVIGNON [18.2] *Colour:* medium purple-red. *Bouquet:* complex, powdery aromas with touches of mint and leather. *Palate:* strongly reminiscent of a fine Bordeaux; a finely structured wine of light to medium weight and a long, lingering finish. Drink '85–'89.

1982 ZINFANDEL [18] *Colour:* light cherry red with a touch of purple. *Bouquet:* clean and perfumed spicy aromas. *Palate:* lively, crisp positive varietal flavours with elegant spice characters; similar to high quality light-bodied Californian Zinfandel. Drink '85–'87.
(All wines tasted June 1984.)

STRATHAYR VINEYARD

p. 561

Location:
Richmond, 7025.

Winemaker:
Tom Crossen.

1985 Production:
Negligible.

Principal Wines:
Rhine Riesling, Chardonnay, Traminer, Pinot Noir and Cabernet Sauvignon.

Distribution:
No commercial releases yet made.

Glossary

The *Australian Wine Compendium* contains a large glossary of common wine terms, grape varieties and the like. The glossary which follows is intended to supplement that of the *Compendium*, and is directed mainly to the at-times arcane terminology of the tasting notes. It also covers in a little more detail some of the background to wine faults.

Acetic: A wine with an excess of acetic acid, a volatile acid present in virtually all table wines in small quantities. Acetic volatility, and volatile acidity, are alternative terms.

Aggressive: An unpleasantly obvious component of wine flavour, e.g., aggressive tannin.

Aldehyde: A volatile fluid deriving from the oxidation of alcohol, present in most wines but undesirable in any appreciable quantity; hence, aldehydic.

Armpit: A colloquial term used to describe the rather sweaty and stuffy smell of a wine which is showing the after-effects of a highly controlled fermentation and maturation in which oxygen has been rigorously excluded. It is a condition which usually passes after the wine has spent a year or so in bottle. For some reason, sauvignon blanc seems to suffer particularly from the character.

Aroma: The scent or smell of the grape variety; aroma decreases with age as bouquet builds; hence, aromatic.

Astringent; Astringency: Sharpness or bitterness deriving usually from tannin and sometimes from acid; particularly evident in a young wine, and can be an indication of the keeping potential of such a wine. Can also be associated with mercaptan, and overall is not a desirable characteristic.

Autolysis; Autolysed: The breakdown of internal barriers within dead cells to allow enzymes present in those cells to digest components of the cell, producing both flavour and structure changes in the wine; a marmite-toast flavour is often noted, while the surface tension of the wine is decreased, leading to smaller bubbles in the sparkling wine in which the process of autolysis occurs.

Backbone: A term used to describe a wine with a core of strength, which derives from acid (in the case of white wine) or from tannin and/or acid (in the case of a red wine).

Back-palate: The point in the tasting cycle shortly before or shortly after the wine is swallowed.

Balance: The harmony or equilibrium between the different flavour components of wine, and the first requirement of a great wine.

Barrel Fermentation: The practice of conducting the primary fermentation in the small oak barrels in which wine is normally stored at the end of fermentation; a common practice in making French white burgundy, but of recent introduction in Australia.

Body: A term used to describe the weight or substance of a wine in the mouth and deriving from alcohol and tannin. Softens and mellows with age.

Bottle-development: A reference to the secondary characters and flavours which develop after a wine has been cellared for some years.

Botrytis; Botrytised: Reference to the effect on the taste of the wine of Botrytis Cinerea, a microscopic fungus or mould and which leads to the great sweet wines of the world. It tends to impose a lime/tropical fruit aroma and, in high concentrations, to mask substantially the natural varietal aroma and flavour of the grape it attacks once made into wine.

Bouquet: The smell of the wine (as opposed to simply the aroma of the grape) produced by the volatile esters present in any wine. Bouquet becomes more complex during the time the wine needs to reach full maturity and finally softens and dissipates with extreme age. Much work still remains to be done to understand fully the very complex chemical changes which take place in a wine as it matures and which contribute to the changing bouquet.

Bready: Literally the smell of freshly baked bread, often associated with the influence of yeast, and probably, but by no means necessarily, a pleasant aroma.

Broad: A term used to describe wine which is soft or coarse, lacking in refinement.

Camphor: A smell which can develop after a wine has spent a number of years in bottle; usually quite pleasant unless it becomes too marked.

Caramel: Literally, a caramel flavour found in wine, usually white wine, and often indicating either oxidation or over-ripe fruit.

Carbonic Maceration: A winemaking method which involves a substantial portion of the primary fermentation taking place within whole berries, which have not been crushed in the usual method. It results in very soft wines with a distinctive aroma of spice and well-hung meat.

Cassis: A dark purple liquor made from blackcurrants, chiefly near Dijon in Burgundy. The aroma of cassis is often found in high-quality cabernet sauvignon as the smell of sweet blackcurrants.

Cedar: An oak-derived aroma or taste reminiscent of the smell of cedar, usually developed in older red wines.

Chalky: A rather dry, dusty aroma or taste, often found in young wines made from chenin blanc in the Loire Valley of France; may also be due to solids fermentation (see hereunder).

Character: The overall result of the combination of vinosity, balance and style of a wine.

Charred Oak: A particular taste deriving from oak which has been deliberately charred during the heating process needed to shape the wooden staves into barrel form. A complex, pleasantly smoky/toasty aroma and flavour is often the result.

Cheesy: A smell (and very occasionally a taste) which principally occurs in white wines and which tends to diminish fruit aromas. Its most likely cause is a degree of oxidation or perhaps yeast problems. Not particularly desirable.

Chewy: A term used to denote the structure (rather than the flavour) of a wine which just stops short of being thick or heavy; generally a term of qualified approval.

Cigar-box: Literally the smell of an empty cigar-box, usually manifesting itself in older red wines and deriving from oak. Sometimes present in young wines. Usually a term of approbation.

Clean: The absence of any foreign (or "off") odour or flavour; an important aspect of a wine of quality.

Closed: A wine lacking fruit aroma and possibly flavour; normally affects young wines and diminishes with age.

Cloying: The characteristic of a wine which lacks acid.

Coarse: Indicates a wine with excessive extract of solids, particularly tannins, and probably affected by oxidation during the making process.

Coffee: An undesirable taste or aroma reminiscent of coffee, normally indicating oxidation.

Complex: A term of commendation, but otherwise having its normal English meaning.

Corked; Corkiness: Refers to a wine affected by microscopic moulds (chiefly of the penicillin family) which penetrate corks in the cork factory and which subsequently impart a sour, mouldy taste in the wine.

Cosmetic: A somewhat imprecise term used to indicate a foreign, and often faintly sickly, aroma (or possibly flavour).

Creamy: A term used particularly in relation to sparkling wine and intended to denote texture more than flavour.

Crisp: A term of commendation, but otherwise having its normal English meaning.

Dull: Denotes a wine either cloudy or hazy in colour, or with a muted or flawed bouquet or palate.

Dumb: A wine showing either no aroma or distinct varietal taste, or no development; closed.

Dusty: Used to describe both the bouquet and taste of red wine, and normally denoting a character caused by long storage in big, old (but sound) oak casks.

Earthy: Bouquet and flavour reminiscent of certain soil types; a smell of fresh earth can often be identified in young vintage port.

Extractive: A coarse or heavy wine with excessive extract from skins and pips.

Fading: A wine past its peak, losing its bouquet, flavour and character.

Finesse: A term denoting a wine of elegance and subtlety.

Finish: The flavour or taste remaining after the wine leaves the mouth.

Firm: A term usually applied to the finish of a wine, and denoting the impact of tannin and possibly acid.

Flat: Similar to dull and flabby; a lack of freshness, character or acid.

Fleshy: A youthful wine with full-bodied varietal flavour.

Flowery: The aroma reminiscent of flowers contributed by certain aromatic grape varieties. Thus also floral; usually a term of commendation.

Fore-palate: Used to describe that part of the tasting cycle as the wine is first taken into the mouth.

Fresh: An aroma or taste free from any fault or bottle-developed characters, usually characteristic of a young wine but occasionally of older wines.

Furry: A term used to denote a particular aspect of the texture (rather than the taste) of a red wine, almost invariably deriving from tannin and akin to the sensation of soft fur on the side of the tongue.

Generic: A term used to denote a wine falling within a general style (e.g. chablis, white burgundy, claret) and not made from any particular grape variety or from any particular region.

Grassy; Grassiness: Literally the smell of freshly cut or partially dried grass, found very frequently in sauvignon blanc and in cabernet sauvignon grown in cooler areas or in cooler vintages. Can also occur occasionally in other varieties, particularly semillon. Provided it is present in moderation, is more likely to be desirable than not.

Gravel; Gravelly: Denotes a slightly flinty, slightly sour, taste akin to the taste (or sensation) of sucking a pebble.

Green: Term applied to a young wine which is unbalanced because of excess malic acid deriving from unripe grapes.

Green-yellow: The colour of white wine in which green tones predominate over yellow, but both are present. Highly desirable.

Grip: A component of the structure of a wine which probably has marked acid, but usually a term of qualified approval.

Hard: An unbalanced and unyielding wine suffering from an excess of tannin and/or acid (if red) and acid (if white).

Harsh: Usually applied to red wine suffering from excess tannin, often when young.

Herbaceous: Similar to grassy, but indicating a slightly broader spectrum of grass and herb-like flavours, usually a little richer and more complete. As in the case of a grassy wine, should not be excessively marked.

Hollow: Applies to a wine with initial taste and with finish, but with little or no flavour on the middle palate.

Honeyed: Denotes both the flavour and the structure (or feel in the mouth) of a mature white wine, particularly aged semillon but also sauternes.

Integrated; Integration: Used in relation to a wine in which (most probably) fruit and oak flavours have blended harmoniously and merged imperceptably into each other; a most desirable characteristic.

Intensity: Applied in particular in relation to fruit aroma or flavour; very different from weight; normally used in relation to a high-class wine.

Jammy: Excessively ripe and heavy red grape flavours, sweet but cloying.

Lactic: Refers to lactic acid, seldom present in grapes but formed during the alcoholic and malolactic fermentations. Also occurs in faulty wines as a result of bacterial decomposition of sugars; the slightly sickly, sour-milk aroma is very unpleasant.

Leafy: Yet another variant of the grassy/herbaceous spectrum of flavours, usually the lightest in weight. May or may not be pleasant.

Leathery: A slightly sour, astringent smell or taste, almost certainly deriving from small concentrations of mercaptan.

Lift; Lifted: Usually applied in relation to a wine with a degree of volatility, but in which that volatility is not excessive.

Lime: A lime-juice flavour commonly encountered in rhine riesling, and often (but not invariably) indicating that the fruit has been affected by botrytis.

Limousin: A particular type of French oak with a distinctive spicy aroma and taste.

Malic: A rather tart, green flavour deriving from higher than normal levels of malic acid, an acid found in all grapes but usually converted to lactic acid during the secondary fermentation.

Malty: Literally, the taste of malt; not a particularly desirable wine characteristic.

Matchbox: Literally the smell of a box of matches, a slightly sulphurous/woody smell; not at all desirable.

Meaty: The smell of slightly aged, raw meat, usually although not inevitably a form of mercaptan.

Medicinal: A somewhat vague term used to describe childhood recollections of cough mixture; not desirable.

Mercaptan: Produced by ethyl mercaptan and ethyl sulphides in wine, deriving from hydrogen sulphide produced during the fermentation. It manifests itself in a range of unpleasant odours ranging from burnt rubber to garlic, onion, gamy meat, stale cabbage and asparagus. While hydrogen sulphide can easily be removed, once mercaptan is formed it is much more difficult to eliminate.

Mid-palate: The mid-point of the tasting cycle, as the wine rests in the centre of the mouth.

Mint; Minty: An aroma and flavour of red wine in the eucalypt/peppermint spectrum, and not garden mint.

Modulated: A wine in which varietal aroma or flavour is very well-balanced between the extremes such aroma or flavour can on occasions take.

Mouldy: Off flavours and aromas derived from mouldy grapes or storage in a mouldy cask or from a bad cork.

Mousy: A peculiar flat, undesirable taste resulting from bacterial growth in wines, most evident after the wine leaves the mouth. Its precise cause is not yet known.

Mouth-feel: Literally, the feel rather than the taste of the wine in the mouth; a wine with good mouth-feel will be pleasantly round and soft.

Nose: The scents and odours of a wine, encompassing both aromas and bouquet.

Oily: Oils deriving from grape pips or stalks and not desirable in wine. May also derive from poor oak.

Oxidised; Oxidation: Used in respect of a wine which has been exposed to too much oxygen, resulting in coarseness and loss of flavour.

Pastille: The flavour of a fruit pastille, not totally unpleasant but nonetheless undesirable.

Pencil Shavings: A rather bitter and raw oak aroma or flavour caused by the use of poor oak or unskilled use of oak maturation.

Phenolic: Deriving from phenols, important flavour contributors to wine, but denoting a hard or heavy coarse character; not desirable.

Powdery: Similar to dusty, and almost inevitably deriving from prolonged old oak storage. Can be quite attractive.

Pressings: Wine recovered from pressing the skins, stalks and pips after fermentation. It is higher in tannin and may be deeper coloured. Often back-blended into free run wine to add strength and colour.

Pungent: A characteristic of a very aromatic wine with a high level of volatiles.

Purple-red: A red wine colour in which the purple hues dominate the red; usually a young wine colour, and desirable.

Rancio: Distinctive, developed wood character of an old dessert wine stemming from a degree of oxidation. Highly desirable.

Raw: A term used to describe a sharp and aggressive oak flavour, due either to poor, unseasoned oak or to wine which has been removed from new oak barrels too quickly.

Red-purple: Applies to a wine in which the red hues are more dominant than the purple; usually the first stage of colour change.

Reductive: A term used to describe a wine which has been rigorously protected from oxygen, and in which the fruit aroma may well be suppressed.

Residual Sugar: Unfermented grape sugar remaining in white wine in the form of glucose and fructose. Can be tasted at levels in excess of 5 grams per litre. Many so-called dry rhine rieslings have 6 or 7 grams per litre of residual sugar.

Robust: Usually applied to a young red wine which needs further time in bottle.

Rough: Astringent, coarse tannin taste in red wines indicating lack of balance and maturity.

Round: A well-balanced, smooth wine showing good balance of flavours, and particularly of acid.

Rubbery: The most common manifestation of hydrogen sulphide in the form of mercaptan.

Sappy; Sappiness: A touch of herbaceous or stalky character often found in young wines, particularly pinot noir, and usually a sign of potential quality.

Scented: Characteristic of a wine having a highly aromatic smell usually associated with flowers or fruits.

Smooth: Agreeable and harmonious; opposite of astringent, harsh or rough.

Soft: Refers to a wine with a pleasing finish, neither hard nor aggressive. May indicate fairly low acid levels, but not necessarily so.

Solid: A wine which has ample depth of flavour but which probably lacks complexity and subtlety.

Solids; Solids Fermentation: The particular aroma and flavour of a white wine in which the fermentation has been allowed to commence immediately after the grapes are pressed, and in the presence of a large number of particles of skin and flesh. Modern technology in Australia usually calls for the juice either to be cold settled for a number of days or centrifuged. White wines fermented on solids tend to be longer lived, but to be much less aromatic as young wines, and can appear heavy and harsh (or chalky).

Sorbate: A chemical used to control oxidation but which imparts an unpleasant aroma and flavour.

Spice: A term used to denote any one of the numerous spice flavours which can occur in wines, deriving either from oak or from the grape itself. Most spicy characters are very pleasant and add to complexity. The actual spectrum is as broad as the name suggests, running from nutmeg to black pepper.

Spritz; Spritzig: A German term indicating the presence of some carbon dioxide bubbles in the wine, frequently encountered in Australian white wine and occasionally in reds. Often an unintended consequence of protecting the wine from oxidation during storage and/or bottling. Can be felt as a slight prickle on the tongue.

Stalky: Bitter character deriving from grape stalks, mainly appearing in red wines and indicative of poor winemaking.

Straw: Refers either to colour (self-explanatory) or to taste; in the latter context usually denotes a degree of oxidation.

Structure: An all-encompassing term covering all aspects of a wine other than its primary flavours, and includes alcohol, body, weight, tannin and acid, even though some of these also manifest themselves as flavours.

Stylish: A somewhat imprecise and subjective term to denote a wine which attractively conforms to varietal or generic style.

Sulphide; Sulphidic: The generic term given to hydrogen sulphide and mercaptans.

Sulphur Dioxide (SO_2): An anti-oxidant preservative used in virtually every wine, red, white or sparkling. In excessive quantities imparts a disagreeable odour and may artificially retard the development of the wine. Dissipates with age.

Supple: Denotes a lively, yet round and satisfying, wine.

Sweaty saddle: A description most frequently accorded to aged Hunter Valley reds, probably indicating the presence of some mercaptan, but curiously a term of commendation more than condemnation.

Tannin: A complex organic constituent of wine deriving chiefly from grape pips and stalks, and occurring in greater quantities in reds than in whites. Plays an important part in the self-clearing of young wines after fermentation, and thereafter in the period of maturation the wine requires: a full-bodied red, high in tannin, requires a longer period than does a lighter-bodied wine. Easily perceived in the taste of the wine by the slightly mouth-puckering, drying, furry sensation, particularly on the side of the tongue and on the gums. Some red winemakers add powdered tannin to wine to increase the tannin level artificially.

Tart: Characteristic of a wine with excess acid.

Thick: Denotes an excessively heavy, and probably jammy, wine.

Thin: Lacking in body, almost watery and probably excessively acid.

Toast; Toasty: Literally the smell of fresh toast, occurring almost exclusively in white wines, and usually developing with bottle-age. Applies particularly to Hunter Valley semillon, but curiously, also to many rieslings.

Tobacco: Literally, the smell of tobacco.

Vanilla; Vanillan: A sweet aroma usually derived from American oak, but also occuring in old bottle-developed white wines.

Varietal: (i) Character of wine derived from the grape.
(ii) Term for wines made from a single or dominant variety and identified by reference to that variety.

Vegetative: Normally indicates a rather dank, vegetable-like aroma, sometimes reminiscent of cabbage, and seldom desirable.

Velvety: The softly rich and smooth feel of an aged wine which has retained strong fruit flavour.

Vinosity; Vinous: A term relating to the strength of the grape character in a wine (though not necessarily the varietal character) and linked to the alcoholic strength of the wine. Denotes a desirable characteristic.

Volatile: A characteristic of a wine spoiled by an excess of acetic acid.

Volatile Acid: A group of acids comprising acetic, carbonic, butyric, propionic and formic.

Volatility: Relating to the release of acetic acid and other esters, and may be present to excess in a faulty wine.

Weight: Normally a measure of the strength of the wine in terms of alcohol and possibly tannin.

Yeasty: A smell or aroma deriving from the action of the yeast used to ferment the wine; except in the case of sparkling wine, should not be discernible to any degree.

Yellow-green: A white wine colour in which the yellow hues are more dominant than the green.

Zest; Zesty: Used in relation to a wine which is very fresh and pleasantly lively and acidic.

Index

The Australian Wine Compendium is the most complete account ever of winemaking in Australia. Written by highly respected wine writer, wine judge and winemaker James Halliday, this invaluable work about the wine industry in Australia has been acclaimed by the critics:

"... by far and away the best book I have ever read on Australian wine ..."

TONY LORD, *Decanter* Magazine, London

"Nearly 600 mostly double-column pages of ... indisputable reference value."

JOHN BEETSON, *Sydney Morning Herald*

"If you take an interest in wine, you must have a copy ... It has immediate indispensable status."

TONY BAKER, *Adelaide News*

"This is the best and most comprehensive reference available on Australian wine ..."

PETER WILSON, *Sun*, Sydney

"Halliday says what he thinks. No words are minced or punches pulled. Because of this, it is the most valuable work of its kind published."

HUON HOOKE, *Wine & Spirit Guide*

"... as complete an account as it's possible to achieve on wine-making in Australia ... Serious, informative, opinionated and possessed of great authority."

DAVID BRAY, *Courier Mail*, Brisbane

This magnificent volume encompasses the history of the wine industry in Australia and examines over 400 vineyards and wineries individually, evaluating soil types, climate, vineyard practices, winemaking techniques and, of course, the wines. More than a reference book, however, it is also a very personal work, full of unexpected anecdotes and insights into the personalities that give the industry its vitality and variety.

Complete with colour and black-and-white photographs and maps, *The Australian Wine Compendium* is the perfect partner to *James Halliday's Australian Wine Guide.*